REAL BOYS

WILLIAM POLLACK, PH.D.

REAL BOYS

RESCUING OUR SONS FROM THE MYTHS OF BOYHOOD

RANDOM HOUSE

NEW YORK

Grateful acknowledgment is made to Simon & Schuster and A. P. Watt Ltd. on behalf of
Michael Yeats for permission to reprint four lines from "A Dialogue of Self and Soul"
from *The Collected Works of W. B. Yeats, Volume I: The Poems,* revised and edited
by Richard J. Finneran. Copyright © 1933 by Macmillan Publishing Company.
Copyright renewed 1961 by Bertha Georgie Yeats. Rights outside of the
United States are controlled by A. P. Watt Ltd. on behalf of Michael Yeats.
Reprinted by permission of Simon & Schuster and A. P. Watt Ltd. on behalf of Michael Yeats.
Grateful acknowledgment is also made to Doubleday, a division of the Bantam Doubleday
Dell Publishing Group: "For My Son Noah, Ten Years Old," from *Man in the Black
Coat Turns,* by Robert Bly. Copyright © 1981 by Robert Bly. Reprinted by permission
of the author and Doubleday, a division of the Bantam Doubleday Dell Publishing Group.

Pollack, William S.
Real boys : rescuing our sons from the myths of boyhood / William
Pollack. — 1st ed.
p.   cm.
ISBN 0-375-50131-2
1. Boys.   2. Sons.   3. Masculinity.   4. Child rearing.   I. Title.
HQ775.P65   1998
305.23—dc21   98-15282

Random House website address: www.randomhouse.com

4 6 8 9 7 5 3

Book design by Tanya Pérez-Rock

To Marsha and Sarah—
who have sustained the man and nurtured the inner boy

To my parents and grandparents—
who knew how to make a boy feel special and loved

And to the boys and their parents—
who opened their hearts and gave voice to their feelings

ACKNOWLEDGMENTS

A work of this scope rarely involves the toil or ideas of just one person. The author inevitably stands on the shoulders of many strong personal, professional, and creative pillars, including many friends, family members, and professional colleagues. Therefore, I'd like to take this opportunity to offer my sincerest gratitude to the some of the many people who helped make *Real Boys* possible.

First, I'd like to thank my editor at Random House, Kate Medina, whose perspicacity, energy, warm support, and critical thinking were central to making this book come to life. From our first meeting in Cambridge I sensed her deep connection with my work and her hopefulness about how my research—and this book—could help make an important difference in how we think about and raise boys. Her editorial comments and suggestions were nothing short of brilliant, and I shall be forever grateful for her creative guidance in taking these chunks of ideas and shaping them into the big picture of this book. Her dedication and expertise at publishing this book cannot be too deeply praised.

Also at Random House Meaghan Rady has been essential to making this book happen and I am deeply grateful. In every way the people at Random House have shown the highest standards of professionalism and excellence.

This work would hardly be a paper, let alone a complete book, without the foresight, energy, and love for this endeavor that my literary agents at Zachary Shuster—Todd Shuster and Lane Zachary—brought to the party. They were the first to see the potential for a book relating to work with boys, and helped me enormously to shape its movement from research notes to the written page. Their agents and staff, especially Jennifer Gates Hayes, Esmond Harmsworth, and Allison Murray, provided me and *Real Boys* with a level of support and encouragement an author has almost no right to expect—but which I did receive, cheerfully and regularly, almost daily.

Although as author one must take ultimate responsibility for the hypotheses, findings, suggestions, and results of his work, there are debts of intellectual gratitude that, though they cannot be completely repaid, must be acknowledged. Dr. Fran Grossman first invited me to study families with her Boston University Parenthood project, which led me in the direction of defining and researching the world of fathers, at a time when the world was just beginning to perceive the meaning of men in family life. Dr. Ronald Levant then felicitously invited me to join him on a journey to understand the struggles men were having in our society and to band together with other like-minded individuals to study, help, and treat men and boys. Our intellectual collaboration has given birth to two professional books on gender, a continuing collaboration toward understanding men and boys, and a friendship for which I'm very grateful. I am appreciative too of my collaboration with Dr. Bill Betcher, with whom I have coauthored a book and now codirect the Center for Men at McLean Hospital.

The International Coalition of Boys' Schools recognized the significance and need for a new psychology of boys and has also been generously supportive of my work. I would like to thank John Farber, who first invited me to speak; past president Rick Hawley, who has been a constant intellectual supporter; and the Reverend Tony Jarvis whose spiritual understanding of boys is both erudite and uplifting. I must especially thank Dr. Rick Melvoin at the Belmont Hill School, who with his staff (especially Connie MacGillivary) opened many doors in helping my recent research project come to fruition. Diane Hulse and John Bednall also collaborated with suggestions and ideas that have been very helpful to our project. I would like to acknowledge and thank the Research Committee of the Coalition for a grant that partially funded some of the early analysis of the data from the "Listening to Boys' Voices" study.

Likewise, I must express my gratitude to the superintendents and educational leaders of the key suburban and smaller city districts in New England who (although they must remain nameless) have been of inestimable value in bringing balance to my understanding of the educational needs of boys today.

Several graduate assistants who aided in the analysis and gathering of data at different phases of the work—namely, Judy Chu, Chuck McCormick, and Roberto Olivardia—are to be thanked most heartily. In addition, I would like to express my sincerest gratitude to John Butman, Nancy Roosa, Becky Shuster, John Delancy, and Mark Zanger for their assistance in gathering data and preparing materials to be included in this book.

I would also like to acknowledge the gracious input of my colleagues at Harvard Medical School/McLean Hospital, including its former chief Dr. Steven Mirin and his successor, Dr. Bruce Cohen, for their support for the Center for Men; Dr. Joseph Coyle, chair of the Consolidated Department of Psychiatry at Harvard Medical School for his recognition of the psychology of boys and men as a legitimate field of specialization; and the support of the Department of Continuing Education at McLean Hospital, especially Carol Brown and Cathy Toon. Carol Brown's and Patti Brown's aid with the typing of portions of the manuscript is also gratefully recognized, as is the research assistance of Lynn Dietrich and Ann Menashi, the chief librarians at McLean Hospital and the Boston Psychoanalytic Institute, respectively.

My colleagues and teachers in psychoanalysis have also played a dynamic, formative role in enhancing and deepening my appreciation of boys' inner lives. On this score, I would particularly like to thank Drs. David Berkowitz, Arnold Modell, Gerald Adler, Dan Buie, Jim Herzog, Ralph Engle, Tony Kris, Lynn Layton, Paul Lynch, Risa Weinrit, Dianne Fader, Laura Weissberg, Rita Teusch, and Steve Rosenthal.

I must also express my gratitude to Dr. Shervert Frazier, psychiatrist in chief, emeritus of McLean Hospital, who has been an incredible mentor, helping me to develop my "voice" in a field of psychological study that was once largely overlooked. Never before or since have I had the opportunity to absorb such sagacity about the inner lives of boys and men.

I must acknowledge how much I have learned from my colleagues in gender and adolescent studies in general, and in particular, from my friends at the Society for the Psychological Study of Men and Masculinity, namely: Gary Brooks, Sam Cochran, Michael Diamond, Richard Eisler, Jeff Fischer, Marion Gindes, Glenn Good, Corey Habben, Marty Heesacker, Richard Lazur, Richard Majors, Neil Massoth, Larry Morris, Gil Noam, Jim O'Neil, Marlin Potash, Jerry Shapiro, Denise Twohey, Lenore Walker, and many others. Jim Barron has honored me with an editorial role on his journal *Gender and Psychonalysis,* and my consulting colleagues Jef Connor and Ken Settel have listened patiently to my theories about boys. Also, the members of the Men's Studies Seminar and Play

Group, a personal/professional development group, have created a wonderful environment in which I have been able to discuss new ideas and hear about the experiences of others as they discover more. Specifically, I would like to thank Joel Eichler, Alan Gurwitt, Steve Krugman, Ron Levant, David Lisak, Jon Reusser, and Bob Weiss.

As the book itself will show, "real boys" have much in common with "real girls"—more than we often tend to believe—and scholars and writers in the new psychology of men and boys owe an enormous debt of gratitude to those researchers who went before us to create a "revolution" in women's studies. Although my research derives from many years of work with boys and men, it is important to recognize the important influences that the "new" psychology of women has had on this entire field. I would like to mention my particular appreciation of the seminal work of Carol Gilligan on girls' "voices" whose influence is clearly noted in this work, and that of the core faculty of the Stone Center at Wellesley: Jean Baker Miller, Irene Stiver, Judith Jordan, and Janet Surrey, all of whom have helped to shape a concept of a "connected self" in women that bears much relevance to my own theories of premature separation in boys and the possibilities boys have to heal from it. Dr. Judith Jordan, my colleague, collaborator, friend, and "fellow traveler," has had a tremendously positive impact on my thinking in this field. Her deep intelligence and creative inspiration may be felt throughout my work.

Researching and writing this work would have been impossible without the patience, love, and understanding of my family. I am deeply indebted to my wife, Dr. Marsha Padwa, for her invaluable insights about adolescents and their families and important input into earlier drafts of this work; and to both Marsha and my daughter, Sarah Faye Pollack, for their unwavering love and support—juggling schedules, borrowing laptops, and sustaining my spirits during times of distress.

To our boys who participated in the study, their parents, and my patients, who have opened their lives to us, and who have taught me so much through their struggles, I extend my personal gratitude and thanks.

Most especially, however, *Real Boys* would never have seen the light of day without the special dedication, tenacity, creativity, and love for this work manifested by my agent, Todd Shuster. Beginning with an innocent breakfast in Belmont and continuing through weeks of reviewing, reediting, haranguing, and kibitzing through draft after draft, Todd shared his heart and soul with me in this project. This book bears much more of his imprint than he is ever willing to take credit for. But such credit must be given, and it must be acknowledged. As literary agent and creative critic, sometimes arguing vigorously and thoughtfully with me about points in this book, Todd worked tirelessly to support me in a project that I can only hope will have an important impact on the lives of boys. I cannot thank him enough for his special contribution to my work.

CONTENTS

LISTENING TO BOYS' VOICES:
RESCUING OPHELIA'S BROTHERS

Boys today are in serious trouble, including many who seem "normal" and to be doing just fine. Confused by society's mixed messages about what's expected of them as boys, and later as men, many feel a sadness and disconnection they cannot even name. New research shows that boys are faring less well in school than they did in the past and in comparison to girls, that many boys have remarkably fragile self-esteem, and that the rates of both depression and suicide in boys are frighteningly on the rise. Many of our sons are currently in a desperate crisis.

We now understand that girls lose their voices as they enter their teens, and are becoming lost not only to themselves but also to us, mostly as a result of society's gender stereotypes about girls. Spurred by these insights, we are starting to make some progress in helping girls gain greater freedom, speak in their true voices, be heard, and become empowered so they can better develop their individual capacities and strengths as they grow into women.

But what of their brothers? And what of our sons?

Over the last several years, I and other professionals who work with boys have become increasingly aware that even boys who seem OK on the surface are suffering silently inside—from confusion, a sense of isolation, and despair. They feel detached from their own selves, and often feel alienated from parents, siblings, and peers. Many boys feel a loneliness that may last throughout boyhood and continue into adult life.

In my work I have tried to understand what boys are really saying about their lives and to get behind the mask of masculinity, a mask that most boys and men wear to hide their true inner feelings, and to present to the world an image of male toughness, stoicism, and strength, when in fact they feel desperately alone and afraid. This book is the result of listening to and learning about boys, and thinking about what we can do to help them become happier, more successful boys and men.

What is the fundamental nature of boys? How are boys different from girls? And how are they the same? What should we expect of and for our boys—in school, in play and sports, with their friends, during adolescence, in the family? And what happens when boys are faced with challenges such as divorce, depression, violence, and so on. These are questions I have studied and will address in this book.

I believe that most of us are at a disadvantage when we talk about boys, because our view of boys is so influenced and distorted by society's myths about them. Over the years a thousand models of boyhood have accumulated and become melded into an all-purpose stereotype.

A myth has been created of the young boy as the rascal and the scamp, the mischievous lad who loves to run and be loud, whose pockets are filled with junk that he considers treasure, with a frisky puppy as his constant companion. He considers girls to be "yucky." He likes to go fishing and ride a bike. The mythical teenage boy is obsessed with himself, sports, cars, sex, and—above all—being cool. He's tough. He breaks the rules. He talks back to his teachers. He would rather hang out with his hip friends than spend time with his "dorky" family.

Yet, if you know boys, are a parent or teacher of boys, you know in your heart that these stereotypes are false and limiting, as all stereotypes are. Even so, the power of these stereotypes and the myths that perpetuate them are bound to be profoundly affecting the boys you know and your relationships with them. They are hindering the development of boys, our raising of them, and a boy's ability to function at his best.

These myths start to fade, in the light of emerging new information about boys, but much of this knowledge is unknown outside academic circles. I will show that while there is often a grain of truth in myths about boys—which is why these myths have endured—the full truth is more complex and considerably more positive.

Real Boys is based on my twenty years of working with and thinking about men and boys as codirector of the Center for Men at McLean Hospital, a faculty member of the Harvard Medical School, and a fellow and founding member of the Society for the Psychological Study of Men and Masculinity of the American Psychological Association. Much of this book is derived from my recent study called "Listening to Boys' Voices," in which research colleagues at Harvard Medical School and I are studying hundreds of young and adolescent boys, observing them in various situations, conducting empirical testing, and talking with their parents. This study is intended to gather critical data relating to the new psychology of today's boys and to evoke their candid responses to a broad range of questions regarding not only their everyday experiences at home, at school, and with friends, but also to reveal the true depth and complexity of their inner emotional lives as boys.

The findings of "Listening to Boys' Voices" added new evidence to support my experience as a psychologist and my belief that many boys are deeply troubled. The picture becomes more alarming when one considers the findings of the study in light of other statistics that are now surfacing.

Consider the following: in the educational system, boys are now twice as likely as girls to be labeled as "learning disabled," constitute up to 67 percent of our "special education" classes, and in some school systems are up to *ten* times more likely to be diagnosed with a serious emotional disorder—most especially attention deficit disorder (for which many boys receive potent medications with potentially serious side effects). While the significant gaps in girls' science and math achievement are improving greatly, boys' scores on reading are lagging behind significantly and continue to show little improvement. Recent studies also show that not only is boys' self-esteem more fragile than that of girls and that boys' confidence as learners is impaired but also that boys are substantially more likely to endure disciplinary problems, be suspended from classes, or actually drop out from school entirely.

Boys are experiencing serious trouble outside school as well. The rate of depression among today's boys is shockingly high, and statistics now tell us that boys are up to three times more likely than girls to be the victim of a violent crime (other than sexual assault) and between four to six times more likely to commit suicide. In the summer of 1997 a string of suicides took place just miles from where I live in a small working-class neighborhood known as South Boston, or "Southie." All of these self-inflicted deaths took place within the same community and within the span of a single summer. And all of the victims were boys.

Why? What's going on? That is the subject of this book.

I'll discuss how and why society places boys in a "gender straitjacket." Without being aware of doing so, society is judging the behavior of boys against outmoded ideas about masculinity and about what it takes for a boy to become a man. These models (many of which date from the nineteenth century) simply have no relevance to today's world.

Yet if boys don't conform to these ideas, society has ways of shaming them into compliance. By placing a boy in this gender straitjacket, society is limiting his emotional range and his ability to think and behave as freely and openly as he could, to succeed in the ever-changing world in which we live.

Boys are pushed to separate from their mother prematurely. Mother is expected to "cut the apron strings" that tie the son to her and, indeed, that connect him to the entire family. As early as age five or six, many boys are pushed out of the family and expected to be independent—in school, camp, at all kinds of activities and situations they may or may not be ready to handle. We give our boys in early adolescence a second shove—into new schools, sports competitions, jobs, dating, travel, and more.

The problem is not that we introduce our boys to the world—that's what parents should be doing—it's how we do it. We expect them to step outside the family too abruptly, with too little preparation for what lies in store, too little emotional support, not enough opportunity to express their feelings, and often with no option of going back or changing course. We don't tolerate any stalling or listen to any whining. That's because we believe that disconnection is important, even essential, for a boy to "make the break" and become a man. We do not expect the same of our girls. In fact, if we forced our daughters to disconnect in the same manner as we do boys—with so little help and guidance—we would expect the outcome to be traumatic.

I believe that boys, feeling ashamed of their vulnerability, mask their emotions and ultimately their true selves. This unnecessary disconnection—from family and then from self—causes many boys to feel alone, helpless, and fearful. And yet society's prevailing myths about boys do not leave room for such emotions, and so the boy feels he is not measuring up. He has no way to talk about his perceived failure; he feels ashamed, but he can't talk about his shame, either. Over time, his sensitivity is submerged almost without thinking, until he loses touch with it himself. And so a boy has been "hardened," just as society thinks he should be.

Even as we continue to harden our boys the old-fashioned way, we expect them to live up to some very modern and contradictory expectations, particularly in their relationships. We want them to be "new men" in the making, showing respect for their girl peers, sharing their feelings in emotionally charged circumstances, and shedding their "macho" assumptions about male power, responsibility, and sexuality. In short, we want our boys to be sensitive New Age guys *and* still be cool dudes. Is it any wonder that a lot of boys are confused by this double standard?

All of this gets absorbed by boys and promulgated by the society at large as an unwritten Boy Code, which is the sum total of this disturbing cycle. The code is a set of behaviors, rules of conduct, cultural shibboleths, and even a lexicon, that is inculcated into boys by our society—from the very beginning of a boy's life. In effect we hold up a mirror to our boys that reflects back a distorted and outmoded image of the ideal boy—an image that our boys feel under great pressure to emulate. When a boy tries to see his own genuine attributes, his true self, in the mirror, he can't; he only sees how he falls short of this impossible and obsolete ideal. Is it any wonder, then, that he may later become frustrated, depressed, or angry, suffer low self-esteem, fail to succeed in intimate relationships, or even turn violent?

Through this book I would like to help families, communities, and boys themselves better understand what a real boy is and, most important, how to help boys flourish and succeed in our society. In Part I of the book, "Real Boys," I explore these and other myths about boys and discuss the true nature of boys, using boys' voices and stories. In Part II, "Connecting with Boys," I discuss the "how to"—what we can do to help boys break out of society's gender straitjackets, express a wide range of their true feelings, and function more successfully as confident, open, and caring young men in a difficult world. In Part III, "When the Bough Breaks," I outline more serious consequences of the Boy Code—depression (including the crisis of boy suicides), violence, and divorce—and emphasize not only how we can detect these problems, but also what we can do to make a positive impact in our boys' lives despite these challenges. In the Epilogue, I propose ways in which we can strengthen the connections we have with boys by suggesting how we might replace the old Boy Code with one that is more consonant with our new understanding of real boys.

Although it's not always easy to tell, many adolescent boys—just like adolescent girls—suffer from a crisis of self-confidence and identity. There is, however, a major difference between the plight of boys and that of girls. Even when their voices are stifled in public, girls generally feel comfortable speaking in private to one another about their pain and insecurities. By contrast, though boys may exhibit bravado and braggadocio, they find it more difficult to express their genuine selves even in private, with friends and family. Their voices, as loud and forceful as they may sound, may not reveal what is really in their hearts and souls. Instead, most boys—whether in public or private—tend to act confident and contented, and even brag about their abilities. While we may joke about how adult males won't ask for directions when they're lost, it is no laughing matter that so many of our boys feel they can't reach out for the emotional compass they so desperately need.

What can we do to change all this? How can we help boys adjust to today's world and social environment and learn new ways of seeing and relating to other people? What can we do to draw boys out, to get boys to trust us, to let us join them inside their worlds, and help them be and become more fully the people they really are?

As we will discuss in detail in this book, there is much we can do to support and connect with our boys. We can become aware of the boy stereotypes even the best of us carry in our minds, and consciously work to eliminate them from society, from our thinking and our language. We can learn to recognize the words that boys use when something is troubling them but feel they can't talk about—the "I'm fine," that actually means things are really not fine. We can learn how to get our sons to talk, without demanding or pressuring them to, by finding the safe spaces that will allow them to open up and express themselves. We can better anticipate the situations that might cause feelings of vulnerability and fear—the first day of school, the big test, the first date, the gym class, the school trip, the illness of a friend, the breakup of a romance, the move to a new place, the doctor's appointment, the onset of puberty—and find ways that will prepare a boy for them in advance, and allow him to talk about them after the fact. Above all, *we can begin to teach connection* as the basis of a new male model.

Boys themselves can lead us in this process, if we'll only let them. In this book, I want to let you hear the true everyday voices of *real boys*. They have so much to say to us, to teach us, about themselves and what their inner worlds and daily lives are really like. Many boys will speak in this book. They can guide us, telling us what they genuinely need from us in the way of attention, love, listening, and caring. When you get behind the mask boys typically wear, many of them are beautifully articulate about who they are and how they feel and what they see in the world around them.

PART ONE

REAL BOYS

I remember the gleams and glooms
    that dart
Across the schoolboy's brain;
The song and the silence in the heart,
That in part are prophecies, and in
    part
Are longings wild and vain.
And the voice of that fitful song
Sings on, and is never still:
"A boy's will is the wind's will,
And the thoughts of youth are long,
    long thoughts."

There are things of which I may not
    speak;
There are dreams that cannot die;
There are thoughts that make the
    strong heart weak,
And bring a pallor into the cheek,
And a mist before the eye.
And the words of that fatal song
Come over me like a chill:
"A boy's will is the wind's will,
And the thoughts of youth are long,
    long thoughts." . . .

—HENRY WADSWORTH LONGFELLOW
  "My Lost Youth"

_1_

Inside the World of Boys:

Behind the Mask of

Masculinity

"I get a little down," Adam confessed, "but I'm very good at hiding
it. It's like I wear a mask. Even when the kids call me names or
taunt me, I never show them how much it crushes me inside.
I keep it all in."

THE BOY CODE: "EVERYTHING'S JUST FINE"

Adam is a fourteen-year-old boy whose mother sought me out after a
workshop I was leading on the subject of boys and families. Adam, she
told me, had been performing very well in school, but now she felt something was wrong.

Adam had shown such promise that he had been selected to join a special program for talented students, and the program was available only at a
different—and more academically prestigious—school than the one Adam
had attended. The new school was located in a well-to-do section of town,
more affluent than Adam's own neighborhood. Adam's mother had been
pleased when her son had qualified for the program and even more
delighted that he would be given a scholarship to pay for it. And so Adam
had set off on this new life.

At the time we talked, Mrs. Harrison's delight had turned to worry.
Adam was not doing well at the new school. His grades were mediocre,
and at midterm he had been given a warning that he might fail algebra. Yet
Adam continued to insist, "I'm fine. Everything's just fine." He said this
both at home and at school. Adam's mother was perplexed, as was the

guidance counselor at his new school. "Adam seems cheerful and has no complaints," the counselor told her. "But something must be wrong." His mother tried to talk to Adam, hoping to find out what was troubling him and causing him to do so poorly in school. "But the more I questioned him about what was going on," she said, "the more he continued to deny any problems."

Adam was a quiet and rather shy boy, small for his age. In his bright blue eyes I detected an inner pain, a malaise whose cause I could not easily fathom. I had seen a similar look on the faces of a number of boys of different ages, including many boys in the "Listening to Boys' Voices" study. Adam looked wary, hurt, closed-in, self-protective. Most of all, he looked alone.

One day, his mother continued, Adam came home with a black eye. She asked him what had happened. "Just an accident," Adam had mumbled. He'd kept his eyes cast down, she remembered, as if he felt guilty or ashamed. His mother probed more deeply. She told him that she knew something was wrong, something upsetting was going on, and that—whatever it was—they could deal with it, they could face it together. Suddenly, Adam erupted in tears, and the story he had been holding inside came pouring out.

Adam was being picked on at school, heckled on the bus, goaded into fights in the schoolyard. "Hey, White Trash!" the other boys shouted at him. "You don't belong here with *us*!" taunted a twelfth-grade bully. "Why don't you go back to your own side of town!" The taunts often led to physical attacks, and Adam found himself having to fight back in order to defend himself. "But I never throw the first punch," Adam explained to his mother. "I don't show them they can hurt me. I don't want to embarrass myself in front of everybody."

I turned to Adam. "How do you feel about all this?" I asked. "How do you handle your feelings of anger and frustration?" His answer was, I'm sad to say, a refrain I hear often when I am able to connect to the inner lives of boys.

"I get a little down," Adam confessed, "but I'm very good at hiding it. It's like I wear a mask. Even when the kids call me names or taunt me, I never show them how much it crushes me inside. I keep it all in."

"What do you do with the sadness?" I asked.

"I tend to let it boil inside until I can't hold it any longer, and then it explodes. It's like I have a breakdown, screaming and yelling. But I only do it inside my own room at home, where nobody can hear. Where nobody will know about it." He paused a moment. "I think I got this from my dad, unfortunately."

Adam was doing what I find so many boys do: he was hiding behind a mask, and using it to hide his deepest thoughts and feelings—his real self—from everyone, even the people closest to him. This mask of masculinity enabled Adam to make a bold (if inaccurate) statement to the world: "I can handle it. Everything's fine. I am invincible."

Adam, like other boys, wore this mask as an invisible shield, a persona to show the outside world a feigned self-confidence and bravado, and to hide the shame he felt at his feelings of vulnerability, powerlessness, and isolation. He couldn't handle the school situation alone—very few boys or girls of fourteen could—and he didn't know how to ask for help, even from people he knew loved him. As a result, Adam was unhappy and was falling behind in his academic performance.

Many of the boys I see today are like Adam, living behind a mask of masculine bravado that hides the genuine self to conform to our society's expectations; they feel it is necessary to cut themselves off from any feelings that society teaches them are unacceptable for men and boys—fear, uncertainty, feelings of loneliness and need.

Many boys, like Adam, also think it's necessary that they handle their problems alone. A boy is not expected to reach out—to his family, his friends, his counselors, or coaches—for help, comfort, understanding, and support. And so he is simply not as close as he could be to the people who love him and yearn to give him the human connections of love, caring, and affection every person needs.

The problem for those of us who want to help is that, on the outside, the boy who is having problems may seem cheerful and resilient while keeping inside the feelings that don't fit the male model—being troubled, lonely, afraid, desperate. Boys learn to wear the mask so skillfully—in fact, they don't even know they're doing it—that it can be difficult to detect what is really going on when they are suffering at school, when their friendships are not working out, when they are being bullied, becoming depressed, even dangerously so, to the point of feeling suicidal. The problems below the surface become obvious only when boys go "over the edge" and get into trouble at school, start to fight with friends, take drugs or abuse alcohol, are diagnosed with clinical depression or attention deficit disorder, erupt into physical violence, or come home with a black eye, as Adam did. Adam's mother, for example, did not know from her son that anything was wrong until Adam came home with an eye swollen shut; all she knew was that he had those perplexingly poor grades.

THE GENDER STRAITJACKET

Many years ago, when I began my research into boys, I had assumed that since America was revising its ideas about girls and women, it must have also been reevaluating its traditional ideas about boys, men, and masculinity. But over the years my research findings have shown that as far as boys today are concerned, the old Boy Code—the outdated and constricting assumptions, models, and rules about boys that our society has used since the nineteenth century—is still operating in force. I have been surprised to find that even in the most progressive schools and the most politically correct communities in every part of the country and in families of all types, the Boy Code continues to affect the behavior of all of us—the boys themselves, their parents, their teachers, and society as a whole. None of us is immune—it is so ingrained. I have caught myself behaving in accordance with the code, despite my awareness of its falseness—denying sometimes that I'm emotionally in pain when in fact I am; insisting that everything is all right, when it is not.

The Boy Code puts boys and men into a gender straitjacket that constrains not only them but everyone else, reducing us all as human beings, and eventually making us strangers to ourselves and to one another—or, at least, not as strongly connected to one another as we long to be.

OPHELIA'S BROTHERS

In Shakespeare's *Hamlet,* Ophelia is lover to the young prince of Denmark. Despondent over the death of his father, Hamlet turns away from Ophelia. She, in turn, is devastated and she eventually commits suicide. In recent years, Mary Pipher's book on adolescent girls, *Reviving Ophelia,* has made Ophelia a symbolic figure for troubled, voiceless adolescent girls. But what of Hamlet? What of Ophelia's brothers?

For Hamlet fared little better than Ophelia. Alienated from himself, as well as from his mother and father, he was plagued by doubt and erupted in uncontrolled outbursts. He grew increasingly isolated, desolate, and alone, and those who loved him were never able to get through to him. In the end, he died a tragic and unnecessary death.

The boys we care for, much like the girls we cherish, often seem to feel they must live semi-inauthentic lives, lives that conceal much of their true selves and feelings, and studies show they do so in order to fit in and be loved. The boys I see—in the "Listening to Boys' Voices" study, in schools, and in private practice—often are hiding not only a wide range of their feelings but also some of their creativity and originality, showing in effect only a handful of primary colors rather than a broad spectrum of colors and hues of the self.

The Boy Code is so strong, yet so subtle, in its influence that boys may not even know they are living their lives in accordance with it. In fact, they may not realize there is such a thing until they violate the code in some way or try to ignore it. When they do, however, society tends to let them know—swiftly and forcefully—in the form of a taunt by a sibling, a rebuke by a parent or a teacher, or ostracism by classmates.

But, it doesn't have to be this way. I know that Adam could have been saved a great deal of pain if his parents and the well-meaning school authorities had known how to help him, how to make him feel safe to express his real feelings, beginning with the entirely natural anxiety about starting at a new school. This could have eased the transition from one school to a new one, rather than leaving Adam to tough it out by himself—even though Adam would have said, "Everything's all right."

HOW TO GET BEHIND THE MASK

As we'll discuss throughout this book, there are many ways that we can learn how to understand a boy's deepest feelings and experience, to come to know who he *really* is, and to help him love and feel comfortable with his genuine self. The starting place for parents—as well as for teachers and other mentors of our boys—is to become sensitive to the early signs of the masking of feelings. These signs include everything from bad grades to rowdy behavior, from "seeming quiet" to manifesting symptoms of depression, from using drugs or alcohol to becoming a perpetrator or victim of violence; and sometimes, as in the case of Adam, the mask may accompany the mantra that "everything is fine."

The second step to getting behind the mask is learning a new way to talk to boys so that they don't feel afraid or ashamed to share their true feelings. For example, when a boy like Adam comes home with a black eye, rather than saying "Oh my God! Just *what* is happening to you at school?" or "What the heck happened to you?" less intimidating language can be used, such as "What is going on—can you tell me?" or "I've noticed things seem a little different for you lately—now I can see something's wrong. Let's talk about it."

The third step is to learn how to accept a boy's own *emotional schedule.* As we'll discuss more in this book, boys who do share their feelings often take longer to do so than girls do. Whereas a girl might share her feelings as soon as she's asked what's going wrong, a boy will often refuse (or ignore us) the first time he's approached. We have to learn how to give the boy the time he needs and how to recognize in his words and actions the signals that he is ready to talk.

A boy's need to be silent—and then his subsequent readiness to share what he is feeling—is what we will call the *timed silence syndrome.* It's the boy who usually needs to set the clock himself—to determine how much time he needs to remain silent before opening up to share his feelings. If we learn to become sensitive to each boy's unique timing, we become better at respecting how he copes with emotions and make it more possible for him to be honest about the feelings behind the mask.

The fourth step involves what I call *connection through action.* This means that rather than nudging a boy to sit down and share his feelings with us, we begin by simply joining him in an activity that he enjoys. Often by simply *doing* something with the boy—playing a game with him, joining him for a duet on the piano, taking him to an amusement park—we forge a connection that then enables him to open up. In the middle of the game, the duet, or the Ferris wheel ride, a boy may often feel close and safe enough to share the feelings he'd otherwise keep hidden.

Finally, we can often help boys take off their masks by telling them stories about our own experiences. We can tell them "war stories" about when we were young and had to deal with life's ups and downs, or we can share recent experiences that challenged us. Even if our boy groans or rolls his eyes when we begin to share our story, he almost always benefits from the empathy that telling the story inevitably conveys. By discovering that, yes, we too have felt scared, embarrassed, or disappointed, the boy begins to feel less ashamed of his own vulnerable feelings. He feels our empathy and discovers that we understand, love, and respect the real boy in him.

For schools, getting behind the mask to help a boy like Adam requires several specific additional steps. First, as we'll learn throughout this book, teachers, school administrators, guidance counselors, and others all need to learn about how the Boy Code operates. They need to be actually trained to understand how this code restricts boys from being their true selves and how it pushes them to put on the mask. Second, I often suggest that schools assign to each boy an adult mentor who is sensitive and empathic to that boy's unique personality and interests. For example, the mentor for a boy who loves sports might be one of the gym teachers, whereas the mentor for the boy who loves poetry might be the English teacher. By assigning a mentor whose interests mirror those of the boy, the boy gains an adult friend with whom he can talk, somebody with whom he might feel comfortable sharing his deepest feelings and thoughts. Third, schools need to monitor closely those areas where the Boy Code operates most intensely. These include bus rides (where boys are often completely unsupervised), gym class, recess, and extracurricular sports. In such situations, teachers and other supervisors need to be especially vigilant about making sure that each boy is doing all right. Fourth, when teachers or others do intervene to help a boy who seems to be hurting behind the mask, it's important that they use the kind of nonshaming approach I discussed above. For example, when a boy seems to be the victim of a lot of teasing, rather than intervening suddenly by saying "Hey, what's going on here? Cut that out!" the adult supervisor might take aside the boys involved, individually and at separate times, and investigate what's happening in the particular situation. Finally, as I'll discuss more in this book, schools need to give boys a "report card" that covers not only their academic progress and classroom conduct but also their social life. By keeping an eye on a boy's social adjustment, schools are much better able to stay in touch with a boy's genuine emotional experience.

PREPARING A BOY FOR CHANGE

In addition to learning how to get to know the real boy, it's important for us as adults to anticipate situations such as important life changes—a move, a divorce, the birth of a new sibling—that are likely to bring up the kinds of painful feelings that force many boys to retreat behind the mask. For example, a new school, knowing that a boy like Adam was coming there from a less advantaged neighborhood, might have anticipated difficulties, assigned a buddy or mentor to Adam, an older boy who could teach him the ropes, introduce him to other boys, help him to become an insider rather than remain an outsider, and be a friend to ease him through the first weeks of school. The school counselors might have been in contact with Adam's mother from the first sign of an academic dip. Adam's teachers, too, might have been encouraged to help him get acquainted. Adam's parents might have spent more time with Adam during the first few weeks, and also prepared him in advance for his new experience, talking with him about what to expect, meeting with other parents and boys who had been involved in the same program, looking for another parent with a boy in the new school who might befriend Adam or talk with that parent about the school, visiting the school with Adam before his first day, and exploring the new neighborhood so he could adjust to the scene. Once he began to experience academic difficulties, which was the first indication to them that something was amiss, his parents might have tried to create safe spaces or activities to do together in which Adam might have felt able to open up and share his feelings; they might also have talked about their own memories of going away to college or feeling alone in a new experience.

A MOTHER'S INSTINCTS

One of the things I especially noticed in Adam's story is a hallmark of other boys' stories too—the mother's instincts were accurate; she *knew* in her heart that something was wrong. But she distrusted her own knowledge, and went along with the Boy Code and with Adam's saying, "Everything is all right." In her denial of what she in fact knew, and in her acceptance of society's code for boys, she disconnected from her own instincts, not realizing she knew better; she didn't feel empowered to listen to her own intuitions about her son or take action that might have been outside the code but could have helped Adam before the situation came to a crisis. With the very best of intentions, everyone involved—the parents and authorities at both schools—had pushed Adam away from help and connection, from the full range of expressing himself. Everyone believed that the special school program represented a great opportunity for him, as indeed it did; but they failed to realize that it also represented a change in his social setting that needed to be handled for and with the boy.

Adam tried to tough it out on his own, the way boys do. It's part of the code.

BEHIND THE MASK OF MASCULINITY: SHAME
AND THE TRAUMA OF SEPARATION

Just as Adam and his parents unwittingly adhered to the Boy Code, most parents and schools do the same. It has been ingrained in our society for so long, we're unaware of it. One educational expert recently suggested that the way to achieve equality in schooling would be by "teaching girls to raise their voices and boys to develop their ears." Of course boys should learn to listen. They should also speak clearly, in their own personal voices. I believe, however, that it's not boys who cannot hear us—it is we who are unable to hear them.

Researchers have found that at birth, and for several months afterward, *male infants are actually more emotionally expressive than female babies.* But by the time boys reach elementary school much of their emotional expressiveness has been lost or has gone underground. Boys at five or six become less likely than girls to express hurt or distress, either to their teachers or to their own parents. Many parents have asked me what triggers this remarkable transformation, this squelching of a boy's natural emotional expressiveness. What makes a boy who was open and exuberant unwilling to show the whole range of his emotions?

Recent research points to two primary causes for this change, and both of them grow out of assumptions about and attitudes toward boys that are deeply ingrained in the codes of our society.

The first reason is the use of shame in the toughening-up process by which it's assumed boys need to be raised. Little boys are made to feel ashamed of their feelings, guilty especially about feelings of weakness, vulnerability, fear, and despair.

The second reason is the separation process as it applies to boys, the emphasis society places on a boy's separating emotionally from his mother at an unnecessarily early age, usually by the time the boys are six years old and then again in adolescence.

The use of shame to "control" boys is pervasive; it is so corrosive I will devote a whole chapter to it in this book. Boys are made to feel shame over and over, in the midst of growing up, through what I call society's shame-hardening process. The idea is that a boy needs to be disciplined, toughened up, made to act like a "real man," be independent, keep the emotions in check. A boy is told that "big boys don't cry," that he shouldn't be "a mama's boy." If these things aren't said directly, these messages dominate in subtle ways in how boys are treated—and therefore how boys come to think of themselves. Shame is at the heart of how others behave toward boys on our playing fields, in schoolrooms, summer camps, and in our homes. A number of other societal factors contribute to this old-fashioned process of shame-hardening boys, and I'll have more to say about shame in the next chapter.

The second reason we lose sight of the real boy behind a mask of masculinity, and ultimately lose the boy himself, is the premature separation of a boy from his mother and all things maternal at the beginning of school. Mothers are encouraged to separate from their sons, and the act of forced separation is so common that it is generally considered to be "normal." But I have come to understand that this forcing of early separation is so acutely hurtful to boys that it can only be called a trauma—an emotional blow of damaging proportions. I also believe that it is an unnecessary trauma. Boys, like girls, will separate very naturally from their mothers, if allowed to do so at their own pace.

As if the trauma of separation at age six were not wrenching enough, boys often suffer a second separation trauma when they reach sexual maturity. As a boy enters adolescence, our society becomes concerned and confused about the mother-son relationship. We feel unsure about how intimate a mother should be with her sexually mature son. We worry that an intense and loving relationship between the two will somehow get in the way of the boy's ability to form friendships with girls his own age. As a result, parents—encouraged by the society around them—may once again push the boy away from the family and, in particular, the nurturing female realm. Our society tells us this is "good" for the boy, that he needs to be pushed out of the nest or he will never fly. But I believe that the opposite is true—that a boy will make the leap when he is ready, and he will do it better if he feels that there is someone there to catch him if he falls.

This double trauma of boyhood contributes to the creation in boys of a deep wellspring of grief and sadness that may last throughout their lives.

MIXED MESSAGES: SOCIETY'S NEW EXPECTATIONS FOR BOYS

But there is another problem too: society's new expectations for boys today are in direct conflict with the teachings of the Boy Code—and we have done little to resolve the contradiction. We now say that we want boys to share their vulnerable feelings, but at the same time we expect them to cover their need for dependency and *hide* their natural feelings of love and caring behind the mask of masculine autonomy and strength. It's an impossible assignment for any boy, or, for that matter, any human being.

THE SILENCE OF LOST BOYS

Often, the result of all this conflation of signals is that the boys decide to be silent. They learn to suffer quietly, in retreat behind the mask of masculinity. They cannot speak, and we cannot hear. It's this silence that is often confusing to those of us concerned about the well-being of boys because it fools us into thinking that all is well, when much may be awry—that a boy doesn't need us, when in fact he needs us very much.

The good news is that we now know of many ways that we can help boys, and they are based on various patterns we now understand about typical boy behavior. Understanding these patterns, these ways of a real boy's life, will, I believe, help us raise boys of all ages in more successful and authentic ways. For the truth is that once we help boys shed the straitjacket of gender—once we hear and understand what a real boy says, feels, and sees—the silence is broken and replaced by a lively roar of communication. The disconnection quickly becomes reconnection. And once we reconnect with one boy, it can lead to stronger bonds with all the males in our lives—our brothers and fathers and husbands and sons. It can also help boys to connect again with their deepest feelings, their true selves.

LIVING WITH HALF A SELF—THE "HEROIC" HALF

Until now, many boys have been able to live out and express only *half* of their emotional lives—they feel free to show their "heroic," tough, action-oriented side, their physical prowess, as well as their anger and rage. What the Boy Code dictates is that they should suppress all other emotions and cover up the more gentle, caring, vulnerable sides of themselves. In the "Listening to Boys' Voices" study, many boys told me that they feel frightened and yearn to make a connection but can't. "At school, and even most times with my parents," one boy explained, "you can't act like you're a weakling. If you start acting scared or freaking out like a crybaby, my parents get mad, other kids punch you out or just tell you to shut up and cut it out." One mother told me what she expected of her nine-year-old son. "I don't mind it when Tony complains a little bit," she said, "but if he starts getting really teary-eyed and whiny I tell him to just put a lid on it. It's for his own good because if the other boys in the area hear him crying, they'll make it tough for him. Plus, his father really hates that kind of thing!"

Boys suppress feelings of rejection and loss also. One sixteen-year-old boy was told by his first girlfriend, after months of going together, that she didn't love him anymore. "You feel sick," confessed Cam. "But you just keep it inside. You don't tell anybody about it. And, then, maybe after a while, it just sort of goes away."

"It must feel like such a terrible burden, though, being so alone with it," I remarked.

"Yep," Cam sighed, fighting off tears. "But that's what a guy has to do, isn't it?"

Jason, age fifteen, recently wrote the following in an essay about expressing feelings:

> If something happens to you, you have to say: "Yeah, no big deal," even when you're really hurting. . . . When it's a tragedy—like my friend's father died—you can go up to a guy and give him a hug. But if it's anything less . . . you have to punch things and brush it off. I've punched so many lockers in my life, it's not even funny. When I get home, I'll cry about it.

I believe, and my studies indicate, that many boys are eager to be heard and that we, as parents and professionals, must use all our resources to reach out and help them. As adults, we have both the power and perspective to see through the boys' false front of machismo, especially when we know enough to expect it and to understand it for what it is—a way to look in-charge and cool.

A four-year-old boy shrugs and tries to smile after he is hit in the eye with a baseball, while blinking back tears of pain. A ten-year-old boy whose parents have just divorced behaves so boisterously and entertainingly in class he's branded the "class clown," but underneath that bravado is a lot of suffering; he longs for the days when his parents were together and he didn't need that kind of attention. A fourteen-year-old flips listlessly through a sports magazine while his school counselor discusses the boy's poor conduct. When the counselor warns the boy that his behavior may well lead to failure and suspension from school—trying to discipline through shame, through a threat of rejection—the boy retorts, "So what?"

Unfortunately, at times we all believe the mask because it fits so well and is worn so often it becomes more than just a barrier to genuine communication or intimacy. The tragedy is that the mask can actually become impossible to remove, leaving boys emotionally hollowed out and vulnerable to failure at school, depression, substance abuse, violence, even suicide.

BOYS TODAY ARE FALLING BEHIND

While it may seem as if we live in a "man's world," at least in relation to power and wealth in adult society we do not live in a "boy's world." Boys on the whole are not faring well in our schools, especially in our public schools. It is in the classroom that we see some of the most destructive effects of society's misunderstanding of boys. Thrust into competition with their peers, some boys invest so much energy into keeping up their emotional guard and disguising their deepest and most vulnerable feelings, they often have little or no energy left to apply themselves to their schoolwork. No doubt boys still show up as small minorities at the top of a few academic lists, playing starring roles as some teachers' best students. But, most often, boys form the majority of the bottom of the class. Over the last decade we've been forced to confront some staggering statistics. From elementary grades through high school, boys receive lower grades than girls. Eighth-grade boys are held back 50 percent more often than girls. By high school, boys account for two thirds of the students in special education classes. Fewer boys than girls now attend and graduate from college. Fifty-nine percent of all master's degree candidates are now women, and the percentage of men in graduate-level professional education is shrinking each year.

So, there is a gender gap in academic performance, and boys are falling to the bottom of the heap. The problem stems as much from boys' lack of confidence in their ability to perform at school as from their actual inability to perform.

When eighth-grade students are asked about their futures, girls are now twice as likely as boys to say they want to pursue a career in management, the professions, or business. Boys experience more difficulty adjusting to school, are up to ten times more likely to suffer from "hyperactivity" than girls, and account for 71 percent of all school suspensions. In recent years, girls have been making great strides in math and science.

In the same period, boys have been severely lagging behind in reading and writing.

BOYS' SELF-ESTEEM—AND BRAGGING

The fact is that *boys' self-esteem as learners is far more fragile than that of most girls.* A recent North Carolina study of students in grades six to eight concluded that "Boys have a much lower image of themselves as students than girls do." Conducted by Dr. William Purkey, this study contradicts the myth that adolescent boys are more likely than girls to see themselves as smart enough to succeed in society. Boys tend to brag, according to Purkey, as a "shield to hide deep-seated lack of confidence." It is the mask at work once again, a façade of confidence and bravado that boys erect to hide what they perceive as a shameful sense of vulnerability. Girls, on the other hand, brag less and do better in school. It is probably no surprise that a recent U.S. Department of Education study found that among high school seniors fewer boys than girls expect to pursue graduate studies, work toward a law degree, or go to medical school.

What we really need for boys is the same upswing in self-esteem as learners that we have begun to achieve for girls—to recognize the specialized academic needs of boys and girls in order to turn us into a more gender-savvy society.

Overwhelmingly, recent research indicates that girls not only outperform boys academically but also feel far more confident and capable. Indeed the boys in my study reported, over and over again, how it was not "cool" to be too smart in class, for it could lead to being labeled a nerd, dork, wimp, or fag. As one boy put it, "I'm not stupid enough to sit in the front row and act like some sort of teacher's pet. If I did, I'd end up with a head full of spitballs and then get my butt kicked in." Just as girls in coeducational environments have been forced to suppress their voices of certainty and truth, boys feel pressured to hide their yearnings for genuine relationships and their thirst for knowledge. To garner acceptance among their peers and protect themselves from being shamed, boys often focus on maintaining their masks and on doing whatever they can to avoid seeming interested in things creative or intellectual. To distance themselves from the things that the stereotype identifies as "feminine," many boys sit through classes without contributing and tease other boys who speak up and participate. Others pull pranks during class, start fights, skip classes, or even drop out of school entirely.

SCHOOLS AND THE NEED FOR GENDER UNDERSTANDING

Regrettably, instead of working with boys to convince them it is desirable and even "cool" to perform well at school, teachers, too, are often fooled by the mask and believe the stereotype; and this helps to make the lack of achievement self-fulfilling. If a teacher believes that boys who are not doing well are simply uninterested, incapable, or delinquent, and signals this, it helps to make it so. Indeed when boys feel pain at school, they sometimes put on the mask and then "act out." Teachers, rather than exploring the emotional reasons behind a boy's misconduct, may instead apply behavioral control techniques that are intended somehow to better "civilize" boys.

Sal, a third-grader, arrived home with a note from his teacher. "Sal had to be disciplined today for his disruptive behavior," the teacher had written. "Usually he is a very cooperative student, and I hope this behavior does not repeat itself."

Sal's mother, Audrey, asked her son what he had done.

"I was talking out of turn in class," he said.

"That's it?" she asked. "And how did your teacher discipline you?"

"She made me stay in during recess. She made me write an essay about why talking in class is disruptive and inconsiderate." Sal hung his head.

"I was appalled," recalls Audrey. "If the teacher had spent one minute with my child, trying to figure out why he was behaving badly, this whole thing could have been avoided." The teacher had known Sal to be "a very cooperative student." It seems that, the night before, Sal had learned that a favorite uncle had been killed in a car crash. "I told my son that I understood that he was having a really hard day because of his uncle, but that, even so, it's wrong to disrupt class. He was very relieved that I wasn't mad," Audrey said. "The episode made me think about how boys get treated in school. I think the teacher assumed that Sal was just 'being a boy.' And so, although what he really needed was a little understanding and extra attention instead she humiliated him. It reminded me to think about how Sal must be feeling when something like this happens, because he often won't talk about what's bothering him unless we prompt him to."

As a frequent guest in schools across the country, I have observed a practice I consider to be inappropriate, even dangerous—and based on a misunderstanding of boys. Elementary school teachers will offer the boys in their class a special "reward"—such as a better grade, an early recess, or an extra star on their good-behavior tally sheet—if the boys will *not* raise their hand more than once per class period. They find that some boys are so eager to talk and so boisterous in clamoring to be called on that their behavior disrupts the order of the classroom.

High school teachers sometimes adopt the same practice with their adolescent boy students, particularly those who act up or talk out of turn in class. The teachers will let the boys leave early or take a short break from class if they demonstrate that they can keep quiet and "behave." In other words, instead of trying to look behind the behavior to the real boy, to what is going on inside him, teachers assume a negative, and ask these boys to make themselves even *more* invisible and to suppress their genuine selves further. Ironically, they're asking boys to act more like the old stereotype of the passive, "feminine" girl. The teachers may get what they want—a quiet classroom—but at what cost? Such approaches silence boys' voices of resistance and struggle and individuality, and serve to perpetuate boys' attention-seeking acts of irreverence.

We need to develop a new code for real boys, gender-informed schools, and a more gender-savvy society where both boys and girls are drawn out to be themselves.

If we want boys to become more empathic, we must be more empathic toward them.

THE POTENCY OF CONNECTION—A NEW CODE FOR BOYS AND GIRLS

Growing up as a boy brings its own special difficulties, but the good news is that boys can and do overcome them when and if they feel connected to their families, friends, and communities. My research demonstrates that despite society's traumatizing pressure on boys to disconnect from their vulnerable inner selves, many, if not most, boys maintain an inner well-spring of emotional connectedness, a resilience, that helps to sustain them. Sometimes these affective ties are formed with special male friends—boys' "chumships." Boys may also forge empathic and meaningful friend-ships with girls and young women, relationships that are often platonic.

The fact is that boys experience deep subliminal yearnings for con-nection—a *hidden yearning for relationship*—that makes them long to be close to parents, teachers, coaches, friends, and family. Boys are full of love and empathy for others and long to stay "attached" to their parents and closest mentors. These yearnings, in turn, can empower parents and professionals to become more deeply connected to the boys in their lives, much as Professor Carol Gilligan at Harvard and researchers at the Stone Center Group at Wellesley College have so eloquently advocated we do for girls. This intense power to connect of parents and others is part of the "potency of connection" that needs to be at the heart of a revised real-boy code. Through the potency of connection a boy can be helped to become himself, to grow into manhood in his own individual way—to be fully the "real boy" we know he is.

—2—

STORIES OF SHAME AND THE HAUNTING TRAUMA OF SEPARATION: HOW WE CAN CONNECT WITH BOYS AND CHANGE THE "BOY CODE"

"It's really hard being a guy," fifteen-year-old Calvin Branford recently explained to me, "because you're really expected not to talk about your feelings. You've got to deal with everything yourself. With girls, everybody expects they'll go off and talk to somebody. When you're a guy you're really not allowed to do that. I guess it's pretty hard being a guy because there are so many things a normal person would probably do, but you're just not expected to!"

JOHNNY: THE TRAUMA OF SEPARATION AND SHAMING A BOY

Johnny Martin was a boy of not quite five years of age who went for his first day in kindergarten. He was one of the smaller boys in the class. I spied him across a crowded room of five- and six-year-olds, all accompanied by their parents on this first day at a public primary school in a middle-class, educationally sophisticated suburb.

The voice of the school principal came over the loudspeaker with a special greeting to all the new kindergarten students. He reminded them of the school's core principles: learning, respect for self and others, and diversity. Parents and children alike seemed too dazed and confused by this momentous occasion to take in much of this. My ears perked up when he said that all parents would be expected to leave at the ten-minute bell, but for today, and this day only, parents could stay with their kindergart-ners for five extra minutes to say good-bye. I guess that's when Johnny really came into view. He began to cling to his mother, and she with great animation was whispering something I could not hear.

I understood from past painful experience that a child would do fine if he or she could let go of his mother at his own pace, be allowed to remain connected for as long as necessary each day or until he was ready to make the developmental leap of separation on his own.

Johnny was not so lucky. Surrounded by a group of five boys who couldn't wait to start playing with the trucks and crayons, Johnny stuck out like a sore thumb, a sensitive and still very young boy who wasn't ready quite yet to let go, who feared separation from his mother.

When the bell rang, most of the parents drifted away, leaving only those who seemed to know from experience that their kids would need them to be there for a while longer or some parents who probably just felt deep inside it was wrong to go quite yet. I asked the mother of another lit-tle boy, Sean, who was playing enthusiastically but continuing to look over his shoulder to see if his mommy was still there, what she thought.

"I don't know much about these things, but Sean just looks like he needs to be with me some more, so I'm staying," she said.

Johnny's mother was more confused. She looked to Rachel, Johnny's teacher, who offered the traditional prescription: "A clean break and he'll be OK."

The mother whispered to Johnny, "Now, be a big boy—not like your crybaby little sister—and you'll be fine." With misty eyes, she kissed him on the head and started to leave. But before she reached the door, Johnny started to cry—his wailing could be heard all the way down the hall in the office of Mr. Bartlett, the school's principal. In a flash he was on the scene, and suggested that Ms. Friedland, the school nurse, get involved.

Ms. Friedland, a woman in her late fifties, came and advised that Rachel would need to be stricter with the students.

"You'll learn, Rachel, that setting a firm limit is the best thing, espe-cially for boys!"

When Rachel asked, "Why boys?" Ms. Friedland delivered a perfect summary of the Boy Code. "Separation is hard for girls," she explained with authority, "since they're so close to their mothers. Boys, however, have to be more independent or their peers will call them sissies and make fun of them. It's our job to help boys deal with this, especially if their mothers haven't done it themselves." She glanced at Johnny's mother. "You don't want Johnny to become overdependent, do you?" she asked. "Let's see if we can get him to handle things on his own."

Now that the "experts" were involved, Johnny's mother was told that she could feel free to leave. Johnny was still crying, though less frantically, and as the nurse began to read him a story, Mom left.

Later that week, when I had the chance to observe the classroom again, I asked Rachel how things were going. "Well, some parents wait to leave until their kids give them a signal that they're ready to be on their own," she explained. "Most of these kids have adjusted beautifully, and each day they let their parents go sooner. I wish I could say the same for all the other kids. Some of the boys, especially those who were so brave on the first day, spend a good deal of time crying for their mothers, and I have to comfort them, often in a group."

"What about Johnny Martin?" I asked.

"You'll see for yourself in a minute. . . . I've got to get ready for the class."

The bell rang and almost all the parents scattered. Sean's mother was still staying behind, and now was enlisted in comforting some of the other boys who looked sad when their dads and moms left the room at 9:05. I heard what at first I thought to be a loud coughing noise in the corner, and when I turned around, I saw Johnny Martin, isolated from his classmates on the side of the room, vomiting into a small wastepaper basket.

"What's the matter, Rachel?" I asked.

"He's been doing that every day after his mother leaves—crying and throwing up!"

"What did the school nurse have to say?"

"Well, Ms. Friedland thinks he's 'overattached to his mother,' that if this disruption continues, he may need a special class or therapeutic counseling." As we spoke, Johnny kept vomiting, and the class fell silent as if awed by the sight. There and then I broke a vow I had made to myself— never to give a teacher advice when I was only invited to "observe" his or her classroom—but Johnny was traumatized and Rachel, a novice at her job but empathic at heart, knew something was wrong. I explained that vomiting was a stage two response to unbearable separation, an escalation from the crying that had led to no adequate response, and that next might come a more dangerous withdrawal. Then the nurse and principal would have a self-fulfilling prophecy of a "special needs" boy on their hands. I told Rachel that all kids separate at their own rates and that boys need not be pushed to separate more quickly than girls. At first I worried about the impact of my blunt comments, but Rachel's response reassured me.

She breathed a sigh of relief, and when Ms. Friedland came to check in, Rachel told her that since the present plan wasn't working, and since it was her classroom, she would try a technique of her own. Johnny's mother would be invited back and would stay until her child felt more comfortable—and felt less pressure—to separate.

A month later I saw Rachel again. "Thanks for your advice," she said. "It worked wonderfully. Johnny's mother felt less guilty, Johnny seemed more self-assured, and after about ten days he let his mom leave without any fuss. Now if I can only get up the courage as a second-year teacher to confront Mr. Bartlett and Ms. Friedland about this policy and the needs of the boys in my class, I'll be all set."

THE BOY CODE: FOUR INJUNCTIONS

Boys learn the Boy Code in sandboxes, playgrounds, schoolrooms, camps, churches, and hangouts, and are taught by peers, coaches, teachers, and just about everybody else. In the "Listening to Boys' Voices" study, even very young boys reported that they felt they must "keep a stiff upper lip," "not show their feelings," "act real tough," "not act too nice," "be cool," "just laugh and brush it off when someone punches you." These boys were not referring to subtle suggestions about how they "might" comport themselves. Rather, they were invoking strict rules they had absorbed about how they "must" behave, rules that most of them seemed to genuinely fear breaking.

Relying on well-known research, Professors Deborah David and Robert Brannon divided these kinds of do-or-die rules, or "injunctions," boys follow into four basic stereotyped male ideals or models of behavior. These four imperatives are at the heart of the Boy Code.

The "sturdy oak." Men should be stoic, stable, and independent. A man never shows weakness. Accordingly, boys are not to share pain or grieve openly. Boys are considered to have broken this guideline, for instance, if they whimper, cry, or complain—or sometimes even if they simply ask for an explanation in a confusing or frightening situation. As one boy in the "Voices" study put it: "If somebody slugs you in the face, probably the best thing you could do is just smile and act like it didn't hurt.

You definitely shouldn't cry or say anything." The "sturdy oak" require-ment drains boys' energy because it calls upon them to perform a constant "acting job"—to pretend to be confident when they may feel afraid, sturdy when they may feel shaky, independent when they may be desperate for love, attention, and support.

"Give 'em hell." This is the stance of some of our sports coaches, of roles played by John Wayne, Clint Eastwood, and Bruce Lee, a stance based on a false self, of extreme daring, bravado, and attraction to vio-lence. This injunction stems largely from the myth that "boys will be boys" (more on such myths later)—the misconception that somehow boys are biologically wired to act like macho, high-energy, even violent super-men. This is the Boy Code requirement that leads many boys to "dare" each other to engage in risky behaviors and that causes some parents to simply shrug their shoulders if their sons injure themselves or others.

The "big wheel." This is the imperative men and boys feel to achieve status, dominance, and power. Or, understood another way, the "big wheel" refers to the way in which boys and men are taught to avoid shame at all costs, to wear the mask of coolness, to act as though everything is going all right, as though everything is under control, even if it isn't. This Boy Code imperative leads many boys and men to push themselves exces-sively at academic or career-related work, often in an effort to repress feel-ings of failure or unhappiness.

"No sissy stuff." Perhaps the most traumatizing and dangerous injunction thrust on boys and men is the literal gender straitjacket that pro-hibits boys from expressing feelings or urges seen (mistakenly) as "femi-nine"—dependence, warmth, empathy. According to the ideal of "no sissy stuff," such feelings and behaviors are taboo. Rather than being allowed to explore these emotional states and activities, boys are prematurely forced to shut them out, to become self-reliant. And when boys start to break under the strain, when nonetheless they display "feminine" feelings or behaviors, they are usually greeted not with empathy but with ridicule, with taunts and threats that shame them for their failure to act and feel in stereotypically "masculine" ways. And so boys become determined never to act that way again—they bury those feelings.

And so in several fundamental ways the Boy Code affects the ability of boys and adults to connect.

First, it separates boys from their parents too early, before most boys are actually emotionally prepared for it. When boys encounter some of early childhood's most trying times—when they sleep alone in a crib for the first time, are sent away for two weeks of summer camp, or separate from their parents for the first day of kindergarten—they are often being pushed toward pseudo-independence before they're really ready.

Yet when boys rebel against this push to separate—when they cry, get injured, or tell friends that they'd rather stay at home than go outside and play—society's Boy Code makes them feel ashamed of themselves. Shame haunts many boys all their lives, undermining their core of self-confidence, eroding their fragile self-esteem, leaving them with profound feelings of loneliness, sadness, and disconnection. Moreover, it affects our ability to fully connect with our boys.

Even when boys appear sad or afraid, our culture lets them know in no uncertain terms that they had better toughen up and "tough it out" by themselves. The feelings boys are forced to repress become so troubling that some boys may show the apparent symptoms of attention deficit disorder and serious conduct disorders, become depressed, and—when they're older—turn to alcohol or drugs. Indeed, the same kind of shame that silences adolescent girls from expressing their true voice affects boys at a much younger age—at the age of five or six.

But the good news, I also believe, is that neither boys nor the adults who care for them need to live by these rules. Boys can rebel against them and revise the code for boys and girls so that they can experience a broad range of feelings and behaviors. Parents do not have to resist their deepest feelings for their sons or let myths about boys overwhelm the wisdom of their own instincts. Together we can unlearn the Boy Code. Together we can insist on enjoying close, emotionally rich relationships, based on connection instead of disconnection.

ROGER: BOOT CAMP FOR LONELINESS AND SHAME

Roger's mother sent him to a three-week "sleep away" summer camp program for the first time. "I guess I wasn't really thinking about how hard it might be for him to be away from me at age seven," his mother, Jaye Waters, explained. "Later, when I thought more about it, I realized I would never have been ready for that at his age. I guess I thought a boy would like to have an 'independent' adventure on his own. As a single parent, I was really looking forward to a few weeks to myself. I forgot that he is as attached to me as I was to my mother when I was seven years old."

Roger was miserable from the moment his mom dropped him off at the camp. "I didn't know anybody. I kept looking at my mom's picture, but it wasn't enough. I hated camp," Roger told me tearfully.

Jaye saved the heart-wrenching letter Roger mailed on his third day there. "Dear Mom," it read, "I hate it here. The food makes me throw up. Nothing we do is fun. I am crying every day because I miss you so much. I think of you all the time. I know you love me so please come get me right now. Love, Your Son."

"I considered driving the three hours to get him that day, but I decided to wait until visiting day over the weekend. I wanted to make sure he wouldn't get used to it and start liking it after a few more days," Jaye explained. "I tried to call on the phone, but the camp director explained it would be better to let him 'tough it out.' "

Roger came back with her that Saturday. "I'll never know how damaging it was to him to be there for that whole week. I hope that he got something out of it, but I'm afraid all he got was a lot of pain that probably nobody would have expected him to put up with if he were a girl. . . . I realize some separations can be painful and are necessary for kids, but it was just too soon and nobody saw it—not even the supposed expert of a camp director!"

"I don't ever want to go to camp again," Roger maintains. "I'd rather just hang around here while my mom goes to work, than go anyplace else."

PREMATURE SEPARATION—THE TRAUMA OF BOYHOOD

Both Roger Waters and Johnny Martin were suffering the trauma of premature separation, the source of much of their pain today—the disconnection they feel and their fear of being shamed. For all of society's mandates to boys to act like invulnerable superheroes, among all the subtle messages given to boys to downplay their sadness and pain, premature separation is the deepest hurt of all.

At the heart of society's beliefs about boys are the ideas that, early on, boys need to achieve "masculine autonomy" and that even today this is a prerequisite for a boy's healthy psychological development.

Since young boys are taught that staying close to their mothers is something shameful, one of their natural responses is to turn to their fathers for love. Yet for some boys, mother may offer a special kind of nurturing, loving interaction that even the most caring father may not be able to replicate. And for many other boys, father may simply not be there to meet them. Fathers often work long hours, tend to leave parenting to the mother, or are not able to nurture their sons' emotional development. Many fathers *want* to be there for their sons, but fear that doing so will only bring their sons further shame or distress. In a later chapter I'll have more to say about the empathic relationships of fathers and sons.

At a very young age, a boy may feel emotionally abandoned, without knowing that's what he feels. Or he may know—as eleven-year-old Jake described this part of his early childhood: "I felt left out in the cold. I was all alone and just had to fend for myself." Or as seventeen-year-old Jamal explained, "My dad always seemed jealous and would throw these real temper tantrums if my mom let me lean on her. So by the time I was five, neither one of them acted like they really understood what I was going through, even if they really did."

This painful separation process by which many very young boys are shamed into withdrawing from their mothers more than they naturally want to, and then are only partially nurtured by their fathers, is a devastating disruption in a boy's emotional life. It is too often vigorously defended or even celebrated as a natural movement forward for the young boy, an inevitable step away from childlike dependency toward so-called "healthy" masculine identity. Yet many people who advocate this attitude toward boys believe it would be a tragedy if such a schism were to happen so early in a young girl's life.

This relational rupture, this *trauma,* profoundly affects the psychology of most boys—and of most men—forever. To understand what it is like to experience this trauma, we needn't go any further than the trauma adults experience when their hearts are broken—the trauma of unrequited love. In my clinical practice, I have found that deep in the psyche of older boys and men lies the formative experience of a little boy struggling to maintain an early independent masculine sense of self. That little boy is *not* fending off too close a tie to mother, but rather is forever longing to return to her, and to the "holding" connection she once provided him, a connection he now feels he can never regain. If a boy had been allowed to separate at his own pace, that longing and sadness would not be there, or would be much less.

WISHING TO REMAIN IN MOTHER'S REALM IS NORMAL

Although by kindergarten age many boys are already taking on the persona of their favorite superwarrior, replete with space-age weapons and other high-tech equipment, other boys of that age, and certainly many boys in preschool, are still in the corner playing with dolls and small trucks, and with the girls. For parents who ask me whether this is "normal," I usually share with them research pioneered by New York psychoanalyst John Ross. In a study in which he explored young boys' fantasies about pregnancy and birth, Ross found that healthy boys—boys with a clear sense of masculine gender identity—still believed that, like their mothers, they could get pregnant, carry a child in "their tummies," and give birth. This is not at all surprising when we stop to realize that the lion's share of child care for both girls and boys is given by mothers and female caregivers, and, naturally, young boys identify with their earliest role models. So it is equally unremarkable to see a younger boy playing with a doll or even dressing up in Mom's dress. But woe be unto him if this behavior continues beyond the age of five or six.

By the time boys are ready to enter school they receive numerous messages—in the media, from the toys they are given to play with, from older boys, parents, and teachers—that they must become different from their mothers in order to have a healthy male mentality. Toy manufacturers pour resources into creating "boy toys"—weapons and warriors and games of destruction. Schools still offer gender-specific activities, even when there is no valid reason for doing so. The cultural imperative to achieve this differentiation lies under the push toward separation.

Nancy Chodorow, a feminist sociologist, did research that looked at how boys and girls connect with their mothers. She showed that because, in our society, women are still largely responsible for child care, boys appear to have a harder time than girls in integrating their identification as males, their initial "gender identity." Girls can remain comfortably bonded with mother, she explained, but boys are threatened with a danger of remaining too close and not consolidating a safe enough sense of a "different," more masculine self. Following from her argument, then, being a boy or being masculine is not so much based on the positive identification with father but on the negation of the male child's tie to mother. Becoming masculine is defined as avoiding the feminine. *Being a boy becomes defined in the negative: not being a girl.* And this requires a more rigid separation from the close-touch world of mother and all things feminine or maternal—including warm, tender feelings, such as vulnerability, empathy, and compassion.

Some professionals still believe that this push for separation is good and necessary, that it provides a healthy way station in boys' growth toward manhood. This kind of separation is called "dis-identification," since the boy, by separating, is renouncing his earlier identification with mother and replacing it with a supposedly "healthier" male self-image now borrowed from his father. But, in my opinion, this model of dis-identification is not healthy but damaging. If girls were emotionally separated from the caring people in their young lives and thrust into a world hostile to their dependency needs, we'd probably say these girls were in deep trouble, that they would fail unless they were rescued. Yet when it is boys whose development we are contemplating, this ruptured connection is celebrated and is called a manifestation of "health."

BOYS ARE ALONE

Let's imagine what this experience of ruptured connection must actually feel like for a little boy. Let's imagine the sense of loss a boy must feel as he is prodded to separate from the most cherished, admired, and loved person in his life, the shame and embarrassment he often encounters whenever he's asked to "act like a man" but doesn't yet feel equipped to do so, the destructive feelings—of self-hatred, inadequacy, loneliness—that become deeply embedded within the definition he creates of his own nascent masculine identity.

A recent poll taken of children as young as *nine years old* showed that only 40 percent of boys spent almost all weekend with their parents, as opposed to 50 percent of the girls.

While not quite one tenth of the girls sampled said they spent few or no hours with their families on the weekends, almost 25 percent of the young boys polled reported that they were already out on their own! Given the young age of many of the boys involved in this study, these statistics are staggering. They suggest that the schism between boys and their parents most often thought of as taking place at adolescence actually begins at a much earlier age. And the younger boys are when this separation is first thrust upon them, I believe, the more traumatic they may find the experience.

CHRISTOPHER: LONELINESS AND SADNESS BEHIND A YOUNG BOY'S MASK

Sometimes a boy must undergo an unexpected and painful separation from his caregivers that is not related to a first day of school or time away at camp.

Christopher Benson is a ten-year-old who came to see a colleague of mine. His parents were baffled as to how he could have become so depressed. An energetic, upbeat, extremely well-liked boy for most of his childhood, Christopher had undergone, a year earlier, a series of operations after a major bicycle accident had seriously injured his right foot. After the accident, Christopher had had to undergo months of medical treatments and physical therapy. He had missed weeks of school, and his whole family had rallied behind him to help him through the process.

His parents couldn't figure out why only now, a year later, after Christopher had almost completely healed, he had suddenly become so depressed. According to his parents, Christopher had dealt with the accident and its aftermath with a positive attitude. He had rarely complained about the acute pain, never put up a fight when he had to undergo medical treatments, and had always joked about his condition with doctors, nurses, and family members. Everybody had loved Christopher. During his year of recovery, his parents had taken off a lot of time from work to be with him. For the months that Christopher was hospitalized, one of Christopher's parents had visited him in the afternoon every day, and many times one of them had spent the night with him at the hospital.

About eleven months after the accident, Christopher had recovered almost a hundred percent of the use of his right leg and was otherwise in top health. His doctors told him he could return to school on a full-time basis. His parents resumed their full-time work schedules and Christopher went back to school. But instead of rejoicing in his recovery and slipping back cheerfully into his life at school and with his friends, Christopher became deeply depressed. He virtually stopped eating, became extremely quiet, and refused to cooperate with his parents or his teachers. He lost most of his energy, didn't respond when spoken to, and protested each morning when his parents tried to wake him up to send him off to school.

For weeks Christopher refused to say much of anything in his psychotherapy sessions. When asked how things were going for him, he either ignored my colleague or simply said that things were "fine." But about six weeks into his therapy, Christopher finally opened up. When asked how his foot was doing, he stood up, kicked over his chair with his once-injured foot, and shouted, "I wish it were broken again. I wish it were broken! I hate this!"

"Tell me about what you hate. Do you hate having everything seem like it's OK when it really isn't?" my colleague asked him.

"Everything *was* OK when I was at the hospital," he explained, his words cut off by tears. "But now, everything sucks. I hate school. . . . I hate everything."

"Have you spoken to your parents about this?"

"They wouldn't care. They only cared about me when I was in the hospital. Now that I'm all better, they spend all their time with my little sister, Jessica. They hardly even talk to me."

"Then you miss having special times with your parents?"

Christopher responded by sobbing.

In future sessions with Christopher, his parents were invited to come along. What emerged through these discussions was that once he returned from the hospital, Christopher still sought the extra attention his parents had given him when he was undergoing medical treatment. Christopher wanted to keep receiving the extra love, affection, and support they had given him when he was in the hospital. Although they loved him very much and wanted to see him happy, his parents were concerned about Christopher's apparent need for this kind of special attention. So instead of talking to him about it, instead of reassuring him about how much they loved and cared for him, they both nudged him away. They were, in effect, doing exactly as Johnny's mother and Roger's mother had done with their boys—forcing him to make "a clean break" and "tough it out" without adequate preparation or support. They both felt certain that if they continued to "baby" him, he would become overly dependent on them. "I didn't want to treat him like we treat his younger sister anymore," his father, Chip, explained, "because I felt that he should begin to learn how to handle things on his own. It was one thing when he was at the hospital. But once he had come home, I just didn't think he needed me or his mother to treat him like a little boy anymore."

"I really wanted to continue to take time off from work and spend it with Chris in the afternoons," his mother added, "but Chip convinced me that this would just make it harder for him to adjust to going back to school. I don't know. Maybe we were wrong not to stick in there longer for him."

Christopher's parents were gentle, thoughtful people. They wanted what was best for Christopher. But what they were unable to do was feel comfortable staying emotionally connected to their son once an emergency had passed. Something made them feel that it was time to nudge this boy toward independence. This impulse, I believe, is "normal" in that many parents feel and act upon it. But as common as it may be, I believe that pushing boys to separate, to be on their own, when they signal they need something else, is a mistake with serious emotional consequences. It is so traumatic that it can lead, as it did in the case of Christopher, to depression.

SHAME: THE CONSEQUENCE OF EMOTIONAL DISCONNECTION

As boys reach adolescence the traumas of early childhood can persist in forms that do not look like normal sadness or loss. So masked are boys' feelings by the teen years that many of the inexplicable bouts of anger or wild mood swings parents see may be produced in part by earlier, unrequited longings for connection and a fear of the shame such longings produce.

Shame, it turns out, is with most of us throughout our lives. It begins to be experienced very early on, and is perhaps one of our most primitive feelings. Infants show the precursors to shame—physical responses such as painful blushing and "heat"—when their vocalizations for parental response or gestures for recognition go largely unacknowledged. In some psychological research, shame is associated primarily with these types of early physical sensations. But I have come to believe—following Judy Jordan, my colleague at Harvard Medical School—that shame can also be described as the feeling state that accompanies an emotional disconnection.

We all experience such emotional disconnection. Two common examples come to mind. The first one, suggested by a patient some years ago, involves what happens when we see somebody we know across a crowded street and wave to them—this is a simple reaching out for connection. But, instead of returning the greeting, the other person stares in our direction, looks away, and keeps walking, as if to say, "Who the hell are you?" We realize he may not have seen us. But still, we give a furtive glance to those around us. Do they see us looking foolish with our hand waving in the air? We blush and try to melt into the sidewalk. We don't want anybody to see us because we feel too embarrassed. The isolation and humiliation we feel—and the feelings of emotional disconnection that result—are what psychologists call "shame."

A second example involves the feelings of shame experienced in the workplace. You've created an important presentation for your manager.

The key points of the presentation are rejected, however, and the boss derides them in front of your colleagues. You feel stupid, foolish; you want to disappear. You don't want anybody to exacerbate your feelings of vulnerability, so you shun any help. Instead you turn inward and become emotionally disconnected from others.

These examples are mild in comparison to what a boy experiences when he does not measure up to the Boy Code, but they help demonstrate what shame is all about. It is about feeling such a fear of humiliation and embarrassment that we prefer to be alone with our pain.

GIRLS ARE SENSITIVE TO SHAME, BUT BOYS FEAR IT

Because shame is such an undesirable experience, I have found that most boys (and men) will do anything to avoid the possibility of experiencing it. I recall attending a Little League game where my friend's son, Peter, was participating in one of his first baseball games. Before the second inning, Peter was hit in the head by his first hardball. Small for his age and only in the first grade, he looked absolutely mortified. The helmet drooping over his brow gave him the look of a miniature punch-drunk fighter about to go down for the count.

His mother rushed out to the field to comfort her son. "Not here, Mom," she later told me he had whispered to her, stifling his tears, "Big guys don't cry on the field."

For many years, traditional psychologists thought that exquisite sensitivity to shame was mostly characteristic of girls, especially at somewhat older ages. But what I have found after years of working with boys and their families is that the same kind of shame that silences girls from expressing their true voice as adolescents takes its inhibiting and self-suppressing toll on their brothers at a much earlier age. And while girls may be shame-sensitive, boys are shame-*phobic:* they are exquisitely yet unconsciously attuned to any signal of "loss of face" and will do just about whatever it takes to avoid shame.

Rather than expose themselves to this kind of potent embarrassment, boys, in the face of suffering shame, engage in a variety of behaviors that range from avoidance of dependency to impulsive action, from bravado and rage-filled outbursts to intense violence.

GABE: TRYING TO BE THE STURDY OAK IN A FRIGHTENING FOREST

Boys can feel separation and disconnection—and a resulting shame—from an isolated experience, as well as from a more prolonged separation, such as going off to kindergarten.

Gabe, sixteen, was usually a thoughtful boy, bright and cheerful. But this morning he was fidgeting in his chair like a much younger child, reminding me of a little kindergarten boy sitting still with difficulty in the classroom. Gabe's parents had brought him in to see me this time because of a sudden outburst of irritable and tearful behavior. All they had done was mention the idea of a tennis camp in a distant city. Gabe had good friendships and excellent grades, no prior history of emotional or behavioral problems, and he had mentioned getting serious about his tennis. So why such a radical response, a change from his usual cool composure?

Gabe was as puzzled as everyone else. I thought about some indirect ways to find out what was on his mind, and remembered we had previously discussed dreams, but he had said he usually couldn't remember them. Today, however, Gabe could remember one from the previous night.

"It was very scary—a nightmare, I think," he said. "A strange place all dark and quiet, maybe in the woods. I felt all alone, but there were others there—my parents, I think. We were camping. All of us were in sleeping bags, but mine was missing. All of a sudden there was a noise at the edge of the tent—a wild animal maybe? I freaked, then I screamed—and that's when I woke up."

The vividness with which he told the dream, the liveliness of his feelings in comparison to his day-to-day cool attitude, gave me a hunch that perhaps this dream was more than a complex piece of fantasy from Gabe's unconscious. Here, instead, was a memory emerging from repression. "Gabe," I asked, "Does the dream remind you of anything similar that ever happened to you, perhaps not recently, but long ago?"

"No." Gabe paused. "Well," he started again, "I guess the only thing that comes to mind is that first camping trip in the Adirondacks, the summer I was five. It was my first time away from home, my first time in a tent, but my whole family was with me. I remember now. The door of the tent was mosquito netting, and whoever slept next to it had to contend with cold drafts, the buzzing of mosquitoes, and the sounds of animals out in the woods—they sounded like wolves and bats. On our first night, my father slept next to the door. But on the second night my father said that I should sleep next to the door—I should "stand guard" and protect the family from intruders. I didn't want to. I complained. But they told me I should be the 'big boy' of the family and tough it out. I tried to tough it out, but then I heard a noise. I thought it was a bear or something, and I got very upset and started to cry. Dad told me not to be such a 'wimp' and act like a man; I think he even told me a story about him and his dad roughing it in the woods."

"Were you afraid?" I asked.

"I guess it was actually pretty safe or they wouldn't have let me stay out there all alone, but I remember being scared to death for days afterward. A funny thing, though—my mom told me that after that trip I stopped begging her and Dad at bedtime to stay in my room with me, and my dad told her he thought I really had grown from the camping experience. Jesus, I must have been scared shitless and pushed it all away until now."

GABE REVISITED: HOW PARENTS CAN HELP EASE THE PAIN OF SEPARATION

Gabe's dream—and the memory the dream evoked—are significant in that they reveal a boy who was afraid but was embarrassed to show he had been made to feel ashamed of his feelings at such a young age. While most boys may not have any such clear-cut nightmares nor horrifying memories of camping trips to report, many of them, like Gabe, may harbor unconscious memories of premature separation, of being pushed in a shameful, unexpected way toward pseudo-independence. All three- to five-year-olds suffer somewhat as they begin to spend more time apart from their primary caregiver. But society's gender stereotypes permit daughters to linger with their mothers, while little boys are urged out of their comfort zones and into a premature separation. When the little boys resist, another set of stereotypes—that boys need to be toughened up—leaves them with an additional burden of inner shame.

As they grow up and face later challenges to their self-reliance or self-confidence, boys only allow these repressed emotions of early childhood to surface symbolically, as Gabe did when he reported his dream, or symptomatically, as Gabe did when he began to act unusually irritable and tearful, when his feelings of fear, frustration, and sadness became so overwhelming that they punctured his outer psychological armoring. But in most cases, boys hide these feelings behind their masks of "cool." And as boys grow into men, they continue to hide their feelings, and an ever-intensifying sense of shame and disconnection develops within them.

ACTING OUT: IS IT ATTENTION DEFICIT DISORDER—OR LOSS OF CONNECTION?

For Johnny, Christopher, and Gabe, dealing with the trauma of separation—and with the intense shame they felt about the feelings it produced—meant turning inward, trying to handle their problems quietly and alone. Yet in many cases, boys deal with the pain of separating from their parents and the shame they feel by "acting out," by using dramatic or disorderly conduct to call for help. I believe that an overwhelming number of elementary school boys diagnosed with conduct disorders or with what is often called attention deficit disorder, or ADD, are misbehaving not because they have a biological imbalance or deficit but because they are seeking attention to replace the void left by their mothers and fathers. Their problems paying attention or regulating impulses may not be "faulty wiring" or "testosterone poisoning," but simply the result of accumulated emotional wounds and years of paralyzing shame. These desperate last-ditch efforts to assuage the pain or resist the thrust of premature autonomy are frequently misread as symptoms of an illness rather than as a natural part of coping with the trauma of separation. When boys act rambunctious and their activities spiral into aggressiveness and violence, what they are often expressing is far from some sort of macho desire for power or vindication but rather a longing to be nurtured, listened to, and understood, to engage in all of the needy, dependent behaviors they're being told are girl-like and forbidden.

Certainly there are boys with significant psychological disorders in need of appropriate diagnosis and treatment. Attention deficit disorder is a real illness (actually a constellation of psychological syndromes housed under one name). In fact, in 1995 more than five million children were classified as "learning disabled," 25 percent greater than a decade ago. Within these categories of disability, ADD is the fastest-growing illness, with numbers doubling over the last five years.

Perhaps most shocking, the ratio of boys to girls of such newly diagnosed ADD cases can range as high as 10 to 1.

But when millions of boys are diagnosed as having attention deficit disorder, and when far fewer girls are given the same diagnosis, I begin to wonder whether this diagnosis is sometimes being applied inappropriately to what are normal episodes of boy behavior. I also wonder whether diagnosing boys as having this disorder reflects society's tendency to misunderstand how the trauma of separation affects school-age boys. The diagnosis of "hyperactivity" is often made on the basis of a checklist of behaviors that, in reality, could reflect boys' grief over losing emotional connection—a loss that we have learned cannot be fully expressed or mourned but rather expresses itself through action or anger. In short, a combination of biologically influenced "boy temperament" plus a boy's resistance to the Boy Code may lead to a diagnosis of ADD.

RUSTY: SETTING THE WORLD ON FIRE

Rusty was my first "fire setter." Children who start fires frighten psychologists even more than extremely violent children, because the impulse is poorly understood and may lead to serious harm to large numbers of people. But this didn't seem to jibe with little Rusty's sad eyes, meek demeanor, and sudden outbursts of tearfulness when he was confronted with his "crime."

Sent to a locked psychiatric unit after he had induced two older boys to pour some lighter fluid on a pile of old wood behind his housing project and to light a fire, Rusty, age seven, did not deny his actions. He didn't show remorse either. Rather, Rusty seemed to be in a dreamlike state, disconnected from the seriousness of the events. People began to throw around diagnoses and suggestions for treatment, and it was determined that Rusty's conduct disorders could involve ADD as well.

Rusty's parents were of little help, as his mother felt that Rusty was "too clingy," being the "baby" of the family, so she had pushed him to spend more time at school and Little League. Rusty's father had divorced his mother when Rusty was five, and he rarely, if ever, visited.

I made a request: that we bring Rusty together in one room with his mother and father and talk about this boy's pain. Arranging the meeting wasn't easy, but it did finally take place. As might be expected, Rusty clung to his mother as soon as she entered, with her gently trying to redirect his attention. Then his father arrived. Rusty's whole face appeared to change in structure: he beamed as he ran to embrace his father. Rusty's dad was wearing some kind of badge—no surprise, as we had been told he worked as an investigator for the police department. All of a sudden I got one of those hunches you just can't easily explain. "Mr. McDonnell, what kind of work do you do exactly?" I asked.

"Didn't Rusty tell you," he replied, "I investigate fires of suspicious origin for the city. Gee, I'm surprised Rusty didn't talk about it—I'd often take him along when he was a small boy. I think it fascinated him."

No victim of ADD, no veteran "fire setter," Rusty was a sad little boy who had lost his emotional bonds with mother and father and was calling out through conduct and action—typical boy approaches—for love and response. Luckily most boys diagnosed with conduct or activity disorders don't light fires. But perhaps by acting out, these boys are attempting through the language of behavior to light a fire under us, to give us a wake-up call to their pain and desperation, feelings that will not be cured with medications or behavior modification.

THE SLOW POISON OF PREMATURE SEPARATION: BOYS AND MEN STILL LONGING FOR CONNECTION

As the boys' voices I've shared reflect, the trauma of separation manifests itself in myriad ways. In many cases the loss boys feel causes them to experience diminished or rocky self-esteem. They may become unhappy and disaffected, much in the way that Gabe did. In some cases, they may actually become clinically depressed, as Christopher did. Sometimes they may manifest psychosomatic diseases such as the vomiting and crying spells that little Johnny endured. And sometimes, like Rusty, they may seek reconnection by acting out, behavior that may lead us, in the first instance, to diagnose them as "hyperactive" or as having "attention deficit disorder." But perhaps most often, boys give the impression that every-thing is going just fine by effectively hiding behind the mask of an invul-nerable personality. For years they may suppress the angst they feel, and in many cases, boys become so skilled at pushing this trauma out of their memories that it is not until years later, as adults, that they remember what they went through.

Many of the adult male patients I see still grapple with the aftermath of the trauma of separation. Many men still unconsciously long for con-nection with mother and the nurturing "holding" environment she once provided.

For example, when Paul, a thirty-five-year-old man, recently lost his mother to cancer, he told me that even though he hadn't felt dependent on his mother as an adult, his mother's death made him feel terrible about himself. His mother, who lived in Italy, where Paul was born, had never received a college education and in many ways was not a central figure in Paul's daily life as an adult. Despite all this, Paul reported a sense of incredible loss. "I feel as though my only anchor in life is gone," he told me, explaining that after his mother's death he had lost the energy to make love with his wife and felt little motivation to go to work. As we spent more time talking, it emerged that the pain Paul felt was linked less to any recent experiences he had had with his mother than to his memories of how she had nurtured him as a very young child. The warm, loving environment she had once created for him was now forever beyond his reach. As I discussed with Paul what I had learned about the trauma of separation and how this trauma continued to affect boys and men throughout their lives, Paul said, "Dr. Pollack, you just hit the nail on the head. I can't believe this. I've actually been dealing with these problems for years and only now realize how much it had to do with my mother. I forgot how painful it was when my father first separated me from her to send me off to school. I never would have thought any of that could still matter now."

While Paul's response to the trauma of separation was to feel a lack of sexual drive and to experience the early symptoms of depression, other adult patients of mine have experienced far more severe responses.

For example, David, a forty-year-old client of mine, was hospitalized when, after years of "normal" mental health, he attempted to commit suicide by consuming sedatives and an entire bottle of aspirin. As we worked together in therapy sessions, David recounted the acute pain he felt when Helen, his live-in girlfriend of three years, decided she "couldn't take him anymore." David described how in all his relationships with women he inevitably reached a point where he felt something was missing. "There's always at least one thing about each girlfriend," he explained, "that just really gets in my way of continuing the relationship."

"Was it you who initiated breaking up with Helen?" I asked.

"No," he whispered, his voice beginning to crack, "And for the first time, it wasn't me. Helen left me and I don't know how I'll live without her."

As our sessions progressed, David shared details about his relationships with women and what went wrong in each relationship. Each of these friendships ended, he confessed, because he always found at least one critically important trait missing in the women he dated. One woman he found too independent and self-absorbed; another was somewhat guarded in the affection she gave David; and with Helen, he felt, she just wasn't as interested in starting a family as David was—she wanted at most one child, while he hoped to have many. As we pieced together the qualities David found missing in these relationships, he himself realized that the qualities he was seeking were in fact those he associated with his idealized mother.

"In some ways," he explained, "I always hold up my girlfriends to the image I have of my mother and they just never seem to hit the mark."

As I began to explain to David the trauma of separation and how the wound it leaves can affect us throughout our lives, he injected angrily, "I'm not interested in marrying my mother! I just want to be with somebody who will be as warm, caring, and loving as she was—someone like Helen!"

EMOTIONAL SHAPING IN A MOTHER'S REACTIONS: INFANTS BEING FITTED FOR THE FIRST GENDER STRAITJACKET

I believe the trauma of separation is one of the earliest and most acute developmental experiences boys endure, an experience that plays a large role in the hardening process through which society shames boys into suppressing their empathic and vulnerable sides. What few people realize is that this shame-based hardening process begins as early as the first months of a little boy's life as a narrowing of emotional expressiveness and then continues during early childhood, following boys right through adolescence and manhood. It is, in other words, a lifelong process.

Research on interactions between mothers and their babies illustrates how the process begins, revealing that, totally unaware of their actions' consequences, genuinely loving caretakers prematurely dampen their sons' sensitive emotive sides. Boy infants, at birth and for months afterward, are much more expressive emotionally than girls—they startle, excite, cry, and fuss more than girls—though caretakers sometimes believe this infant emotionality is a sign of "fragility" or a lack of self-control, rather than an enhanced communication of feelings. Haviland and Malatesta, in studies conducted at Rutgers University, found that in order to keep their sons' more volatile emotions in check, mothers tend unwittingly to mimic and overly reinforce smiling in boys while discouraging more unhappy emotions. Hence without realizing it, in their attempt to be "soothing," mothers are participating in the earliest phases of emotional straitjacketing in boys—they are teaching them to smile when they may not feel like it. Even infant boys are subject to the Boy Code!

In general, the researchers found, mothers were far less likely to mirror their infants' unhappy feelings; but when mothers were interacting with infant boys, the mothers were particularly resistant to recognizing their sons' negative emotional states. When girl infants expressed painful states, mothers responded only 22 percent of the time, but when their sons showed negative feelings, they ignored them altogether. Haviland and Malatesta concluded that when mothers notice their baby boys showing greater emotionality, many of them fear their sons are psychologically off-balance or unwell. To calm their sons, therefore, many of these mothers, often without realizing it, take steps that squelch their young sons' emotional expressiveness.

While this difference between how mothers respond to the emotions of their infant sons and daughters is startling, I feel it is very important not to misinterpret these findings. The mothers studied, in my opinion, were *not* insensitive or indifferent to their sons' feelings. They were not neglecting their young sons' pain. Quite to the contrary, these mothers, based on cultural imperatives about boys and masculinity, were struggling to do what they felt was best, manifesting a knee-jerk reaction to their sons' expressions of distress. They were trying to smooth over their boys' emotions not out of callousness or a lack of caring but out of empathy, because they loved their sons and wanted to see them happy and fulfilled. Far from being unsympathetic or neglectful, these mothers were concerned that if they let a boy express too much grief, pain, or vulnerability, somehow he would become something less than a "real," fully functional boy, in accordance with our society's rigid code.

The study conducted by Professors Haviland and Malatesta also investigated how mothers respond to their babies' expressions of "surprise" or "special interest." Here mothers more exactly "mirrored" their sons' feeling states by making surprised or excited faces whenever their sons made these kinds of faces. Hence, when a boy raised his eyebrows in surprise, so did his mother. When he acted startled, so did she. In other words, she kept the situation comfortably neutral and provided no additional stimulus of any kind. By contrast, mothers responded to their daughters' expressions of surprise or interest in ways that did not exactly mimic those of their daughters. In doing so, these mothers led their daughters to experience joyful stimulation, broadening and deepening the range of these girls' emotional responsiveness and experience. Again researchers understood this difference, *not* as a maternal deprivation of boys, but as a struggle on mothers' part to "go to great lengths to ensure that their sons remain contented." In other words, just as mothers ignore their infant sons' sad faces in the hope their sons will simply "snap out of it" and feel happier, mothers try to closely mimic their young sons' expressions of surprise or special interest simply to avoid pushing their boys toward more distressing emotions such as embarrassment, sadness, or fear.

But it is my view that by encouraging their boys to achieve such narrow "contentment," mothers—*while they clearly do not intend to*—are actually pushing their sons toward premature disconnection from the wide range of their true inner experience, and teaching them that experiencing certain kinds of emotions is either inappropriate or unnecessary. By suppressing their sons' vigorous expression of spontaneous vulnerable feelings, mothers give boys the subliminal message that it is dangerous or shameful to manifest such feelings and that these feelings do not have an important place within their mother-son relationship. Without any forethought, mothers, by coaching their sons in this way, unwittingly "socialize" their boys' natural emotional states into our highly limited repertoire of emotional expression for males—another early gender straitjacket.

This is particularly unfortunate since my research shows that *what "real" boys actually need from infancy forward—and what mothers in their hearts are often longing to offer—is complete and unconditional empathy and understanding for a full range of feelings.* Ideally, when a mother sees her infant son looking unhappy, she would simply gaze gently into his eyes, hold him close, and ask him something like "What's going on? Are you OK? You're feeling tired, aren't you?" These expressions of love and empathy are truly what most boys (like most girls) need when they are feeling discomfited or afraid.

Regrettably, research shows that the suppression of emotions in boys continues through childhood. For example, not only do mothers allow girls to express a greater range of emotional states as infants, but, as girls get older, mothers also simply communicate more with them than with boys. Leslie Brody, at Boston University, summarized her own and others' research as demonstrating that mothers not only speak more to daughters about feelings but actually display a wider range of feelings to them as well. Mothers, in communicating with their daughters (as compared with their sons), may actually use more vivid facial expressions, allowing both girl and mother to develop better skills at recognizing each other's emotions. But with sons, Brody explained, perhaps to adjust to these boys' more intense emotions (such as anger or irritability), mothers tended to hold back, to respond less expressively. This is a set of complex findings, precisely because, as Brody reminds us, these "natural" styles of interaction tend to conform to "the cultural . . . stereotype that girls should be more emotionally expressive and that boys should be more emotionally constrained."

As their sons grow older, caretakers use a greater variety of emotion-laden language when they speak to their preschool daughters than to their sons. These studies show that mothers talk more about sadness or distress with daughters, and about *anger* with sons—tending to minimize the extent to which their sons might attempt to dwell on their sadness. For example, if a girl begins to cry when she gets a bad grade at school, her parents might tend to say things such as "Oh, you must feel awful" or "Are you all right?" whereas if a boy begins to cry when he suffers the same fate, they might say, "How unfair—that's ridiculous" or "You march right in there and tell them this just isn't right."

Though it is unintentional, such gender straitjacketing takes its toll. By the time they reach school age, little girls expect mothers to respond positively to their expression of sadness while little boys expect both mothers and fathers to respond far less warmly to their expression of the same emotion. Also, by the time girls and boys have reached this age, boys simply express less sadness than girls and thus "self-regulate" how much they show negative or vulnerable emotions. Indeed research shows that the older a boy is, the less emotionally responsive he will be and the harder it will be for his mother to tell how he is feeling.

Lest anyone begin to believe that mothers are alone in this emotional shaping process, it is important to point out that when fathers become actively involved in their children's care, they too—perhaps especially so—push boys to limit their expression of emotional vulnerability. Fathers use many more emotion words with daughters than with sons, with only one exception. With their sons they use one word they rarely say to their daughters: "disgust." The language of fathers in general, with boys or with girls, has more demands and teasing in it than in the mothers' language, and the demands and teasing are even more persistent and intense when the father is addressing his sons. Such verbal jousting by fathers with their sons—for example, the use of a taunt such as "you ding-a-ling"—is usually playful, uttered in jest. But when we think about how such "teasing" affects boys in combination with all the other social pressures they face at such a young age, it is hard not to conclude that such jousting serves only to further *toughen up* boys, adding heavy plating to their already weighty emotional armor, and pushing their more tender feelings underground.

ANGER: THE OK MALE EMOTION

While studies show that boys at a very early age are pushed to suppress their vulnerable and sad feelings, they also demonstrate that boys are pressured to express the one strong feeling allowed them—*anger*. Several research centers have documented that parents speak more about sadness with daughters; but when it comes to sons, parents speak mostly about anger. In Professor Esther Grief's work with colleagues at Boston University, mothers were asked to create a story with their children. When performing this task, mothers never used the word "angry" with girls, but frequently used it with boys. In Professor Robyn Fivush's laboratory at Emory University, parents not only focused on anger more frequently with their sons, but also, when guiding their sons and daughters through conflict situations, they favored the reestablishing of harmony when their daughters were involved, but accepted retaliation as a reasonable solution for their male progeny.

Unfortunately, it is through anger—the final common pathway for a boy's strong feelings, what Professor Don Long at Washington University has called an "emotional funnel"—that most boys express their vulnerability and powerlessness. In the face of a premature separation, boys turn most to anger in order to mute and rein in the full range of emotional responsiveness they would otherwise exhibit. The more tender feelings seem too shameful to show and thus boys turn to anger. When I consider these studies—when I think about how difficult it is for many of the adolescent boys and men I know to cope with intense emotional situations—it becomes clear why anger has always been the easiest feeling for men to express. Understandably, it is very challenging for most men to express or experience emotions other than anger, since, as boys, they were encouraged to use their rage to express the full range of their emotional experience.

SAM AND OSCAR: HOW SHAME-PHOBIC BOYS BECOME HARDENED MEN

Starting during infancy with the trauma of separation and persisting during early childhood and adolescence, the shame-hardening process continues throughout the lives of our boys and men. It is a process that causes boys and men to develop a thick skin, a strong resistance to showing any emotions that might lead them to feel ashamed. This hardening comes not from a boy's desire to be either courageous or coldhearted, but rather from an intense wish to protect himself from "losing face" or feeling otherwise dishonored.

Sometimes, especially with adult men, it is easy to misinterpret this hardening as a kind of typical male boasting or bluster. Sam Gash, described as a "fierce" blocker for the New England Patriots football team, bemoaned the knee injury that had placed him on the bench. Watching the action without being part of it, he explained, "was the worst thing I've ever had to endure." When asked how he might cope with a more serious injury that could end his career—let alone leave his body paralyzed—he responded as if from behind a typical male mask, "Hey, if that's God's will, that's the way it will be. I approach the game as if I have a big shield around me—God's armor. I'm not really afraid of anything." If we were to take Sam Gash's testimony at face value, it would be hard not to think he was just a thoroughly tough, powerful, self-confident man.

But when we look closely at the behavior of young boys, and when we listen closely to their stories, we realize that what in men or older boys is often interpreted as a macho sense of rigor and cockiness, in reality often has much more to do with hardening. This hardening takes place, and the mask goes up, not because boys or men feel particularly strong or self-assured, but rather because they *don't*—they feel anxious to protect themselves from wounds to their already fragile male psyches. Once they've been shamed enough for failing to be fully masculine, once they've been told enough times that they should suppress their vulnerable feelings, once they've actually been *physically injured* for failing to meet the mark, boys allow the wounds to scar over, cover any remaining soft tissue, and act as if everything is going all right.

Take, for instance, Oscar De La Hoya, who today is an Olympic gold medal winner and known as a Golden Boy of boxing. As a young boy, Oscar was pushed into the sport by his father as a result of an unhappy childhood episode. Oscar recalls that during his third birthday party, he became frightened by the violence of the traditional piñata game. This is the game in which he and each of his friends were blindfolded and then, using a long wooden cane, were asked to take turns whacking the multi-colored toy-stuffed doll that was suspended above them by a cord. "I got scared," Oscar remembered. "I started to cry hysterically and ran away in panic." Oscar's parents not only threatened but punished him, but nothing could get him back to that fearsome scene.

Later his father saw Oscar fleeing from other boys when they threatened to punch him. His father felt that Oscar's lack of manliness was a "disgrace," a shame upon the family. The "best medicine" for his son, he felt, was to teach him to box. After all, that's what Oscar's grandfather had done one generation earlier with Oscar's father, when he too had seemed "unmanly."

Oscar vividly remembers his first attempt at boxing when he was just five years of age. The match began, he recalls, and "the next thing—WHAM—the first punch thrown lands smack on my nose." Oscar ran home in tears. But from that time on, he recalls, "I learned to manage my fears."

Like so many boys, Oscar learned how to harden himself, in this case with the encouragement of his father. By training himself in a sport where he would need to withstand both emotional and physical pain, and by resolving to no longer allow himself to experience or show his fears, Oscar, at the ripe age of five, was already mastering the hardening expected of boys.

HARDENING'S RISK: BECOMING ANESTHETIZED TO PAIN

When boys become hardened, they become willing to endure emotional and physical pain—even to risk their lives—if it means winning the approval of their peers. Boys can become so thoroughly hardened that they literally anesthetize themselves against the pain they must cope with. And because they are left unsupervised at an earlier age than girls and are usually discouraged by adults from engaging in help-seeking behaviors at their time of greatest vulnerability or need, boys learn to remain silent despite their suffering.

Studies show, for instance, that though by the time boys reach junior high school, one in ten of them has been kicked in the groin, and though 25 percent of these boys actually suffer injuries to their groin area, the majority never tell an adult. One year after the trauma, 25 percent show signs of depression and 12 percent manifest post-traumatic syndromes. And in a study the Navy recently commissioned to understand the history of childhood sexual abuse in its female recruits, researchers made the entirely unexpected finding that as many as 39 percent of its *male* recruits had experienced some form of physical violence (beyond spanking) at the hands of the parents before they reached the age of eighteen. While this statistic is disturbing in and of itself, what is particularly striking is that, unless the Navy had decided to commission this study, this abuse by parents of their sons would never have been revealed. Once boys have become hardened, they often cover their pain so masterfully that we, as a society, become utterly incapable of seeing it.

"It's really hard being a guy," fifteen-year-old Calvin Branford recently explained to me, "because you're not supposed to talk about how you feel. There's nobody you can depend on. With girls, everybody expects they'll go off and talk to somebody. When you're a guy you're really not allowed to do that. I guess it's pretty hard being a guy because there are so many things a normal person would probably do, but you're just not expected to!"

HELPING BOYS RECONNECT: A PRIMER FOR PARENTS

As powerful as the cultural imperatives of the Boy Code may be in pushing boys of all ages to separate from their parents, toughen themselves up, and restrict their emotional lives, there is a lot we can do as adults to help boys overcome these conventional pressures. Here are some basic guidelines I would suggest:

At least once a day, give your boy your undivided attention. This means you're not speaking with someone else, you're not simultaneously trying to cook, clean, read, or do some other task. You're listening closely. He's got your attention. While sometimes he may not want to talk—while he may just want to play a game, get some help on his homework, or complain about having to do chores—showing him this attention, even if he doesn't always soak it up, gives him the message that you're there, that you care, and that he has a daily time and place when he can share things with you. It's not important that he always unload heavy emotions on you. And he may signal that he prefers to talk about things at some later point. He just needs to feel your regular loving presence and know that you're eager to know what's happening in his world.

Encourage the expression of a full range of emotions. From the moment a boy is born and throughout his life, it's important he gets the message that all of his emotions are valid. With an infant, this means we need to mirror back all of the feelings the baby expresses. Rather than forcing him to constantly smile or laugh, we also need to show him we're receptive to his sadness, fear, or other painful emotions. So when a young infant begins to frown, yawn, kick, or cry, rather than trying to "cheer him up" or "smooth things over" by making happy faces at him or ignoring his displays of discomfort, show him your empathy, let him know you understand how he's feeling, and show him with your words, facial expressions, and gestures that you respect and understand his genuine feelings. With toddlers and school-age boys, we need to ask questions—"What happened?" "Are you feeling sad about something?" "Tell me what's making you unhappy"—and, again, express our empathy—"Gee, that sounds unfair!" "I'm sorry it hurts so much." We also need to use a broad range of emotion words—happy, sad, tired, disappointed, scared, nervous—rather than limiting our discussion of emotions to words such as "anger" that force boys to channel the gamut of their feelings into one word and one emotion.

In our daily attention-giving time with our sons, we need to pay close attention to what he's saying and how he's acting. If he complains, expresses fears or anxieties, cries, or otherwise shows emotions that reveal he's hurting, ask him what he's going through and let him talk about all that he is experiencing. With an older boy, be sure to ask him questions about his relationships with girls, with other boys, with his siblings, teachers, and other friends and acquaintances. Ask him to share with you not only what's going well in those relationships, but also what's going less well. Ask him what he enjoys about them and what he finds difficult. By probing about both the "positive" and "negative" sides of these relationships, older boys will begin to discuss a broad array of thoughts and feelings.

When a boy expresses vulnerable feelings, avoid teasing or taunting him. While it's natural to want to be playful with our sons, and though showing him a sense of levity and good cheer sometimes helps him to overcome unpleasant feelings or situations, by and large it's important that we not "cut off" his painful emotions by teasing or taunting him. So, for example, when he comes home and complains that his teacher told him he needs a haircut, rather than teasing that he "sure looks like a real fuzz ball," ask him how his teacher's comments made him feel, hear him out, and tell him that you too don't appreciate what the teacher said. Or if your teenage son announces despondently that his sweetheart just "dumped him," rather than joking that it must have been his bad breath that got to her or that his heart "must just be totally broken," instead ask him if he'd like to talk about it and, if so, listen to what he'd like to share with you and try to mirror back in an empathic way the feelings you sense he's trying to convey. Teasing and taunting rarely heal the boy. Empathy, however, goes miles to help him learn how to express and cope with a broad range of feelings.

Avoid using shaming language in talking with a boy. Research, as well as everyday observation, reveals that parents often—although unintentionally—use shaming language with their male children that they do not use with girls. It's important to find ways to talk with boys that do not shame them, and that they can respond to. If a boy does something that surprises or concerns you, a natural reaction is to ask, "How could you do that?" But that implies that the act, whatever it was, was wrong and casts the boy in the role of the evil perpetrator. Rather, you might ask, "What's going on?" or "What happened?" which suggests that you have not formed a judgment about the situation under discussion.

If a boy comes home with a less than stellar report card, a parent—understandably concerned—may challenge him and deliver an ultimatum, "You're going to have to work harder than this. These grades won't get you into a good college." Undoubtedly, the boy knows he is not performing as well as others or as well as he would like. The better parental response might be "You're still struggling with math, aren't you. What could we do to help?"

Or suppose a boy declines an invitation to visit a friend or go to a party. Rather than say, "It would do you good to get out of the house. Besides, that boy is really nice," you could try to find out why the boy no longer wants to be with his friend—"Has something happened between you two guys?"—or what it is about the party that doesn't appeal to him— "Will somebody be there you don't get along with?"

Such language carries tremendous power to make a boy feel shame and to reinforce his own conception that he is somehow toxic.

Look behind anger, aggression, and rambunctiousness. In so many cases, a boy who seems angry, displays a lot of aggression, or is constantly rambunctious is indirectly asking for our help. If you notice a boy who's acting in such ways, try to create a setting where he'll feel comfortable talking with you and then ask him how things are with him. With a young boy, you might not be able to ask him a lot of direct questions—and he may not yet be able to talk about feelings in a clear way—but try your best to get a sense of what he's feeling. For instance, if you notice that your son has seemed angry a lot lately, you might say, "Gosh, you've seemed upset a lot. Is everything OK? Have things been rough for you lately?" Or, if you're a schoolteacher and you notice a boy who's constantly roughing up and provoking other kids, rather than chastising the boy, ask him how things are at home. Ask him if he's upset about something. Try to get a sense of whether there might be deeper, more vulnerable feelings that are motivating his anger or rowdy behavior. You might even tell him that sometimes when we act irritably or show aggression, we might be feeling sadness or other upset feelings.

Express your love and empathy openly and generously. Despite all the messages you might receive about "letting go" of your son, of not staying too attached to him, of not "babying" him, you simply can never show him too much love or empathy. Cutting off your affection and support, to let him "stand on his own," as we've discussed in this chapter, can actually traumatize him.

Tell your boy that you love him as often as you like. Give him hugs. Tell him you're proud of him and that you care about him. Stay involved in his emotional life. Seek opportunities to connect with him for moments of playful closeness and emotional sharing. If he asks you to let him alone, give him the space he needs, but let him know that you love him very much and that when he's ready to spend time together, you'll be up for it. You cannot "spoil" your son with too much love or attention. You will not make him "girl-like" or "feminine" by maintaining a close relationship. There's simply no such thing as too much love!

Let boys know that they don't need to be "sturdy oaks." So many boys, even at a very young age, feel that they need to act like a "sturdy oak." When there are problems at home, when he suffers his own failures or disappointments, or when there's a need for somebody who's physically or emotionally "strong" for others to lean on and he feels he has to be that support, the boy is often pushed to "act like a man," to be the one who is confident and unflinching. No boy should be called upon to be the tough one. No boy should be hardened in this way. So through thick and thin, let your boy know that he doesn't have to act like a "sturdy oak." Talk to him honestly about your own fears and vulnerabilities and encourage him to do the same. The more genuine he feels he can be with you, the more he'll be free to express his vulnerability and the stronger he will become.

Create a model of masculinity for him that is broad and inclusive. Despite all the narrow messages about "being a guy" that they may get at school, on television, or elsewhere, you can help boys to create their own model of masculinity. Try to help them develop a model that is broad and inclusive. Try to do for them what we have done for girls by valuing them as people before evaluating them as a distinct (and therefore restricted) gender. This means encouraging boys in all their interests, relationships, and activities. It means letting them know that "big guys *do* cry." It also means exposing boys to people who bend society's strict gender rules—to men who are nurses, women who are plumbers, girls who are "jocks," boys who cook, and so on. Boys especially benefit from getting to know adult male "role models" who exude masculinity in a genuine and expansive way. When you give your son a sense that there's no one single way of being "manly," you're helping him develop confidence about who he really is. You're letting him know that no matter what he enjoys doing, whom he likes spending time with, and what sorts of feelings he experiences, he's a "real boy" on his way to being a "real man."

_3_

REAL BOYS:

THE TRUTHS BEHIND THE MYTHS

*"Sometimes just because you're a guy, people treat you like you're
a little hoodlum. I think if they opened up their eyes, they'd see that
most of us are actually pretty good people."—Dirk, age seventeen*

Though the stereotypes about what boys are and how boys should behave
continue to be perpetuated, in our hearts many of us know that these outdated ideas are simply untrue. And we now have research confirming what
most of us have always known.

There are three major myths about boys that persist in all kinds of situations and among all sorts of people, even among the most thoughtful and
progressive families, schools, and communities. They are so deeply
embedded in the culture, that without realizing it, they often short-circuit
our ability to see and love the real boy before us—the true boy behind
these old-fashioned ideas.

MYTH #1: BOYS WILL BE BOYS: NATURE AND TESTOSTERONE WIN OUT OVER NURTURE

One myth, which recent studies, including my own, show to be untrue, is
that nature controls much about a boy's behavior. More specifically, that
where there are boys there is testosterone, and where there is testosterone
there is aggression, and where there is aggression there is violence, or at
least its potential. The phrase "Boys will be boys" is saying, in effect, that
boys are prisoners of biology, that their behavior is predetermined, an
inherent part of their nature. "Typical" boy behavior is assumed to involve

insensitivity and risk-taking. The phrase is used when a little boy breaks a window with a baseball and runs away laughing. Or when a teenager skateboards into traffic, narrowly avoids a collision, and zooms away. Or when an older adolescent stays up until four in the morning playing Doom, and drags himself to school the next day.

"Boys will be boys" is not said, however, when a little boy brings a present to his teacher or gives his crying mother a hug. Or when a teenage boy obviously feels racked with guilt for breaking up with his girlfriend—unless he covers it up with a convincing show of apathy. Or when an older boy spends time with a dying parent in the hospital—unless he takes the opportunity to watch football on the hospital-room television.

The great danger in subscribing to the myth is that it tends to make people assume that they have less power to affect a boy's personality, behavior, or emotional development than in fact they do.

TRUTH #1: A BOY'S BEHAVIOR IS SHAPED MORE BY LOVED ONES THAN BY NATURE

Underlying the "boys will be boys" myth, is a misconception about the role of testosterone. Testosterone does contribute to a boy's natural patterns of behavior, but testosterone is not necessarily the major factor in determining a boy's behavior.

It's true that many boys enjoy being active. For most little boys, running hard across the playground, kicking a soccer ball, or zooming down the slide is action enough. I might add that plenty of little girls take delight in these very same activities. We don't apply the "boys will be boys" myth to that kind of "typical" boy behavior until it takes on a careless edge—when the running turns into a race, when the ball gets kicked *at* someone, or when the boy leans over the edge of the slide daring himself to fall off.

The unfortunate effect of the myth is that it allows us to shrug off a boy's behavior when it crosses the line from active to aggressive. We are more inclined to throw up our hands and say, "We can't do anything about it—that's the ways boys are!" But I strongly believe that a boy's behavior *can* be shaped, that any natural need for action can be encouraged and satisfied, and any impulses toward violence and aggression can be discouraged and channeled in creative, positive directions. The case of Kyle illustrates my point.

Kyle was six when his sister, Charlotte, was born. "We expected Kyle to show the usual sibling jealousy," says his mother, Roberta. "But he was much worse with her than we'd expected. Kyle showed no delight in having a new member of the family, and demonstrated no affection for her. He would poke her with his toys, and make faces at her as if he was completely disgusted with her existence.

"One day, we put Charlotte down for a nap. She slept longer than usual, and my husband, Don, went in to check on her. He found Kyle in the room with her, with his hands close to her neck. It looked for all the world like Kyle might strangle his baby sister. Don rushed to grab him, and realized that Kyle was just pretending. The baby was fine—she hadn't even woken up—but both Don and I completely lost our tempers.

"I rarely yell at my kids, but this time I just went over the edge. I felt as if there was something horribly wrong with my son, that he had a violent nature or something, and this incident had revealed his true self. I didn't try to understand what prompted his action. I viewed my baby daughter, a girl, as a helpless victim, and my boy as the aggressor."

Roberta told her friends about what had happened, and asked them for advice. "I was very worried about Charlotte's well-being. Don was an only child in his family, and I was the youngest child in mine, so neither one of us could really relate to what Kyle was going through. Finally, my friend Gloria helped me understand how Kyle might be feeling."

Gloria, the oldest of three children, explained how her life had changed when her two siblings came along. She had not been consulted in the decision to bring other children into the home—children rarely are. When her siblings first arrived, Gloria lost her status as the special, the only, child. She received far less attention than she'd had before. She had to share her parents and their limited resources of energy with two other children. "Gloria made me understand how much better things were for Kyle before Charlotte appeared, and I had to admit it was true. Kyle got our undivided attention before. Now it was hard to find the time or the energy to play with him."

Roberta and Don determined to work with Kyle to change his attitude toward Charlotte, to curb his "aggression," and to help him understand that his parents still loved him as much as ever. Together, the three of them read stories about big brother/little sister relationships, which sparked lots of conversation about the topic. "Once we convinced Kyle that we weren't going to blame him or punish him for his natural feelings," Roberta recalled, "he opened up. We had some really good talks with him, and we told him he would always be our special boy."

"Kyle's become a very caring brother," Roberta now says. "One day, he spent an hour drawing an elaborate picture of our family—including Charlotte—and he told me he wanted to give it to his baby sister as a present. Today, he's the kind of brother I'd hoped he would be. He knows that we're not going to abandon him for Charlotte, and he feels comfortable enough to share us with her. I can even laugh now at the memory of him pretending to strangle Charlotte, because I know he never would and never could do such a thing. He's not a violent person. He was just in a very difficult situation and couldn't express his feelings about it, and we certainly weren't helping him any."

My clinical experience and research—as well as work done by others—have shown that most boys, when lovingly nurtured themselves, will in turn nurture and show empathy for others. We have learned that the way parents care for their sons has an even more powerful effect on a boy's behavior than we had realized, an effect at least as strong as biology in determining a boy's nature. How you treat a boy has a powerful impact on who he becomes. He is as much a product of nurturing as he is of nature.

THE MYTH ABOUT TESTOSTERONE

The idea that high levels of testosterone equate with high levels of violence stems from a mistaken assumption that testosterone is the only force that inclines boys toward both active, rough-and-tumble play and violent behavior. This is not the case. Boys do play differently than girls, but their style of play is not solely a function of testosterone and it certainly does not prove a proclivity for violence. Boys, in general, like play that is competitive, physically rough, and forceful. They like games that involve interaction in large groups and take place in large spaces (such as playing fields, gymnasiums, stadiums) as well as those that follow rules and have a hierarchy of authority. Girls, on the other hand, generally enjoy play that is more interpersonal, often one-on-one, and less physically aggressive.

Although scientists have long recognized the differences between the play styles of girls and boys and continue to debate the evolutionary and hormonal influences, they have not been able to establish a clear link between boys' rough play and aggression or violence.

While testosterone does, in fact, contribute to boys' proclivity for action, scientists over the years have tried without success to establish an unequivocal link between testosterone and violent behavior. The fact is

that testosterone is just one of many biological factors (including serotonin) that have an influence on aggression. In addition, testosterone can
have a variety of different effects on boys' behavior. A high testosterone
level in one boy may enable him to play a chess match with great intensity
and alertness; in another, it may give him the energy and concentration to
make complicated arrangements for a political rally. In a third case, it may
contribute to his involvement in a brutal fistfight. But the amount of testosterone in a boy's system fluctuates depending on when it is measured and
the activities he has been involved in—rather like the pulse rate. In older
men the effects of testosterone vary from man to man. Research has also
shown that when older men are given supplemental testosterone they
become calmer and less aggressive than before. By contrast, when athletes
take anabolic steroids, the cousins of testosterone, they become ornery and
excitable. No simple scientific link has been made between testosterone
levels and the tendency for aggression and violence.

The level of testosterone in any boy—and the way that testosterone
affects him—has less impact on his behavior than how the boy is loved,
nurtured, and shaped by his parents and by the context of the society
within which he lives. The hormone may well predict a certain type of
energy in boys. But the way in which that energy is funneled and
expressed lies in our hands.

THE POTENCY OF CONNECTION: THE POWER OF PARENTING
TO AFFECT OUR BOYS' BRAINS

Parents, and others who love and look after boys, are empowered in their
efforts by their boys' own deep yearning for connection. This is what I call
the *potency of connection*. The power of love can dispel the myth that, in
boys, nature and nurture are at odds, or, indeed, have distinct separate
influences on a boy and his life. The way we interact with boys, and the
connections we make with them, can have a permanent effect on a boy's
biology, his brain, and his social behavior. Scientists have found that early
emotional interaction can actually alter a boy's brain-based biological
processes.

When a boy (or girl) is born, the baby's brain—unlike the brain of any
other primate—is not fully developed. In the first year of life a child's brain
doubles in size, and then doubles again. By the time a child reaches the age
of two, his or her brain has as many synapses (connections between brain

cells) as an adult's. During this period of development, the human brain is very pliable and plastic, and—more than in any other species—is very open to learning from emotional and cognitive experiences. The human brain can, in fact, be permanently altered by its environment in these early years of its life. Scientists have demonstrated that at birth the human brain is wired to accommodate developmental interactions that further shape the nervous system after birth, with profound consequences for lifelong functioning.

How we respond to our baby boys and young sons—the manner in which we cuddle, kiss, and reassure, teach, comfort, and love—not only determines a young boy's capacity for a healthy emotional start in life but deeply affects a boy's characteristic style of behavior and the development of his brain. Our behavior fundamentally, and at times irrevocably, alters a boy's neural connections, brain chemistry, and biological functioning. The capacity to use language, to tolerate distress, to show and name feelings, and to be timid or eager to explore are all dramatically affected by the emotional environment created for a boy during early childhood. While nature creates boys whose behavior is influenced by biological proclivities—more than we used to believe—nature also creates boys who are more receptive to interaction with their caretakers than we had ever imagined.

Bruce Perry, a developmental neurobiologist at Baylor College of Medicine, summarizes it this way: "a child's capacity to think, to laugh, to love, to hate, to speak—all of it is a product of interaction with the environment. Sensory experiences such as touching . . . literally stimulate activity in the brain and the growth of neural structures."

The people in a boy's life—moms and dads, teachers and siblings, coaches and ministers, day-care providers and doctors—may have an effect equal to that of testosterone in shaping a young boy, not only by influencing his formative experience but by affecting his brain structures and neurotransmitters. The potency of connection is not just about the power adults have to create safe, nurturing, "holding environments." It is also about how these caring environments, in turn, affect the biological development of infant and toddler brains. Modern science has demonstrated how easily nurture becomes nature; there is no rigid dichotomy between the two.

So, let's rid ourselves of the myth that boys can never escape their biological fates. The truth is that we can do a great deal to shape how a boy behaves. We can search for ways to celebrate our boys' energy and chan-nel it into positive and productive activities. If they feel the urge to hit, let's give them a punching bag and help them learn to box. If they want to scream and yell, let's play a game that gives them a chance to cheer. If they want to argue, let's engage them in a conversation that allows them to develop their debating skills. If they refuse to do what's on the family agenda, let's challenge them to come up with an alternative plan.

MYTH #2: BOYS SHOULD BE BOYS

The myth that "boys should be boys"—that they *must* fulfill the stereotype of the dominant and "macho" male—inhibits some parents and their sons from living in the way that comes most naturally to them. The Boy Code says that boys should be tough, should demand respect from others, and should never act "like a girl." As soon as a boy behaves in a way that is not considered manly, that falls outside the Boy Code, he is likely to meet resistance from society—he may merely be stared at or whispered about, he may be humiliated, he may get a punch in the gut, or he may just feel terribly ashamed.

When eight-year-old Ethan tells his physical education teacher that he would rather jump rope than play basketball with the boys, some of his second-grade classmates cannot contain their laughter. The teacher smiles indulgently but pushes Ethan firmly in the direction of the basketball courts.

Thirteen-year-old Steven arrives at school with flesh-toned acne lotion covering an embarrassingly large pimple on his nose. His peers tease him about how "pretty he looks." They humiliate him by asking whether he "forgot to put on his lipstick," or what color dress he plans to wear to the dance that night.

When seventeen-year-old Brad reads a poem in English class with dra-matic intensity, there are a few sniggers from the back row. Later, someone mocks his recitation, adding an exaggerated lisp, and whispering loud enough for all to hear: "Faggot."

When boys act in less than conventionally "masculine" ways, their peers—both boys and girls—can be quick to tighten the laces on their gen-der straitjackets. Some parents, teachers, coaches, and other mentors also act in ways that reinforce society's myths about masculinity by letting boys know when they are violating the Boy Code.

Jennifer, a teacher at a Boston-area preschool, is thirty-six years old and holds degrees in childhood development from Wellesley and Harvard. She asked for my advice about one of her students, four-year-old Benjamin. "He still wants to play the mother and put on jewelry in the dress-up corner," she told me. "When I suggest something else for him to do, he cries in front of all the other kids. He seems perfectly healthy otherwise," she explained, "but I'm getting worried about whether he's really ready for kindergarten."

"Didn't I see Lisa wearing a cowboy hat and slapping her thigh like a horse the other day?" I asked.

"Sure," Jennifer said, "but *all* the girls do that."

Even this well-educated, highly competent, and sensitive teacher was influenced by the "boys should be boys" myth—playing mother and putting on jewelry did not constitute "healthy" boy behavior.

I witnessed similar attitudes at another private school that prided itself on being progressive. Recently they had instituted a coed program called Boxing Can Be Safe, designed to help kindergarten kids express their anger. I attended one of these kindergarten boxing matches and watched as five-year-old Michael, who stood no taller than three feet, made an awkward attempt at a punch. "Not like that, Michael," the coach admonished him. "You're swinging like a girl!"

It's hard to imagine how damaging these reproaches must be for boys. As a therapist—working with young people as well as adults—I have been through countless sessions with adult men who shared painful memories about being shamed as children for not being "manly" enough, for not being "like the other boys." Especially for very young boys, the humiliation leaves them feeling that there is no place to turn.

Without safe places where they can voice their pain or discuss their shame and deep embarrassment, many boys begin to toughen themselves up into little men. They become cut off from their own feelings, and their voices no longer fully connect with their emotional selves.

As difficult as the shame-hardening process is for boys, it is almost equally difficult for parents to watch. In many ways the myth that "boys should be boys" shields us, as adults, from dealing with our own pain and frustration as we observe our boys going through this extremely upsetting process. Perhaps by accepting the myth that boys must learn on their own how to act, must be like other "masculine" boys, and "tough it out," we somehow make ourselves feel more comfortable that this process is a necessary rite of passage, a natural part of growing up as a boy. Adult men in particular may rely on this myth to protect themselves from remembering how hurtful this "hardening" process was in their own childhood.

TRUTH #2: THERE ARE MANY WAYS TO BE
A BOY—THE DIVERSITY OF MASCULINITY

The truth is that the Boy Code is based on a stereotype unique to our culture and time. There is no *one* correct pathway to healthy masculinity. Boys have been defined very differently in other countries, other cultures, and other eras. For example, in one country crying may be expected of boys and men, whereas in another it may be expressly forbidden. Many parents today feel terribly ill at ease and struggle with the myths of boyhood, knowing in their hearts that they do not truly reflect the true nature of their own boys. Others, who have taken the time to fully examine the validity of the myths, refuse to accept the Boy Code and actively seek to break free of it. Often these parents are able, in turn, to help their sons break free of the code.

When they feel comfortable that they will not be humiliated by girls or other boys for doing so, many boys derive tremendous joy from participating in a full range of playful, expressive, and creative activities—which was how a young man called Kip was able to create a wonderful life for himself. In high school Kip had spent every waking hour—when he wasn't doing schoolwork or helping out at his father's small business—practicing, living, and breathing basketball. He dreamed of being the next Larry Bird, Michael Jordan, or Shaquille O'Neal. He was good enough to make the all-state team and received a basketball scholarship to Duke University. During his first game of the season, Kip's career aspirations came to an abrupt end. An elbow to the ribs caused a hard fall to the parquet and a serious knee injury. That night the Duke doctors told him the bad news: his knee could not be repaired. He would have to forget about a career in the NBA. Kip spent months moping and feeling sorry for himself; he relived the moment when he took the hit, wondering if he could have turned away from that fateful elbow or fallen differently to avoid the injury. Finally, he faced up to the fact that he would not be the next Larry Bird. He decided that he would have to "reinvent" himself. But, because he was a mediocre student, Kip figured that he would not be accepted into business school and that a business career was not an option for him.

One day he had an inspiration. He had another skill besides basketball, although he had never taken it very seriously. He was an inventive cook. He had grown up in a close and loving Italian family and had often helped his mother in the kitchen. She had always said that he had culinary talent, and she loved to tell her friends about his skill with bruschetta and fresh pasta and osso bucco. Kip wondered if he could make a career as a chef. He also wondered if it would be an acceptable career for an ex–basketball player, a jock.

Kip mentioned the idea to his father and hinted at his reservations. "Hey, Kip, there's nothing wrong with wearing an apron," his father responded. "It's a uniform, just like wearing basketball shorts. Maybe even better. Anybody who thinks you can't be a man and be a chef has never tasted a really great fettucine Alfredo."

The next month Kip enrolled at the Cordon Bleu cooking school in Paris. Five years later Kip was one of the most celebrated chefs in Denver and had employment offers from three restaurants in New York City. A well-known food-and-wine magazine hailed him as one of the stars of American cuisine. If you had told Kip when he was ten that he would become a chef, he probably would have scoffed at the idea. But he came to understand that his ability to be effective with the big round ball was not so different from his ability to be creative in the art of cooking.

"I'm not doing what I expected to do when I was a kid," Kip concluded. "But I think I had a very limited view of what a man should do with his life. Now I don't think there's anything less masculine about being a chef than being a forward."

There is no single path to a healthy and mature masculinity. A good school or home environment will send the message that activities like sports, acting in a school play, and volunteering at the local nursing home all provide equally good ways to succeed in the journey from boyhood into manhood.

When I am advising parents about boys, I encourage them to follow their own instincts about their sons' need for love and nurturing. Mothers and fathers need to feel secure that there is no such thing as giving their son too much love. Within appropriate limits you will never spoil a boy by showing him affection or by providing him with the freedom to follow his own path.

The Reverend Tony Jarvis, headmaster of one of Boston's most prestigious independent schools for boys, ends many a private interview with a

troubled high school senior—perhaps a six-foot 250-pound fullback—
with a big bear hug and the words "You know I love you." We can all set
up this kind of caring environment in which thoughts and feelings can be
freely expressed and encourage boys to experience childhood in an
entirely natural way. By doing so, we allow our sons to talk, mourn, and
grieve openly about the shame they may feel when they fail to live up to
the Boy Code. By doing so, we show boys that we love them for who they
really are.

MYTH #3: BOYS ARE TOXIC—THE ANTI-BOY

A third myth of boyhood follows from the first two, but it can be even
more devastating. Not only does society see boys as prisoners of their biological makeup ("boys will be boys"), and as properly confined by the
gender straitjacket ("boys should be boys"), but we also tend to believe
that there is something inherently dangerous or toxic about boys—that
they are psychologically unaware, emotionally unsocialized creatures.
This myth adds a potentially damaging element to the social environment.

Karen decided to send her daughter, Alison, to an all-girls school, but
kept her son in a coeducational environment. The reason, she explained,
was that her daughter needed to learn that "all roles in society are open to
women." Her son, on the other hand, needed to learn in the company of
girls because they would help to make him more "sensitive and polished."
She was saying, in other words, that the presence of boys might have a
toxic effect on her daughter, while girls could help mitigate the noxious
disposition of her son. Barbara, another parent, put the same anti-boy sentiment a little more directly when she said, "Girls have a civilizing effect."

Such views must be seen as discriminatory to boys, but they are seldom challenged by other parents or by teachers because of the prevalent
myth that boys *are* in fact toxic. This myth manifests itself in both subtle
and dramatic ways. When a seven-year-old boy impulsively plants a kiss
on a somewhat unwilling female playmate, he is branded a sexual delinquent and suspended from school. A fifth-grade boy coming directly from
a "sex education" class jokes with a girl that her sagging belt looks like a
penis and gets accused of "sexual harassment." It is as if we are in the
midst of an irrational society-wide backlash against boys and young men.

Put aside for the moment the obvious double standard of how teenage
girls who joke about the "bulge" in football players' pants are unlikely to

be branded as sexual harassers, and ask why we have confused boys' child-ish exploratory play with adult predatory behavior. No doubt some com-ponents of boys' and girls' play go beyond the bounds of acceptability and are deserving of redirection or even reprimand. Yet, when it is a *boy* involved, we seem to forget his need to play, experiment, and fail in order to grow. Instead, we respond as though he is a full-fledged aggressor.

TRUTH #3: BOYS ARE EMPATHIC

Although empathy is considered to be one of the strongest attributes of girls, there is ample evidence that boys are highly empathic as well. An interesting study was conducted of boys raised in a two-parent household in which the father was the primary emotionally nurturing parent. In addi-tion to all the other typical traits of well-adjusted male children—self-confidence, exuberance, action-orientation—these boys also showed a greater flexibility of personality and a positive attitude toward girls and the ability to connect with them. In other words, men are capable of rais-ing their boy children to have empathy in all their relationships. Even when raised without a predominant female presence, boys can learn to be sensitive and to care deeply about other people, including girls, and their feelings.

Seth's friends were just such boys.

Seth was a slight sixteen-year-old who excelled at soccer. In his junior year in high school he was elected cocaptain of the varsity soccer team. Not only was he respected by his teammates, but he was a model student and high achiever. But Seth had a sadness in his eyes, and an uncertainty in his bearing that seemed at odds with his popular and physically confi-dent self. However, it was not difficult to see why he seemed to be bearing a burden. His mother, a warm and active woman named Cindy, had been diagnosed with a severe and rapidly growing form of breast cancer.

The entire family—Seth, his thirteen-year-old sister, Amy; his father; and Cindy herself—had met with Cindy's oncologist. Seth talked about that meeting with great emotion. His father, who owned an insurance busi-ness, had broken the ice by asking the doctor for some straight answers about Cindy's condition and her chances. "There's no good way to tell you this," said the doctor. "Your wife has a very serious form of breast cancer. We're going to do everything we can, but the average life expectancy from tumors like this is less than five years."

The family rallied around Cindy as best they could. Seth seemed particularly able to provide her with special comfort and support. He was aided in his efforts by an unexpected source—the members of his soccer team. The boys pitched in, helping with the formidable day-to-day tasks of caring for a seriously ill person. They hosted a bake sale to raise funds for the hospital, donating the proceeds in her name. Perhaps most important, Seth's buddies offered him their shoulders to cry on. And cry on them he did. When his mother's hair fell out from chemotherapy, when radiation treatments didn't work, Seth wept openly, at lunch hour, at study hall, or on his way to soccer practice in the afternoons. By his side were one or two, sometimes three or four, of his friends—tears streaming down their cheeks, as well.

His mother died four years later, when Seth was a sophomore at Yale. Although the news came as no surprise, it still hit him like a fist in the chest. He remembers doubling up with pain, worrying that he couldn't make it through the funeral. That night he called his best buddy from high school, Bill, a student at Stanford.

"Don't worry, Seth," Bill assured him. "We'll be there for you."

Seth assumed that Bill meant that his friends would be thinking of him, there for him in spirit. But on the day of the funeral almost all of the twenty-five young men who had composed Seth's soccer team showed up at the church to attend the funeral. Outside the church, they joined together in a circle of shared love and grief, poured out their sadness to one another, and gave Bill the strength he needed to get through the service.

The priest remarked to me that he had never seen anything like this. "I'm struck not only by their open affection and caring," he told me, "but by the fact that this is coming from *boys*."

"They're men now, Father," I replied, "real men."

This is just one example of the kind of caring, deeply supportive, empathic behavior that boys can show for their loved ones—their parents, their friends, their families—and that I have seen boys display in a wide variety of situations and circumstances.

ACTION LOVE:

HOW BOYS RELATE

*"We're really not so different from girls," an adolescent boy,
Tim, said. "We just do things a little differently."*

THE LOVE AND YEARNINGS OF REAL BOYS

Boys are immensely loving and they yearn for relationships far more than
we have ever recognized.

There are two reasons boys' inherent loving nature and their yearning
for relationships go largely unnoticed by society. First, when boys relate in
ways that are considered traditionally "feminine"—when they're tender
and affectionate, when they are emotionally expressive, when they talk
sensitively about difficult friendships—society often does not support
them because it sees them as violating the Boy Code of masculine toughness and independence. Second, boys often relate in ways that many of us
simply don't recognize as a means for expressing love. Boys approach
friendships and express love differently from the way girls do, and too
often we just don't get it, because we're so used to assuming that love can
be expressed only through the traditional "female" models. And so we
don't fully understand that boys are reaching out for human relationships
when they actually are.

As we'll learn in this chapter, though some boys show their love and
caring in traditional ways, many have their own "boy-like" ways of doing
so. First, rather than showing love through words, many boys do so
through action. Thus, instead of declaring their love directly through
words, many boys use indirect ways of conveying their feelings by *doing*

things for or with other people. So, for example, rather than telling his mom how much he loves her on Mother's Day, the boy may instead simply ask her if she'd like to go to the movies with him that day. Boys also show love through acts of protection. When they see somebody they love in a vulnerable position or in trouble, they leap to the rescue and do whatever they can to help their friend or loved one through the situation. A third way that boys show love and form relationships is through work: instead of using words to tell his parents that he cares deeply about them, a boy may signal the same feelings by offering to repair the leaky toilet, fix the roof, or drive his younger brother to his trumpet lesson. Finally, many boys express their love and their longing for human relationships through acts of justice and kindness. Whether it's helping an elderly person cross a busy city street or sticking up for the rights of the first person of color to come to his all-white high school, a boy may often show his love and caring by standing up for what he believes is right, good, and fair.

LOVE THROUGH ACTION

Even at a very young age, boys may show their love not so much with words but through action. The early ability to "attach"—in the terminology of psychologists—refers to a child's capacity to develop intimate, powerful emotional bonds to others, such as his mother and father and his peers. Research shows that boys have this ability as much as girls do, yet their typical attachment styles often differ from those of girls.

For example, boys and girls show their feelings toward their parents in very different ways. A girl might seek connection with her mother by snuggling up beside her, kissing her, smoothing her hair, or just talking with her. A boy is more likely to ask his mother to *do* something—to play a game, give him a ride. Or he might express love indirectly—give her a playful nudge and then run away, hoping, of course, that she'll give chase. An adolescent girl might seek connection with her mother by giving her a hug or bringing her a small gift for no particular reason or occasion. An adolescent boy typically tries to make connection by offering to help his mother with some task that he normally avoids—taking out the trash, cleaning up his room, agreeing to an errand, or doing his own laundry. Or he may suggest some activity they can do together, such as taking a bike ride together or going to a movie. A girl may seek attachment with her father by asking for help on her homework. A boy in the same family might tease his father—an indirect way of showing love—or initiate a wrestling match.

Similarly, boys and girls often approach other close caregivers, such as teachers, in substantially different ways. While a young girl might seek attachment with her schoolteacher by complimenting the teacher on her special outfit, a young boy might make a connection with the teacher by asking whether he can stay after class and help out by erasing the blackboards. On the whole, boys tend to seek attachment less through asking for it directly and more by trying to bring it about indirectly or through action.

LOVE IN ACTION: MRS. KOSLOWSKI'S CLASS

Mrs. Koslowski was flabbergasted when the boys in her all-boys English class began asking her questions about her upcoming wedding. She recounted a striking story about how boys' love is expressed through action.

"I already knew these boys were gutsy to take a class devoted to poetry, but *this, this* I never expected." The boys had become concerned that she be able to take time off to buy the matching shoes and veil to go with the wedding dress, which she had not been able to do. So they volunteered to clean up the classroom and read extra chapters in their textbooks so that she could take the day off. Two of the boys offered to go with her.

"I knew they cared," she said, "but I never imagined they'd feel so close to me that these concerns would matter to them too!"

Mothers, too, report ways in which boys use action to promote closeness. Mrs. Schwartz told me the following story about how her son Jamie connects with her each day. A serious student and captain of his local soccer club at age fourteen, Jamie takes time every morning to send a loving E-mail message from the school-library computer; and every afternoon during "half-time," he calls her up to check up on how her day at work is going. "He knows this new job at the hospital is very stressful, and we're so close, he just wants me to know he's thinking of me."

"When he was born," Mrs. Schwartz continued, "his grandmother told me, 'He's a beautiful child, but boys just don't think of their mothers the way girls do, once they're grown up.' I prayed my mother would be wrong, and now I know that she was."

Boys show their yearnings for attachment in a unique way, but as different as their attachment styles may sometimes be, boys, like girls, benefit enormously from both feminine and masculine forms of mentoring, and they rely significantly on their connection to the women and men who raise and educate them.

THE INDIRECT APPROACH—AND ITS USE WITH FRIENDS

To initiate or deepen a friendship, girls may tend to do so directly through open verbal communication, but boys may take an indirect route, through an action or activity of some kind, as in the case of Brian. Wanting to be friends with David, Brian might plan an activity and offhandedly ask David if he wants to come along or join in, acting as if it doesn't really matter whether David accepts. The activity may be a game of pickup basketball, a saxophone rehearsal, or simply hanging out at the local hub. Though the approach looks different, the feelings behind it—the longing for closeness—are the same.

Little boys, too, may seek emotional bonds in indirect ways. With other boys, these bonds may be forged through exuberant, rough-and-tumble play. With girls, they may start with teasing—a method of seeking connection that is usually motivated far less by malice than by a fundamental desire to stir up possibilities for friendship.

And sometimes boys may surprise us with how innovative they can be in drumming up relationships. Consider, for example, the other creative approaches by Jason and Aaron, discussed below.

A "GUY PLACE"

Jason, a "four-letter man" (he qualified for four varsity sports in high school), had proposed that the school set up a place where the boys in his class could create an after-school "peer support group" talk center. "There are so many pressures on us, and no place to talk. I thought if we had a 'guy place' with rules that no one could come there and poke fun at what anyone said—just listen and help—it might help take a load off us."

Jason's school implemented his idea, and soon the idea was so popular that extra groups had to be added. Mr. Hanritty, the school principal, commented to me, "Who would have thought that boys would want their own space to 'relate'?"

Aaron Spencer, another high school student, created his own relationship-building project. Tired of hearing all the ranking down of the "nerds"—bright but slightly weird science whizes in the tenth grade—Aaron, as class president, decided to create a forum with representatives of girls and guys, popular and unpopular, brains, jocks, feminists, cheerleaders, nerds, "artsies," liberals, and conservatives. He brought them all together to talk, and encouraged them to form relationships that transcended their basic differences. Aaron's program, it turned out, was a great success. But perhaps the most striking result was that Aaron found a new friend—Jake, a science "nerd."

"We just got to talking at the forum," Aaron said. "Then we went to a movie, and now we do all kinds of stuff together. I've really learned that to find a true friend you've got to stretch yourself a little."

As these stories reveal, boys—if we read their signals correctly, and if we encourage them—not only want to form close relationships but actually are often very creative and successful in doing so. Habits of thought in society confuse us into imagining that close relationships are not central to boys' normal growth and development, and that a boy's only possible path to healthy adult masculinity is through self-reliance, autonomy, and solitude. Yet in reality, boys yearn for close relationships just as much as girls do.

PROTECTIVE LOVE

Boys' love and protectiveness may show themselves through a unique form of action. One middle-school teacher told me the following story. One of his students, Jeremy, heard a rumble of voices in the cafeteria that sounded like an argument in progress. He ambled over, shouldered through the crowd, and saw two girls in the middle of the group screaming at each other—both shaking with anger and on the brink of physical violence. One of the girls was Jeremy's sister, Cassie, a freshman. The other girl, Tara, was a junior, a bigger girl and one of the most popular kids in school. In fact, Jeremy had dated her a couple of times and had wanted to continue the relationship, but Tara had started going out regularly with a senior.

The situation was a difficult one for Jeremy. He cared for his sister, but she was very independent and might not appreciate his getting involved in the argument. He also had little interest in making a scene in front of Tara. Everybody knew that he liked her and that she had "dumped him." He didn't want any more embarrassment. But the argument was getting more intense and he knew that Tara, who was a weight trainer and center of the girl's basketball team, could do some real physical damage to Cassie if she felt like it.

The confrontation had reached the breaking point. Rather than allow his sister to get involved in a fight, Jeremy stepped into the center of the circle. "Hey, Tara!" he shouted. Tara looked at him, startled. "What do you want?"

"Want to go out Saturday night?" Jeremy asked her.

Tara was thrown off-balance. "I told you I didn't want to go out with you anymore," Tara said. The crowd tittered nervously.

"No. I guess you'd rather beat on my little sister," he said calmly. The crowd laughed with him.

"Yeah, as a matter of fact, I would," taunted Tara. "It's more fun than making out with you." A big laugh from the crowd.

"But, Tara, what did Cassie do that makes you want to fight her?"

"It's none of your business," Tara replied.

"OK. I just can't imagine why someone as smart as you would want to beat up a freshman. Why can't you talk it out?"

"Just stay out of this," Tara insisted and turned back to Cassie.

Jeremy looked at his sister. She was holding her ground, but he could tell she wouldn't mind some help in getting out of her predicament. Jeremy simply took her by the arm and said, "Come on," he said to her. "This is stupid. Let's go."

The two made their way through the crowd, leaving Tara behind. She watched them go and the crowd wondered what she would do. Finally, she spoke, with a grudging admiration. "If he loves his sister that much, maybe he's not so bad after all." The crowd broke up with laughter.

As they walked away, Cassie said to her brother. "I could have handled that."

"I know," said Jeremy.

"But thanks. That was really nice of you."

"I had to do it." He smiled. "You're my sister. I love you, don't I?"

"I guess you do," Cassie said, marveling, never having really thought about it.

You might expect a brother to protect his sister, especially a younger one, but in today's climate a boy may feel too constrained to express this kind of protective love. He may fear that he will be criticized for being too macho, or think that no boy should presume to intervene in an altercation between two girls. But Jeremy felt he had no choice but to get involved and show his love and support for his sister, and he found a way to do so that did not make her seem foolish or incapable.

Another boy, Kim, expressed a similar kind of protective love—in this case, for a neighbor with a serious illness. "When I was ten," Kim told me,

"I volunteered to help take care of my neighbor kid down the street, named Michael. He had something wrong with his spine, and had to be in a body cast for a whole year. I didn't really know him, but his mother asked my mother if I could come over and just say hi, and I said OK. When I first saw Mike I thought the whole thing was really weird and I wanted to go home. I thought we could never be friends. He's sick and can't walk. But then we discovered that we both liked playing that card game, Magic. That was about the only thing Mike could do besides watch TV. Once we started playing and I got to know him better, I liked him. So, then I really started looking after him. Sometimes I would just go over and read to him. He couldn't walk, but he liked going outside in this cartlike thing. So, I'd push him around the driveway and down the street sometimes. If anybody looked strangely at him, I'd give them the evil eye back. If anybody said anything bad about him at school, or laughed at him, I'd tell them to shut up and say that he was a really good kid."

Kim found it rewarding to be able to help and protect his friend. He felt very close to Mike, and showed it by helping him and defending him to others. "It made me feel really good about myself," said Kim. "Part of being a friend is letting other people know it."

Love is the core of each and every boy.

EXPRESSING LOVE THROUGH WORK: MRS. SUMMERS

Another way boys (and men) express their feelings for others is through engaging in what we call work. A boy's inclination to do hard work and willingness to take on duty and responsibilities—virtues traditionally celebrated as "masculine"—may be shaped into a strong motivation not only for improving academic performance but also for caring for others in a disciplined way.

Just as men will work toward a goal that they believe will please or protect a loved one, boys will undertake a project or a task as a way of expressing affection. Though sometimes we may focus only on the task that's being accomplished, we should be aware that behind the labor there's often the devotion of a boy engaged in what's truly an act of selfless generosity, an act of love.

Bob and Tim had always liked Mrs. Summers, one of the most involved and thoughtful fifth-grade teachers at King Elementary School. She liked to regale her students with stories of her vacation adventures, and always brought back some sort of live animal to show the class. Over the years, the classroom came to look like a zoo, filled with cages containing small furry creatures with Latin names the boys could not remember. Mrs. Summers joked that if she brought in any more animals, the children would have to go. It was a warm, inviting, caring, and nurturing environment.

One winter weekend, vandals sneaked into the school. When Mrs. Summers's students arrived in class Monday morning, they found the room in a shambles. Most of the animals had been let out of their cages and had escaped; others had been killed. Mrs. Summers was devastated, as were the kids. They talked about what had happened, and why. During the day a few of the girls used photos of the animals to make a collage and pinned them up on the bulletin board. Other students talked about having a party to cheer up Mrs. Summers. But Tim and Bob came up with a different idea.

Both boys did odd jobs in their neighborhoods—shoveling snow, moving lawns, walking dogs, and baby-sitting. They each managed to save about five dollars a week, which they deposited in their own checking accounts; they had promised their parents they would save the money to help with the cost of their college educations. The boys' first thought was to withdraw the money and give it to Mrs. Summers to buy some new animals. But, after some discussion, they decided that it wouldn't make sense to spend all their hard-earned money, and, besides, they had made a promise to their parents.

Finally, they came up with a clever idea. They realized that they had more time in their weekly schedules that they could devote to work. They enlisted several other boys from their class, and made posters advertising their services. Their earnings would go to the Summers Wildlife Fund, established to restock the animal kingdom in Mrs. Summers's fifth-grade classroom. They even created a website that detailed their services and enabled their classmates to follow their progress.

For three months Bob, Tim, and their friends devoted every Saturday and Sunday afternoon to do the work for the Wildlife Fund. By June, they had accumulated seventy-five dollars. On the last day of school, the boys surprised Mrs. Summers with a check. She was overwhelmed. "You boys are unbelievable!" she exclaimed, hugging them, tears streaming down her cheeks. "I have never seen such a hardworking, caring bunch of guys." Bob and Tim felt tremendous joy that their hard work had been appreciated by a person they cared very much about.

Bob and Tim had found a way to express their love for Mrs. Summers through action, a way to use their inclination to do hard work to benefit another person. And she received their message very clearly. Seventy-five dollars, even for a public school teacher, did not represent a significant sum of money. But three months of free time spent on work by five young boys represented not only a real sacrifice but a tremendous investment of love and energy—all for her benefit. No wonder she wept.

It's important for parents, for all of us, to be aware that boys often choose to express their love through action and work, and to recognize and respond to it when they do. When father and son team up to create a homeless project for Scouts, or when brothers tackle a snowed-in driveway together for a disabled neighbor, we are seeing the traditional male work ethic buttressed by a demonstration of love and affection.

DEDICATION TO JUSTICE AS A FORM OF CARING

Another way boys show love that often falls outside stereotypical expectations is through their strong sense of fairness and justice. Boys will often sacrifice their own personal interests in an effort to be fair to others, especially those they care most about. This characteristic often surprises me when I encounter it. "Yeah, I really wanted to go to the game," a boy will tell me. "But my mother needed me to look after my sister. It was fair, because she left in the middle of a dinner party last weekend to care for me when I got that terrible flu."

When boys analyze their own behavior in light of what is fair and just for all involved, they are showing how important their relationships are to them—and that they are willing to put aside their personal interests, to sacrifice in order to maintain an emotional connection with someone they love, respect, or wish to protect, or to defend a principle that affects the quality of people's lives.

Take, for instance, Eric, a boy who sought me out when he was facing what he saw as a moral dilemma. Eric was trying to decide whether to cut school to attend a demonstration in Washington, D.C., against the proposed American military involvement in Iraq. A loving son and an excellent student, he cared deeply about issues of politics and ethics. His parents had brought him up to do what was "right" as well as to "do good"; and although they didn't disagree with him on the issue itself, they did not want him to miss school and attend the demonstration. He would be holding a placard and handing out flyers.

"Why do they need *you* to do that work?" his mother asked. "Anyone could do it."

"It could be dangerous," added his father. "You could be tear-gassed. There might be a riot."

Eric was tormented by his decision. On the one hand, he felt very strongly about the prospect of innocent women and children being killed if the United States were to attack Iraq. At the same time, he did not wish to go against his parents' wishes. He loved them and understood their point of view.

He discussed his decision with his two sisters. They, too, were disturbed by the situation and felt tremendous empathy with the Iraqi people who would be the innocent victims.

But Eric didn't feel the urge to cry or talk about the problem. He felt, instead, a deep urge to right the wrong that he believed was being perpetrated. He wanted to show his empathy through action.

"I hope you can help me sort these things out," Eric said to me. "I really feel like I've got to stick to what's right. As my dad used to say, 'Actions speak louder than words.' "

The sense of justice, of moral responsibility, with which he had been imbued since childhood had welled up inside him, and he felt forced to take action in this Iraq protest. The potential damage to his honors record as a result of skipping school and the struggle with his loving family would have to take second place to his sense of justice and of what he felt was right.

Like Eric, many boys express their sense of fairness by trying to solve problems, by making decisions, and especially by taking swift, decisive action. Girls sometimes express their sense of fairness quite differently— for instance, by speaking about their feelings with adults or by talking among themselves about their sense of outrage. Adults sometimes expect the same kinds of behavior from boys and thus misinterpret boys' justice-seeking actions as mere bravado. When we observe boys closely, we discover that many of them feel strongly about making a difference in the lives of the people for whom they care deeply and about "doing what's right" for them. They do this, in most cases, by planning and implementing hands-on, proactive measures—their own way of showing love through action.

REAL BOYS SHOW A LOVING RESPECT FOR GIRLS

When given proper support, boys develop a loving respect for others in general, as well as a platonic affection for the opposite gender in particular. In coeducational peer settings in which they feel pressured to compete against one another for the attention of girls, boys may sometimes behave, on the surface at least, as though they do not respect girls. In these settings, for instance, boys may tease girls, taunt them, or brag to other boys about their interactions with girls or women. But when they are placed in an environment where they believe they won't be harassed for showing respect to girls—or in a gender-sensitive all-boys environment such as a boys' school or the Boy Scouts where they are temporarily freed from the pressure to compete over girls—many boys can come to understand and empathize with what makes girls and women feel vulnerable and unsafe. If properly encouraged, boys show a natural inclination to honor these feelings in girls and women with compassion and respect.

In my interview with Guy, a sixteen-year-old honors student from an all-boys school, he explained to me that Ellen, the girl he had met at a dance through his younger sister, was first and foremost a "good friend." There had been some romantic stirrings on both sides, but Ellen, he specified, "was very nervous about touching, and I could tell she wanted her space—so we'd just talk." But the talking was more than he had ever imagined. "Ellen has a way of listening, of caring about what I say, that I never thought I'd find. She makes me feel so good about myself—like I really matter. And it makes me want to share with her, too. It's a new thing for me, and it's great."

"Have you told the other guys about Ellen?" I asked Guy.

"Some of the other guys understand. They have girls they're close to but it's not romantic, not girlfriends. Some guys tease me—they push me to tell them if we're making out, having sex. I let them know it's none of their business. Ellen's a great girl and I'm lucky to know her; and for now that's just fine with me."

Many boys are less solid than Guy, and often try to fool themselves and others into thinking that girls are just objects to be taken advantage of. Do they really believe it? In many cases, the answer is no. The pressure to be "cool," "tough," and "together" pushes many adolescent boys and young men to hide their deepest connected feelings, mask the empathy that comes naturally to them, and instead assume the roles of unthinking sexual predators. If we removed that pressure from boys' lives, I believe they would feel safer to express their inherent respect for girls and women and their yearning to relate closely and meaningfully with them.

EACH BOY'S VOICE IS UNIQUE

There is not one single healthy path to mature masculinity. Boys' self-esteem—which is, of course, as essential to their emotional growth and academic achievement as it is to girls—is dependent not upon macho displays of competitive aggression but on having their "real" voices heard and genuine selves responded to with deep understanding.

If we offer "comfort zones" free of shame and humiliation—if we let them know that all of their attributes and yearnings are not only acceptable but *cherished*—we discover sides of our boys that we never knew existed. The boy we always thought was "shy" delivers a Shakespeare soliloquy with exuberance and conviction. The boy who never before had felt close to his father reaches out to him and makes a new, strong connection. The boy everyone had branded as a troublemaker breaks down in tears and speaks for the first time of his abusive alcoholic mother and how lonely and afraid he feels. When we really give boys the chance to share *everything* they're thinking about and hoping for, when we work to understand the diverse ways they use to show their yearnings for closeness and connection—whether they use more traditional "feminine" approaches or some of the special ways of loving others discussed in this chapter—and when we give them our full nonjudgmental support to pursue exactly what they want for themselves, their masks finally come off and we begin to discover the virtues of our "real boys." It's then, too, that we realize that so much of what boys do for and with us is more than just random boyish activity. It's the way that so many of them relate—the way that they love.

REAL BOYS LIKE KEVIN—ONE FINAL STORY OF HOW BOYS EXPRESS ACTION LOVE

Kevin Loranger, a lanky, blond-haired twelve-year-old boy, was playing with his two best buddies, John Jr. and Charlie, along a sandy California beach that was deserted that morning. The surf was dangerously high, way too high for swimming, as the lifeguard's red warning flag indicated at the rescue station just one mile up the road. Charlie, a freckle-faced redhead and the most daring of the group, challenged the "three amigos," as they were called by their parents, to strip off their clothes and jump in for a swim. Before Kevin could object, Charlie had plunged into the surf. John Jr., hesitant and uneasy, and Kevin, weighing the risks involved, suddenly heard cries of Charlie's distress. Kevin could see waves crashing on the shore and Charlie, his arms flailing, bobbing up and down.

"Help! Help!" Charlie shouted, his voice shrill.

Kevin yelled over to John to run for help, and without any apparent thought for his own safety, yanked off his shoes and ran to the water, diving into the surf toward his friend in trouble.

With massive effort, several times almost succumbing to the choppy waves himself, Kevin managed to drag Charlie out of the surf and pull him onto the beach. He looked at Charlie and found he was barely breathing. Images of their past moments together flashed through Kevin's mind: the time they wandered off on a Boy Scout hike and spent a cold night in the Sierra Nevada; the cool, breezy Sunday afternoon their Little League team won the local championships; the time Charlie's sister Amelia was dying from leukemia and he stood by as Charlie cried in the waiting room of Mount Zion Hospital. While these images came to him, he cleared Charlie's mouth of water, and began to perform mouth-to-mouth resuscitation. Happily, he was soon interrupted by the paramedics, who ran up to him along with John Jr.

Kevin was interviewed later that day on the ten o'clock news. Bashfully Kevin answered the reporter's question of how he'd had the courage to risk his own life to save his friend.

"It wasn't anything really," he said. "Charlie's my best buddy and when he needed help, I just did what I had to do. I'm sure he'd do the same for me. And the mouth-to-mouth, well that's what Coach Larson had taught on the swim team, and I just followed his instructions exactly. I'm sure glad everybody's OK."

While in some ways Kevin's story celebrates some of the traditional virtues of boys that we often take for granted—their enormous energy, how they revel in physical contact, their ability to compete with admirable gusto—it also reflects many of the kinds of love we've been discussing. Kevin takes action to show his love for Charlie. He's loyal to his friends and will do whatever it takes to protect them. Boys, this story tells us, will risk their lives for a buddy. Boys, it assures us, very much need friends, and will put their lives on the line to keep them.

PART TWO

CONNECTING TO BOYS

Night and day arrive, and day after
*   day goes by,*
and what is old remains old, and what
*   is young remains young and grows*
*   old.*
The lumber pile does not grow
*   younger, nor the two-by-fours lose*
*   their darkness;*
but the old tree goes on, the barn
*   stands without help so many years;*
the advocate of darkness and night is
*   not lost.*

The horse steps up, swings on one leg,
*   turns his body;*
the chicken flapping claws up onto
*   the roost, its wings whelping and*
*   walloping,*
But what is primitive is not to be shot
*   out into the night and the dark,*
and slowly the kind of man comes
*   closer, loses his rage, sits down at*
*   table.*

So I am proud only of those days that
*   pass in undivided tenderness,*
when you sit drawing, or making
*   books, stapled, with messages to*
*   the world,*
or coloring a man with fire coming
*   out of his hair.*
Or we sit at a table, with small tea
*   carefully poured.*
So we pass our time together, calm
*   and delighted.*

—ROBERT BLY
    "For My Son Noah, Ten Years Old"

THE

POWER OF MOTHERS

"I don't think I'd be much without her."
—Clint Westfield, age fifteen

NEVER TOO MUCH OF A GOOD THING

Mothers help make boys into men.

Contrary to society's traditional misgivings about a close relationship between mother and son, I find that, in reality, boys benefit tremendously from the love of their mothers, especially the kind of unshaming parenting we've been discussing as the way to bring out the best in boys.

I believe that by empowering the mother you empower the son. And I believe empowered mothers are a key to resolving society's confusion about masculinity and creating a new real-boy code.

Far from making boys weaker, the love of a mother can and does actually make boys stronger, emotionally and psychologically. Far from making boys dependent, the base of safety a loving mother can create—a connection that her son can rely on all his life—provides a boy with the courage to explore the outside world. But most important, far from making a boy act in "girl-like" ways, a loving mother actually plays an integral role in helping a boy develop his masculinity—the self-esteem and strength of character he needs to feel confident in his own masculine self.

THE DOUBLE STANDARD OF MASCULINITY

In our contemporary world, the old Boy Code still holds our sons to a double standard of masculinity—on the one hand, boys are told they should act in tough, conventionally "guy"-like ways, and on the other, they are chastised when they don't act "sensitive," "caring," or "empathic" enough. My research shows that amid these confusing double messages to boys it is often a boy's empathic, active, undaunted mother who is in the best position to help him reconcile these conflicting messages about who he should become and how he should or shouldn't behave. In other words, it is mothers—the first women who are deeply involved in the emotional lives of most boys—who are in fact the earliest teachers of today's masculinity. It is they who first instruct boys about how to integrate *both* components of our split model of masculinity, and who therefore imbue boys with a sense of confidence about the wash of feelings, behavior, and experiences that add up to being an emotionally balanced and satisfied man.

Then too, it's generally the mother who is still mainly responsible for creating a home, that warm, loving environment to which a boy can retreat when his spirits run low or when the outside world seems overwhelming. As we'll see in the next chapter, most fathers have a special ability to bond with their sons through high-energy activities that teach them how to stretch their capacity for handling the intensity of such experiences. Most mothers, by contrast, seem to connect with their sons just by being with them, by giving them their undivided attention, and by making themselves available as an unfailing source of love, comfort, and support.

As discussed in Part I, I don't think a boy's separation from mother at a very early age and again at adolescence should ever be sanctioned. Instead, I believe that mothers should be encouraged to trust their own instincts over society's misgivings—that the love of a mother, in most cases, is what will help a boy launch himself into a healthy masculine life.

My research also shows that the absence of a close relationship with a loving mother puts a boy at a disadvantage in becoming a free, confident, and independent man, a man who likes himself and can take risks and who can form close and loving attachments with people in his adult life. In their early years as well as during adolescence, I think boys will benefit enormously from spending time in the loving environment created by his mother *and her friends*—the happy, nurturing world of women. So I'm in favor of more of mother, not less, especially at those times in a boy's life when our culture typically pushes for the premature separation of boy from mother.

CLINT: A STRONG BOY WHO STILL NEEDS MOM

Clint Westfield, age fifteen, speaks passionately about how his mother gives him strength and courage to face the future:

"When I start freaking out, it's my mom who puts down everything and comes around to help me. She explains things to me—you know, comforts me—and then I feel strong again. Like sometimes I'm so upset I don't want to go outside anymore—I just want to go hide in my room. My mom tells me that what I'm going through is normal. After we spend some time together—or sometimes we hang out with some of her friends in the neighborhood—I feel like I can go outside again to be with my friends."

"What makes you afraid in the first place?" I asked, surprised by the candor of this tall, well-built teenager who looked as if he was probably the biggest and strongest kid on his block.

"My dad. I mean my dad's the best. But he's an agent with the FBI and lots of times he leaves really early in the morning to go on these dangerous missions. I get nervous, and so does my mom, because he puts on his body armor and wears a gun on his belt. He tells us these wild stories at night. Friends of his have been wounded. I love his stories—but they get us worried because his life is just about always on the line. Sometimes Dad just goes to work in an office and I don't have anything to worry about. But on the days when he wears his body armor, I know something bad might happen. When I go into his bedroom and the armor is missing from his closet, I know something's up."

"Have you ever spent a day at work with your dad?"

"It's not allowed. But anyway, I don't want to be an FBI agent. My grandfather was an agent and now my dad is too."

"So, is there pressure on you to become an agent? That must make you scared too."

"Well, I look up to my father a lot and in some ways he probably wishes I'd become an agent. But my mom tells me that I can do whatever I want. When we talk about my future, she always says 'you don't have to be just like your father and take risks and put your life on the line to be a man. You can be just as much a man by being yourself and doing whatever seems the easiest and the most fun for *you*—*that* is what you should do.' "

"That sounds pretty fair."

"Yup. My mom's pretty cool. She always knows what to say to make me feel good about myself. I don't think I'd be much without her."

"So, do you have an idea of what you'd like to do in the future?"

"I'm thinking about law school—maybe I'll become a criminal lawyer. I like the whole law enforcement world as long as I don't have to go through what my dad does. But I'm not really thinking so much about careers these days."

"That makes sense," I told Clint.

"Yeah," he explained, "I'm more worried about finding the right girl. If I could find someone just like my mom, I'd be golden."

Clint's story is important, I believe, because it shows how his mother could not only talk openly with her son and help him deal with his most vulnerable emotions but also be instrumental in helping him to feel confident, to feel he's a good, competent, "normal" boy. Moreover, by encouraging him to choose whatever kind of career he'd like (despite the family history of FBI work) she also gives Clint the message that he can become a man according to his own definition.

WHAT'S A MOTHER TO DO? THE BOY OF THE FUTURE

Fortunately, many of today's mothers are no mindless enforcers of gender stereotypes. After all, this generation of mothers was raised in the bracing atmosphere of feminism. Many have embraced the ideal of equality between the sexes, struggled to rediscover their own voices and to find qualities of toughness, assertiveness, and competitiveness within themselves. Today's mothers have successfully battled for the right to work, think, and compete as men do. They have battled for the right of their daughters to be outspoken and strong, to succeed in math class, even to play football if they want to. And at home, these women have struggled with their male companions to rework their most intimate relationships on a more equal basis. Today's mothers demand from their partners more than help with the diapering and vacuuming—they want empathy and sensitivity.

Yet I find that these women, who are so confident about so many gender issues, are frequently still unsure of themselves when it comes to raising their own sons.

Time after time women have voiced to me their doubts and confusion. Yes, they say, we want to raise boys who are sensitive to others, who can play with girls, who are aware of their vulnerable emotions and not afraid to express them. But, they add, we also don't want to raise a boy who will be branded as a wimp, who will have to endure teasing and beatings from other boys, who will have no friends and no dates in high school. How can we raise a son to be the kind of sensitive man we'd want to have a relationship with and still have him survive the relentless peer pressure of grade school and the adolescent years? How far ahead of the gender curve can we be? they wonder.

Mothers who try to ignore gender stereotypes often find they have a rocky road. Society is quick to let them know that the old Boy Code is still in effect, that mothers too must abide by the rules. Whether it's a little boy who runs home crying when his peers tease him about his long, curly hair, the adolescent who complains that Mom's alternative dispute-resolution techniques just aren't working at school, or the husband or other family member who implores her to stop trying to make the boy so "sweet," a mother receives constant outside reminders that she must comply with society's rules about boys and masculinity.

ELLEN AND JACK

Take, for example, Ellen, who discovered that her husband, Jack, was concerned about her relationship with their son. When I first got to know them, they were struggling over "how to set limits" for Christopher, their fourteen-year-old son—each of them was advocating a different way of disciplining the boy when he was acting out.

But as Ellen and Jack talked things through with each other, they realized that underneath the problem of discipline was a more volatile, more emotionally charged difference of opinion. Ellen and Jack disagreed over the Boy Code's rules about tenderness between mother and son and what this might mean for Christopher's development:

"You let Christopher get away with murder," Jack said to Ellen, "especially with all that hugging in public. He's all over you like a monkey in heat—it's so inappropriate."

Ellen responded with passion: "It's one of the most wonderful things about our son. In this world of guns and TV violence, Christopher can still show his love openly by hugging me and his friends. We should reward that, encourage this gentle, loving side."

I attempted to empathize with both: to support Ellen in her courageous stance and to help her husband understand its benefits. Jack grudgingly agreed that he would want his son to be well loved by Ellen. Yet Jack was unable to let go of his fears for the boy's masculinity and his nagging sense that there was something "inappropriate" about their physical show of affection.

GRACE AND DINO

Mothers tell me they feel pressured to cut off their close relationships with their sons from many sources, both intimate and institutional: peers, teachers, coaches, in-laws, grandparents, and fathers. But years of psychological research confirm what we all know—that the more love small children receive from their mothers, the more confidence they gain in themselves as individuals. A mother's love can help a boy become more self-reliant and more adventurous.

Study after study has shown that small children who have a close relationship with their primary caregiver—so-called securely attached children—are psychologically healthier and stronger. The more nurturing children receive, the braver they can be. Secure attachments to mother, concluded Megan Gunnar at the University of Minnesota, work as a buffer against new, frightening situations. And Gunnar's colleague Alan Stroufe found that those who in their infancy were securely attached to their mothers may enjoy greater self-reliance, have lower rates of psychopathology, do better at school, and have higher self-esteem throughout their lives.

Yet in the face of society's relentless pressure to make them disconnect from their sons, even the most nurturing of mothers feel the need to limit their love.

Grace, a mother of two sons, spoke to me of the guilt and confusion she felt: "My first boy and I were as close as any two humans could be. It was a difficult pregnancy and a tough few months after birth. But we felt really bonded. Then, when Alexander turned four, I'd notice that sometimes he'd get an erection when he was in the bathroom with me. I got worried. Was I doing something wrong, something hurtful?"

"How did you handle that—the worry you had?" I asked Grace.

"I turned to my husband, Dino. But he wasn't much help. Both he and his parents seemed like they were out to get me."

"What do you mean exactly?"

"Well, Dino just told me: 'Of course—what do you expect? You baby him too much. He still has that baby doll you bought him years ago. If we don't do something right away, he'll turn into a sissy. You've got to give him more space. I'll sign him up for karate classes and when he asks you to hold him on your lap or in bed at night, try to discourage it—at least a little.' And his parents told me I should stop 'babying' Alexander."

"And how did that feel for you?"

"Well, I followed all the advice, and Alex did seem a little more independent. He said good-bye at preschool with less fuss, stopped asking to have me wash his hair in the tub, and forgot all about that doll set when his dad bought him a Batman costume. But somehow in his eyes and in my own heart I could perceive a subtle sadness, like a little flickering light had gone out. He's in college now, a fine, healthy young man; but our relationship is limited and we seem to talk less and less about the things that matter in life."

THE MOTHER'S CATCH-22

The net result of society's conventions is that a mother like Grace or Ellen who's trying to raise a healthy son finds herself in a difficult Catch-22 situation. She is held responsible for a boy's emotional growth and development, and yet she's also expected by society to push him away so he can learn how to survive in a culture that may shame him for showing the very feelings she's teaching him to express. She's supposed to hold back the amount of physical affection she shows him and limit the emotional intensity of her interactions with him, especially as he grows older—yet she's also expected to consistently nourish her son's self-esteem so that he'll know how to cope with the Boy Code.

It's a painful bind for mothers. Again and again, mothers like Ellen and Grace ask me: "How can I give my boy the love and attention he craves and still prepare him for the tough male culture?"

ARE MOTHERS CONFUSED, OR IS IT ALL OF US?

Many mothers I know would love to fight for the right to stay connected to their sons, but part of the reason they hold back is that they become overwhelmed by society's myths about boys—especially the myths we've spoken of, that "boys will be boys" and that "boys should be boys."

Some moms throw up their hands, mutter something about testosterone, and turn to their husbands and other "experts" about how to raise their sons. The advice they get is usually similar to what Grace and Ellen heard from others—things like "Don't be so close and mushy with him,"

"Stop babying him," and "Let him be more independent." Mothers may find it easier to engage in battle for the sake of their daughters. We know what little girls need, they say firmly. But boys, well, boys are a different story. And so mothers learn to distrust their best instincts, curb the natural flow of love and empathy they feel for their young boys, and participate in the push to prematurely separate from their sons.

Michael Gurian, a leader in the new men's movement, believes that mothers are simply confused by boys. "We don't educate moms very well in how to raise kids, especially how to raise boys. Moms weren't brought up in male cultures and don't have male bodies, so that's harder for them. We don't educate them about how active their little boys are, how testosterone affects them. The boys will act up in ways that don't make sense to them."

I disagree. The problem for boys is not that mothers are confused by them. Mothers, today and throughout history, are simply *part* of a culture. And it is our *entire culture* that is confused about masculinity and therefore about how to raise boys. Mothers have been confused by mixed messages about boys and masculinity in the same way that teachers, coaches, clergy, grandparents, children, and *men themselves* are confused. So if mothers are to be helped—mothers who are usually given primary responsibility for raising our sons in their earliest years and who must first struggle with these mixed messages about boys and masculinity—it is society as a whole that must clarify the best way to support our boys as they grow toward manhood.

A NEW KIND OF MOTHER, A NEW KIND OF BOY

If we really think carefully about it, many of the qualities today's mothers are trying to develop in their boys—far from being "feminine" qualities or qualities that women will tend to reject in the men they choose to love— are actually the very qualities most of today's women seem to be urging their male partners to develop. I firmly believe that as a society the time has come to encourage women to trust their instincts when it comes to mothering a boy. For as society begins to put a premium on "emotionally intelligent," verbally capable, empathic, loving men, there could probably be no better way to cultivate such "new men" than by starting to cultivate such "new boys." So if we're beginning to officially revise the Boy Code so that it's considered a plus for boys and men to have these special qualities, let us also revise this code so that it's considered a real plus for boys to remain close to the people who are often best positioned to teach them these qualities—their mothers.

But how can this be done? How, you may wonder, can we simply revise the Boy Code? What happens when I teach my son to be sensitive and empathic and he comes home with a broken nose?

While it certainly is not easy, many mothers are indeed finding ways to fight back, buck the code, and foster sons who are both close to them as mothers and successful within their contemporary peer culture.

SARAH AND EVAN

Sarah, the forty-something mother of two, had let the Boy Code talk her into constraining her feelings for Max, her first son. A lot of her friends (including her first husband) had chided her for being too "clingy" with Max, and so she had decided to back away from the boy, to be less "soft" with him. Max had grown distant from her, gotten involved in drugs, and ended up going to college thousands of miles away from home. Disappointed in herself for letting society's old-fashioned rules tell her how to raise her son, she decided that when she gave birth to another boy in her second marriage she would listen to her own intuitions about being a mother:

"This time I did things differently. Evan was a lot like Max was—rambunctious, independent, high-energy. But for all his rough play, he's always loved to run back to my lap, have me stroke his hair and tell him stories about my childhood. With Max, I wasn't allowed to indulge in this. My first husband would never have allowed it. But my second husband, Jim, encourages me, and now Evan is twelve, and he and I are superclose."

"It sounds like you're doing a great job this second time around," I told Sarah as she proudly smiled back at me.

"Well—it hasn't always been easy, but we're doing it. I'll never forget this one time when his third-grade teacher wrote me a note expressing concern that Evan seemed to enjoy playing the 'girls' games' at recess and wanted to try out for the starring role in the class play, even though it was the Wicked Witch in *The Wizard of Oz.* I thought to myself—Oh, God, here we go."

"That sounds pretty tough. What did you do about it?"

"Oh, I dealt with that teacher and the other parents, all right. Evan and I have always had too much of a meaningful relationship to sacrifice to their rigidity. All I had to do was think about how difficult things had become with Max, and I found the courage to go in there and tell them that Evan could play the Wizard, the Scarecrow, or Dorothy as far as I was concerned!"

"It sounds as though you handled the situation pretty well."

"Well, in private, I remember explaining to Evan that sometimes society is hard on boys—that girls these days are usually allowed to be more experimental and expressive. You know, if some girl wanted to play the Wizard, can you imagine anybody complaining? If anybody did, they'd probably be labeled a 'sexist.' So why couldn't Evan play a female role if that's the one he found most interesting? I told him he might get teased if he played the Witch, but that it was fine with me."

"So what did he decide?"

"Well, actually, he decided to be the Lion instead. After we discussed the way other people might have tried to make him feel, he thought it wouldn't be worth the trouble. I was pleased with myself, because instead of just snapping at him and telling him he'd have to play a different part, we talked really openly about the situation and he decided to handle it how he thought best."

"Not bad for a boy who was only in the third grade at the time," I told Sarah.

"You bet," she said. "In fact now that he's a teenager, he's just this really great kid. He seems like he's much more popular with his peers than Max was, he's close to a number of girls, and his teachers report he's one of the best behaved and most caring boys in the whole class."

Of course, Sarah and other mothers who are bucking gender stereotypes worry that such a wonderfully empathic boy will barely survive within the peer culture, where conformity and macho ideals may still squeeze out boys whose emotionally expressive and caring capacities are still intact. Yet though this is a very real challenge for mothers, Sarah shows us that it's not an impossible one. As Sarah and I discussed, by not shaming Evan for his dependency needs and meeting his desire for a close mother-son relationship, and by standing up for him when his teacher tried to hit him with the Boy Code, Sarah gave her son wonderful gifts that will last his lifetime: strong social skills, empathy for others, and the kind of positive, self-confident personality that attracts friends. And because he remained connected with his mother and was comfortable discussing things with her, Evan will probably have richer, more satisfying relationships with women than most men do. Since he has not been straitjacketed by the rigid code of masculinity, Evan will be more flexible in his behavior.

But it's no mystery that gentle, so-called feminine attributes still do not have widespread approval, especially among adolescent boys, many of whom are hiding their own tremendous insecurity about their masculinity behind a mask of coolness, and are all too willing to taunt and abuse anyone who drops the pose of cool. But I believe that even for adolescent boys, women like Sarah can continue to play a very important role, helping them adjust to peer culture and the Boy Code in a healthy way.

The crucial thing to remember is that simply because a boy like Evan *can* be gentle and low-key doesn't mean he always *has* to be. In short, Evan can learn to choose when and how to express his full emotional capacities. For instance, Evan deliberately chose not to play the role of the Witch to avoid the taunting he'd face if he followed through with his original choice. Likewise, Evan can learn to temporarily hide his vulnerable emotions when he's out with the football team and express himself more freely in safer contexts, such as when he's among his closest friends or with his mom.

In a similar way, women have learned to compete in previously all-male arenas by learning new codes of behavior that they apply in a limited context, such as on the job. When a woman is the head of a bank, she doesn't cry on the job, but she might very well cry if her close friend went bankrupt and couldn't pay her debts. In short, women have learned to broaden their emotional repertoire and apply responses that are appropriate for the situation in which they find themselves. Boys obviously can too.

In fact, Evan will probably feel freer than other adolescent boys who have been more constrained by gender straitjackets. He may feel freer than most boys to pursue whatever interests he may have—football, cooking, or even playing female parts in theatrical productions. If his passions lead him outside the few rigid areas that the Boy Code says are appropriate, he will probably have the self-assurance to buck the stereotypes with humor and grace.

When I talk about a boy choosing when to show his more sensitive side, I don't mean the process I described of boys adopting a mask, a forced persona, to hide shame and insecurity. There's a crucial difference between the two. Evan will not be forced to wear a mask out of fear or shame, because he has been allowed to develop a genuine, deep sense of self that enables him to freely and selectively choose when it's safe to show the side of his personality that is outside the Boy Code.

Some parents actually stand up for their boys and try to encourage other adults to see the downside of gender straitjacketing. For instance, when Sarah and I spoke further, she explained that when she met resistance from Evan's third-grade teacher she scheduled a talk with her and Evan's other teachers. She thought carefully about how to explain her position. She told the teachers that she valued Evan's creativity and his caring quality and that she had worked hard to ensure that they survived. She gave a few examples of things she loved about Evan and after a while the teachers joined in. They talked for a while about how cooperative, empathic and fun Evan was. Then Sarah asked the teachers to help her maintain the development of those qualities and to communicate with her about them. "At first I don't think I changed their minds a bit," says Sarah. "I'm not sure I could have done that. But I started a good discussion among us. And now Evan is doing wonderfully."

Like Sarah, other mothers can become a new breed of coach for the less open-minded and help make the world safer for sensitive boys. Her love and unconditional support of her son can be a powerful counterpart to the shaming messages society delivers.

BOYS WITH SINGLE MOTHERS

Among some of our best coaches in this area are women who raise sons without fathers, due to divorce, a father's death, or simply the choice of single motherhood. Because they are even more likely to be subjected to our culture's discomfort with close mother-son relationships than women in two-parent families, single mothers tend to focus very carefully on what they are doing to raise their boys and how this affects them as they grow into men.

Single mothers say they are almost universally counseled to find the boy a male role model, as if a mother cannot possibly raise her son alone, as if she will be unable to convey some vital secret about masculinity. Single mothers are particularly warned against being physically affectionate with their sons, as if any physical contact will automatically become sexual, simply because there's no father in the house. Many single mothers I've met and counseled find it extremely hard to sort through this issue, to trust in their own ability to raise a son and to feel comfortable showing him affection. As a result, they may be more likely than other mothers to pull back from intimacy with their sons, which is unfortunate because these boys have no other parent to turn to for a closer relationship.

But I believe most single mothers have excellent instincts about what to say and do—and about when to ask others for help—to ensure that their sons will grow into healthy young men. Single mothers, I believe, have a lot of good things to teach the rest of us about boys and masculinity.

OLIVIA AND GEORGE

Olivia found there was really only one time she needed to call on her ex-husband for help with George, now fourteen years old:

"I remember calling my husband when George was still toilet-training and saying, 'When you're up here, can you show George how to stand over the toilet and pee? He's getting to the age where he can do that, but he's never seen a man naked, so how is he supposed to know how?' "

It wasn't that there weren't other times Olivia wished her husband were around to handle specific parenting issues, but who among us, male or female, hasn't occasionally wanted to hand tough parenting challenges to someone else? For example, Olivia remembers her reluctance to talk with her son about sex.

"I'll never forget it. A year ago when George was only thirteen years old, I came home from work one day and found him and his girlfriend in his room by themselves. I knew I had to talk about sex with him again—and *soon*. At that point, I really, really wished his father were there to do it. I wish I could have just gone off and made dinner and said, 'Dear, you handle this. You know how to handle boys.' But I couldn't."

"What did you end up doing?" I asked.

"Well, the upside is that we had a good talk—all about sex and relationships. We got through it. If we could get through that, we'll get through anything!"

OTHER SINGLE MOTHERS TAKE CHARGE

Olivia is not alone in her gifts as a single mother. Another mother told me she found it difficult, as a woman, to intervene in the supreme bastion of masculinity—sports. But she handled it well. When a coach verbally abused her son, Chad, after he fell and injured himself, Deborah took action:

"I called the athletic director of the school, which is not something that a mother does," she explained. "Certainly you don't do it lightly. For a year afterwards I had parents come up and say that was a very courageous thing to do—and very risky."

"That *was* quite courageous," I agreed.

"Well," Deborah told me, "sports directors and coaches hate to see mothers meddling. They can get quite condescending and patronizing to mothers. And I think parents fear they will take it out on their sons. But it actually had positive results. The coach was remorseful about what he did to Chad, and the athletic director has been working on coaching styles. It still has a long way to go, but I'm glad I stuck up for my boy."

Deborah has also had to manage Chad's tendency to feel that he should be the man of the family:

"Occasionally Chad has tried to advise me on what to do with the family money or tell me how I should be running my business. I think he gets it in his head from somewhere that a family needs a male in charge. I tolerate it and he gets over it pretty quickly. He figures out I'm doing OK."

Clearly these single mothers are managing, and managing well. Single mothers face challenges to their authority from coaches, other parents, and especially their sons. While facing down these challenges and defying the gender stereotypes that say women can't raise sons, single mothers open doors for all of us.

Of course, any parent knows that a second set of hands, a second adult presence, is helpful for surviving and thriving, and it probably helps if the two adults have complementary capacities, to better split up the work and present a model for a broader range of behavior for children. But in many respects the gender of those individuals is less significant than we had often imagined.

The real issue for the son of a single mother—or the son of any mother, for that matter—is not the presence or absence of a man in the house but the mother's attitude toward men in general. A woman who exudes hostility toward men can confuse her developing son's sense of his own gender. A son can also be confused if his mother is passively dependent on men and gets involved with men who are controlling and aggressive. (But then, similar damage to a son's development is done by fathers who exhibit unhealthy aspects of masculinity, such as aggressive, controlling behavior toward their wives.) In short, a single mother with adequate self-esteem and a healthy attitude toward men can be a wonderful parent of a son.

We witnessed the phenomenon of well-adjusted families headed by mothers during World War II, when many sons had fathers who were absent for years. The boys did not become emasculated or effeminate in the predominantly female world in which they lived, but were perfectly able to develop healthy attitudes about their masculinity. I would suggest that they were helped because of their mothers' overwhelmingly positive attitude toward their soldier-fathers. The entire country, mothers included, were proud of their men, sure that their strong masculinity was enabling them to fight effectively for a just cause.

Mothers who have a positive attitude toward other men in their lives will naturally allow them into their mother-son relationship, thus broadening the boy's exposure to father substitutes. This is helpful not because single mothering interferes with the development of masculinity or because boys somehow require testosterone-charged models, but rather because bringing adult male friends into a boy's life simply means there will be more love to go around. By exposing her son to several empathic adult mentors, a single mother can shepherd her son along a healthy journey toward manhood.

THE INTERNAL CONFUSION—WORKING ON YOUR OWN ASSUMPTIONS ABOUT BOYS

Most mothers, whether single or not, know just the kind of boy they want to raise, and their struggle involves reconciling that ideal image with the one the old Boy Code still tells them is more appropriate. But sometimes it's not society that's affecting a mother's attitude, but rather her own internal confusion about what *she* considers a good, healthy, "masculine" boy. Sometimes a mother's own best ideals about equality between the sexes are tainted by her own unresolved confusion over masculinity. A mother might *say* she wants her boy to be sensitive, but her deeper, sometimes unconscious feelings might want her boy to be tough and athletic. In the same way, a woman might state that she wants a kind, sensitive man for a partner, but she might instead consistently choose to date men in the Rhett Butler–macho style. She may be so imbued with society's ambivalence about masculinity that she has trouble giving her son a consistent, helpful message. Mixed messages increase a son's confusion and sense of shame over his own masculinity, as he finds himself unable to live up to a mother's ambiguous messages about what a man should be.

To avoid this painful dilemma, I suggest moms try to look within themselves to examine their own ideas about masculinity. That journey is probably not complete until they have examined their own histories and thought about the men who probably taught them the most about masculinity: their fathers. If a woman grew up with a silent or absent father, as was common, for instance, in the 1950s, she may be uncomfortable with men who are expressive. She may find herself unconsciously, yet consistently, blocking her son from expressing his feelings.

Another common role that fathers in the previous generation adopted was the covertly seductive father, the one who adored his little girl and felt free to comment on her appearance, clothes, and figure. As Ellen Kaschak has argued, this covert seductiveness has damaged many women in our culture, leaving them with the idea that their self-esteem is wrapped up in their ability to be attractive to men. A mother with this sort of history may find herself unconsciously being flirtatious with her adolescent son, believing in some deep-seated way that this is the only way to relate to a man.

Far more common than the sexually seductive mother, however, is the mother who pulls back from a relationship with her boy out of fear of being inappropriate or simply out of a sense of strangeness. The most well-meaning mother may feel that she doesn't know how to achieve intimacy with a boy, especially when he reaches puberty and suddenly begins to look very much like a man. Fear of Freud's Oedipus complex haunts the most healthy of mother-son relationships. And yet, at this point, a boy may vitally need his mother as a mentor as he negotiates this all-important life passage.

Much of a mother's inner conflict and confusion could be eliminated, I believe, if we as a society were to clarify our expectations about what it means today to be a "man"—what we really hope for from our boys and men. My years of counseling boys and their parents make it clear that we don't really want our boys to move across the country, live apart from us, and never call, although part of a mythic view of manhood is that boys must go through some solitary hardening ritual, some heroic mission, to prove their courage and solidify their masculinity. In Greek legend Odysseus doesn't see his family—including his son Telemachus—for twenty years as his journey home from the Trojan War is extended by adversity and many adventures. In our more recent mythology, we have figures such as the Lone Ranger, who ride around the West performing heroic feats, unfettered by wives and children. And commercials tell us that any young boy can become a real man by joining the Marines, getting physically tough and proving himself on the battlefield.

But these mythic images of solitary men no longer serve us. We live in an *interdependent* world, so that even the best corporate executives, heroic men of strong vision and action, sink or swim on their ability to work with others. We also live in a world where traveling even long distances is relatively quick and easy—and communicating over these distances is even quicker and easier—so that we don't need to be training our boys (or any other group of our citizens) to withstand long, lonely, dangerous journeys. It's time we rethink the merits of our old-fashioned male archetypes—the distant "warrior," the "lone adventurer," the "fearless hero"—and reconsider what we really want from our boys and men.

I would suggest that most people's image of a healthy male is one who can succeed on the job, on the athletic field, *and* in relationships, and change diapers. What we really want is for our boys to become strong, authentic individuals, to become capable both of acting heroically and of maintaining strong affectionate relationships to spouses, children, parents, co-workers, neighbors, and friends. Mothers are a key to this, and to helping our boys mature into self-respecting men who don't need to cut off relational ties. If they refuse to give in to society's outdated myths about the need for separation and instead let it be known loudly and clearly that they want to nurture boys to become emotionally open human beings, mothers give the message to young and adolescent boys that there's no reason to sever their mother-son ties, no reason to harden themselves, and no reason to become the kind of emotionally disconnected adult male who will be disliked by many women.

CARL: A REAL BOY

A good example of a real boy is Carl, a bright, gregarious, and athletic high school senior who is extremely close to his extended family of Russian-Jewish heritage and an expert at negotiating within it. Carl spoke about how he chose to attend a prestigious college in a nearby state.

"My guidance counselor told me that with my grades and my football record I had a lot of places to choose from, which is just great, but it made my decision really hard," Carl explained. "When I told my parents about what he said, chaos broke out at the dinner table. Dad told me that I should try for an Ivy League school. I mean here's someone who stowed away on a boat at age twelve to get to this country and has busted his butt ever since. I could just see the stars in his eyes as he thought Yale."

"Then my mother jumped in," he continued. "She started praising N——, the local university, which is good but not as good as she wanted to think. I could almost see her thinking, 'My baby's moving away.' "

"My brother Danny started yelling at me to choose a school with a good football team. You know what was on his mind. He wanted me to be a star so he could tell all his friends. I mean it was pretty funny, all these people talking at once, each telling me what they wanted for me. I started teasing them about it. I said, 'C'mon, Dad. You just want to drive around with one of those Yale stickers on your car. And, Danny, you just want to watch me on TV. And aw, Ma, don't you think I'll survive without your cooking?' We all ended up laughing, and, of course, in the end I didn't choose any of the schools they wanted. *But,* I am at a school Dad's proud of and I'm close enough to come home on weekends. As for football, who needs it? It gets too rough at the college level."

As Carl impressed on us, the presence of supportive relationships does not hamper a boy's ability to become his own individual self. Carl is easily able to identify and act on his own interests, despite the fact that his family is close and all too ready to offer their own opinions.

THE LASTING POSITIVE BENEFITS OF A CLOSE
RELATIONSHIP WITH PARENTS

When I counsel couples, I am often struck by the fact that many of the skills required to succeed in adult relationships are those we resist teaching to growing boys—skills of connection (empathy, negotiation, and compromise), instead of competitiveness; the ability to be dependent and vulnerable and to share one's troubles, instead of the ability to keep a stiff upper lip and handle pain alone. And these are the very skills mothers are told by society *not* to encourage in boys, who may therefore grow into men who, in turn, insist that their boys also do without these skills.

I cannot stress enough that it's not mothers who are crippling our boys' masculinity—it's society's myths about manhood that are preventing boys from being seen and trained as whole human beings, men who can work effectively and live in close relationships with other people.

Research actually shows that men who are able to develop their emotional lives more fully are physically and psychologically healthier than men who are not. For example, in a study conducted at Wellesley College, Rosalind Barnett found that young adult men with close relationships to their parents had lower levels of psychological distress. In addition, such men reported that they did not feel that their parents were too intrusive. Clearly, these men had found ways to continue relating closely with their parents and to rely on this closeness in a healthy way to succeed in their adult lives.

Other Western cultures are now teaching us about interesting aspects of masculinity and the positive impact mothers may have on their sons. For instance, for adult sons in Italy, *mammismo*—meaning "being a mamma's boy"—is not a mark of shame. According to the Italian National Statistics Institute, in 1997 over 58 percent of Italian "boys" between the ages of eighteen and thirty-four may live with their mothers. And these mothers and sons vehemently support their right to stay connected. As one young man argued: "It's better to be loved at an older age than abandoned at an early age. . . . The kids who leave home at thirteen or fourteen in England are the ones missing something in terms of affection." An Italian mother agrees: "The problems come more from a lack of affection than an excess of it. You don't find people who are psychologically unbalanced because they got too much love or protection at home."

INTERDEPENDENCE: A DELICATE BALANCE BETWEEN PARENT AND SON

In healthy mother-son relationships, there simply does not seem to be anything as too much love. Yes, some mothers and sons can potentially fall into a relationship in which parent and child vacillate between extremes of dependence and independence in an unhealthy way. But I believe most mothers and their sons are capable of creating strong, healthy relationships based instead on *interdependence,* the recognition that each of us has ties to and relies on other people but that each of us is also responsible for our own actions and selves. Parents simply need to be careful not to put *their own* needs and desires ahead of their son's and not to attempt to manipulate his emotions—to guilt or shame him into doing what they want. Faced with a demanding and controlling parent, a son may feel he has no choice but to either knuckle under or move across country and forget to leave a forwarding address.

In short, mothering—and fathering—involves striking a delicate balance between supporting a child and allowing him to grow on his own. A mother operates most effectively on instinct, on when to intervene and when to let go. The best guide, in almost every case, is the child himself. A mother naturally learns to read the child's cues, remaining as a steady, secure base while the child negotiates the next step of independence. She doesn't intrude when the child is doing well on his own. She doesn't move away when the child reaches out for comfort. She doesn't flee if he momentarily pushes her away. A mother's best guide is her own knowledge of her child, gained through countless daily interactions.

But this process of learning a healthy interdependence, which seems so simple in theory, may be quickly inhibited when our boy, and his mother, fall under the inevitable sway of the Boy Code. As we saw in Chapter 2, little Johnny Martin clearly still very much needed to lean on his mother, yet he was not *allowed* to need his mother on the first day of kindergarten. He was humiliated by the depth of a normal dependency that others, including all the experts, were telling him a five-year-old shouldn't have. And so what happens is that the boy himself begins to pull away from his mother. It's not just that mother feels pressured by society to "let go" and does. A boy also feels this cultural pressure and he too may push mom—and many of the emotional skills she's trying to teach him—far, far away. And so what should be a son's process of learning a healthy interdependence becomes instead one of learning an abrupt, unhealthy, even traumatic independence. Because of the Boy Code, instead of teaching connection, we end up teaching disconnection.

DIFFERENT STYLES AND LANGUAGES OF LOVE: TALKING VERSUS DOING

Another result of the Boy Code is that boys, as we've seen, tend to develop their own style of showing their love and affection that is generally quite different from that of girls (and thus from that of their mothers). This is critical for a mom to remember because—though it may hardly look like what *she* would do to rekindle a relationship—a boy, even after a traumatic separation from her, may reach out to reconnect.

He may do this, rather than asking for it, by seeking out his mother's company in playful activities. As we've already discussed, a boy's natural language is usually action language. He tends to be best at showing his love, affection, and empathy through action. Thus for boys who create friendships by doing things together, empathy and love can emerge simply from a shared game of baseball, a joint building project, or a walk around the block.

Sometimes mothers may make the mistake of discounting such activities because they seem to involve little of the verbal intimacy—the talk—

that most women prize. But many boys gain a significant sense of support and comfort from these activities. And, ideally, a mom is attuned to this fact.

Which is why I believe mothers can learn to connect with their sons simply by hanging out and sharing an activity.

"HOW CAN I GET HIM TO TALK TO ME?": RECONNECTING THROUGH CAR THERAPY

Gwen learned about boys' relational styles quite accidentally. She had been saddened that David, her thirteen-year-old son, didn't talk to her as openly as he used to, but she was stymied in her attempts to change that. One day when her husband was working late, she took on his job of driving David to hockey practice. In the car on the way home, after talking about the scrimmage, David started talking about his friends on the team and eventually wandered into a discussion about marijuana.

Gwen was surprised when he opened up so much. "Something about the car," she mused. "The darkness outside, the coziness inside, the way he could just stop talking and look out the window if he wanted to—all of it created a setting where he felt more comfortable talking." From now on, she says, she makes sure she shares the driving duties with her husband. "It's car therapy—for both of us," she says, laughing.

Many mothers find that if they engage in action-oriented activities with their sons, their boys begin to open up and talk. Claudia, for instance, spoke to me of her ten year-old Scott, who often comes home from school in what she refers to as a "really bad mood." When he's in one of these moods, she explains, "he just seems to want to turn on the TV and tune out from reality." If she asks him what's wrong, "he either ignores me or tells me to get lost." But Claudia soon developed a strategy for getting Scott to share the feelings behind the mood. "I can usually get him to be much more expressive if I invite him to just do something with me. Like we'll play Ping-Pong in our family room, go outside and throw a Frisbee, whatever. Once we get going, his mood seems to change. Lots of times, after we've been playing for a while, he'll come over to me and start talking about stuff. He doesn't always tell me everything that's going on with him, but I often have the feeling he's getting the emotional release he really needs."

THE TIMED-SILENCE SYNDROME OF BOYS

Mothers are usually more willing to sit down and talk about their feelings, and so a boy's relationship pattern might seem frustrating. But in fact the pattern can in some ways be anticipated and planned for. And it is different from what is typical for girls.

The most challenging time for communication, the time when mothers and sons are most likely to disconnect (although in their hearts they may long to connect even more closely), is when a boy is hurting. I have found that when boys suffer a blow to their self-esteem or otherwise feel sad or disappointed, they often follow a pattern that I call the "timed-silence syndrome."

A boy's first reaction is to retreat and be alone to nurse his hurt. If a mother presses him with concerned questions at that point, it only intensifies his sense of shame and causes him to retreat further or more angrily. In many cases, it's only after he has had time to sit with his own pain that he becomes ready to come back and talk about it. At that point his approach might be so subtle that his mother could easily miss it. And my studies show that if a parent misses that moment, the opportunity to connect about that episode might take a while to come around again.

A caring mother could misunderstand this pattern. When her son walks into the house obviously upset about something, a sympathetic mom may immediately want to talk about it. When the boy says "Leave me alone," she may feel rebuffed or she may push for connection when it simply won't happen. Then, when the boy comes back to her and makes a cautious overture, indicating he might want to talk, she may miss his subtle cues, particularly if she's still bothered by the previous rebuff, angry that her son was rude, frustrated that she doesn't know how to help him. In fact, his initial gruff "Leave me alone" may simply be an indication of how badly he's hurting and may really be an indirect call to his mother to be there for him—but later.

MARIA AND CARLOS

Maria Cortiz, a Boston mother who participated in my study, told me the following story:

"Carlos came home one day and told me that he had lost a soccer game at school. In the past, whenever something like this happened, I tried to get him to talk about it. 'Leave me be,' he would tell me. 'I don't want to talk about this.' I used to try to pressure him, but then he would get really mad, go into his room, and slam the door."

"So how did you handle things this time around?" I asked.

"Well," Maria continued, "this time I tried something else. I just said, 'Sorry to hear that,' and then waited for a chance to just hang out with him. After he took his shower and got into some fresh clothes, I asked him if he wanted to go take a walk and get some ice cream. We started walking together and making jokes about some of the goofy people on the street. When things felt comfortable, I simply said, 'Hey, sorry the game didn't work out today.' "

"How did that go?" I asked.

"I could not believe it," Maria said, her eyes widening, her head nodding. "Carlos looked at me—you know, right in the face with those puppy-dog eyes of his—and said, 'Ma, I feel so bad about it. I feel like such a failure.' I gave him a big hug. I realized that the best way to get him to talk to me and tell what's up for him is to just go out walking or something. From now on, that's what I'm always going to do!"

As Maria found out, boys often respond best to their mothers' attempts at closeness when they can set the timing—when they're free to follow a period of silence with one of action. Maria learned that she can't push her son into talking when he doesn't want to. And this is particularly true for adolescent boys, who feel a tremendous need for personal space and privacy. Mothers need to listen closely to a boy's more subtle, action-oriented language and be available to talk on the boy's schedule, not on their own.

THE MOTHER TONGUE

Of course, a woman's more typical style of relating, through talk, is useful too. At times a mother will be able to bond with her son through sharing her feelings verbally, and her talent for this will serve a boy well. I think a mother should take every opportunity to teach her boy the "mother tongue" (as psychoanalyst Jim Herzog refers to it), gently pushing a boy to stretch his capacity to talk about feelings, a process that ideally starts when boys are very young. A mother might say, "I remember how awful I felt when I didn't make the softball team. I felt like the biggest klutz." Or a mother might take the opportunity to acknowledge uncomfortable feelings, such as sadness and shame, in everyday life, with a statement such as "I was so upset when my supervisor criticized me at the meeting today, in front of everyone." In this way a mother demonstrates that sadness, shame, and vulnerability are natural, inevitable feelings, a part of living, and that they feel just a little less awful when they can be put into words and shared with a friend. Finally, a mother can often use her specialized skills to help her son find words to express his deepest feelings. So, for example, when her son comes home and punches the wall to relieve his anger, she might help him explore other feelings, such as sadness and disappointment, by asking, "Are you OK? Are you feeling disappointed about something? Could something be getting you down?"

MOTHERS AND FATHERS—WORKING TOGETHER
TO TRANSCEND THE STEREOTYPES

Obviously, the best parenting of sons will be achieved when mothers and fathers transcend gender straitjackets in actions as well as words. Unfortunately, in real life, couples tend to split up roles, with each partner doing whatever he or she feels most comfortable with. This can lead to a pernicious pattern where mothers do more nurturing and daily care and fathers do more disciplining. The real problem with such a pattern is that it perpetuates the rigid gender stereotypes we hope to teach boys to overcome.

One way gender stereotypes get stuck is that some mothers unconsciously play the role of gatekeeper, preventing a father from getting involved in parenting.

NINA AND MARK

When they entered counseling, Nina and Mark epitomized the dilemma of gatekeeping—a phenomenon we'll discuss in greater detail in Chapter 6—with Nina complaining bitterly that Mark was not more involved with the children.

Mark exploded: "What am I supposed to do? Every time I try to help, she tells me I'm not doing it right."

"What do you mean exactly?" I asked Mark.

"For example," he explained, "The other day I was trying to diaper the baby. The Velcro stuck to his leg and he gave a little squawk. In a flash Nina was there, scooping the baby out of my hands, asking, 'What did you do to him?' as if I were torturing him, for God's sake."

"How did you respond to that?"

"I left Nina and the baby and tried to help Matthew, our nine-year-old with his math homework, and before I knew it, she was criticizing that too, telling me I was helping too much and giving him all the answers. Whenever I do something, I can just see her in the background, wincing, as if I'm ruining the kids for life."

"Do you feel you do have an important role with the boys?" I asked.

"The only thing she lets me do is be the bad guy. I come home and she tells me I have to talk to Matthew about his manners. Why can't she do it?"

"You're his father," Nina responded. "You know how to talk to boys better than I do."

In this case, we had to address Nina's strong desire to be the perfect mother to her children. She was a professional woman who had chosen to stay home with her two boys, and it was hard for her to admit that her husband, who saw his children only in the evenings and weekends, could be as good a parent as she was. And in truth, she was quite right when she said that Mark was not as skilled at physically taking care of a baby or at reading his older child's emotional needs.

Mark, in turn, finally realized that sometimes he colluded with Nina, playing dumb at child care, so she would take over and let him return to his newspaper. We emphasized that Mark had the right—and the need—to learn his own style of interacting with his children. Over several weeks, Nina learned to ask Mark for help with the children, and then to be less hypervigilant about how he accomplished it. They found it worked best when Nina physically left the room, so she wasn't wincing and shrugging in the background and, also, so that Mark had no possibility of getting help. He struggled through on his own and found he enjoyed the sense of accomplishment and intimacy that resulted.

Nina and Mark also had to address what they had learned from their own families about parents' roles. Nina's father had been a strict, distant man. She remembered her father would yell and punish her, and afterward she could always run to her mother for a hug and cuddle. She realized she was replicating that pattern, which allowed her to always be the good, loving parent, by forcing Mark into being the authority figure. But this ultimately undermined his ability to be intimate with his children. Mark, in turn, resented playing the role of authority figure because his own father had been so ineffectual. When Mark's father was home, which was rare, he had read a book to the children or kissed them good-night so absentmindedly that Mark wasn't sure he even knew which child he was dealing with.

Mark's mother had run the house with a firm hand. So Mark really felt, subconsciously, that Nina should take care of all discipline problems.

Nina and Mark were able to recognize these patterns and gradually work to improve them. Nina learned to set limits more effectively. Mark learned to take a greater role in all areas of parenting. Of course, they did not magically become equal partners. Nina will always have a somewhat fierce protectiveness of her sons, as compared with Mark's lackadaisical style. Changing one's typical style takes constant work. In their case, as in many others, the reward for the work is a greater sense of comradeship as parents and a greater sense of intimacy with their children. In addition, the boys are learning something about appropriate gender roles—i.e., that both mother and father can be responsible for nurturing *and* setting limits. Such modeling will help the boys keep an open mind toward gender roles.

Parents should discuss issues of masculinity and agree in principle on how to raise their sons, but they need not worry if they don't do things exactly the same way. As Nina and Mark show, parents can have very different styles. A son can get different things from each parent, ultimately learning more.

TIPS ON TODAY'S MOTHERING: HOW TO STAY CLOSE AND STILL PREPARE HIM FOR THE "REAL WORLD"

We've seen that moms face several hurdles in raising boys today. First, they must struggle with the constant pressure they feel to separate from their sons when in their hearts they yearn to stay close to them. Second, they're put into a Catch-22 situation because though they're expected to raise boys to be loving and sensitive, they're also expected to prepare their sons for the "real world" where they may get teased, taunted, or shamed if they show their loving or sensitive sides. And third, as their boys get older, moms have to deal with the ways in which their sons—in response to society's shaming messages about masculinity—begin to harden themselves and thus resist their mothers' overtures at closeness and connection.

I often suggest that a mother use the following strategies to deal with these challenges and to forge a closer more successful relationship with her sons:

Talk openly about the Boy Code. It's just about impossible to conquer any problem if it's never discussed. So talk openly about the Boy Code with your son. Tell him what you like and don't like about it. Discuss the new double standard of masculinity that calls on boys to be "nice guys" but then pushes them to act like "toughies." Tell your boy about the bind that places you in as a parent. Explain how much you'd like him to become an empathic, caring man, but also be sure to discuss what you know about the "real world," and share with him how hard a place you know it can be. If your son believes that you really do understand what it's like for him within male peer culture—that you understand the ways that he can get teased and mistreated for breaking the old Boy Code—he'll be more open to learning the empathy and other emotional skills you're probably eager to impart to him.

This may sometimes mean admitting defeat. In other words, sometimes you may suggest an approach to a problem a boy is experiencing with his peers and your solution may simply fail. For example, suppose one of your son's best friends begins to turn on your boy, to tease and taunt your son rather than continue to be friendly with him. Suppose too that, when your son shares this problem with you, you advise him to simply remind his friend how much the friendship means to him and to insist that his friend cut out the teasing. And, finally, suppose your son comes home and tells you that he tried out your advice but that the teasing only got worse.

Here lies the rub. Your boy will tend to feel betrayed—and alone with his pain—if you follow all this by simply insisting that your suggested solution will work. Instead, tell your son how sorry you are that your approach didn't work out. Suggest other ideas or, perhaps better yet, ask him how *he* thinks he should handle the situation and try your very best to support him. His approach might be quite different from the one you might tend to propose. Perhaps he'll try ignoring his friend for a while. Perhaps he'll tell his buddy that if he doesn't cut out the teasing, he'll be in for it! Your son's approach may not be quite the one you're most comfortable with, but it simply can't be forgotten that your son is doing the best he can to deal with the Boy Code with all its harsh imperatives about masculinity. So just as it is important to discuss and critique the Boy Code with your son, it's also critical to remember that your son is under enormous pressure to conform to it. So speak openly about the Boy Code and stand behind your son as he does all he can to rebel against it and to succeed within it.

Teach others about the problem of the Boy Code. As they confront the old Boy Code, mothers often tell me with a sigh of resignation that they feel there's nothing they can do to change it. I constantly hear things such as "You can't change boys!" or "If they hear it at school, it's all over!" or "Once adolescence hits, it's in their blood—that's it!" These kinds of helpless statements derive directly from the myths of boyhood we've already discussed.

But in my opinion there *is* a lot mothers can do to change things. First and most important, talk to your friends, neighbors, and families about the Boy Code. Tell them what you know about how it operates and what it does to limit our boys. Explain your approach to handling it.

Second, educate the educators about the Boy Code. As we'll discuss later in this book, teachers and school faculties need to learn about boys' peer culture too. Boys spend years of their lives in these institutions. If you sense that the schools your boys attend are not focused on boys' emotional needs and aren't attuned to how these needs can get ignored because of society's rules about masculinity, take the time to teach what you know to the men and women who spend their days educating your sons.

Finally, a big part of teaching others about society's harsh imperatives about boys and masculinity is to stand up and rebel against them! In other words, it's not enough simply to talk in a neutral way about them. In this chapter, we heard from several mothers who successfully bucked the stereotypes. Much in the way that mothers led the way to paving new opportunities for their daughters, it may be mothers who will show us the way to help boys feel freer as they grow into men.

Teach your son about masculinity by talking about the men you love and why you love them.   One of the best ways you can help give your son a clear healthy message about masculinity is to talk to him in a *positive* way about the men you and he care about—your husband, your father, an uncle, a close friend of the family, or any man both you and your boy can feel good about. As your boy struggles to fulfill society's confusing expectations about masculinity, you can provide clarity by discussing the qualities you admire in these men. "What a warm person your uncle Charlie is," you might tell your son. Or: "What I really love about your father is that he ignores what everybody says about how to dress and just does his own thing. Don't you love that funny hat he wears?" Or: "You know that Pete next door? I just think it's great the way he blasts that opera from the windows when he's mowing the lawn. What a neat, creative guy!" By hearing the way you appreciate these men, your boy can develop his own sense of the kind of man *he* would like to be and feel more confident about breaking the rigid stereotypes he's bombarded with all day long.

On the flip side, be careful not to add to your boy's confusion by saying what you don't like about the men around you—at least, not in a hostile tone. While it may be appropriate to share, in a limited way, aspects of these men that disappoint you, it can be very damaging to a boy's sense of male confidence if he's constantly forced to hear about what you dislike in men. So, for example, it might be OK, in limited doses, to say things like "I feel really hurt when your grandfather gets so quiet and distant" or "I don't understand these body-building magazines—don't guys get how great they look just the way they are!" But it simply is not acceptable—and again, can be seriously detrimental to a boy's development—if he hears you making negative remarks about the men closest to him: "Your father is such a jerk the way he acts like such a know-it-all!" or "Your older brother thinks he's Hercules—I wish he'd stop spending so much time lifting weights and just get over himself!" Or more subtle things such as "Does your friend John think he's cool with those silly unlaced shoes?" or "Those flowers your father bought me are not going to make up for the fact that he always comes home so late from work." All of these negative messages about men only obscure what you really want for your boy. So avoid them as best you can.

Rotate parenting responsibilities. If you're in a two-parent family, rotate the tasks of parenting with your partner. For instance, don't always make your husband the disciplinarian, and don't allow yourself to be the only one whose job it is to nurture your boys when they're feeling down. When each parent shares the tasks of parenting in a gender-neutral way, it gives a boy the message that being empathic and nurturing is not just a "woman's job" and that being strict and tough is not only for men. The way that we divide our responsibilities as parents really does give boys powerful messages about gender roles and masculinity. Just think—if we're telling our boys that they should be more gentle and sensitive, but then relegating all of the sensitivity training to mom, it's no wonder that our sons will begin to internalize a sense that this a purely female agenda. By contrast, if dad too is pitching in on the empathy training and if mom takes on some of the roles and responsibilities traditionally assumed by dad, naturally the boy will become more flexible and feel far more confident about his male identity.

When your son is hurting, don't hesitate to ask him whether he'd like to talk. Even though your son may not respond right away, there's nothing wrong with asking him how things are going and whether he'd like to talk to you. Simply engaging him in a frank conversation is often effective in helping him work through difficult feelings. Sometimes it works well to initiate this somewhat subtly—for instance, rather than saying, "Gee, you seem like you're in a terrible mood. Do you want to talk about how you're feeling?" you might instead say something like "Hey, we haven't hung out and talked about things for a while. Do you feel like spending some time together this afternoon?" Especially by focusing away from your son as the "one with problems" and gently suggesting some time together for intimate sharing, at the very least you're showing that you care, that you're interested in connecting with him. Depending on his particular personality and the feelings he's experiencing at the time, he may accept your offer or perhaps tell you he's uninterested or unavailable, or that he needs some time alone. The key here is to wait until he's ready to talk with you.

But avoid shaming your boy if he refuses to talk with you. If your boy indicates he's not interested in talking with you right away, try to avoid saying or doing anything that might shame him for his refusal. Saying things like "Oh, you're just like your father" or "If you knew what's best for you, you'd sit right down and talk to me NOW," are both examples of typical shaming statements. Slamming the door behind you or walking off in a huff are behaviors that give your boy the same kind of message. In reality, there's nothing wrong with his need for some time on his own. It may be his best way of coping with difficult feelings, or it may just be the way he thinks the Boy Code expects him to behave. As much as you may feel rejected—or eager to help him—try to avoid punishing him for his decision to spend time alone. Instead, simply let him know that you love him, that it's all right if he doesn't want to talk right away, and that you'll be there for him if he wants to talk later.

Honor your son's need for timed silence. If your son prefers not to talk right away, give him the chance to spend some time on his own. He may get into a quiet mood—sit down in front of the television, listen to music, or go off to be by himself. Do not interrupt him right away. As in almost every other case, he'll come out from his place of isolation and seek out some attention.

When your boy seeks reconnection, try your best to be there for him. It's important to make yourself available when your boy finally emerges from his self-imposed period of silence and isolation. He may not provide you with a long "window" of connection, so it's best that you pay close attention to him and try to notice when he's reaching out for you. It may be subtle—he may simply ask you, "What time are we having dinner?" or it may be explicit—"Mom, can we talk now?" In either case, your best response is to let him know—without embarrassing him—that you'd be happy to spend time with him.

Experiment with connection through action. When you first approach your boy, or when he approaches you following a "timed silence," you may find it helpful to try to connect with him through action-oriented activities. Thus, instead of encouraging him to talk with you right away, invite him to do something active with you. Whether it's taking care of a chore, playing a sport, or going for a walk, doing something together can often provide subsequent opportunities for talking together. Not only is this a good way to reconnect with many boys, it also gives them another message that you understand their style of relating, that you respect it, and that you're eager to experience it together.

Don't hold back. Finally, and most important, don't feel you need to hold back. It's fine to show your son your love and affection. It will only make him feel stronger and more capable of handling the outside world. While we've spoken of the problems that can arise if any parent is too dependent, controlling, or domineering, the psychological literature overemphasizes the frequency of this kind of parent. My years of working with boys and their parents suggest that moms need not worry. Their love is tremendously valuable, and it truly helps boys become confident, powerful, successful men.

THE POWER OF MOTHERS

In many ways, Western society has traditionally celebrated the powerful connections that develop between mother and son. For instance, Freud—whose later followers often distorted many of his brilliant insights—recognized the positive power of mothers, the potency of maternal connection. As he put it: "If a man has been his mother's undisputed darling he retains throughout life the triumphant feeling, the confidence in his success, which not seldom brings actual success with it." In past centuries, sons were indeed *expected* to remain closer to their mothers. According to historian Anthony Rotundo, "Mothers were encouraged to maintain intimate ties with sons for as long as they lived and were expected to shape their sons' moral character."

Today we have somehow lost touch with this wisdom, with the reality that mothers can and do have such a profound positive impact on the emotional lives of boys, an impact that lasts a lifetime. Mothers have an awesome power to allay the shame-based hardening process that too often claims the psychological souls of our boys, and they model—and influence their sons to give vent to—vulnerable emotions such as sadness, fear, and anxiety.

I strongly believe that both a boy's ongoing natural yearning for his mother's love and the mother's deep-seated desire to continue loving her son should be permitted to find appropriate expression. Mothers should feel free to follow what they have always known in their hearts to be the truth—that when he maintains an ongoing connection to his mom, a boy is taking an important, healthy step toward becoming a man.

As we've seen, a mother is often an expert at coaxing a boy to be more emotionally expressive, feel more confident about himself, and reveal his complete personality with more courage and honesty. But she's also especially talented at showing how boys can merge these new "sensitive" qualities with some of the traditional qualities celebrated as typically "masculine."

By giving her son the love and support he needs to satisfy society's two-sided rules about masculinity while still being the person he truly is, a mother is training him to become a man who can share his feelings in an authentic way, a man who can be forthright about what he likes and doesn't like, a man who's able to share his genuine self with friends, family, and colleagues alike. By connecting closely with her son, she's giving him the energy, confidence, and savvy he needs to meet all of society's expectations of him, old and new, while still honoring his true self, the *real boy* behind the mask.

REAL FATHERS/REAL MEN:

THE EMPATHIC RELATIONSHIPS OF

FATHERS AND SONS

"I've got a couple of pretty good friends who I can count on for some of the small things. But when something big comes up or I'm feeling really down, I go to the one guy who really understands and who can really help—and that's my dad."
—*Tyler Williams, age twelve*

THE SPECIAL ROLE OF FATHERS

Fathers are not male mothers.

Interactions between father and son are, as we know, crucially important in a boy's life, but they don't always look the same as those between mother and son. Fathers tend to develop their own loving style of teaching, guiding, and playing with their boys.

ENTHRALLMENT: FATHER-SON PLAY

Beginning very early in the lives of boys, fathers show a special ability to enliven and broaden their sons' play activities and to teach their sons how to feel and express certain emotions. Research shows that while mothers tend to soothe their children and shield them from too much stimulation, the average father is inclined to arouse the emotions and *stimulate* a boy, playing with him zestfully and "jazzing" him up.

In studies observing interactions between fathers and babies, Professor Ross Parke, at the University of California's Riverside Center for Family Studies, discovered that dads are just as responsive to infant cues as mothers are, although their style with their sons is remarkably different. Parke found that when fathers spend intimate recreational time with baby boys, the fathers show a unique capacity to draw out the infants' emotional expression along a wider scale of intensity and to help the infants to learn how to tolerate a wide range of people and social situations.

When their sons become toddlers, fathers boost the stimulation ante, revving up the emotional systems of their sons by playing games such as tag or wrestling. Martin Greenberg, a child psychiatrist, referred to a father's early emotional investment in his newborn as "engrossment." I call active father-son play *enthrallment,* since in my experience a boy becomes enthralled by the loving, playful attention of his father, and dad becomes enthralled by the responses of his son.

This gift that fathers have—this enhanced ability to evoke a son's diverse emotional responses—is invaluable to boys. With the help of their dads, boys can learn how to engage in a broad range of appropriately spirited behaviors. In fact, when fathers take the time to play zestfully with boys during their infancy and as youngsters, at adolescence these children often need less guidance from adults when handling difficult feelings and are more capable of handling emotionally intense situations in a graceful and socially acceptable way.

THE BENEFITS OF FATHER-SON ENTHRALLMENT: LEARNING HOW TO READ ANOTHER'S EMOTIONS

While perhaps some of this fatherly rough-and-tumble play—what Harvard psychiatrist Jim Herzog calls "kamikaze play"—drives mothers up the wall, research shows that such father play, or enthrallment, has many developmental benefits because it forces children—and this is especially significant for young boys—to learn to regulate and tolerate their feelings when interacting with a different special caregiver, to identify these feelings more clearly, and to adapt to a variety of complex social situations.

How does this learning occur? A father's playful and vigorous type of play forces a boy to learn to read his father's emotions. Is dad joking or is he seriously in the mood to roughhouse? a boy might ask himself, closely observing his father's facial expressions and body language to figure out his father's mood. Then, too, by playing with his father, a boy is prodded to learn how to communicate his own fluctuating emotional states to adults and to other children. Is this roughhousing going too far for me? he may ask himself. If so, the boy may begin to cry. Is this getting boring? he might ask instead. If so, the boy may withdraw to signal that he needs more stimulation.

And perhaps most important, through interactions with father, a boy learns to "listen" to his own inner emotional states, identifying which ones are overwhelming, out of control, tolerable, or intolerable.

EMOTIONAL MANAGEMENT

Dad play, then, leads to important *emotional mastery skills*. As a father coaxes a son to cope with interactions that test his limits and stretch him emotionally, the boy starts to feel empowered to effect change in his environment by analyzing what he is feeling and then communicating these feelings to his parents and others.

As nine-year-old Bradley, a boy in my recent study, explained: "My dad and I play rough and horse around; and sometimes we wrestle and then one of us has to just give up—has to stop. Sometimes it's me and sometimes I'll be laughing and sometimes I'll be crying. But it's good because then at school I'm not afraid of anybody or anything; and I know when I'm going too far!"

These early father-son lessons in emotion management can actually be of lifelong importance. They have been linked to later capacities in the boy to manage frustrations, explore novel circumstances, and persevere in academic problem-solving. Even more important, they have been tied, by Ross Parke and others, to the ability older boys have to master "social encounters" and to better handle interpersonal strife with communication skills and cooperation rather than with fighting. To put it simply: that roughhousing between father and son that may make mom cringe is actually the rudimentary beginning of a boy's management of his aggression and his ability to substitute emotional mastery and mutual cooperation for violent interaction. As Jay Belsky at Penn State University—a pioneer researcher on the impact fathers have on their children—has quipped: "If Adam had been a better father, things would have turned out differently for Cain and Abel."

FATHERS AND SONS: EMPATHIC RELATIONSHIPS

In addition to teaching critical emotional management skills, fathers— through the warm, playful, empathic relationships they forge with their sons—imbue boys with an important sense of safety and well-being that bolsters a boy's feelings of masculine self-confidence. As twelve year-old Jackson told me: "I have to go to these 'extra help' reading classes at school on Saturdays. I don't think I need those stupid classes. But when my dad drives me there and waits until I'm done, I really don't mind going as much." Or as seven-year-old Tommy explained: "I like it best when my dad comes to my Little League games because he cheers for me and then I feel like I've hit a home run, even if I strike out!"

Feeling empathy for a child, studies show, seems to come naturally to most dads. Though they may express it differently than mothers do, studies show that many fathers feel deep empathy for their sons and want to stay closely connected to them. This was not always believed to be the case. For instance, in early studies that measured how fathers and mothers reacted when a baby began to cry, mothers seemed more sensitive and caring than fathers did in how they responded to the crying infant. But in recent studies that look at *biological* (rather than behavioral) markers of empathic response—factors such as heart rate and rhythm, changes in blood pressure, skin responsivity, and so on—*researchers have found that when responding to the urgent cries of a young infant, there are no differences between how men and women react.* Though women may behave on the outside as though they are more thoughtful and concerned about their baby's feelings than men are (or at least may be perceived by researchers in this way), in reality both men and women have a full range of biologically based empathic reactions toward their sons.

Because of the way we as a society view boys and men, when they act in a way that is open, caring, or expressive, many fathers, especially in public settings, may feel inhibited about showing the empathy they *naturally* feel for their sons. So, on the surface, it may seem as though fathers just can't be as close to their sons as mothers often are. Yet in my twenty years of work with fathers and sons, what is most striking is the genuine and profound feeling that boys and fathers have for each other throughout their lives. I believe that boys and their fathers both feel immense natural empathy for one another and yearn to develop closer, more connected relationships.

As twelve-year-old Marco expressed it, "I like going to school every day. But what I love the most is going to my house, doing my homework with my mom, and then—then I wait for my father to come home. When my dad walks in the door, it's always a really special feeling."

Jack, a father in one of my studies, put it this way: "When my boss makes me stay late at work, I just hate it. I can't stand the feeling of missing out on one extra moment of seeing my son, on being able to go home to play with him and then see that special glimmer in his eye when I tuck him into bed."

Or as twelve-year-old Tyler Williams said when asked to describe whom he turns to when he's feeling unhappy, "I've got a couple of pretty good friends who I can count on for some of the small things. But when something big comes up or I'm feeling really down, I go to the one guy who really understands and who can really help—and that's my dad."

Just as boys yearn for the special kind of companionship and nurturing that many fathers provide, their fathers, in turn, long for the chance to coach and educate their sons, participate closely in their emotional lives, and, through intimate connection with their boys, perhaps achieve the loving responsiveness that they may have lacked in their earlier relationships with *their* own fathers. Within our current social and family contexts, however, for a variety of reasons these natural, mutual longings sometimes remain unfulfilled or only partially satisfied. Yet my research shows that many fathers and sons are discovering new ways to forge close, active, caring relationships.

"HERE I AM!": THE GENERATIVE FATHER

Fathers have a natural ability (as mothers do) to be what Erik Erikson, the well-known psychoanalyst, called "generative." The generative father is one who cares a lot about the next generation, who wants to help guide his children and give them what they need to be productive, creative, and happy. The generative father enjoys being needed by his children and thrives on giving them what they require. Although some fathers may focus their generative impulses more traditionally toward working hard and striving for financial and professional success for the family, many fathers also apply their generative efforts toward developing close, attached, deeply loving relationships with their daughters and sons.

When I think about the importance of fathers and the emotional connections they can share with their sons, I recall the biblical father-son pair of Abraham and his firstborn son, Isaac. Coming late in Abraham's life, through the intercession of Sarah's prayers to God, Isaac represents a much loved and special son, the inheritor of all the future promises to the Hebrews, and the beginning of a paternal line that leads from the Old Testament into the Christian world of the New.

Although the story is still read today as testimony to a man's faith in his God, as reflecting the monotheistic ethic of ending human sacrifice on behalf of God, it also could symbolize the bonds between fathers and their sons. While Abraham's love for Isaac was tested by God, in the end Abraham and Isaac—father and son—were reunited in a profound and meaningful way.*

A beautiful poetic phrase, used repeatedly in the ancient Hebrew text, when God calls upon Abraham to be his spiritual son, is the reply *"Heneini*—here I am." On another level, Abraham, more than just responding to God, is announcing to Isaac, his one and only son, *"Heneini*—here I am!"*; and perhaps today, in quite a similar way, most fathers are trying to let their sons know that they are there, ready to love, comfort, and protect them.

And recent statistics reflect that's what fathers *want.* In a large poll recently conducted by *Newsweek* magazine, 55 percent of men interviewed felt that parenting was more significant to them than it had been to their own fathers; and while over 60 percent felt they did it better than their dads, 20 percent said their fathers did it "much better." Seventy percent said they spend more time with their children than their fathers did with them; and 86 percent of the mothers who shared parenting responsibilities with these men rated them as doing a "good" or "very good" job at parenting.

As these findings indicate, not only do most fathers today want to be close to their sons, they *are* close to them. Fathers also seem to feel more confident about these emotional bonds and to have the support of their wives in making them. My research shows that now more than ever before, contemporary fathers are putting aside old ways of passive fathering, turning with confidence toward their sons, and crying out loudly and clearly: *"Heneini*—here I am!" This is the pronouncement of the generative father, the father who rejoices in the need he shares with his son for love and connection.

---

*The story of Abraham and Isaac is most clearly centered on God's command to Abraham to bring Isaac, his only son, to be sacrificed. God calls upon Abraham to have his son killed presumably to test Abraham's faith in his newfound God. In the original Hebrew rendition of the tale, the story is called the "binding" of Isaac, referring to Isaac's attachment to the sacrificial pyre prior to the angel's intervention and the substitution of an animal by God in order to save the father from such an intolerable loss.

THE LASTING DADDY EFFECT

A boy whose father stays close to him during infancy and early childhood benefits from this fundamental father-son connection for a lifetime. Studies show that a father's empathy and his involvement with his son at early stages pays off all through a boy's life—especially during the turbulent years of adolescence. We know from the work of Leslie Brody at Boston University, for example, that when fathers are actively involved in their sons' lives, the boys turn out to be less aggressive, less overly competitive, and better able to express feelings of vulnerability and sadness. Brody's research suggests that boys with active, caring fathers don't feel the need to act out or show aggression in order to win their fathers' love and attention. It also suggests that boys with such fathers observe how their dads handle various life situations and thus learn how to deal with such situations thoughtfully and appropriately. Hardesty and her research group at Morehead State University in Kentucky corroborated these findings with a sample of boys followed from ages seven through twenty-two. Fathers who were "close and nurturing" had adolescent boys who had more flexible attitudes about gender and life. First-grade boys whose fathers participated in their care showed greater capacity for empathy in a study conducted at Santa Clara University; and in a study of preschool children and their fathers in Alabama, fathers who were closely involved in the nurturing of their children were shown to have sons with increased self-esteem and low incidence of depression.

The profound and lasting impact of fathers upon their sons' emotional lives has also been demonstrated by several longitudinal studies—studies conducted with the same group of boys and men over decades. In work done by Robert Sears, young men who at the age of twenty-three were best able to compromise to resolve conflicts were the ones whose fathers were most sharing in their care at the age of five. As adults, this group of the "well-fathered" boys also showed the effects of their fathers' early parenting when their capacity for empathy was assessed at age thirty-one and the health of their social relationships and capacity for intimacy was evaluated in their forties.

Along similar lines, the Glueck Study, first undertaken over four decades ago with 240 fathers and their sons in the Boston area (and later followed by John Snarey at Harvard) demonstrated that fathers who were supportive of their sons' "social and emotional development" during their sons' first ten years of life had boys who excelled in high school and college; and when fathers kept up this nurturing through adolescence, their sons' career success was also influenced positively. Indeed, it was virtually impossible for fathers to be "too involved" with their sons—barring any overt misuse of the time together. *The more time the fathers stayed close to their boys, the better the boys did.*

A Different Way of Relating: Love Through Action

Because in the past relatively few men had fathers who participated actively in their day-to-day emotional development as children, it is hard for many of them to know exactly how to initiate a close relationship with their own sons. Many fathers I talk to feel passionately about getting involved with their sons but wonder about the best way to get started. They feel love and empathy for them but feel nervous or unsure about how to convey these feelings.

But fathers—and, as we've discussed, this is often true for mothers too—are often most effective when they simply join in their sons' activities. Whether the son is hammering a nail, cleaning a very dirty car, or printing and collating multiple sections of an overdue term paper, many boys enjoy the feeling of doing something requiring a good deal of energy—working hard or accomplishing a difficult task—with the help and support of their fathers. Fathers, I have found, often discover they can most effectively tap into boys' emotional worlds by joining their sons in this kind of work-related, goal-oriented activity or supporting them in their efforts. Because our society places tremendous emphasis on the conventional female approach of bonding verbally by sharing feelings through words, we often lose sight of what my research illuminates—that fathers frequently show that they care and nurture their sons through *action*. Young boys, for instance, love the intimate sharing and camaraderie in helping dad to change a younger sibling's diaper, going outside and throwing a football, shopping together for a saxophone, and so on. Older boys enjoy being together with their fathers, for instance, on a long bike ride, at a movie, or on a Sunday-morning mission to prepare a surprise soup-to-nuts brunch for the whole family. The specific activity does not matter so much as the connection that develops through sharing in an action together. While words and emotions may be exchanged openly, many times it's just being "at the same time at the same place" and doing some activity together that help father and son grow close to one another.

THE ACTION-ORIENTED LANGUAGE OF FATHERLY LOVE

Especially during the stormy period of boys' adolescence a dad's capacity to "hang in" with his son and remain active in a boy's daily activities makes all the difference. In an eleven-year study that followed boys beginning at ages seven to eleven through ages eighteen to twenty-two, the more shared activities a boy had with his father, the more education he completed; and the closer the emotional bond between father and son, the lower was the incidence of social delinquency. Indeed this study showed that fathers had more of an effect on their teenage sons in their academic and social functioning than mothers did, and boys reported receiving greater emotional support from fathers than mothers in well-functioning two-parent families.

By contrast, when D'Angelo and colleagues at Case Western Reserve studied over eighty adolescent boys, they found that boys with fathers who had the poorest self-control—boys with fathers who easily lost their tempers or who frequently acted out in impulsive ways—demonstrated significant difficulties in almost all areas of their lives. These boys had problems doing well at school (or showing up to school), were poor at resolving conflicts in an appropriate way, and found it difficult to get along with their peers. They also tended to have problems with drugs and alcohol, were relatively inept at handling intimate relationships, and tended to be sexually promiscuous.

Fathers provide a flexible surface for their sons to bounce off, a play space with elastic but firm limits, a secure sense of love expressed not just in words but through actions. When they refrain from disciplining their sons in heavy-handed ways and from emotionally overreacting to the inevitable provocations boys use to test their emerging masculinity, fathers can neutralize their sons' rebelliousness and teach boys (and often mothers too) an action-oriented language of fatherly love.

A bright and sassy thirteen-year-old has a prickly debate with his father, a fifteen-year-old argues about curfew, a seventeen-year-old tears through the house yelling and screaming about his girlfriend and cursing under his breath. Before all hell breaks loose for any of these boys his dad grabs him up and says, "Hey, let's go out back and shoot some baskets." To all of this potential aggression spinning out of control, the involved and nurturing dad will provide a loving "holding environment." He will good-naturedly maintain reasonable expectations and express his love through action.

BOYS AND NONVERBAL LOVE

In addition to doing things together with his son, with genuine cama-raderie, a father can also convey his love by doing things *for* his son, through nonverbal gestures. As Jerome, a forty-nine-year-old African American man and the father of two boys, reminisced about his own father: "We never really said much at all . . . because my father was never much of a talker. It was what he *did* that mattered. I remember that when I was younger, sometimes I'd get all balled up about something, really unable to do anything but go to my room and cry. Soon after my retreat, I'd hear a knock on the door and I'd know it was Dad."

"What would your dad say when he came in to see you?" I asked.

"He wouldn't say anything," Jerome offered. "Without saying a word, he'd just slide up beside me on the bed and begin to gently *rub my back*. It was a firm, soothing sense like he knew I was hurting. Neither one of us had to say much . . . I'm not sure we could have, really. But I knew my dad was there for me, that he cared. But Dad is dead now—he died of cancer when I was fifteen. When I think of him, though, I always remember those back rubs. He didn't have to say 'I love you.' . . . Somehow I just always knew it."

I was touched by Jerome's story and told him I could understand why the back rubs were so memorable for him. He then began to tell me about his experiences as a soldier during the Vietnam War. Jerome was in the thick of the fighting, and the patrols would go out on overnight missions, digging foxholes, and lying in them two or three soldiers at a time, waiting to ambush the enemy. The waiting time was excruciating, the tension unbearable, and the men had to stay relatively silent so as not to attract enemy fire. Since Jerome and his buddies couldn't talk—all they could do to support each other and relieve the pain was to give one another back rubs. This imbued Jerome with a sense of fraternal love and safety he hadn't felt for years. Today, when his own boys have had a hard day, or gotten into an adolescent tiff about power and control, he'll often wait until evening, knock softly on their door and ask if they'd like him to rub their backs. He says, "They've never said, 'No.' "

TAG-TEAM PARENTING: THE FATHER'S ROLE
IN SUPPORTING THE MOTHER

Fathers also strengthen their relationships with their sons indirectly by supporting the children's relationships with their mothers. Indeed an important component of effective fathering is the ability to weave comfortably in and out of his son's relationship with the mother. It is that important skill of knowing whether—if, for example, an argument is about to break out—one should quietly intercede, helping both mother and son, or whether one should give them space to work things out without their feeling crowded; it is also about recognizing the need—when father and son have just about had it with each other—to bow out gracefully and give mom a turn at finding a resolution (something a colleague once called "tag team" parenting after those wrestling matches which co-parenting a boy may often bring to mind).

Mothers and fathers need to leave their gender-based fortresses and develop mutually acceptable arrangements to parent their sons. It's just as essential that fathers spend some of their time *supporting* their wives and children by being physically and emotionally present as it is that their wives facilitate their husbands' learning how to take care of a newborn and how to parent a young child. Men need to accept that wives can mentor them in nurturing skills. At the same time, wives need to recognize that male ways of parenting can be a valuable complement to mothering.

As discussed in the the last chapter, mothers and women perform a central role in very young and teenage boys' adaptation to masculinity. But one of the most essential ingredients in mother-son bonding is the father's capacity to know when and how to intervene in his boy's relationship with the mother. Ideally, a father's involvement in rearing his adolescent son need not include imploring his son to "stand on his own two feet," spurring him on to become an independent boy-man. Instead fathers need to strike a balance between supporting the boy's growing sense of independence, his sense of the "I," as well as the boy's continuing need for connection with *both* parents—the "we" aspect that is also a natural and important part of his maturing masculine self. While the boy should be encouraged to explore the bounds of autonomy, he must also be made to feel welcome to return to dad as well as to mom for love, support, and affection—to maintain his relational ties.

BARRIERS TO FATHERHOOD

Beginning in early youth when the premature push away from mother creates both a crisis and an opportunity for father and son, many well-meaning dads—even though they're eager to get involved in their young sons' lives—discover they are ill equipped to supply the male mentoring that then becomes critical. The difficulty fathers have in embracing their young sons stems from a variety of factors, some internal (such as how confident a father feels about his abilities as a dad) and some external (such as how well mom deals with dad's attempts at fatherhood). Some of these factors are easy to overcome, some less easy.

WHEN DAD'S DAD WAS ABSENT—"FATHER HUNGER"

First, many fathers find it difficult to become closely involved in parenting their sons because during their own upbringing they themselves lacked a father who sought this kind of closeness. "It's a hard thing being a dad," Steven, one of the fathers in my study, told me, "because so often our own fathers weren't there in the way we wanted them to be, and there are so few role models."

Reporting on male sexuality, the sociological researcher Shere Hite found in her sample of more than seven thousand men that almost none of them could claim they were close to their fathers. Likewise, Jack Stern-back, a Massachusetts psychologist, recently found in an informal survey of seventy-one clients that almost one quarter had physically absent fathers, another 40 percent had fathers who were psychologically or emotionally absent, and 15 percent had fathers they found frightening or dangerous. Such statistics are even more staggering when we look at the African American population. Between 1970 and 1994 the percentage of black children living in single-parent families nearly doubled; and by 1994, *60 percent* of black children lived in one-parent homes.

Growing up without a father or with an ineffectual father inevitably leaves its mark. In recently conducted research, the majority of the men I studied consistently expressed that they wished "to be a better father" than their own fathers had been.

What we may be hearing from fathers is an unrequited yearning that generations of men have experienced—what psychiatrist Jim Herzog has dubbed "father hunger." But when men say that they wish to be better fathers to their own sons than their fathers had been to them, I believe they are not uttering mere rhetoric or trying to vicariously satisfy their own childhood hunger, but in fact expressing a genuine wish, a wish that is carried out, at times, against difficult odds.

Father absence has been correctly linked to a host of ills for boys: diminished self-esteem, depression, delinquency, violence, crime, gang membership, academic failure, and difficulties with emotional commitments. But what this absence also does is provide boys with a warped model of parenting—one that teaches them that it's acceptable not to have a father who "stays in the picture." Boys who are raised with this model, not surprisingly, may find it difficult, when they become fathers, to feel confident about being a parent.

For such men—for men whose fathers were not there for them—it's important to take a few steps. First, these dads should spend time with other dads. This can happen informally by doing things with friends or with other families in the neighborhood or by joining a fathers' group at a local school, church, synagogue, or social center. Just as many women go to discussion groups for support on work, parenting, and other issues, many fathers—especially new fathers or fathers whose own dads were either absent or "not there" for them—benefit enormously from sharing stories, ideas, and concerns with other fathers. In addition, dads should try their best to take cues from their wives. By observing how mom handles various situations with a boy and "translating" her approach into his own "dad version," a father can often find the confidence and know-how necessary to deal with situations when it's his turn to take the lead with his son. Not only does watching and modeling himself after mom's approach help make dad feel less anxious, it also provides her with a healthy dose of his loving affirmation and brings mom and dad closer in the process.

WHAT TO DO ABOUT THE GATEKEEPING MOTHER

Yet as close as mother and father may become through mutual parenting, sometimes they can fall into patterns that draw them apart, and actually make it tougher to feel good about themselves as parents. Some fathers may find it hard to stay closely involved in nurturing their sons if their wives engage in unconscious "gatekeeping." As we discussed in the last chapter, gatekeeping is what happens when mothers, despite their very best intentions, unwittingly maintain so close a bond with their sons that there is simply little room left for the father to play a meaningful role—the emotional "gate" has been kept closed. It usually manifests itself in subtle ways, such as when the mother hands the baby to the father at an inopportune moment and says, "Oh, dear, don't hold him like that," or "That isn't the way to rock him." Often the father, who is already feeling inadequate, unconsciously colludes by hastily giving his son back to his wife and backing off. The father's imagined or expected deficiencies lead him to feel shame and thus to shy away from subsequent connecting with his son.

With men and women increasingly sharing one another's traditional turf and often sharing financial responsibilities, it is understandable that some women may feel inclined, often unconsciously, to maintain some control over the historically female-managed realms of household and day-to-day parenting. This may entail significant strain and sacrifice, particularly for career-oriented women who are already juggling the burdens of work and home. But it can also have the completely unintended and unfortunate effect of making fathers—especially those whose own fathers had not been terribly nurturing—feel afraid, incompetent, or unwelcome.

The principal way around this mother-father dynamic is threefold. First, it's important for moms to try to separate those tasks that dads actually do need some coaching on from those that they know how to handle just fine. For instance, if a baby is being fed formula rather than being breast-fed, a father may need to be instructed before he mixes the formula for the first time. But if the father has already learned this task and does it well, he probably does not need to be instructed again the next time he offers to feed the baby. The second helpful step is for moms and dads to share everything they know or are learning about these various tasks. If the doors of communication are wide open and the "teaching" happens in a mutual, positive, consistent way, both father and mother can learn new approaches without feeling as though the other is being patronizing or overcritical. Thus instead of saying, "Honey, you're going to kill him if you burp him that way," the more competent parent might say in a more relaxed way, "Hey, honey, look at the neat way I figured out to burp him— it's really easy and seems to work just great." Finally, I think it's a good idea for each parent to give the other private time with the child so that each can feel more confident about his or her parenting styles and abilities. Thus, when it's time to feed the baby or to comfort him when he cries, sometimes it's best if just one parent takes charge and is allowed to handle the task alone without the presence of the other. When a dad is given this kind of one-on-one "learn by doing it yourself" time, the problem of gate-keeping often evaporates as both father and mother come to fully trust themselves and each other.

ANOTHER BARRIER TO FULL FATHERHOOD: FLEEING INTO NEST-FEATHERING

Just as some mothers engage in unintentional gatekeeping, many fathers engage in a parallel unconscious process—occurring around the time of the birth of the newborn and continuing into the child's early years—that I refer to as "nest-feathering." My research shows that new fathers often feel that the best way to be a parent is to be a competent "breadwinner"—to "feather the nest," to work assiduously to earn greater income or career status, to create a comfortable home for his wife and son.

But there can be a negative side to this approach. As one executive told me: "I think I actually run away to work sometimes. I know how to run a team and make a business plan, but diaper a baby or talk to my son about his feelings? His mother's so good at it, I feel like an oaf."

While this kind of nest-feathering may in fact be a natural instinct on the part of fathers, it seems to run directly against what most mothers wish would happen—and certainly against what a boy would want. Mothers report that what upsets them most during this period of a boy's early childhood is that fathers are emotionally absent. And, in my interviews with fathers, most of them lament the fact that they don't get enough time to relate closely to their sons. It seems that many husbands sacrifice for their wives and their wives sacrifice for them in ways that do not reflect their true yearnings, in ways that seem terribly out of sync.

The predicament of nest-feathering can be solved through two avenues. First, it's important for father and mother to talk openly and regularly about their disappointments in each other. It's too late when mother complains about dad's emotional absence while in the car on the way to dropping off the boy for his freshman year of college. If mom and dad check in with each other on a consistent basis about how their co-parenting is going, speak honestly about how they should divide and share the responsibilities of parenthood and about how well (or poorly) things are working out, it's far more difficult for father to engage exclusively in "nest-feathering," since any resentments he may feel about how hard he may be working—or any resentment she may feel about his absence—will likely be brought to the fore. Second, it's critical that both mother and father talk together to clarify their values about how hard they each want to work, what their career goals are, what their financial objectives may be, how important it is to each of them to spend quality time with their children, and so on. Many times it turns out that both parents, for instance, would happily forego the addition to the house or the new car if it meant they would each have more time to spend as a family. But if these value-clarifying discussions are not taking place, each parent may make separate, often self-defeating decisions, rather than coming to a new understanding based on their shared goals and aspirations. Dad may continue to work around the clock to pay for that new addition to the house. Mom may continue to watch the front door each night, wishing dad would come home earlier and just be with the family (rather than worry about making the extra money). Simply by talking openly about what really matters to them and coming up with approaches that fulfill what both of them want, mother and father can avoid the tragedy that can come from nest-feathering.

THE MYTH OF THE MACHO FATHER

In addition to succumbing to nest-feathering, some fathers resist getting closely involved in nurturing their sons because of the myths about boys that we've already discussed. Many fathers fear that if they don't follow the old Boy Code by acting "tough" around their sons—and by pushing their boys as early as possible to act strong and independent—their sons will become outcast sissies rather than "real boys" destined for success in the mainstream. Closely tied to this fear are fathers' own experiences of being a boy, a son. Research clearly shows that many men feel a "wound" when it comes to the memories of the fathering they received. These can be painful memories, and most men find that before they can work at becoming a "new kind of father" they first need to address these memories head-on.

While some of this emotional work might be best done with the help of a qualified therapist or in the context of a father support group, fathers can often overcome the straitjacket of gender simply by consciously deciding to rebel against it. Consider, for example, the following story of Bill Sandburg, who, by looking honestly at his own internal "demons" and thinking creatively about how to conquer them, helped both his son and himself to escape society's rigid ideas about boys and masculinity and, in the process, become closer as father and son.

Bill had grown up in a family with an alcoholic father. When his father drank, he usually became quiet and reclusive, wanting little to do with Bill. On a couple of occasions—rarely, as far as Bill can remember—his dad actually lashed out at him, mostly just by yelling loudly and uncontrollably, apparently once or twice taking a swing at him with a canoe paddle. In discussions with me as a friend, Bill shared how he still harbors a distinct memory of when, as a sixteen-year-old, he asked his parents whether he might be able to take a pottery course at the local community center, rather than playing soccer, as he usually did each fall. His father, perhaps worried about how other people might respond, not only forbade Bill from taking the course, but one evening, after drinking, bombarded Bill with questions about why he was interested in pottery and whether Bill thought he might be homosexual. Bill defended himself by trying to ignore his father's myth-based (and partially alcohol-induced) questions and by forgetting about pottery and sticking to soccer.

But now as the proud father of fourteen-year-old Alex, Bill confessed how hard he was finding it to deal with his son's newfound interest in painting and sculpting. Bill admitted that the memory he had about his father kept resurfacing and that he was now becoming worried, ironically, that perhaps Alex was headed for many shame-filled years as a possibly less than fully masculine adolescent. Bill also admitted that he felt bitterly envious of Alex, since his son seemed so happy and carefree doing just the kind of hands-on creative work that had once been forbidden to Bill. Because of his anger, Bill had been trying, painful though it was, to keep his distance from his son:

"As much as I really want to be close to Alex, right now I just feel this incredible wall between us. I know he should be allowed to do whatever he wants, but I just want to scream at him whenever he brings home one of his sculptures or paintings. It seems like things are so easy for him and sometimes I hear my father's words in my head and think—*maybe if I don't do something, Alex is going to turn out to be effeminate.* I feel like such a hypocrite. I know I should love my son for whoever he is."

The poignancy of the story comes in the solution that Bill found for himself and for Alex. With a little bit of friendly encouragement from me and a lot of love and support from his wife, Bill decided to buy a potter's wheel and kiln and to enroll in an adult-education course for beginning potters. He also decided to involve Alex in his learning process, so that Alex could feel free, in the afternoons after school, to spend as much time as he wanted making pottery using the wheel and the kiln. Before long, father and son were spending many an evening in the family "pottery basement" turning out a variety of team-produced ceramics. Now Bill has not only soothed much of the hurt about how his father treated him as a child, but also developed a well-deserved sense of pride about how he was able to overcome his own irrational feelings about Alex. Above all, he and his son have found a hobby at which they both excel and one that they greatly enjoy doing together.

THE MARKETPLACE'S MISTAKE

Of course, it's not only a father's internalized feelings that may hold him back from connecting emotionally with his son. Society's traditional expectations of men and the way many workplaces are still run can also often make it difficult for men to even find enough time and energy to be with their sons. Despite a father's best intentions, society sometimes makes it very difficult for a father to stay closely involved in raising his children. Workplace family programs continue to be primarily aimed at women, and when opportunities for choosing family over work are offered to men, they often demur for fear—based on real experience—that opting to use such "family-friendly" benefits will blacklist them for a promotion or raise.

When my daughter, Sarah, was born, only ten years ago, I was working for one of the seemingly more flexible institutions—a teaching hospital associated with Harvard Medical School—where at that time there was no "paternity leave"—in fact, no policy at all for new fathers. I remember my relief when through the underground grapevine of male clinicians, I learned I could take sick time to be involved in my child's birth and early development.

Indeed in one recent study, it was found that men with MBAs who work just two fewer hours per week to help share in child-rearing duties get raises that are 20 percent lower than men who sacrifice their sons for work. Such society-determined systems discourage most men from taking the nurturing plunge, and must be changed if we are to raise the type of healthy, loving boys we want for the next generation.

Other external situational factors can also separate father and son. For instance, when the family model is less traditional—for example, when mom and dad have divorced and dad lives elsewhere—satisfying the yearnings between son and father can, of course, become even more complex. It has been estimated that for the children of baby boomers, 59 percent of their sons will live without their fathers for at least part of their childhoods. In 1990 more than 36 percent of all children were living apart from their fathers, and among those fathers who did not have custody of their children a majority began to lose touch with their sons within three years after moving out of the home, sometimes abandoning them completely. In a study by the Census Bureau it was reported that in 1994 over sixteen million children were living with only the mother, and 40 percent of those kids hadn't seen their fathers in at least a year. Even within traditional, intact two-parent families both fathers and sons complain about a lack of enough quality time together.

But lest we become overwhelmed by some of the negative implications of these statistics, there's also much good news to report. For instance, if past research showed that most fathers spent significantly less time with their young sons than mothers did, the trend is now moving toward expanded commitment, with a greater than 20 percent increase in fathers' overall family involvement over the past ten years. Today fathers spend approximately 30 percent of their time (as opposed to mothers' 70 percent) on family-related activities. And if when analyzing these statistics, one factors out the amount of time that mothers spend on family chores not directly related to child care, such as washing baby clothes or shopping for food, it turns out that fathers' actual proportional involvement with their children is now even larger.

Perhaps of greater importance, it appears that more and more fathers—even if they still have limited time away from work—are making significant strides in relating closely and connecting emotionally with their sons in the time they do have available. My research shows that for many fathers still struggling with the balance between work and parenting, what ends up mattering the most is not necessarily the *quantity* of time they get to spend with their children but the *quality* of such time. For example, many fathers who were highly involved with and satisfied by their work— what I call "job-satisfied fathers"—were able to affect their sons' self-esteem and emotional stability directly and positively. One young attorney in my study, extremely busy and pressured to make partner, always set aside time for dinner with his young son on Wednesday evenings and breakfast on Sunday mornings. It was a special "daddy-son" time as sacrosanct as any religious ritual and never violated by anything other than an extreme emergency or illness. Although there was no doubt for either of them that more hours spent like this would be even better, both father and son came to feel a special bond through this biweekly men's dining club for two. Because such job-satisfied fathers spend quality time with their children despite their outside time commitments, these dads are able to make an enormous difference in the overall well-being of their sons.

PRIMARY FATHERS: WHEN DAD IS NO. 1

Another interesting contemporary trend is the growing ranks of fathers who are not only active family team members but the primary parents. Kyle Pruett, a child psychiatrist at Yale, studied a number of these primary nurturing dads and their families—where fathers stayed home and moms went to work—for over ten years. His findings were striking: in observing these very active primary fathers, he discovered the formative emotional impact that one man, a father, can have on another male, his son. First, he found that even more than traditional dads, these primary caregiver dads used play as a way to teach valuable moral lessons, ideas about respect, and rules about handling emotion and dealing with loss. He discovered that boys who have such a high dose of "loving" from their dads seem to identify early with this nurturing role and thus themselves show more caring behavior toward friends and siblings.

These boys, Pruett found, also experience a different type of primary discipline. As one boy in his study remarked, "When I'm being a pain to my little brother or not listening to her, Mom says, 'How do you think that makes me feel'?" The boy's mother, in other words, personalized how the boy's behavior could affect her. She asked a question that focused on how unhappy *she* might feel if the boy continued to tease his brother or to fail to listen to her. By posing this question, she was thoughtfully nudging her son to think about how he would affect her world if he continued to misbehave. The boy's father, by contrast, focused on what the here-and-now consequences of the boy's behavior would be for *others*. The boy explained: "Dad tells me to stop because it looks like I don't love my brother or care about my mother's feelings. . . . Sometimes Dad just says 'No,' while Mom gets all emotional." Unlike his wife, who related the boy's behavior to her own emotions and used a question to push the boy to examine his motivations, the primary-care father in Pruett's study employed what seemed to be a practiced, matter-of-fact way of reproaching the boy. With a few quick words from father, the boy appeared to understand that he would need to adjust to his "real" world.

These boys with an extra dose of dad also seem to be more relaxed about gender roles, feeling less afraid to bend traditional rules about masculinity while maintaining a confident sense of self. Apparently because their fathers had such a strong and consistent presence in their lives, they were more sure of themselves as boys and thus felt freed from wearing gender straitjackets. When this set of boys in Pruett's study was in preschool, for instance, they seemed to be equally comfortable staying in the doll corner with the girls or playing in the block room with the boys. Also, as they grew up they were able to keep girls as close friends, not needing to exclude them from "all-guy play." One middle-school boy remarked: "I love to see the ways boys and girls talk about stuff in different ways. . . . It's just neat."

This impressive maturity and flexibility about gender didn't seem to cloud these boys' clear sense of identity. "As a group," Pruett explains, "they tend to be more in touch with who they are . . . [and have a sense of] self-assurance of being accepted for who they really are." So, quite to the contrary of our myths about boys and men—especially the myth that so much male "rubbing together" would somehow create fires of toxic aggression—boys with fathers as the primary parents may actually be much more calm, flexible, and empathic than boys without this extra dose of dad.

ACTIVE FATHERS, LUCKY SONS—THE WIN-WIN BENEFITS OF FATHERING

If one piece of good news is that active, loving fathers have a lifelong positive impact on their sons' development, and that fathers as primary parents seem to raise eminently well-adjusted, self-confident boys, another is that these loving men themselves seem to derive ample benefits from their endeavors as fathers. Just as nurturing, generative fathering offers a powerful alternative to the limited love and support boys tend to experience in their outside emotional lives, research now shows that being such a father also has substantial positive repercussions for the men themselves. In our study, fathers who could give their sons even a small portion of the kind of caring, time, and love they had longed for from their own dads—but often did not receive—got a great personal emotional boost of self-esteem. They were giving something to the next generation of boys—a legacy—and repairing something from their own boyhood simultaneously. It was a second chance for male-based caring and love.

One father described it this way: "Being a . . . [father] has helped me get away from a self-centeredness. My sense of identity feels complete now."

Another father who had received very little love from his own dad explained: "Getting up to change my son's diaper in the middle of the night . . . it makes me feel like a hero."

And as a third father—whose own workaholic dad was "never home while I was awake as a child"—said after he had made the decision to work three-quarters time: "I feel like something empty inside has now been filled with my son. At least my child will know his father!"

My research shows that in taking their sons' emotional development seriously, active fathers not only satisfy their longing to do better for their sons than their own fathers did for them, but also bond with their wives in a new and different way—sharing a task for too long considered feminine, valuing it together, and putting their own masculine value-added spin on it as well. Their wives tend to see them as more relaxed and loving, and their sons have the positive experience of observing dad—an adult male— enjoying what society often tags as "girls' or women's work." And in families where dad is both present and participative, there are generally more hugs and play.

But I believe that no matter how influential the scientific research, no matter how meaningful its impact on the psychological development of one's son, the fact of becoming a sensitive, playful, outgoing father—a different kind of dad—is ultimately mediated by a father's "generativity"— the pure psychological pull that fathers feel toward their sons. This is a way that nature has of joining the need many men have to experience the "selfish joy" of being a nurturing father with their immense natural capacity to love and support their sons and thus to provide abundantly for the next generation of men.

The confluence of these fatherly drives—of feeling the intense *need* to love and generously offering that love—can work out quite well. Not only does nurturant fathering help boys develop intellectually and improve their later academic and professional performance, and not only does it provide a second chance for adult men to break through their own gender straitjackets, but such loving fathering—such "masculine success"—also appears to redound to the father's benefit in other important ways. My research shows that loving fathers—especially those with the capacity to *balance* their sons' need for autonomy (by letting their boys roughhouse, show aggression, handle tasks on their own) with their need for affiliation (by staying involved in their boys' play, intervening when their boys become too rambunctious or break family rules, and encouraging relational ties to family life)—were also the dads who were more successful at work. In other words, success at home with the boys also predicted professional success.

This of course makes sense, since the "new" workplace—just like the "new" two-parent family—is known to demand less hierarchical, more flexible, interpersonal styles for achievement. One succeeds these days with empathic skills that support colleagues and staff and leadership capacities that subordinate self-interest to the goals of the team—all the skills honed by nurturant dads. I've even quipped that generative dads may be the best executives we can find in the next century and that perhaps fathers should request letters of recommendation from their sons! Professor Snarey's interpretation of the long-term Glueck study found similar results: "Having been active fathers in raising their sons, these men," according to Snarey, "are better managers, shop stewards, mentors—concerned with the . . . [next] . . . generation. This contributes to the life of society and to the survival value of their own particular family." In addition, these generative fathers of the Glueck study had greater marital stability and experienced greater happiness in middle age. Having successfully negotiated the Sturm und Drang of their sons' adolescence—remaining connected to the teenage boys despite their adolescent struggles and a tendency to push dad away—these fathers enjoyed better promotions at the workplace, as well as the satisfaction of ongoing involvement as coaches and civic leaders. Indeed, in a large-scale research study on dual-earner couples by Barnett and Marshall at Wellesley College, fathers' positive relationships with their children was also the best predictor of the men's physical health.

There appears to be an important payback system here, a two-way street. When fathers invest early in nurturing their sons and keep at it throughout adolescence and adulthood, not only will their boys be better off emotionally and intellectually, but they, as fathers, will feel enhanced self-esteem, enjoy a critical second chance for father-son bonding, and receive the bonus of increased marital satisfaction and of greater personal and professional success.

FATHERING PIONEERS

Men from all walks of life, all social classes, backgrounds, races, and religions are struggling to be generative, connected fathers, to be a new "different" kind of parent. For instance, at the age of forty-nine, Jeffrey Seiler resigned as president of American Express to spend time with his children. Father of four, he let go of one of the most prestigious jobs in the United States to become more of a dad. When he was interviewed six months later, Mr. Seiler was still working hard as a consultant, but could be home "sixty percent more time," having more dinners with his kids, meeting their teachers and feeling "much more engaged in their lives."

And it's never too late. Glenn McCloud, manager of a Canadian bank, felt he had been away from his sons too much when they were young. So one day he decided that he'd take a full "workday" off per week to be with his boys, now teenagers. He even became active as their Boy Scout leader. In the years that followed, McCloud saw his relationships with his sons grow in strength, and felt better about himself as a father and a man.

Robert Reich, former U.S. labor secretary, discussed his priorities this way when he left his powerful post to be more active as a father: "There will be ample opportunities for me to sink myself 200 percent into another job. But there will never be another opportunity to be a father to a twelve-year-old and a fifteen-year-old."

Peter Lynch, a successful mutual funds manager at Fidelity, explained that even though he shocked the business community with his resignation from his job, he received "hundreds and hundreds" of letters from other men supporting his actions. Ultimately, too, his decision was deeply personal. On his forty-sixth birthday, "I remembered that my father died when he was forty-six." He recalled the old adage made famous recently by the late Senator Paul Tsongas: "That no man on his deathbed ever said: 'I wish I had spent more time at the office!' " This change in life also shook loose Peter Lynch's own father hunger as a motivator to new fathering. His father died when Lynch was only ten: "I have . . . [only] a vague picture of him. He was always a very busy man, a math professor . . . then a senior auditor . . . I didn't get to do anything with my father. We never went camping or climbed a mountain together. I remember meeting him at the train sometimes and walking with him. . . . Maybe that's why I take so many photos, because I don't even have any pictures of him with the family."

Charles McDuffie, a divorced African American man who became estranged from his wife and lost contact with his own son, takes part annually in a father-and-son Father's Day March in Roxbury, Massachusetts. He explains: "I decided to march . . . because I want to assume my duties as a father but cannot be with my son. I think I should help other people's kids as much as I can because somebody may be helping mine." An eighteen-year-old, Wesley Braithwaite, marches beside him to show that young African American males want to feel connected to their fathers and the community: "I'm marching on behalf of my neighborhood . . . the crime . . . I want people to see that we all don't have guns in our hands."

Curtis Jones has a sandwich in his hand. Taking part in a special annual Father's Lunch at his sons' elementary school, he explains, "More fathers should participate in their children's education. It's about time . . . [our sons] . . . see their fathers as heroes, just as they see sports figures."

Co-owner of a small pest-control firm, he adjusts his hours to spend time coaching and reading to the kids at school. The school's principal, a woman, talks about the importance of a male presence: "We want these men to know the important role they have in their children's lives and how crucial it is to have male role models in a child's [early] education."

HOW TO BE A WELL-CONNECTED FATHER:
WHAT CAN A DAD DO?

For many fathers it all still feels so confusing, this new type of generative, nurturant fathering. Often in my research or workshops on fathers and sons, dads approach me to ask a myriad of questions: how to reconnect with sons, how to show their love, what to do about discipline, how to teach, how to nurture. Although it's impossible to touch on all these issues in this book, to give the personal answers many dads need, I will try to highlight some important advice—gleaned from listening to both boys and their fathers, as well as to moms, siblings, teachers, and other experts.

STAY ATTACHED—NO MATTER WHAT

My research and clinical experience highlights one central point: be nurturing and stay attached. And I'll say it again: boys are never hurt by too much love! The styles of love and affection you use will vary as your child progresses from toddler to teen—and may well be different from those of the significant women in your son's life—but your continued investment and love is essential. Don't be frightened off by lack of experience or even by estrangement from your son's mother. The natural yearnings you have, plus the learning you can receive from other caring parents or a fathering course in the community will see you through.

It's amazing what even the smallest gesture of love and connection can do for a boy. Even if you're very busy with career or other obligations, try to take time at least once each day to spend a few moments with your son to let him know you love him and that you care about him. If you can't do it in person, do it by phone. As trite as it may sound, a little love will go a long way. Even spending a relatively short amount of time connecting with your son each day is far better than giving up and spending no time with him at all.

DEADBEAT DADS—OR DEADPAN DADS?—RECONNECTING AFTER SEPARATION

Single dads are particularly at risk for losing touch with their sons, but struggle with all your heart and might not to let this happen to you. With the only exception being when an abusive relationship exists, fathers are still so necessary to their sons! Many men with difficult or estranged relationships with their ex-wives confide in me the pain they feel in disconnecting from their sons, but for some reason become persuaded that "it's in everyone's best interest." Rarely is that true. You and your son are longing for that same contact of the heart—it's important not to deny it to either of you.

Mark Bryan, at Harvard Graduate School of Education, speaks eloquently about "the prodigal father"—the 50 percent of divorced fathers who see their children but once a year and the 30 percent who never or rarely do. According to Bryan, the sons of these fathers, even their almost adult boys, are longing to re-embrace their dads. He quotes one of his interview subjects: "If only the old bastard would say he's sorry and tell me he loves me. I could forgive him for everything."

In reality, I believe, most so-called deadbeat dads are actually deadpan dads—dads who are depressed and confused about their isolation from their boys. Many actually long to find a healthy, genuine way to return. When they find a way to reconnect with their sons, they come to feel better about themselves, their sons' mental and emotional states improve, and ultimately they genuinely change the world for "real boys" and for all of us who love them.

So, if you are temporarily separated from your son, try as best you can to negotiate a new relationship with him and to work as hard as possible to maintain it. While it certainly isn't easy, if you commit yourself to the importance of your relationship with your son and think creatively about how to keep it alive, you are likely, at least over time, to be successful.

Take, for instance, Patrick Lynn, father of three boys, whose wife, Deborah, recently left him for another man, named Art. After separating from and then divorcing Deborah, Patrick fell into a depression. He still loved his former wife, but knew it was best that they end their relationship, and though he had very much hoped to obtain exclusive custody of the boys—especially since he hadn't initiated the separation with Deborah—he was granted only joint custody.

Initially, the three boys were shuttled between Patrick's home and Art's house, where Deborah now lived. Since Art lived in the same town, the boys could spend some nights with Deborah and Art and some nights with Patrick. But six months later when Deborah and Art moved to a town several miles away, the boys went to live with them because the schools there were arguably much better than those where Patrick lived. Patrick, it was agreed, could visit with the boys on alternate weekends.

The arrangement worked out all right for a while; but as time went on, Patrick's resentments began to fester. He felt the emotional distance growing between him and his sons, and became convinced Deborah and Art were doing little to improve the boys' opinions of their father. When he saw his boys on weekends, Patrick felt as though they didn't love him anymore. They seemed quiet, distracted, numb. After a few months of visiting his boys, Patrick's unhappiness deepened. Not only did he stop seeing them, but he also failed to send child-support payments on a timely basis.

When he came to me for help, Patrick expressed his utter dismay: "I can't stand seeing my boys anymore. They act as though they don't love me. It's just too painful and doesn't seem worth it."

Having become seriously depressed, Patrick needed several months of therapy before he was able to come to peace with the boys' move. Yet as Patrick began to accept this change, with it came a new resolve, a new strong desire to deepen his relationship with each of his boys. Patrick realized that it wasn't enough to see his boys only on the weekends—that it simply led them, and him, to feel distance and disconnection. Though he had been resisting leaving the house where he, Deborah, and the kids had all started out together, Patrick made the brave decision to move into an apartment in the same town where Deborah and Art now lived. Patrick began to spend every other night with the boys, and to have the boys to his new apartment on weekends.

As his depression lifted, Patrick was pleased with his new life. "As difficult as it is to deal with all these changes," he explained to me, "I actually feel closer to my sons than I ever did before. When we were together, Deborah and I used to have so many disagreements over them that it was hard to get any peaceful time with the boys. Now that I get to see them more often, and see them on my own, the boys and I are doing just great together. I love them to pieces—and now I get a sense that they care about me too."

STAND BY MOM

In addition to maintaining his own connection to his boys, it's important for a father to encourage his sons to stay close to their mother. A father who respects the love that the mother gives her son and who does not

shame his boy for taking in that love can help remove or soften the trauma
that happens when the boy is pressured by society to separate prematurely
from his mom. By honoring and supporting the boy's relationship with his
mother, a father also helps teach his son the general importance of male
respect for girls and women.

Standing by mom doesn't only mean defending her when she disciplines or reproaches her son. Instead, ideally a father seizes all sorts of
opportunities to encourage the relationship between mother and son. So,
for instance, if your frightened five-month-old boy begins to cry for his
mother, rather than teasing the boy about his fear, let him know that mom
is right there, and bring him to see her if he seems to need a dose of her
love and attention. If your three-year-old draws a picture for his mom, tell
him what you like about the picture and say how nice it was that he gave
his mom a present. When you arrive home one day to find your twelve-
year-old son sobbing, his head buried in your wife's shoulder, avoid saying anything that will shame the boy. Ask him if there's anything you can
do to help out; and if he prefers to get help from mom, assure him that his
decision is good, that his relationship with mom is valuable and important, that she's a great person to have at such difficult moments. By conveying a sense of loving approval and supporting his natural yearning to
stay close to his mother, you give your son the message that his relationship with mom is important, that in your eyes it doesn't make him any
less strong or manly, and that it won't change anything in his relationship
with you.

IT'S WHO HE IS RATHER THAN WHAT HE DOES

As best you can, try to value your sons for who they are rather than for
what they do. This means that instead of loving your son based on any particular quality or competency you *wish* he had, ideally you will love him
for the qualities and competencies that he already has, those that come naturally to him.

For any child, disappointing a parent is an incredibly painful feeling,
and for most boys, letting down dad is particularly devastating. As a father,
when you set up rigid expectations about who the boy must be, about what
will make him "good" or "masculine," it's easy for him to fall into a pattern of constantly disappointing you. Conversely if you make it clear that
you'll always love him for just the person he is and that there's no single

definition of "goodness" or "masculinity," he'll be spared the agony of feeling he's consistently falling short of your expectations.

Adopting this open-minded approach helps fathers to break the force of the Boy Code. So, for example, rather than enforcing the "big wheel" stereotype that spurs on boys to show endless aggression and competitiveness, you can develop your own creative rules about cooperation, negotiation, and friendship. Rather than frowning if your boy isn't smart enough, athletic enough, tough enough, you can instead focus on noticing what does make your boy the special guy he is—his great flair for well-timed one-liners, his quick instinct to help out others, his winning smile, whatever. As the boy's first and probably most important male role model, the more unconditional love and encouragement you give your son and the more you work to convince him that he is indeed a hundred percent masculine—a "real boy"—the better he will feel about himself, the more confidence he will feel to take on life's challenges, and the closer he will feel to you.

DEVELOP YOUR OWN STYLE

Feel free to develop your own style of playing, teaching, and nurturing your son. As research has shown, your personal style—though it may be different from that of your spouse—is extremely valuable to your son. While it's a great idea to get parenting tips from your boy's mother or from friends or other family, the style you develop to connect with your son is your own creation and doesn't need to match anybody else's.

If spending quiet time talking with your son feels comfortable, then enjoy those special father-to-son discussions. If the language of "action empathy"—using action to connect emotionally—works better for you, feel free to use this approach. As the research I've discussed makes incredibly clear, what matters most is that you simply do something—just about anything positive—with your son. Ideally, try to find activities that both of you enjoy. Thus if he likes contact sports, and you prefer quieter sports such as golf or bowling, compromise by finding a sport, such as tennis, with which both of you feel comfortable. If he loves all things cultural, and you're more of a sports and fishing sort of person, find an activity—such as going to a movie or waking up early for a Saturday-morning bird-watch—that both of you will find fun and interesting. It's not so much the activity that counts as your being by your son's side, showing your friendship, fulfilling the yearning for connection that comes naturally to most fathers and sons.

DO NOT BE THE POLICEMAN DAD

Try to avoid becoming the "heavy" or "bad cop"; instead, work closely with your spouse to provide discipline jointly and cooperatively. By co-ordinating with her to set clear rules and limits, you can avoid falling into the trap of being the parent who is always expected to be the one to punish, the one who must always take on the attitude of goading and restricting your boy's sense of personal freedom. If you come to share the disciplinary role with your spouse, you'll probably notice that it becomes that much easier to develop a close and affectionate relationship with your son.

In a study by Professors Anja Jain, Jay Belsky, and Keith Crnic at Penn State, four basic categories of fathers were identified—caretakers, playmate-teachers, disciplinarians, and disengaged fathers. *It was only the caretaker and playmate-teacher dads who had a positive effect on their sons.* Disciplinarian and disengaged dads, by contrast, found it very difficult to develop close relationships with their sons. In my opinion, there's no reason a father should come to be the only parent who hands out the reprimands. In two-parent families, both parents should participate fully and appropriately to discipline the boy not only so that the boy comes to understand and respect his mother's authority, but also so that he is not led to see his father as a stereotypical tough guy, as the parent who feels less empathy.

SHOW RATHER THAN TELL

Another important part of being a well-connected father—and of avoiding the pitfalls of becoming the "policeman" of the household—is to teach lessons by *showing* them rather than by just *telling* them to one's children. Especially with boys, it's important to make the learning process one that encourages the boy to follow "what I do" rather than "what I say." By modeling how things should be done—by using action to show your interest and skill in the activities and undertakings of your boys—you can avoid the appearance of being condescending or patronizing and instead begin to cultivate a close, mutually trusting relationship with your son.

By way of example, if you hope to instill in your boy the importance of respecting girls and women, saying to him things such as "Don't talk to your mother that way" or "Is that the way to treat your sister?" will probably be far less effective than if he actually observes how you respect your wife or your daughter by talking to them gently and thoughtfully when you are displeased of frustrated with one of them. Likewise, telling your son, "Stop watching TV and get going on your homework" is likely to be less successful than if you too forgo watching television and instead perhaps read a book by his side to keep him company as he's getting his school-work done. Not only does showing (rather than just telling) avoid the risk that your boy will somehow see your words as imperious or hypocritical, but it also enables the boy to see one of the adults he loves and respects most—you—model the behavior you'd like him to learn.

BE AWARE OF YOUR OWN "FATHER LONGINGS"

Because our own upbringing has such a powerful effect on how we behave as parents, it's important that you, as a father, try to be cognizant of your own "father longings" and of the pain or confusion you may feel about the ways that you were treated by your father. So many men harbor memories about being teased or mistreated by their fathers for not having been "mas-culine" enough or for having otherwise disappointed their own fathers' early expectations. As hard as it can be, it is very important to try to muster the courage to go beyond these memories and to avoid repeating the same kind of narrow shame-based upbringing for your own boys. In many ways, you are in the best position of all to help your son break out of society's gender straitjacket. Because fathers are often so talented at drawing out the full range of a boy's emotional experience, it's wonderful when you, as a father, are able to give your son the sense of safety and self-confidence he needs to open up and come out from behind his mask.

REAL MEN SHOW EMOTIONS

To help your son feel comfortable sharing himself in this way, try your best, in appropriate doses, to share the full range of your own feelings and experiences with your boy. Let your son know that, even as an adult, you sometimes feel lonely, vulnerable, or afraid, that you shed tears, yearn for hugs, and sometimes want to run for cover, that "real men" like you can and do have all sorts of emotions. Explain to your boy that all men, like all boys, are fallible, that there is no hero without an Achilles' heel, and the mark of masculine maturity is a man's recognition of his own inevitable failings and his awareness that he needs other people to love and support him. By expressing these things to your son, by exposing yourself in this way, you show your son that in turn you, as father, can be trusted with all of his feelings and experiences, and that your boy need go no further to find a loving, caring friend.

In recognizing such human limitations, fathers and sons alike are changing what it means to be a "real boy" or to become a "real man." In Homer's *Odyssey,* that quintessential Western epic of the absent, wandering, duty-bound father and the bereft son, the story of Odysseus and Telemachus, we are treated to the poetic recognition of this male-based struggle. Are we and our fathers meant to be invincible or merely mortal and, therefore, vulnerable? The ancient poet suggests another prescription, a shared male humility. Odysseus tells his son: "No I am not a god . . . But I am your father . . . No other Odysseus than I will ever come back to you. But *here I am,* and I am as you see me, and after much hardships and suffering have I come . . . back to my own country." Then, his son "folded his great father in his arms and lamented, shedding tears . . . and desire for mourning rose in both of them; and they cried shrill . . . and the tears their eyes wept."

In this harbinger of connection and change, in this echo of Abraham's *"Heneini"*—here I am—is the recognition of father and son, reunited in connection.

—7—

THE ADOLESCENT CRUCIBLE:

GROWTH, CHANGE, AND SEXUALITY

*"I think there is a 'thing,' that boys should be tough and mean. . . .
There are girls that are tough; and just because you are a boy
doesn't mean that you have to be the strongest kid in the world
or the tough guy."—Ken, age fifteen*

*"You've gotta really keep your guard up. If you don't, the guys
will . . . tell people that you're not cool."—Ian, age fourteen*

THE SECOND TRAUMA OF SEPARATION OR THE FIRST STEP TO ADULT INDIVIDUATION

During adolescence a boy naturally seeks to define his own identity, establish his independence, and determine what kind of man he intends to be. The conventional view of society is that, to do so, a boy must separate from his family and learn to stand on his own. My view, however, is that a boy can become a distinct and unique individual without separating from his family. In fact, I believe that the best and perhaps the *only* way he can successfully define a strong, independent, and individualistic masculine identity is with the help, support, and love of his family, friends, teachers, and caregivers.

You would not expect a baby to stand up and take his first steps unassisted, to tough it out no matter how many times he falls over or how many pieces of furniture he crashes into. You would not plunk your five-year-old on a bike and expect him to ride to the next county. You would *be there* for the toddler and the tyro bike rider—to protect them from harm, to stabilize them, to teach them how to balance, encourage them to keep on trying, praise them when they succeed, rejoice with them when they master the skill. Yet, many of us expect our teenagers to face the far more daunting complexities of sexuality, relationships, career choice, peer pressure, and academic performance without similar support, guidance, and "being there."

The idea of adolescence has changed enormously over the years. Since the turn of the century, when the term was first used, adolescence has been considered a safe haven, a period between boyhood and manhood when boys would be sheltered and protected, eased out of the world of toys and books into the world of work and family.

But, today, adolescence is anything but a time of safety and protection—it often is, in fact, the most perilous and confusing time of a boy's life. These are the years when a boy attempts to develop a firm sense of self, of who he is, of what "makes him tick," and of what he hopes for in life. The psychoanalyst Erik Erikson suggested that during adolescence the child must choose between forming a coherent identity or falling prey to a sense of despair and confusion.

As my recent research findings on male adolescence reflect, this adolescent confusion and peril is due primarily to two underlying psychological factors. First, boys receive conflicting messages about men and masculinity from society, their peers, and even their parents. During adolescence they become especially susceptible to the double standard of masculinity, which, as we've already discussed, challenges boys throughout their lives. On the one hand, society tells boys they should be cool, confident, and strong. At the same time, society tells boys they should be egalitarian (particularly in relation to girls), sensitive, and open with their feelings.

It is not impossible to be both manly and empathic, cool and open, strong and vulnerable, but it is certainly a difficult and complex task. Most boys have a very difficult time trying to sort out these conflicting messages and determining what masculine model to pattern themselves after. This is a painful process of self-clarification, much of which, however, occurs outside conscious awareness.

Second, boys have ambivalent feelings about male adulthood—they're not at all sure that being a man is going to be such a great experience. They may not see any male role model that appeals to them and they feel is within their reach. Must they spend their whole lives chained to a job they don't love in order to support a family? And they may suspect that the double standard will not abate in its influence as they become adults, that they will be expected to navigate through dating, marriage, work and family-making (or choosing not to do those things) while being bombarded by similarly conflicting messages about how the ideal man behaves.

A boy's ambivalence toward manhood and his confusion about the double standard are further complicated with the emergence of his sexuality and its concomitant dangers such as fatherhood, sexually transmitted diseases, especially AIDS. Is it any wonder that boys are in intense need of support, guidance, and love from their parents?

But, as difficult as adolescence can be for boys and their families, it can also be a particularly wonderful and rich time for both. As a boy broadens his intellectual and emotional reach, parents find that their relationship with their son can become newly intriguing and rewarding. A boy begins to articulate his own and original ideas about people, society, and the world that may stimulate a parent's thinking in some new way. A boy may take part in activities that the parent finds genuinely gratifying to watch and encourage—anything from sports to community volunteering to academic studies to artistic achievement. A boy may begin to truly excel at some pursuit, bringing a rush of pride and respect that will surprise a parent. During adolescence a boy begins to make a personal contribution to the world; a parent learns that the son is genuinely valued by his friends, teachers, and members of the community. It is during adolescence that all the prior years of parenting begin to show tangible result—you begin to see the outline of the man you have helped to create. The boy, too, can feel a new sense of self-esteem during adolescence, as he understands that he is his own person and he is valued—not just as a member of the family but as a member of the community at large.

THE DOUBLE STANDARD OF MASCULINITY

As discussed above, our society has unknowingly created two dominant and opposing images of masculinity. The traditional image is of the man who does not express his emotions freely and favors a traditional role toward women; the "new man" is empathic, egalitarian, and sensitive. As with all such stereotypes, no one fully believes in them, nor does any man completely embody them. Yet it is difficult to argue that these images do not exist and do not influence our thinking. Our boys are constantly matching their own behavior, and that of others, to the stereotypes to see how it conforms and where it differs. At the same time, peers, teachers, parents, and society "in general," do the same thing—we assess how our boys measure up to the stereotypes. The process is mostly unconscious, and even if we are aware of it and try not to make comparisons, it is a very difficult habit to break.

It's as if our sons are unwittingly mirroring back to us our own adult ambivalence about masculinity and trying in vain to accept and internalize two diametrically opposed views of manhood.

My research shows that many adolescent boys are crumbling under this millstone of our adult ambivalence about masculinity, and that the confusion and uncertainty these boys feel about becoming men is eroding their self-esteem.

"Lots of times I feel like I've got to be two different people," Jamie, a sixteen-year-old, told me.

"What do you mean exactly?" I asked him.

"In our social studies class, we had a forum on gender roles. The teacher brought in a female airplane pilot and a male makeup artist. After we listened to the speakers, we had discussion groups and then wrote an essay. I wrote something I knew the teacher would like about equality and all that."

"But how did that make you feel like two different people?" I inquired.

"Because my discussion group was all guys. Our real reaction to the makeup artist was, 'Oh my God. What a wimp this guy is!' None of us would ever want to do a job like that. But I knew that I couldn't say that in the essay. I knew I had to say how I learned that a man or woman can do any profession, that men and women should be equal when it comes to work and pay, and that lots of people do jobs that you wouldn't expect them to. My real reaction was that I never wanted to be a makeup artist, and thought the guy was a jerk, but I knew what our teacher wanted to hear. So, I had to be two different people—one with the guys, one with the teacher."

I imagine that this exercise had merit, in that it broadened the students' thinking about professional gender roles. But, for Jamie, the learning was overshadowed by his discomfort with having to play two conflicting roles. Perhaps that discomfort will eventually lead him to think more deeply about his reaction to the makeup artist, but for the time being it made him feel irritated and confused. The difficulties associated with this inner struggle can be even more acute for other boys because many of them will remain completely unaware that it is taking place. And because they can't tell where their unhappiness is coming from, they may become even more lost and afraid.

THE DOUBLE STANDARD AND SEXUALITY

The double standard becomes especially hard to deal with when it comes to issues of sexuality. What other area causes boys to be so vulnerable, so open, so naked before girls? In what other area are boys so scared, yet seen as such aggressors?

On the one hand, the boy is becoming a man, with a man's body and a man's sexual appetites. He feels pressure, from society and his peers, to perform as a man—to make out, have a girlfriend, have sexual intercourse. On the other hand, we as parents and teachers encourage our boys to focus on the emotional bonds they can develop with girls and young women. We ask them to respect their female peers' feelings about what sexual behavior feels appropriate, comfortable, and right. As a result, adolescent boys wonder when and whether it is appropriate to begin having sex and how they should go about it. What will their peers think of them if they respect a girl's wishes and "wait"? What will their parents think if both girl and boy agree to have sex?

"At school," Ralph, sixteen, told me, "they teach us to respect girls. We're supposed to treat them like women. They also teach us about AIDS, which is very scary. They say we shouldn't rush into sex. But, if we do have intercourse, they tell us, make sure you wear a condom. Everybody listens very carefully, and agrees in class. But, then, a lot of guys go around bragging about how many girls they've done it with. Everybody wants to know if you've scored or not. There's just a lot of pressure to have sex with a girl."

"How do you handle the pressure?"

"Well, I think I want to wait, but I'm not really sure why. I feel pretty messed up about it."

The decision of whether and when to have intercourse is perhaps the most daunting one, as regards sexuality, that a teenage boy may face. But his life is made up of a thousand other concerns and questions about how to behave in situations that involve girls and sexuality.

Much of the fear and uncertainty he will feel may have to do with the difference in physical maturation rates between boys and girls in general. Especially around the ages of twelve to fifteen, girls are physically and, sometimes, emotionally more mature than boys. Unlike girls, whose sexual maturity is clearly marked by the onset of menstruation, boys have no clear idea when they're actually physically capable of having sex. The onset of puberty for boys is slower, the physical changes more subtle. His voice changes. He begins to develop pubic hair. His muscles and torso increase in size. But there is no change in boys' bodies that directly lets them know they're capable of sex and reproduction. Indeed, the only real way for boys to know they can have sex is to have it. This increases the pressure to have sex as proof of maturity and amplifies the anxiety surrounding that first act. Boys worry that they won't be good at making love, and the fear of impotence—the ultimate humiliation—runs through every boy's mind.

Now put a boy with these kinds of confusions with a girl who physically matured several years earlier and you can only imagine how intimidated he will feel. Unfortunately, as we know, the more insecurity boys feel, the more compensatory bravado they'll exhibit. Hence, there is locker-room talk, reducing girls to objects, and bragging about conquests.

And even worse, the motives of a young boy and a young girl thinking about having sex for the first time are very different. Girls look at sex as signaling an act of love and the ultimate connection. Boys tend to view it, at least partially, as a way of confirming their masculinity. Boys only relax and become emotionally vulnerable after they are able to feel secure about their sexual ability and feel secure that the act of sex won't shame them in any way. Girls want boys to be emotional and loving, *before* sex. Boys, with a very different pace and philosophy around emotionality, often find they can't open up until *after* sex—sometimes long after sex. Before that time comes, it looks to girls as if boys don't care.

The silence of teenage boys on emotionally laden topics and their defensively macho approach to sex has gained them a spotty reputation among girls and parents, who too easily come to view them as sexual predators, interested only in stealing the hearts and virginity of young girls, then slipping back into the underbrush. In our current discussions of safe sex, date rape, and sexual harassment, boys are seen, more than ever, as sexual aggressors, driven by their frantic biological urge for sex into all sorts of uncivilized acts.

But it's important to understand the attitude of teenage boys toward sex. It's important to remember that they're operating under a different, sometimes difficult code. Their behavior is a compromise between a desire for connection and the fears of rejection, additionally fueled by unconscious shameful fears of earlier abandonment, of which the boy is not consciously aware. They're passing through an extraordinarily difficult phase of life, when the ultimate humiliation as a man is possible and the least amount of real honesty is allowed.

Now, I'm not suggesting that, in our sympathetic attitude, we convey the message to our boys that it's OK to be sexual aggressors. My point is only that if we want to reach our boys and help them develop mature and responsible attitudes toward sex, we need to understand their motivations. As a culture we are much more aware of and sympathetic to the pressures around sexuality that girls feel. The confusion boys feel is hidden, hidden under their own masks of macho posturing and under the weight of our misconceptions of toxicity about boys. We are all too ready to offer advice to girls and to blame boys. If you doubt this, I suggest you attend, as I have, any of the educational groups on high school and college campuses that focus on safe sex, sexual harassment, or date rape. All too often, girls are legitimately encouraged to explore their feelings and to communicate assertively. Boys, however, are lectured at and told that their job is to respect a girl when she says "No." The attitude seems to be that boys don't have their own confusion, as if they're sexual machines, poised and ready to go at all times.

Martin, age seventeen, has left such sessions confused about what behavior is acceptable, afraid he might be perceived as dangerous. "They told us to always ask a girl before you even kiss her. And it's not mutual. The girls don't ask. Seems like it's the guy's responsibility to make all the moves. Only the guy is worried about doing something the girl doesn't want and only the guy has to think about doing something the girl *does* want. The whole society seems to feel that way. You know it's strange, very old-fashioned in a way that the idea that the guys are the active ones who do everything and the girls just take it or reject it." Martin feels helpless to change the situation. "You just have to deal with it and take it and live with it and if you don't you are going to get into a lot of trouble."

Here again is the double standard of masculinity that pushes boys to feel they need to "prove themselves" sexually and then castigates them when they do so. Listen to Peter: "Being a guy, wow. You don't know when you are going to offend someone—you always have to be watching yourself. It's harder in relationships. Oh, it's still always got to be the guy who approaches the girl, takes the first step. Earlier on, when you're thirteen or fourteen, maybe even now, you don't know exactly what to do. But you still have the urge. You want to talk to a girl but you don't know. You've never done it before. All the pressure is on you, and you've got to do it."

This is not to say that there are no boys who take advantage of their greater physical strength to perpetrate sexual violence on girls. Any educational program should of course condemn the use of physical force in any context. But most boys are not like this. Most boys are honestly seeking connection and are capable of real relationships.

Mitchell, for example, is the son of Dick and Jennifer Harrington, friends of mine who live in a middle-class, socially "progressive" suburb of Boston. Both Dick and Jennifer work full-time, Dick as an accountant and Jennifer as a public relations executive at a large Boston firm.

One Saturday, Mitchell and his classmate Liz went out for an evening of pizza and the movies—the first "real" date for both of them. When Mitchell got home, his father asked how it went.

"OK," Mitchell told him, looking a little embarrassed and shell-shocked. "A little weird."

"What do you mean, weird?" his father asked.

"I didn't know if I should pay for the pizza or whether we should split it."

"What did you do?"

"We split it, but I think she was expecting me to pay."

"Well," said his father, "that doesn't sound too weird."

"No, but then when I was driving her home we kind of ran out of conversation. I think she was expecting me to attack her sexually or something."

"Why did you think that?" his father asked.

"I don't know. The whole good-night-kiss thing, you know. But, sometimes I feel like touching a girl is illegal, if she doesn't want you to. I wasn't sure if she wanted me to. So, then I started thinking that if I tried to kiss her she'd hit me with a sexual harassment suit."

"So, did you kiss her?"

"No, I was so confused I couldn't even figure if I really wanted to or not. So, I figured I'd better just say good night and drop her off. Now she probably thinks I'm a wimp, or that I don't like her." Mitchell sighed. "Now I think I understand how Bill Clinton feels."

Mitchell couldn't figure out whether to play the strong, aggressive man and make a smooth move on the waiting girl, or whether he should be the egalitarian, gentle, sensitive man who waits. Perhaps most upsetting, he really didn't know how he truly felt. Did he want to kiss her or not? Did he really like her or not?

Mitchell was lucky, because his parents tried to help him with his problem.

"You know," his father told Mitchell, "my new manager at work is a woman. I had a similar problem with her when she first arrived. I didn't know if I should hold open the door for her. I thought if I touched her on the shoulder she'd sue me. I didn't know if I should ask her out for a beer. I didn't tell her any jokes because I was afraid she might take them wrong. It took me a long time to figure these things out, and I'm still working on it."

When Jennifer heard about the date, she offered an idea. "Hey, Mitchell, maybe you could just ask Liz what she thinks. Ask her if you could pay for pizza. Ask her if you could kiss her. Talk to her. I'm pretty sure she'll give you straight answers."

Bolstered by this guidance, Mitchell asked Liz on another date to a rock concert. He asked Liz whether he could treat her to the event, and she accepted enthusiastically. At the end of the evening, as the two pulled into her driveway, I am told, they had no trouble agreeing that a kiss would be acceptable.

So, the good news is that when parents like Mitchell's show they understand how hard it is for a boy to deal with the double standard, stay involved with him, convey their empathy in a loving, thoughtful way, they not only help their son handle his confusion but also bring the entire family closer together.

WE JUST DON'T TALK ABOUT IT

Mitchell was fortunate to have parents willing to tackle issues of sexuality. Many boys report that, by the onset of puberty, they have been taught little or nothing about masculinity, dating, sex, and sexuality. Even more distressing, they feel they have no one who can understand what's happening to them and with whom they can discuss their feelings about the changes in their bodies. In one recent study, nearly half of adolescent boys ages fifteen to nineteen years old reported that they did not think that today's average young person receives enough information about sex and reproduction.

But lack of information about sex does not prevent teenagers from engaging in it. Recent research that incorporates data from the Alan

Guttmacher Institute and the National Center for Health Statistics shows that the majority of adolescents begin having intercourse by their mid- to late teens. By age eighteen, 56 percent of young women and 73 percent of young men have had intercourse. (In the early 1970s, 35 percent of young women and 55 percent of young men reported having sex by the age of eighteen.) The percentage of those having intercourse increases from 9 percent for all twelve-year-olds to 70 percent of all eighteen-year-olds. The bottom line is that four out of five teens have intercourse during their teen years. Only one out of five decides to wait.

But, even if parents are aware of these statistics, the knowledge doesn't seem to motivate them into discussing sex and sexuality. Many boys report that they feel they have to handle alone the experiences of puberty and decisions about sex. "When I had my first wet dream" seventeen-year-old Chad says, "I had no idea what was going on. I thought I had wet my bed. It was a really strange feeling for me. I remember liking the dream, but I felt very embarrassed. I thought maybe I had some sort of psychological problem. And, who was I going to ask about it—my mother?"

Sixteen-year-old Ramon told me this story: "When I moved to the United States from the Dominican Republic, I was thirteen years old. I came with my mother and my older sister—my dad died when I was six. I didn't speak any English. When I first started touching myself, I wasn't sure if it was OK. I thought maybe I was weird. I wasn't even sure why it felt so good, or what would happen if I did it. There was nobody I could talk to about it. I didn't speak English, I didn't have any friends back then, and I wasn't gonna talk to my mother or sister. It was really lonely and I was worried that something was wrong with me. I thought that it was wrong and might get me or my mother into trouble somehow. I just didn't have a clue."

Sixteen-year-old Lionel told me: "Mom started working when I was about eight years old. She just wasn't around, so I pretty much went through puberty on my own. I don't spend much time with my parents, except sometimes at night or on the weekends. But it pretty much feels like they just talk to me when they want me to do something or are angry at me."

As these statements demonstrate, many boys feel that beginning at puberty and through the teen years, they don't have the kind of relationship they once had—or wished they could have—with their parents. Many feel distant from their parents or feel that their parents are constantly angry at them. And most seem to feel uncomfortable talking to their parents about sex and sexuality.

But I believe the gulf that develops between the adolescent boy and his parents, the difficulties they have talking about sex, and the frustrations that lead the boy to perceive his parents as being distant and angry, have little to do with what parents actually want in their relationships with their sons. As one father said to me about his adolescent son, "I'd do just about anything to feel close to him again. I don't know what happened to us. Between everything that's gone on for him at school and with some of his friends, we just don't seem able to connect anymore."

It doesn't have to be this way. I have found that parents and sons can have open discussions about sex and experience the kind of parent-child closeness for which they all continue to yearn if they acknowledge that they are interdependent. They need and want to be individuals but they don't need to separate from each other. The truth is that an adolescent boy still needs his parents and his parents still need him. If each can learn to understand the other's needs for freedom without disconnection, I believe that much of the silence around sex could be replaced with lively dialogue and much of the pain and isolation felt by our boys who are about to become men could be significantly reduced.

WHAT HAPPENS WHEN WE DON'T TALK ABOUT IT: THE SPECTER OF DRUGS

When we don't talk about the issues that are bothering our teenage boys, when we force them to separate rather than supporting them as they learn to individuate, they may retreat behind the mask so completely and consistently that it becomes hardened and fixed in place. They may, in fact, find themselves unable to remove the mask, and—just as Mitchell couldn't determine how he really felt about Liz—they may lose touch with their own genuine feelings.

The mask makes it difficult for parents and sons to talk openly about sex and sexuality; what's worse, as we'll see, it may make a boy more likely to take risks with alcohol and drugs. And because the mask makes it appear that everything is fine, it may prevent parents from seeing (or accepting) that a boy is in fact already taking those risks. But whether parents see it or not, many teenagers are involved with drugs. According to the recent National Longitudinal Study on Adolescent Health—a large-scale nationwide demographic study of adolescents' physical and mental health—in addition to the over 25 percent of adolescents who are current cigarette users, nearly 10 percent of students report that they drink alcohol at least one day a week and nearly 18 percent say they drink more than once a month. While over a quarter of the adolescent students in this study reported having smoked marijuana at least once, more than 12 percent said they smoked it at least once during the previous month.

In studies that look at what teenagers say *other* teenagers are doing with drugs, the statistics are even more disturbing. For instance in a 1997 study conducted for the Commission on Substance Abuse Among America's Adolescents by the National Center on Addiction and Substance Abuse at Columbia University, 56 percent of teenagers said they knew someone who used cocaine, heroin, or LSD (up from 39 percent in 1996). Among the *twelve-year-olds* involved in this study, 23.5 percent of them said they knew friends or fellow students who had used these hard drugs.

Other statistics reported in connection with this major study include the fact that among eighth-graders, heroin use doubled from 1991 to 1996. Also among eighth-graders, binge drinking (i.e., drinking continuously to get drunk) went from 12.8 percent in 1992 to 15.6 percent in 1996. The study noted too that teenagers who smoke, drink, or use marijuana—the so-called gateway drugs—are seventeen times more likely to move on to harder, more dangerous drugs, and stressed that boys, taken alone, are twenty-nine times more likely to move on to such substances (whereas girls are eleven times more likely).

Many boys use drugs and alcohol simply to numb the pain of their emotions—the disconnection they feel from their parents, their low self-esteem, their problems at school, with peers, or with their budding sexuality. Some boys turn to drugs like marijuana or cocaine in a vain attempt to ease the pain of being an adolescent, to escape its perils and confusions, to help them slip off the mask and rebel against society's old Boy Code rules about how boys should be and about what is or isn't "masculine." Relying on this ungenuine, drug-induced sense of emotional safety, they feel more comfortable revealing what they are truly experiencing inside, especially the love, affection, and need for connection they feel for others. *I love you, man!*

The problem, of course, is that drugs and alcohol present only short-term and illusory relief from a boy's worries and cares. When the intoxication wears off, the boy retreats behind the mask, the straitjacket tightens, and he begins to repress his true self once again. And now he's added dependence on substances in order to feel real. Drug and alcohol solve none of the root problems and bring with them a whole raft of new difficulties and risks: inability to function academically, depression, low self-esteem, being shunned by nondrinking peers, injuries and accidents, dropping out of school, and more.

A Disconnection for the Parents

For parents and caregivers, dealing with the mask is tough enough; when the boy turns to drugs and alcohol to help him remove it, the relationship becomes even more challenging. Parents are often taken by surprise when the boy who used to be so open and willing to talk seems to have disappeared. Many parents tell me they feel disconnected from and rejected by their sons or confused by a boy's outward rigidity or irreverence. "He's acting like such a macho little idiot, never talking to me anymore about anything that matters," one parent said, referring to her sixteen-year-old son, "I just feel like telling him 'You used to be so nice and now you've become a big block of ice. Why don't you just snap out of it and get real!' "

Or as another parent put it: "Every afternoon, my boy comes home, throws his stuff in his room, and then heads off to hang out with his friends at a local park. I really suspect he's doing drugs. Sometimes when he comes home, he looks really tired and rushes off to be alone in his room. But given how distant and angry he seems these days, it doesn't seem worth it to say anything because he'll probably just get even madder and storm off by himself."

As natural as it may be sometimes to feel like giving up and just let a boy do as he pleases, it simply doesn't work. In my years of counseling adolescent boys and their parents, I've learned that it's always better to be there, to say to your son—as Abraham did—"Here I am!" As parents, we simply must hang in there for our sons, because the risks involved in giving up are too great: we may be forced to deal with drugs, depression, AIDS, violence, and all the rest. It's critical that we let our boys know that as much as we respect their need to individuate, they will always be welcome at home; that as much as they may want to wear a mask of protection in the outside world, they can take it off at home or in other safe spaces.

We must let our sons know that we will be there, and we'll always do our best to provide a place they can return to for love, warmth, and reconnection. We have to help them understand that it is only through the potency of connection—and certainly not drugs or alcohol—that the adolescent years can become a time when a solid self takes shape and when the real boy starts to become a real and successful man.

As Robert Frost understood so well, "Home is the place where, when you have to go there, / They have to take you in."

THE PEER PRESSURE COOKER

Even when parents encourage a boy in his fight to individuate, his peers may not be so supportive. When he first begins to spend time with his peers, the adolescent boy may feel he's entered a whole new universe with its own rules and language.

"When I got to middle school," one boy explained, "everything changed. Kids I used to be friends with who were just nice guys suddenly started acting cool. By seventh grade, a few of them started to drink and smoke. They were totally different from when I knew them in elementary school. You knew that if you didn't act the same way, you'd be an outcast from that group." Or as another boy put it, "Once you're thirteen or older, you can't be the same person at school as you are at home. It's not considered 'cool.' " Their peers will also reproach or reject them if boys act in ways that appear feminine or that could possibly suggest homosexuality. As a result, boys begin to harden themselves and to avoid any person or situation that might bring them shame.

Perhaps an adolescent boy suffers his greatest humiliation when he violates the Boy Code. As fifteen-year-old Ken explains: "I think there is a 'thing,' that boys should be tough and mean; and I think that is a little ridiculous because some people are tough, but some people aren't. There are girls that are tough; and just because you are a boy doesn't mean that you have to be the strongest kid in the world or the tough guy." Or, as fourteen-year-old Ian expressed it, "You've gotta really keep your guard up. If you don't, the guys will call you a dork and tell people that you're not cool."

This code to be cool can also push younger adolescents into dangerous and self-destructive behavior. One boy explained: "At parties I've seen the *cool* kids try to influence the other kids to drink. They say that if those kids don't drink, then they can't hang out with them."

One of the saddest consequences of the Boy Code is the creation of such pressure on a boy to mask his true identity that he loses touch with who he is and what really brings him joy in life. To ensure that he'll be seen as cool, the boy may avoid acting in certain ways, expressing certain emotions, or engaging in certain activities that aren't deemed appropriate anymore. In other words, by purposely changing his behavior to avoid the embarrassment of violating the Boy Code, he completely sacrifices his genuine self.

"My sister and I used to have jump-rope contests," says twelve-year-old Stewart, "but then I started to get teased and stopped. It wasn't worth it anymore."

Fifteen-year-old Lionel told me: "I used to talk a lot—you know, about whatever was happening, whatever I was doing. But at school now, if you talk too much, people tell you to shut up. Like the guys who act tough and don't say much are the ones the girls all go for. So now at school I try not to say much. At home, I talk my brother's ear off."

"I think it was when I turned eleven," seventeen-year-old Jake recalled. "Guys just started ranking on each other and picking on the little ones. If you wore some stupid shirt, that was it—everybody would try to do you in. My dad works at a newspaper, so he would always encourage me to keep a journal at home, sort of like a diary. I liked it, because I would write about people and stuff that happened and how I really felt about it. But when things started changing at school, I stopped writing in my journal. I was afraid someone might find it and then I'd be in real trouble!"

During adolescence, Boy Code rules are strictly enforced and the division between those who fit the mold and those who don't can be extremely rigid. Not only can it make the boy disconnect from his genuine self, but it can actually undermine and even destroy his closest friendships.

MATT AND ZACHARY: A FRIENDSHIP BROKEN BY THE CODE

Matt Green, an articulate fifteen-year-old, told me a particularly poignant story about how the Boy Code can push boys apart.

In elementary and junior high school, Zachary Miller was Matt's best friend. When they entered high school, Matt and Zachary began to drift away from each other.

"Zachary does theater and likes to dress in weird clothes," Matt explained. "He couldn't care less about sports. He doesn't watch TV. He doesn't date girls or go to dances. All that might be OK, but he's really sensitive about everything. When kids give him grief, he doesn't know how to respond. He gets flustered and mad. I like him a lot, but a lot of kids think he's a fag and couldn't believe I would hang out with him."

Matt found it tough to keep his other friends and stay associated with Zachary. "I think I could have stuck with him if he had dealt with the flack better. But, one day, he went to the teacher when some kids stole his hat and wouldn't give it back. He should have laughed it off, or punched somebody, or done something for himself. But he turned red and walked away."

What would it take to repair the relationship?

"I don't care if Zachary is into theater or wears purple pants. No one does, really. What matters is that he has to find a way to be himself and deal with everybody else, too," Matt says. "I feel bad about it. I still say 'hi' to him in the hall and everything. But I just can't be his friend right now. If I do, people will definitely get on my case."

SOME BOYS RESIST PEER PRESSURE AND FIGHT BACK

One of the most heartening findings of my "Listening to Boys' Voices" study is that many of the boys I interviewed revealed an eagerness to *resist* the kind of peer pressure that caused Matt and Zachary to split—to come out from behind the mask and to challenge the shame-inducing Boy Code. For some boys, this means creating a safe space where they can all feel free to be themselves. For instance, in Chapter 4, we talked about Jason, who set up a "guy's place" at school where boys with differing personalities and interests could come together to talk about feelings and issues and form new friendships.

Isaiah, a savvy sixteen-year-old, offered this advice to younger boys: "Just be yourselves and don't do anything you don't want to. Because in the long run if you're acting false—hanging out with kids that you don't really like—it's not really worth it. You're only young once. You should do what you want and have fun because that's the way you're going to be happy. You have to be yourself!"

John, another teenaged boy in the study, explained: "There are certain things that boys are supposed to be good at. Boys are supposed to play sports. Boys are supposed to want to make it with girls. Boys are supposed to drink beer. But lots of guys aren't that way. Lots of guys are into computers, some guys like to draw, a lot of guys are into music, many guys do volunteer stuff, or like to hike and camp. I think the stereotypes are wrong.

Whatever a person does should be respected. I don't think a boy should have to play sports at all if he doesn't want to. I think he should do what he wants."

In a similar vein, sixteen-year-old Aaron had an impressively sophisticated understanding of gender straitjacketing and the problem of boys calling one another names like fag or wimp.

"A few of my friends act like you have to be homophobic to prove that you're not gay. You have to say you hate gay people so that everyone will know you're definitely not gay and think you are OK."

At first, Aaron confessed, he and others of his friends participated in the taunting. But then one of his buddies, Bobby, introduced him to a different perspective. "Bobby is the best athlete and a great kid. Everyone loves him and respects him. Bobby isn't gay, but he told me it was wrong to trash gay people. He said being gay is normal. Why should we make fun of them? It got me thinking: he is exactly right."

Aaron concluded, "Now I try to pass the message along. I tell people that gay bashing is stupid. The more people who say that, the more people will get the message and cut it out."

Indeed, boys like Isaiah, John, Aaron, and Bobby sense that there's something wrong with being forced to act in one stereotypical "masculine" way and show that they are willing to take a stand to change how society pushes them to accept a gender straitjacket. But resisting society's code of masculinity is not easy. The boys in my study reported that they have to be cautious about how they go about it.

"I pick my battles," Aaron explained, meaning that he was careful to take on issues that he felt wouldn't risk putting him in a bad place with his peers. Keeping up good relations with one's peers matters a lot to adolescent boys. Many boys report that having close friends—boys and girls— who will support them and their good name, and who will stand up for them if they take a risk by challenging the Boy Code, makes all the difference in the world. In dealing with peer ridicule and mustering the courage to take on the code, boys emphasize that what helps them most is knowing that their friends—and their families—will stand by them.

THE PUBLIC AND PRIVATE SELVES: A BOY SPLIT IN TWO

The disparity between how a boy privately wishes to behave and how he feels he must behave when he is in public may surprise and confuse him.

He feels confused that the way he can act at home, when he's among his family and closest friends, is often different from how his peers expect him to behave. What works in the privacy of his home may not fly in public peer settings. As the boy quoted earlier said, "You can't be the same person at school as you are at home." The schoolyard culture of cool or tough and the family-room culture of openness and authenticity often clash.

The private self—the self that the boy genuinely is within, the self that is reinforced by female peers and often at home by mothers and fathers—may wish to act friendly, be playful and loving, and show a broad range of emotions. But then there is also the pull from society in general, from peers, and especially from other boys, to act strong, athletic, taciturn. Boys are called upon to avoid showing even a trace of vulnerability.

When the pressure becomes too much, some boys will take extreme measures—teasing others, spray-painting graffiti on school lockers, even assaulting another student—to acquire a reputation for being cool and win the kinship and respect of their compatriots. Navigating between the Scylla of "Respect others' needs—stay in connection" and the Charybdis of "Chill out—be your own man," our modern-day Odysseus is likely to falter at the shoals of one extreme or another, striving to master his confusion, frustration, and longing.

My research shows that during adolescence boys voice their desire to remain true to their inner values—to refuse to numb or hollow out their inner voice—while still saving face at school and on the basketball court. For instance, seventeen-year-old Scott Adams told me about the pressure at school to fight with other boys and how he dealt with it in light of what his parents taught him about fighting:

"The worst time I ever had," he started, "was when I was fighting over Sharon with Doug Santos. Sharon was dating Doug, but decided to go out with me, too. Doug, who's really popular, got very mad. One day Doug and a bunch of other guys from his neighborhood surrounded me at school in the parking lot, with Sharon right there. His pals started shouting, 'Come on, Doug, hit Scott. Hit him! He can't fight anyway!' "

"So, what did you do?"

"I try to never get involved in physical stuff. My mother always told me to use my words but not my hands. So, I told Doug I didn't want to fight. I told him I thought we could talk the problem out."

"That was a great response," I volunteered.

Scott rolled his eyes. "No, it wasn't. Doug started shoving me around, saying 'You fucking creep, you little fag, come on, let's see you fight.'"

"So then what?"

"Well, there was no teacher around and I've never really learned how to box or anything, but I just took the hardest swing I could and hit Doug. I guess I got him in just the right spot, because he let out a cry and doubled over, then kind of limped away. His friends started saying, 'Wo, Adams, all right! You got him pretty good.'"

"Did you tell your parents?"

"Yeah, they found out. My mother started lecturing me, but my father just sort of smiled. I feel confused about it, though. I don't think I did the right thing. Mom doesn't think I did the right thing. But Dad thinks it was kind of funny. And Doug never bothered me again."

This conflict between public and private behavior can lead to far more serious results than a minor skirmish in a school parking lot. Research shows that boys who are "split in two" are more at risk developing learning disabilities, severe depression, and impulsive and compulsive behaviors that range from substance abuse to unsafe sex, from acting out in the classroom to committing suicide.

My own study demonstrates that although boys actually work hard to become whole, to resist betraying the inner boy, and to experience vulnerable and painful feelings, they do so under terrible strain to "look good" in front of their peers—to wear their mask.

You're Misunderstood if You Act Tough

It seems that whatever model a boy chooses to follow at any given time— the macho man or the sensitive one—is likely to get him into trouble with somebody. When boys display the kinds of cool, tough behavior they thought society expected of them as young men, adults (especially their parents) reprimand them for seeming distant, rough, or unfeeling. In other words, just when they manage to adopt the behaviors they thought were required of them, many boys find that—far from being admired for their manly comportment—they are actually rebuffed or rebuked. As a result, adolescent boys often feel on the defensive, sensing that others see them as insensitive, violent, uncaring. They don't understand why adults seem so disappointed in them when they're trying so hard to behave in the ways they thought everyone was telling them they should.

Sixteen-year-old Ross relates it this way: "Being a guy today, wow. You don't know when you are going to offend someone. You've always got to be watching yourself. Is this going to get this person upset and is that going to get that person upset? So being a guy, it seems like I'm the enemy to society."

The double standard puzzles and angers thoughtful young men like Craig, a graduating high school senior. On the one hand, his peers expect him to be unflinching. "It's basically what this whole school's about. You try to act like the tough guy. In a sports game, or if someone takes you down, you don't back down, you step toward him," Craig observes.

In other contexts, Craig feels targeted for being a male teenager who may appear too tough:

"People act like guys my age are up to no good half the time," Craig contends.

Craig related two recent examples. "I went to the bank this past weekend, and because I didn't have my bankbook with me, they doubted my identity. Would they have done that if I was a girl? I don't think so. They went through a whole list of questions of who my parents were, what street I lived on, and how old I was. After a while, I was like, 'Why are you still doubting me? Have I done something wrong?' They figure that a *guy* who's a teenager is probably up to no good somehow or other.

"Another time I was about to pull out of a parking lot by Fenway Park after a Red Sox game, and a police officer waved me to stop. I pulled over, and I think just because I was a guy and I'm a kid, he went through a whole list of questions. He asked if I had any warrants out for my arrest or anything like that, and I thought that was kind of unusual that he would do that for no reason. I don't think that would happen to a girl either."

YOU'RE MISUNDERSTOOD IF YOU ACT NICE

Boys can also run into trouble when they try to act empathic, gentle, and connected—to behave, in other words, in the ways that feminist teachings have advocated as healthy and important.

"With all the feminist ideas in the country and the equality, I think guys sometimes get put on the spot," sixteen-year-old Toby said. "Guys might do something that I think or they think may not be wrong at all, but they still get shot down for it.

"If you're not nice to a girl, she thinks you don't care. But if you are nice, she thinks you're treating her too much like a lady. Girls don't understand guys, and guys don't understand girls very well."

I asked Toby to give me an example from his own experience. "For instance, my ex-girlfriend came to one of our basketball games the other day. After the game I went and said 'hi' to her and some other friends. Someone told me later that, just as I was turning to say 'hi' to somebody else, she started to give me a hug. I didn't even know she did it, but she thought I was ignoring her and being a jerk.

"But you know that if I had hugged her first, she would have been mad at me for doing something she didn't want. Instead she ended up mad at me for not hugging her, even though I didn't know what was going on.

"It's a confusing subject because it's just that everyone is different and everyone perceives things differently. Sometimes they want us to be manly or something, but sometimes they don't want us to be manly. You can't really tell how one girl is going to react to certain things. It may be completely different than another girl's reaction.

"Girls want you to be sensitive and everything, but guys call you a fag or a wimp if you act certain ways. Like in my case, I respect all my teachers, I respect adults, and I am always polite, because that is the way I have been brought up. But a lot of the times my friends say I'm kissing ass or being a brownnose, just because I'm being polite and I talk to adults. I say I'm just being polite and they say, 'Oh no, you're a wuss.' It bothers me."

So, What Should I Be? How Should I Behave?

Much of my recent research project consisted of extensive interviews with boys from which many of these comments were taken. But I also gave a series of psychological tests to 150 boys from the ages of twelve to eighteen. The survey included two tests that enabled me to ascertain boys' *conscious and unconscious* attitudes about the way a boy should go about becoming a man and the ways in which they believed a healthy man should act in our society. The first group of boys I surveyed was composed of urban kids from a mid-sized city on the Eastern seaboard, so I suspected that they would convey a fair amount of sophistication about equality for men and women, boys and girls. Indeed, my suspicions were correct.

On a test called the Sex Role Egalitarianism Scale, created by King and King, these boys scored well within the range of men and women who embrace the "new masculinity." This means that they endorsed such statements as "Men and women should be given an equal chance for professional training" and "Courses in home management should be as acceptable for male students as for female students," and strongly rejected such notions as "The husband should be the head of the family" or "It is more appropriate for a mother rather than a father to change a baby's diapers." Here there were no surprises, only confirmation that boys appear to be breaking out of gender rigidities into a new model of manhood, a model that is more open to men doing things and behaving in ways traditionally thought of as more feminine than masculine.

But then I did something a bit unusual. In the past, most research has been either/or—either it has focused on the progress boys have made toward gender equality (by using the Sex Role Egalitarianism Scale or a similar test) or it has analyzed how boys support or reject the characteristics associated with traditional masculinity. In other words, most studies have tested their subjects on just one attribute—where they fall on the scale as regards gender equality (are they egalitarian or nonegalitarian?) or how much they adhere to traditional ideals of masculinity.

But my own theory—that boys are being pushed to be both egalitarian and traditional—led me to take a different approach. I wondered what we would discover if we tested them on both characteristics. So, in addition to testing the boys on the Sex Role Egalitarianism Scale, we also tested the same group of boys on Pleck's Traditional Male Role Attitude Scale. By giving the same boys *both* tests, my research approach allowed for parallel measures, rather than an either/or choice.

The results of this approach showed that the same boys who endorsed the egalitarian values were equally strong when they took the Traditional Male Role Attitude Scale. They supported the following statements: "I admire a guy who is totally sure of himself," "It is essential for a guy to get respect from others," "A man always deserves the respect of his wife and children," "It bothers me when a guy acts like a girl," and "Men are always ready for sex."

So when given the opportunity to bare their souls, these adolescent boys, without knowing it, revealed an inner fissure, a split in their sense of what it means to become a man. On a test that measures their openness to egalitarian ideas, they embraced being egalitarian. On a test that measures how traditional they are about masculinity, they held on to a number of traditional traits. These results point directly to boys' inner unconscious confusion about what society expects of them as males. Because society requires boys to be both traditional and egalitarian, boys are unable to internally consolidate their feelings of masculinity. If they felt consistent and clear about their masculinity, boys would tend to test high on the traditional scale and low on the egalitarian, or high on the egalitarian scale and low on the traditional. But by scoring high on *both* of these diametrically opposed traits, boys revealed profound inner turmoil.

As we will see in Chapter 10, where I will discuss my research on these boys' self-image and how it relates to how well they do at school, this turmoil manifests itself in a growing need to mask their insecurities and an increasingly fragile sense of self-esteem. Specifically, as boys move through adolescence, my research shows that they are more and more prone to distort the extent to which they truly feel confident about their masculinity. More and more they feel they need to *say* they conform to society's ideal of "masculine" self-confidence even though inside themselves they may not feel confident at all.

THE PAINFUL PROSPECTS OF MANHOOD

Perhaps largely because of this festering internal confusion, many adolescent boys appear to feel deeply ambivalent about growing up to be men. If they're not sure what it means to be a man, I wonder, how could they possibly look forward to adulthood? As part of my research, I decided to explore what boys are really feeling about becoming grown men. Discovering this is not easy, of course, because as we've seen, boys tend to bury their deepest, most painful feelings.

One technique that psychologists use to discover the emotions that a person is experiencing subconsciously or is actually suppressing is to show him or her cards with illustrations of people in various emotionally charged situations specifically designed to evoke such feelings, and then ask the person to express what he or she sees happening in the particular illustration. In my recent research I showed boys two such cards and then asked them to write a story about the main character in each picture while concentrating on their feelings. Loosely modeled on a common psychological assessment instrument called the TAT or Thematic Apperception Test developed decades ago by Henry Murray, I used this approach to develop a window into each boy's hidden thought processes, a window through the mask.

What I discovered is that many boys feel profound anxiety about their future as men.

HOW BOYS VIEW A MAN'S WORK

One of the pictures that evoked the most potent responses was a black-and-white sketch of a man dressed in a white shirt and tie, obviously at work, poring over his papers. In the sketch he is sitting at a desk with a neutral expression on his face, gazing vaguely in the direction of a photograph on his desk of a woman and two children (one a boy and one a girl) that could represent his family. Listen to seventeen-year-old Hamilton's story about what we must take to be his expectation of "following the rules" in growing up male:

"This guy," he told us, "is sick of working, and he doesn't want to deal with his job or family anymore. He is thinking about what his life would be like if he hadn't married and how much it sucks to work all the time. He wishes he could leave and be by himself and have fun. But he'll work for twenty-five more years, hate it and then retire. The kids will move out and he'll realize his life was dull and boring. He'll be old then and what will he have to show for all this? Not much."

Hamilton's gloomy tale evokes the depressing, emotionally draining role of the male workhorse "connected" to family but "disconnected" from self. It brings to mind those dray horses that were still around in circuses when I was a child, dragging appallingly heavy loads, wearing blinders, and lumbering for mile after mile with a sense of disgruntled regularity and depressing inevitability. Tragically, Hamilton's caricature is not terribly different from the profile of the disillusioned middle-aged male executives I'm asked to counsel when their suicide plans have failed and they've been hospitalized against their will.

Ninth-grade Roger, rather than focusing on the intensity of a man's workday, hit upon the ways that professional obligations can separate men from family and erode their most important relationships:

"This is the story of a man, construction worker, looking at blueprints, who was divorced by his wife. . . . Now he is staring at the picture and thinking about his family, and how he can get them back. He was probably divorced because he worked too late at night and was never home."

Eighth-grader Bruce had a similar reaction:

"A man is at work, looking at his family. Maybe he was lonely or missing his family . . . because they were killed or he was divorced. . . . Maybe he will rescue them."

As these remarks reflect, though boys still seem to feel hope, it's tempered by a fear that once they become men, work pressures could eventually keep them far from the emotional, intimate world of their families. Adolescent boys, my research shows, are deeply ambivalent about becoming men and dealing with the responsibilities, limitations, and loneliness that appear to go with adulthood.

ADOLESCENT THEMES ABOUT MEN'S WORK

In analyzing the responses of the boys interviewed, I found the results could be divided into at least five thematic categories, one of which reflected positive emotions, and the rest dwelling on the impending pain in becoming "burdened" with the adult role of men at work:

A happy, contented family man. Fifteen percent of the boys told stories that fell into this first and only positive category. These boys saw a happy, contented family man daydreaming at work. They said things such as:

"This is John and he is an engineer, doing quite well at work. Right now he's taking a short break because he's had a hard day; and daydreaming, daydreaming about his family. Soon his day will be done and he'll be home with his wife and kids."

"This man is getting satisfaction that he is able to support his wife and kids."

The lonely career-oriented male provider. Thirty-five percent of the boys told stories that fell within the second thematic category. They viewed the depicted character as a father fulfilling the requisite career-oriented male provider role, a role they saw as leading to autonomy but also to temporary separation from family. They offered the following narratives:

"He's on a business trip, and so he's missing his family. . . . He has to be apart from them."

"He had to work overtime, quite late to make more money, so he's missing his family."

"The architect is looking at the picture of his family . . . worrying about making enough money to support his two children and help them through college."

The alienated breadwinner. Those subjects whose stories were in the third category—about 24 percent of the boys—saw a father who by fulfilling his role as a breadwinner had become alienated from friends and family. Unlike boys from the group directly above, these boys were explicit about the unhappy aspect of having to fulfill this role. For instance:

"A man at work . . . looking at a picture of his family. He misses them terribly because work is taking up all his time. His wife wants more attention. . . . He wants to spend more time with the kids, but he can't. He is feeling depressed and can't get it off his mind . . . maybe he'll try to ask for time off . . . he's not completely hopeless."

"He loves his family very much but has to work to support them . . . therefore doesn't spend enough time with them . . . feels guilty."

The loser. About 21 percent of the boys described a father who had suffered some loss—a death in the family or a similar tragedy—or who was somehow cut off from his family through divorce or otherwise. Most of these boys portrayed the father as feeling vulnerable, as seeking reconciliation and reconnection. Listen, for example, to this story:

"He's looking at his family's picture at work . . . he feels very lonely. Maybe they were killed or he was divorced. He wants his family back. Maybe he will try to save them or rescue them."

"He worked too much and the judge took away his family. He's very sad. He wishes he had a second chance. He'll try to get his family back."

"Alan is staring at the picture thinking how lucky he had once been, having a family. Because he was away at work, the mother was driving while drunk and she and the kids were all killed. He's overwhelmed with grief and wishes he had his family back."

The permanently separated man. Finally, some of the boys we interviewed—about 5 percent—told a tale of a father who, beyond his control, had become permanently separated from his family. In some cases the boys told the story in a neutral way, while in other instances—for example the story of twelve-year-old Jamie—they linked it to deep feelings of pain and longing:

"Bill is staring at a picture of his family who had to leave him. He is writing them a letter telling them how much he misses them, yearns to be with them again, expressing all his feelings. He says, 'I hope we can meet again, live together again, so I can show you all my love.' "

"Harry is looking at the people whom he loved. They have died and he is agonizing over what he could have done to save them. He wants to move on; but he can't. He will probably need to see a doctor for his problems."

"The feeling I get is that this man is lost, is far away from his family. . . . He's in some kind of pain . . . maybe regretting the loss of the custody of his children."

With the limited exception of those in the first category, most of these boys appeared to be telling stories related to separation, isolation, and loneliness. I believe that these boys are reporting how they themselves feel and how they view their fathers and other male figures in their lives. They are also describing memories of how they felt when they were prematurely disconnected from their mothers and early caretakers; they are expressing the longings they may still feel, as adolescents, about the difficulty of maintaining close relationships with parents and other close relatives—

longings for connection they suppress to conform with society's code of masculinity; and that they are telling us, indirectly, "I am afraid . . . I'm not ready to become a man and go to work . . . I am not ready to be cut off from my friends and family."

How Boys View Themselves

These feelings of anxiety and these hidden yearnings for connection—and the deep sense of loss and loneliness that goes with them—also became evident when we analyzed the boys' responses to the second picture we gave them to consider. This second picture is an actual photograph of a young blond-haired boy, sitting by himself at the threshold of an open doorway of an old wooden house. The sun casts generous light upon the boy and the front of the house, but a dark shadow covers whatever is beyond the open door inside the house. The boy is perched alone at the edge of the door, his elbows on his knees, his chin cupped in both hands. His expression is difficult to interpret—he appears to be concentrating, or perhaps the sun is just causing him to squint a bit.

In interpreting this second picture, adolescent boys again told stories that fell into five major thematic categories. While the first two categories were neutral, focused on developmental themes that did not involve particularly positive or negative emotions, the three other categories—like most of those related to the first image—emphasized a sense of intense loss.

A boy in transition. Boys who told stories that fell into the first category—about 13 percent—struck up themes of transition. They recounted things such as:

"A boy who is about to move from one place to another."

"This boy is captured by the photographer while he is waiting to go somewhere."

"He's waiting for someone."

A contemplative boy. About 27 percent of the boys told stories in this second category that involved themes of contemplation. The boys reported that:

"A small boy is sitting on a stoop, thinking about something . . . mulling over a serious matter in his head."

"This is a boy who is thinking very hard . . . he's sitting and sorting out his thoughts."

"[He] just wants to sit and think in the shade."

An abandoned boy. Boys whose stories fell into the third category emphasized abandonment—24 percent of the boys questioned explored these themes. For instance:

"This boy has been left alone, and is waiting for his loved ones to return."

"Arnie is a very young child sitting alone and abandoned in a doorway, starving. . . . His parents abandoned him. . . . His only wants are food and love. Will he die alone on the street?"

"His parents skipped town and left him behind. . . . He'll end up in foster homes."

"A little boy, lost and abandoned. His family lacked money so they abandoned him. He is scared and lonely. He wants someone to love and care for him. He might get adopted."

"The boy is sitting depressed and disappointed. . . . He just pitched a no-hitter and his dad wasn't there to see him. All the other guys' dads seemed to be there. . . . Dad will apologize but nothing will change."

"Missing his mother, crying for her."

The isolated boy. The fourth category involved stories of isolation—19 percent of our subjects.

"It's a boy . . . alone and sad."

"A young boy sitting by himself . . . a sense of loneliness . . . very serious."

"This boy is lonely . . . no friends to be with."

"He's crying and sad, by himself."

The boy as victim. Boys in the final category saw the boy depicted as a victim, and about 17 percent interpreted the picture this way:

"A boy whose father has been correcting him over and over. The boy isn't liking his father."

"This boy was accused of doing something wrong and his father took off his belt and hit him numerous times and he will be emotionally scarred for life."

"The dad is drunk and beating him and his mom."

"This is a boy who has been beat and neglected . . . has no mother and no one to comfort him . . . he'll avoid people now."

"John was just abused and ran away to this cabin to avoid the abuser. He's very depressed. . . . Suicide is going through his mind."

As these anecdotes suggest, for many adolescent boys, making the passage from boyhood to manhood is fraught with profound feelings of inner pain. A boy contemplates his fate all alone. He's restless; he's lonely. He feels abandoned, perhaps stranded by his parents. He is frightened; and he fears he may be injured unjustly or be prone to depression or suicidal feelings. These are the voices of our boys, terribly afraid about becoming men.

My research results do not stand alone. For instance in a national survey of teenagers for the Horatio Alger Association in 1996, many more girls than boys were able to imagine that happiness is what they wanted most from life (32 percent of girls but only 23 percent of boys), and when asked about future plans, 67 percent of the girls expected to attend a four-year college compared with only 54 percent of the boys. As fifteen-year-old Calvin told us in Chapter 2, society's expectations of adolescent boys are not just based on a double standard, they are often inhumane: "I guess it's hard being a guy because there are so many things that a *normal* person would do, that you are not allowed or expected to do." Or to borrow the phrase one Native American tribe uses to characterize its own manhood initiation rites, for many boys adolescence is the Big Impossible.

CONNECTION CAN OVERCOME THE PROBLEMS OF THE SECOND TRAUMA, JUST AS IT CAN THE FIRST

I have found that what boys need most to conquer the Big Impossible—to survive the peer pressure, gender straitjacketing, and the other tribulations of adolescence—is knowing that they have meaningful connections not only with their friends but also with their parents and other family members. Although we are often taught that adolescents—especially male adolescents—need or want to separate from their families, this is another dangerous myth about boys. Certainly adolescents are struggling with issues of identity and growth and will push at us, even push away from us, at times. Certainly they wish to spend some time away from home and develop an individual sense of self. But our sons rarely wish to cut their ties, be on their own, or to separate from us. In fact, most of our boys desperately need their parents, the family, and the extended family—coaches, teachers, ministers, rabbis—to be there for them, stand firm yet show flexibility, and form a living wall of love that they can lean on and bounce off. It's not separation but rather individuation that they want. It's becoming a more mature self in the context of loving relationships—stretching the psychological umbilical cord rather than severing it—that healthy male adolescence is all about.

My research shows that our boys know this only too well. Seth, in describing how he copes with the separation pain many boys experience, replied buoyantly:

"I think . . . [it's] just the *closeness* of my family. The way my parents have brought me up to want to be part of the family. I love going home and spending time with my mom or my dad."

"I'd have no problem going and spending the whole weekend with my family [rather] than going to spend the weekend with my friends," Seth explained. "Sometimes I'd rather be with my family. When I'm with my friends, sometimes I'd say I'd rather be home."

For the adolescent boy, knowing that he has a loving home and that he can tap into the strength derived from positive family relationships is truly key to making it through adolescence. In my research, again and again, boys refer to the importance of family. I firmly believe that it's the potency of family connection that guards our adolescent boys from emotional harm and gives them the most reassurance in the adolescent world of cool.

Other psychologists, too, have corroborated the central role of family connections during adolescence. Feldman and Wentzel, from Stanford University found that the perception boys have of their parents' marital satisfaction directly affected their social adjustment during adolescence. Blake Bowden of the Cincinnati Children's Hospital found that adolescents who shared dinners with their families five times a week were least likely to use drugs or be depressed, and most likely to excel at school and have a healthy social life. Likewise, the recent National Longitudinal Study on Adolescent Health found that what affected adolescent behaviors most were social contexts, especially the family. According to the study, "parent-family connectedness" dramatically influences the level of emotional distress adolescents suffer, how much they abuse drugs and alcohol and, even, to some extent, how involved in violence they become. The study also showed other important factors that affect these behaviors, such as whether an adolescent's parents are present during key periods of the day or whether the child's parents have high or low expectations of his or her academic performance. But these factors paled in significance to the "connection factor." Such connection, according to the study, involves "closeness to mother and/or father, and a sense of caring from them, as well as feeling loved and wanted by family members."

As we discussed in the prior two chapters on mothers and fathers, it is not a matter of being a moral policeman or warden, but rather of offering a boy succor from a world that's rough and creating a niche where he may express his most vulnerable and warm feelings in the open, without fear of ridicule.

ROLE MODELS: REAL HEROES FOR BOYS

For any parent or other family member who doubts the kind of positive influence he or she can have on the adolescent boy it's important to investigate exactly whom our boys say they look up to, who they claim their heroes really are. Despite the prevalent myth that boys' heroes are distant Olympian figures such as sports stars, astronauts, and the muscle-bound stars of action movies, my research reflects that, in reality, most teenage boys find heroes closer to home: brothers, sisters, mothers, fathers. In families with less traditional structures—such as in single-parent families or in families with parents who have separated or divorced—boys often find these heroes in extended family members, such as aunts, uncles, and grandparents. These findings are buttressed by data from other research, such as the Horatio Alger Study I cited earlier, which reports not only that the majority of teen boys respect their parents, but that over 10 percent of them saw their parents as heroes.

Listen to the voices of the boys from our study when asked whom they emulate or see as a hero, and why. Curtis, a sixteen-year-old raised almost exclusively by his divorced mother, named her as his foremost model and inspiration:

"My mom is everything to me. She's sacrificed so much so that I can go to good schools. She got me into art, which is what keeps me going, and what I hope will be my profession someday. She's opened a lot of doors for me. All the opportunities I have now are because of her."

Michael spoke of the male–male mentor bond he felt with his brother:

"Who is my hero? My brother—*definitely* my brother. He is older so I always looked up to him. I try to emulate what he does in my life. There is no doubt in my mind when he came to Hillside School that I was going to come to Hillside School. I still talk to him more than my parents do. He's at college and I call him more, he tells me more stuff. We're best friends and I've always looked up to him. He has really been my role model."

Harry was grateful to his mother:

"Well my mother did everything. She put me in baseball. She took me everywhere. She worked all the time, but she did everything you could ask for—she was always around."

But for some of the boys in my study, moms or dads were around somewhat less, and the earlier family generation became the models to emulate, the heroes of the next generation. As one boy explained when I inquired who his hero was:

"[W]hen my father wasn't around . . . [my grandfather] was the one who taught me how to pitch—he was . . . my father figure and I look up to him, like, even to this day. He is definitely my mentor . . . he's just like a great guy."

Another adolescent boy reports, "I adore my grandparents—they mean the world to me. I spend as much time as I can with them. I admire my grandfather . . . as well as my grandmother. I admire them for completely different qualities. My grandfather was a police officer. He is just like a brilliant man. He reads all the time. He is always cracking jokes just to lighten the situation up. He is a complete people person and everyone seems to love him. He never seems to get on anyone's bad side or anything like that. He always used to take me to the park and play baseball with me and stuff like that. When I was having trouble in Little League he helped me out there and when I was having trouble in school he helped me there too."

"My grandmother," he explained, "is completely different. She is extremely smart. She reads all the time too but she is always forcing me to read. She would always read books to me when I was really young—all types of novels. My grandmother is an amazing cook. Anytime I go down there, they feed me like six or seven times a day." And we can be certain that the sustenance this boy derived was more than culinary.

As the statements of these boys attest, adolescent boys look for role models close to home. By and large, they feel tremendous admiration for the mentors in their family, and more than any other category of people, they see these relatives as their heroes and heroines.

So for any parent or other family members who wonder how much of an impact they can have on their quickly developing son, much comfort should be derived from the fact that they—and not somebody else—are the ones these boys look to most for guidance, love, and support. As volatile as adolescence can be and as frustrating as it may be at times for the parents of sons working their way through this trying period, I believe it is very important for parents to stay attuned to the voices of their adolescent boys and seek as many opportunities as possible to share the potency of connection. When parents do so, they lay the groundwork for a more meaningful relationship with their boys, one that later, when their sons have grown into men, is likely to flourish with a new kind of honesty and a new kind of closeness.

WHAT PARENTS AND FAMILIES CAN DO

When parents ask me how to do this—how to build strong, dynamic, quality connections with their adolescent sons—I stress several things:

Discuss the complexities of adolescence honestly. Though it's normal to want to avoid the complex feelings that arise between boys and adults during the boys' adolescence, do your best to acknowledge these feelings openly. Be honest about not only the confused feelings you think the boy may be experiencing but also about your own mixed-up feelings. For example, if you feel a rush of jealousy when your son is heading off for the prom-night dinner, say to him: "You're not going to believe this, but part of me wishes I was young again and heading off to dinner with you." Or if your son seems to be constantly on the run and you miss spending close times with him, tell him you'd like to respect his need to become more independent but that, yes, you've been missing him lately. There's a big difference between a parent who is trying to control or manipulate the adolescent boy and the parent who's being honest about wanting to reconnect with him. No matter how tough and independent he may act on the outside, you can rest assured that your boy, even as he develops into a man, will greatly appreciate hearing that you want to spend time with him. As you and he learn to balance your respective needs to remain interdependent, his years as an adolescent will become easier for both of you.

Make regular "dates" with your son. While parents often spend a lot of time playing with their sons when they're young boys, many parents forget to find time for such parent-child play when these boys grow older. During adolescence, it's particularly important to make regular "dates" with your son to share in such family activities. Whether it's going out for ice cream, playing a sport together, or just hanging out in the den to watch a favorite television show, spending regular recreational time with your sons creates important opportunities for deeper kinds of sharing and connecting. As we've already discussed, many boys open up emotionally and relate best when they're given the opportunity to *do* something with somebody they love. While it's important to respect your son's need for time on his own (and allow him the time he needs to fulfill his other interests and obligations), be sure to seek him out for shared activities on a regular basis.

Don't wait to talk to him about sex, drugs, or other tricky topics. As we've seen, ignoring tough issues like sex and sexuality, AIDS, drugs, depression, and suicide simply does not help these issues go away for us or our sons. In fact, ignoring them may actually make a boy feel greater shame and be more likely to make unwise decisions. So don't lose any time. As soon as you think he's mature enough (and this age will vary), try to find the right place and moment, make sure it's OK with your son, and then plunge right in! Speak openly to your son about what you know—and don't know—about the perils and challenges of adolescence. Offer to explain anything he's curious about.

If you feel embarrassed or afraid to talk about these issues, tell him so. Your honesty about your own hesitation will make him feel more comfortable talking to you as well. If you don't feel up to handling the talk on your own, do it as a team with your spouse, or have a family meeting with the boy's other siblings (if he has any), or consider getting together with close friends or neighbors to discuss these kinds of topics as a group.

Of course, for both you and the boy, it's never easy to broach subjects like teenage sex or drug use. You're both bound to feel torn about how much to say and to experience moments of shyness or embarrassment. But in the end, resolving and moving beyond these inhibiting feelings is far easier than coping with a boy who's made an inappropriate or even deadly decision because he didn't have somebody he could talk to ahead of time. Setting a good example goes a long way toward instilling your values in the boy. But creating ample opportunities for him to talk with you, ask you a lot of questions, and share his concerns openly is what is most likely to help your son learn and respect the values you'd like to impart to him.

Provide frequent affirmations. As often as possible, try to find opportunities to tell your son that you love him and to emphasize for him, in specific terms, all the things you treasure about him. Be sensitive to the shame he may feel inside himself. Even a boy who acts confident and self-assured on the surface feels vulnerable and needs to hear affirmations from his parents. As we've already seen, many times a boy's external armor of bravado and machismo may be hiding profound feelings of insecurity, loneliness, and low self-esteem. One of the most effective ways to help a boy conquer these demons is to tell him in the most genuine and explicit way all the things we cherish about him.

An important aspect of this process of affirmation has to do with the boy's nascent sense of his identity as a man. Our boys yearn to have us provide clear balanced expectations about masculinity and to say supportive things that will help them build their confidence as they grow toward manhood. As your adolescent son begins to experiment with the behaviors he thinks we see as "masculine" and "manly," stress how great you think he's doing rather than conveying any messages that will make him feel confused or ashamed. So, for example, tell him how good you think he looks (even if that early mustache is a bit fuzzy), compliment him on his personal accomplishments (whether they're in typically male or female domains), and support him as he begins to get involved in dating. By contrast, it's best that you don't do things such as tease him when he brings home a date, harass him about how quiet and cool he sometimes acts in the presence of his peers, or harangue him for acting so macho, or for being an insensitive guy. Likewise, ideally you should not bulldoze him into playing a sport when he doesn't want to, tell him he smells funny when he splashes on Dad's cologne, or tell him to "get a grip" on himself when he comes home in tears one day. These kinds of mixed messages—some exhorting him to fulfill the new ideal of manliness, some pushing him to fulfill conventional ideas about masculinity, and some mocking his valiant attempts to make sense of everything—make it difficult for a boy to forge his own healthy, balanced sense of masculinity.

Show that you understand the adolescent crucible. It's helpful to let your son know that you, as a fellow survivor of adolescence, understand just how rough the adolescent crucible can be. If you don't feel in touch with what the contemporary adolescent experience is all about, it's important to inform yourself as promptly and completely as possible. People who advocate teaching boys to "just say no," or "to agree never to fight" are largely ineffectual because these simplistic directives don't recognize what boys actually experience in the peer-governed world. Ideally you should try to learn what it takes for today's boy to be considered cool, to belong to the central teen social circle, and to avoid being branded a wimp. To protect your boy, you must strive to become empathic to what this adolescent world is all about.

Boys benefit enormously when you show that you appreciate how hard it is to be a boy dealing with peer pressure, society's expectations, and the other challenges of adolescence. So long as you do not "lecture" in a condescending way or exude the kind of pity or sarcasm that will only further shame our boys, often you can best communicate your love and understanding by telling "war stories" from your own adolescence. Sharing your own vulnerabilities as an adult helps the adolescent boy feel that he's not alone, that what he's feeling is normal. It also frequently enables the boy to begin to share his own experience. "But what I'm going through is *different,*" he may begin, and then launch into the kind of open sharing of feelings that is so critical to his happiness and well-being.

Listen empathically. When your boy begins to express what he's experiencing, try to listen carefully and empathically and not interrupt. Once the boy finds the courage to take off his mask and expose his vulnerable feelings, what he needs most is a patient, nonjudgmental, fully attentive listener. While you may feel very tempted to jump right in with advice or to try to "cheer up" the boy, simply try to listen and let the boy know that you sincerely appreciate what he's going through. This helps to make sure that he doesn't just retreat behind the mask and hide painful feelings—including those that might amount to depression—we really should know about. Often by asking further questions about what he's going through, or by simply inquiring "How can I help make things go better?" the boy himself will suggest ways to improve his situation.

Make your home a safe place. Finally, do your best to make family and home an asylum from peer culture and society's ambivalent demands about how to become a man. By remaining available at an optimal distance, moving in or out as the situation demands, you can create *a safe place* in which your boy, protected from shame and ridicule, can explore genuine emotion and vulnerability. Sometimes the sagest advice is that of the late Chaim Ginott: "Don't just do something. Stand there!" Ideally, you will provide for the boy what I call a "revolving door." Don't pester, prod, or cling to him when he's not ready for interaction, but let him know that when the time's right for him, he's welcome to come through the door for a time of closeness. If as he grows you are able to cede control to your adolescent son in this way—allowing him to choose when and how much parent-son relating takes place—you will enable the boy to individuate at his own pace. While it may sometimes feel like an emotional roller coaster, letting your son push and pull, hold on and let go, and seek connection and then retreat is far more effective than striking up a detached laissez faire attitude that communicates a lack of interest in connection or putting your own needs for closeness and companionship ahead of those of a young man striving to become his own person in his own way. So make home a haven for real boys where both you and your sons can enjoy the chance adolescence offers for growth, renewal, and connection. For I believe that by doing so, you're creating the solid foundation for a new kind of closeness that can take shape when your boy becomes a man.

THE WORLD OF BOYS

AND THEIR FRIENDSHIPS

*"I tell him everything. Good things that happen. Bad things
that happen. Everything. It's important to have
someone to talk things over with."*
—*Shawn, age seventeen, referring to his best friend, John*

PUNCTURING THE MYTH OF THE BOY LONER

Because our society is haunted by gender stereotyped ideas about the mythic image of boys and men as stoic loners who thrive on solitude, we tend to misunderstand and greatly undervalue boys' friendships. Psychologists have often failed to see the significant ways in which boys express their yearnings for human closeness and connection. They have underestimated the degree to which boys rely on their closest male and female friends to survive. My research shows that, perhaps beyond what we have ever realized, close friendships are of paramount importance to boys.

Part of the reason we do not fully appreciate the richness and prevalence of boys' friendships is that at first glance, they may not appear as emotionally deep and meaningful as girls' relationships. However, upon a closer look it is clear that boys have friendships of tremendous depth and intensity. Boys' friendships are simply governed by different rules and expressed differently than girls' friendships.

To fully appreciate male friendships, we must put aside traditionally female standards of intimacy and attachment. In doing so, we may be surprised by what the psychiatrist Harry Stack Sullivan termed "chumships"— that is, boys' particular sense of camaraderie and love. For instance, in public—and especially under the watchful eyes of their peers—boys often use action-oriented behavior to express their connection to other boys. They may race each other, climb a tree together, or play against one another in tennis. Such behavior can be seen as "doing together" or caring through action. In these settings, boys generally forgo the kind of quiet one-on-one verbal sharing that we typically associate with girls. Boys do share intimate moments of relating, but they tend to do so privately, away from the group, where such exchanges might expose them to shame or embarrassment.

Furthermore, my research shows that in addition to their same-gender friendships, most boys develop healthy, positive, and deep relationships with girls. This finding undermines the myth that young preadolescent boys are always "less mature" than girls their age and that, because their play styles are different, boys and girls are unable to form important connections with one another. It also debunks the myths that adolescent boys are inept at or uninterested in friendship with girls and that boys this age impart love, affection, and empathy only in the context of sexual conquest. My research reveals that not only are boys capable of forming important platonic friendships with girls, but they are eager to do so and count on these friendships for emotional support and enhancement of their self-esteem.

LEAN ON ME: BOYS HELPING OUT BOYS

Seventeen-year-old Shawn's face softens when I ask him about his friends. "My friends really help me get through," he says gently. As an African American boy living in a predominantly white town, Shawn has had to face prejudice and ignorance. Small in stature, he has encountered a great deal of teasing from other boys.

"It's been easier for me the past two years," Shawn explains, "because now I have a group of friends who know me for who I am and accept me. I don't really need to change the way I act to conform."

Shawn is particularly grateful for his best friend, John, whom he's known since fifth grade. Shawn and John talk every night on the phone. "I tell him everything. Good things that happen. Bad things that happen. Everything. It's important to have someone to talk things over with."

Yet Shawn also expressed appreciation for John's ability—the result of years of close companionship—to communicate without words. "He knows everything about me. I mean it's amazing. He knows more about me than I do. I don't even have to tell him things. It's funny like, even though we can be doing separate things, when we're together it's like we've always been together."

Shawn and John have shared a full range of experiences—good times and bad. Shawn knows that John will always be there for him, no matter what. In fact, he credits John with saving his life. "We were just thirteen or fourteen and boasting to these older guys about how much we could drink. We had some beers and I got really, really drunk and sick. I passed out, threw up all over everything and John took care of me. He put me on his back and carried me home. He took me to his house and put me in his bed. That was a huge thing. I mean, he saved me basically. I was really struggling that night. If I'd been left to myself among those older kids—who we didn't know very well—who knows what would have happened? I could have died."

John is clearly central to Shawn's life. John is Shawn's confidant, his best companion, and even, at times, his protector. Shawn trusts him with his life. Perhaps what is most striking about Shawn's story is that it is *not* atypical for boys today. Nearly all the boys I interviewed in my "Listening to Boys' Voices" project spoke of one or more friends to whom they felt extremely close. They readily described these friends as individuals who support them, care for them, and understand them in ways no one else does.

Boys yearn for friendship with other boys. In our research interviews, when we asked, "Based on your experience growing up as a 'guy,' what advice would you give to younger boys?" Invariably the answers centered on friendship:

"Make some close friends early . . . because people toss things around about you, and if you have a good friend they won't listen to that kind of thing. The friendships you have may be small in number but it's the strength of the friendship that counts."

"When you're younger, try to stay friends with different groups of kids. I think it's really helped me getting through . . . finding out what people are really like, not labeling."

"Don't get caught up with the wrong people. Respect your friends, they're what there is to fall back on. If you lose them you pretty much lose everything." These boy-boy bonds follow a code of fairness and behavior all their own. Our study showed that implicit in this code are rules for being a friend, such as "Keep your cool," "Don't get bent out of shape," and "Stand up for your buddies."

Seventeen-year-old Michael described how his best friend helped him get through the darkest days of being a teenager. He met Chris five years ago, when they started attending the same school. "It was the first dance of seventh grade. I was standing around, like, 'Oh my God, girls everywhere.' I had led a sheltered life so far. All the girls were on one side, the boys on another—you know how it is at younger kids' dances. Chris was actually over on the girls' side. He was one of two or three boys mingling with the girls and I was like "Wow, I should get some pointers.' " So, Michael struck up a friendship with this savvy boy, hoping to learn how to be more sociable.

Though the friendship started on a utilitarian note, it has withstood personal trials and the test of time. Last year, when Michael struggled with a bout of "the blues," Chris was supportive. He listened without shaming Michael. "Chris has been the person I've always been able to confide in and he has always been able to help me out. He's been there for me. I know I can trust him." Lately, Michael has felt unable to confide in his parents and finds he relies all the more on Chris's support. "I don't tell them as much because they tend to treat me as if I'm younger than I am. They want to protect me all the time. They wouldn't be able to understand why I was feeling sad and it would just bum them out."

Michael feels that his friendship with Chris helps safeguard him from further bouts of sadness. "If something really bad happens, then you're bound to feel bad, but you have a sort of *safety net* with your friends which stops the initial cycle from starting up and you getting too down on yourself."

The bond between Chris and Shawn illustrates how boys often cherish and value their friendships. My research shows that boys rely heavily on friends to make it through their emotional ups and downs. Contrary to the image of the reclusive antisocial macho man, most boys have a few good friends they can lean on.

GENDER STRAITJACKETING AND HOMOPHOBIA

Our culture underestimates boys' friendships primarily because we tend to underestimate *all* the emotional needs and abilities of our boys. As we've already discussed, even very young boys are shamed for showing any signs of neediness, dependence, sadness, or vulnerability. According to the old Boy Code, we expect our boys to be little men: tough, independent, autonomous creatures. We restrict how much affection they show one another. Society teaches us that boys—and men—are less in need of friends, close personal bonds, or connections. Furthermore, society often views open displays of empathy and affection from boys as somehow inappropriate.

One boy, Matt, told us he went through a depression last year but felt unable to seek help because of these unwritten rules of masculinity:

"It's hard being a guy because you're expected not to really talk about your feelings. You're supposed to deal with everything yourself. Girls are expected to go off and talk to someone. Guys aren't really allowed to do that." Matt was able to talk to his best friend, Jim, and found relief in doing that, but he never revealed his sadness to his parents or to any other friends. He spoke to Jim only in private, out of earshot of his parents or others.

Boys, early on, are taught to limit the ways they seek out and express friendship. They're encouraged not to talk about problems, especially problems that expose their feelings of worry, doubt, or sadness. In fact, they're discouraged from talking about anything too serious, for fear of being seen as weak, vulnerable, or needy—in short, as not being a "man." As twelve-year-old Alan explains: "I'll talk to Kevin about what's up with me, but only like on the weekends away from school. If we talked about that kind of thing at school, people would say we're acting like girls." Or as fourteen-year-old Scott offered: "They'll say you're a wuss if you're a guy and start talking all mushy like you're on *Oprah* or something." Peter Egan, writer for the teen TV show *Sweet Valley High,* agrees. He says that on his show few scenes show boys engaging in conversation on emotional topics. Egan continues: "It just wouldn't be true. Boys just don't act like that. Boys know that if they say anything sappy to each other they'll be humiliated and called a fag."

Indeed it's this very fear—the fear of being labeled a fairy, a wuss, or a fag, of being perceived as feminine or homosexual—that often prevents boys from feeling comfortable engaging in serious emotional talks with each other. It too often inhibits boys from ever saying they care for each other. It often prevents them from expressing physical affection for other boys. It allows adults to put a low premium on the kind of tender, loving friendships among boys that, with few exceptions, we encourage among girls.

I was recently privy to one sad episode in the lives of two third-graders. The incident illustrates how open displays of affection among boys are often misperceived. Tommy and Charlie became fast friends during the summer after third grade. When they discovered that they were going to be in the same class together in the fall, they eagerly anticipated the start of school.

On the first day, their new teacher, Mrs. Hutchins, asked the students to copy a homework assignment and begin math problems. As the class settled down, Charlie walked in late. Before Charlie could take his seat, Tommy spotted his buddy in the doorway. Tommy excitedly flung himself across the room and gave Charlie a heartfelt hug. Mrs. Hutchins turned around to find the two of them, as she saw it, "struggling and fighting" in front of the entire class. Aghast, she sent them both directly to the principal's office.

"We weren't fighting," the boys explained to Mr. Atkins, the principal. "We were just hugging."

To demonstrate, Charlie planted a kiss on Tommy's head and added, "We're best friends. We like each other."

Mr. Atkins was not impressed. "I guess Mrs. Hutchins was confused in thinking you were fighting. But such sexualized behavior is inappropriate in the classroom. I'm sending you back to class now, but I want you to take these letters home for your parents to sign."

Mr. and Mrs. Simmons, Charlie's parents, later told me they were quite baffled when they received the letter. "What do they mean, Charlie, that you were sexually inappropriate in class? What exactly happened?"

"I just hugged Tommy."

"That's not a problem," Charlie's parents said.

The next morning, Mrs. Simmons found herself sitting in Mr. Atkins's office. "This is the kind of affectionate behavior we love in our son. Why are you punishing him for it?"

"As you will see in the pupils' manual, inappropriate touching and sexual expression are explicitly forbidden," said the principal.

"So you mean that if two girls in the fourth grade were working closely together on a project and one hugs the other, Mrs. Hutchins would be afraid of violence and you would send them home for sexual activity?"

Mr. Atkins's eyes widened and he hesitated. "We would have to evaluate the circumstances of the specific situation," he finally said.

Mrs. Simmons left, hoping the principal would rethink his stance. But she was saddened, too, wondering if she should counsel her son about limiting his displays of affection for Tommy at school to avoid further trouble.

Unfortunately, Mr. Atkins's assumption that the boys' friendship was sexually inappropriate is hardly unusual. The gender straitjacket, combined with the absurd link that is often made between boyhood affection and adult male homosexuality, creates a restrictive environment. Boys are frequently pushed away from one another when they exude even a modicum of overt genuine love or affection for one another. This misguided perception—a form of homophobia—is perhaps most regrettable because it may lead us to undermine boys' friendships before they've even taken hold. Ironically, this may, in turn, cause us to doubt whether boys are capable of intimate friendship. And as we've seen in Chapter 7, it pushes some boys to turn to drugs and alcohol, substances that temporarily mute the shame they feel about their genuine longings for friendship, love, and affection.

Is it any wonder that a society that fails to celebrate boys' friendships breeds men who fail as "friends" in their adult relationships with women? If we separate and shame young boys who show such affection for one another, how can we fault men for being incapable of showing nonsexual affection to their female partners? Similarly, why do we fault men for their inability to empathize with women while we discourage boys from embracing friends in need? The answers to these questions have to do with our gender stereotypes and the shame we heap on boys who rebel against them. I have long felt that a boy able to express his emotions in an open way, far from being a wimp or a sissy, is a *hero* engaged in a true act of courage. Ideally, this kind of uninhibited love and caring between boys would not be seen as unusual, much less courageous. Ideally, it would just be part of every "real boy," and something we'd celebrate in him.

BOYS' PLAY STYLES

On a recent trip to an elementary school playground, I watched as most of the boys engaged in a rowdy game of kickball. At the plate was a small, nervous-looking boy named Brian. From the outfield a larger boy jeered, "Hey, Brian, Brian, Brian. Hey, Brian, why you tryin'." The outfielder grinned at his own cleverness, then started in again, "We got you beat. You can't take the heat." Soon the other boys on his team chimed in. The budding rapper in the outfield was clearly delighted with himself until one of Brian's teammates yelled, "Hey Cruisey, Shuuut uuuup."

When Brian kicked a short, foul ball, Cruisey and his buddies went wild with derogatory yells.

The girls were playing very differently. On the play-gym, four girls raced up the ladder and flew down the slide, usually in pairs, holding one another tightly and shrieking in unison. A second group of three played near the building. One girl demonstrated a dance in earnest: her hands waving in the air, her feet tapping, and her head thrown back dramatically, a schoolyard rumba queen. "OK, you try," she said to the others as she finished. The other two imitated her steps, with a lot of giggles and much less conviction. The dancer clapped and laughed, "Great!" Soon they were all tapping and twirling together.

These scenes are reenacted in playgrounds across the country. Researchers examining play in elementary school children find consistent patterns. Boys and girls cluster in same-sex groups. The play within these groups differs considerably. Boys tend to engage in active, competitive games. Girls, on the other hand, tend to play cooperatively in smaller groups. Boys enjoy structured games, with set rules and procedures. Taunting, boasting, and jousting with one another is part of the fun. Boys argue often during games, but their arguments seldom end the game. When they can't agree, they resort to the rule book or just repeat the play. They seem to value the rules and procedures that govern the game and make it fair for all participants. They learn, as one teacher told us, "to argue and hold no grudges." In other words, boys seem to be good at "agreeing to disagree." Their friendships are resilient, surviving even the roughest play and disagreements.

Boys' games tend to be competitive and inclusive. Their play creates an open arena in which each tests his skills against the others. This competitive attitude pervades other parts of boys' lives. As one junior at an all-boys school told us, "Competition among guys is all over the place, whether in the classroom or athletic field. You see this kind of jockeying for position. Who is better than whom? Who's the best-looking? Who is numero uno? No matter what you do, you're always going to be competing with another guy for something."

This spirit of competition, however, is generally less about one boy triumphing over another and more about engaging in a mutual challenge. Sweating, side by side, boys—as we'll see in Chapter 11—struggle to achieve their personal best. Competition among boys is more about competing *with* another boy than competing *against* him. Boys seem to enjoy asserting themselves with other boys. Boys like making their presence known and appreciated. They like feeling competent at the activities and tasks in which the other boys are participating. In fact, research shows that the men who remember feeling competent in play with other boys have higher self-esteem as adults. Conversely, men who suffer from low self-esteem often recall having felt left out of friendships with other boys when they were growing up, not feeling cared for or loved by other boys, or feeling as though they had failed at boys' competitive play. Donnie, one of the younger participants in our study, put it his way: "I guess what makes the friendship is the fact that we both share common interests in imagination and are both pretty smart, so we can have good talks . . . [But] . . . there is an element of competition with my best friend, being in the same school . . . it's *mild-mannered competition,* very mild."

Less obvious than the competitive and jousting quality of boys' play is the serious nature of the intimate bonds boys form while playing together. Many great friendships are born of shared experiences on the basketball court or on the Boy Scout sleepover. A quirky little movie set in a small Irish town, *War of the Buttons,* is wonderfully illustrative. In the film a group of boys divides into two warring camps. Their pseudo-battles are serious and protracted. When a boy has the misfortune of getting caught by an enemy, he loses his buttons, tie, and belt. Toward the end, the two team leaders, Jerome and Fergus, are left alone. As they sit together, Jerome asks Fergus, "Why were we fighting?" to which Fergus casually replies, "For the hell of it, of course." A raucous pillow fight ensues. The last scene is a still shot of Jerome with Fergus in a head hold, both boys roaring with laughter. The audience feels the boys' powerful connection. Male friendship can arise from the most unlikely circumstances. Amid battling, swearing, and conspiring against one another, the boys' respect and fondness for one another grew.

Girls' play usually centers more on talking and socializing within a small circle of friends. Girls' friendships solidify through shared confidences. Girls are more likely to discuss quietly than to yell and taunt. When a conflict does arise, girls often stop the game until the problem can be resolved to each player's satisfaction. Girls will generally talk it out before they consult the rule book. Their friends' feelings are of greater concern than continuing the game. Research shows that when girls are asked what makes them feel good about themselves, they tend to recall a time when they helped a friend. Overall, where boys care more about fairness and following and enforcing rules, girls worry more about their standing among friends. Girls are especially concerned with whether they are well liked and will be included in their friends' activities.

The comments of a friend's daughter who discussed her Beanie Baby club with me are telling. "We're starting this club for Beanie Babies. We like to collect them and trade them," says seven-year-old Jessie Streeter.

"It's going to be fun because we can do things together and get more Beanie Babies even though my parents won't buy me any more."

Jessie's twin sister, Allison, explained further. "We're figuring out the numbers. We have four members so far and we're trying to pick one more member without hurting anyone's feelings. We don't want it to be too big, because then it won't be as much fun."

"The whole process has been very complicated," their mother said. "Since they thought up the idea a few weeks ago, they've been on the phone every afternoon, planning activities, selecting dates, and going through an elaborate decision-making process about the other members."

"I wanted Sarah, and Ellie wanted Sarah, but Allison wanted Perry," says Jessie. "If we had Sarah, though, then Cynthia might have gotten mad, because Sarah and Cynthia are best friends. And if we had Perry, then Ellie and I would be mad, because we think Perry's too bossy."

Mrs. Streeter has been amused but also impressed by the process. "We've had some good conversations about including people, about compromise, and about people's feelings."

Like the Streeter twins and their friends, many girls are as comfortable talking about and negotiating the process of games as they are playing them. They seem to focus less on the outcome than on who gets to participate and on how that affects the other girls.

Of course, the play of boys and girls does not always fall into neat categories. We are all familiar with boys who shy away from rough-and-tumble play and girls who love getting revved up for a fierce game of basketball, soccer, hockey, or another competitive sport. There are plenty of girls with an ample sense of competition and plenty of boys who care immensely about being well liked and included in the central play group. Recognizing general gender differences in play styles is important, however, because these differences may contribute to our misconceptions about their friendships.

For when it comes to boys, it is often through their rowdy play that they build friendships. Underneath the rough-and-tumble games where boys are seeking to feel part of the action and striving for excellence in the company of their buddies, they are building relationships. Harry Stack Sullivan recognized the importance to boys of these close "chumships." He described boys' friendships as a form of "love." Through these "love" affairs, he said, boys are able to develop a more accurate self-image and a stronger sense of personal worth and enhanced self-esteem.

Intimacy for Boys and Intimacy for Girls

Integral to genuine friendships is intimacy. As we have seen, boys achieve significant intimacy in their relationships with other boys, although they often experience it differently than girls. Because of societal taboos that discourage open displays of caring between boys, their intimate connections get pushed underground. The intimacy occurs quietly, privately, almost invisibly. Researcher Scott Swain has defined men's style of intimacy as "covert intimacy," an intimacy that is expressed unobtrusively and silently.

When a boy's best friend is leaving town for the summer, he is more likely to offer a good-bye hug to his pal when no one else is around. When a quarterback makes a great pass to clinch the game, his teammates are more likely to give him a quick pat on the back or offer succinct words of praise such as "Great pass" or "Nice going" than to tell him how proud they are of him. To help us understand boys' brand of intimacy, Swain talks about "behavior in the context of a friendship that connotes a positive and mutual sense of meaning and importance to the participants." In other words, intimacy encompasses whatever behaviors make people feel close to one another.

It is important to support boys in experiencing these moments of connection with one another. I encourage parents to gently reinforce them. Fathers can tell stories about their own buddies. Mothers can share their own special friendships—with girls or with boys—from childhood. Parents can reinforce behavior by telling a boy, "That was really nice the way you complimented Bobby on his great pass" or "What a great idea to invite Hal over for dinner—he must be glad to have your friendship now that his dad's moved out." Without embarrassing him, we let him know that boy-boy bonding is valuable and that the intimacy he's able to achieve is not only appropriate, but commendable.

Boys Do Talk

One of the most surprising findings from my interviews was how much these allegedly nonverbal boys were talking. In fact, according to some of these boys, they rival their sisters in phone usage.

Guy told us he talks to Conor, his best friend, at least twice a day. "When I get home from school and before I go to sleep. And then in the morning, he picks me up for school and he calls me from the car before he gets here. Yeah, we talk a lot." These boys process everything with the intensity of any two girls. "We talk about everything: sports, girls, school, our parents. We're a lot alike so he can sort of look through my eyes in a situation."

Sixteen-year-old Ed says humor and conversation are what bind his friendship with Jamal. "We think exactly the same and we really make each other laugh a lot. I think that he's probably the funniest kid I know and he thinks I'm the funniest kid he knows. Talking to him is so easy. I know I can call him and talk to him about pretty much anything. Sometimes I just want to talk about nothing—just joke and laugh—and sometimes I have something I really need to ask him about: what should I do and what do you think about that? There are certain things that you don't want to talk about with just anybody and it's good to be able to talk to him."

Once again, however, there is a covert aspect to these conversations. Ed talks to Jamal about things he can't tell anyone else. Guy and Conor talk in the privacy of their homes. No one is aware of the extent to which these boys process their feelings together—except perhaps, the phone company and the parents who pay the phone bill.

At times some boys may expect different things from their conversations than girls do. In particular, they may express their natural empathy in a different manner. When boys are sad, they often expect a friend to try to talk to them and cheer them up. "I always have people around to cheer me up, so I don't get down that often. When things go wrong, I talk to my friends and get it off my chest," says fifteen-year-old Curtis.

As Shawn puts it, "When my friends are feeling down, I try to talk to them, bring their spirits up a bit because I know how much it helps me. There is nothing worse than feeling sad or frustrated and having no one to talk to."

Yet when boys are feeling down they don't always expect their friends to lend a sympathetic ear. Quite the opposite, boys sometimes tease and insult one another when emotions are running highest. When Paul was going through a hard time, he turned to Tim. "We usually end up dealing with our problems in a comical way," says Paul. "We always end up making light of it. It's easier to handle."

Jeremy tells how Brett goofs on him to cheer him up. "One day I was in a really bad mood. I had totaled my car that morning and I was an hour late. Brett was egging me on. Teasing me about stuff. It had nothing to do with the car. I took my shoes off and a moment later my shoes were gone.

I was getting pissed and I would go, 'Just give them to me.' But he kept it up and I finally ending up laughing and punching him."

Indeed boys may also expect contradiction from their close buddies. Contradiction may enhance their friend's capacity for perspective on emotionally charged issues. As Tony explained: "I think it's important [to talk]. . . . Oh, I think it's helpful because it's definitely good to see their perspective on things and it helps to know if they disagree . . . it kind of makes you want to rethink your decision, and that's very helpful."

Boys may avoid direct expressions of sympathy. The "Oh, you poor thing" approach is heard by some boys as condescending, as implying a deficiency in the boy in trouble. And, while it might be all right to admit a weakness to a very close friend, it's not something most shame-sensitive boys dwell on. Boys may far prefer a friend saying, "What a jerk," or "No way! That's ridiculous!" or "That sucks! Now, let's go play ball" to "How can I make you feel better?" or "How are you going to get through this?"

And when boys are confused or upset, they may prefer direct advice. Jeremy says he turns to Brett for advice when he has problems. "I can tell him anything because it's almost like he's going through it too. There are a lot of situations that I can talk to him about and he gives me an honest answer. I know in all seriousness that he would give me the best advice he could."

BIASES AND BLIND SPOTS: OTHER REASONS
WE DON'T VALUE BOYS' FRIENDSHIPS

As we saw earlier, our difficulty in valuing boys' friendships stems, in part, from unwitting biases and blind spots. Researchers of child behavior are certainly not immune to these influences. On the whole, many researchers have missed the importance of boys' relationships because they too have applied what they've known about girls' relationships or adult female friendships as a benchmark to understand relationships among boys. Unfortunately, when researchers misunderstand boys' behavior, we as a society are often led to adopt the same misguided viewpoints.

To get a sense of how highly sophisticated researchers distort our view of boys, let's consider the work of noted psychologist Eleanor Maccoby, who in one widely cited 1990 review study examines the differences in conversational style between boys and girls. In this study Maccoby concludes that a boy tends to use speech to serve egoistic functions, such as to establish and protect his turf. Among girls, she says, conversation is a more socially binding process, used to create feelings of connectedness rather than rivalry.

She labels boys' speech patterns as *restrictive,* a style that tends to derail an interaction. "Examples are threatening a partner, directly contradicting or interrupting, topping the partner's story, boasting or engaging in other forms of self-display," she writes. In contrast, she calls girls' speech patterns *enabling,* which means that, by "acknowledging another's comments or expressing agreement," girls tend to extend the conversation. She concludes: "I want to suggest that it is because women and girls use more enabling styles that they are able to form more intimate and more integrated relationships. Also I think it likely that it is the male concern for turf and dominance—that is, with not showing weakness to other men and boys—that underlies their restrictive interaction style and their lack of self-disclosure."

Clearly Maccoby's statements are based on broad assumptions. She says that the girls' enabling speech style keeps conversations going longer and therefore leads to greater intimacy. This view makes the assumptive leap that conversation equals intimacy. As we have seen, intimacy can arise from any shared activities that bring people closer together. Intimacy can be born of a "doing together" in which caring or empathy finds expression. Maccoby also assumes that behaviors such as "contradicting" or "topping the story" of the speaker will necessarily limit an interaction. However, for boys perhaps more accustomed to teasing, I believe that contradiction can in fact *prolong* a good-spirited argument. Topping another's story can be an invitation for continued storytelling.

Other researchers are equally quick to judge little girls as relational experts and little boys as lagging far behind. Deborah Tannen, author of *You Just Don't Understand,* asked second-grade girls and boys to talk about "something serious." The girls told stories about accidents and illnesses that have hurt people they care about. The boys, however, couldn't seem to settle down and bring themselves to do any "serious" talk. They ran around the room, telling scatological jokes, searching for games to play, for "something to do," and taunted or teased each other. Tannen interprets what happened as showing girls' natural ability to be in relationships and boys' greater need for status, independence, and action, which gets in the way of relationships.

Boys are so competitive with each other, Tannen and Maccoby seem to believe, so concerned with one-upmanship and activity that they ride roughshod over one another's feelings and lose the ability to connect with one another in any meaningful way.

If we understand the developmental path of boys, we view these behaviors differently. For instance, I would suggest that the boys in Tannen's study are less Machievellian princes, concerned with power and dominance, than they are our own "real boys." They are boys trying to make friends, be accepted by the group, and avoid rejection or humiliation. If we shift our focus from friendship to what psychologists call "pro-social activity"—that is, doing something positive with or for a friend—we discover that these boys are in fact in the early stages of what I've called "doing together," or what psychologist Ronald Levant has referred to in adult men as a form of "action empathy."

A boy knows that were he to sit down and talk about his disappointing grades, his mother's illness, or his lonely weekends, he would be breaking the Boy Code, the code of masculinity. Responding to the researcher's demands to talk seriously may bring him shame and humiliation. Why would any boy let down his protective macho mask in front of a researcher he hardly knows and whom he likely doesn't trust? What most boys probably do instead is energetically *not* comply. The boys' rebellious outbursts and foul language may well reflect the tensions of an impossible assignment.

In fact, much of the boys' group behaviors that were observed likely stemmed from this sort of compensatory response. Boys learn they have to put on an act to get by, to wear a tough-guy mask to avoid being teased. "When someone teases you, you learn you can't back down," says Shawn. "You have to step up and show you're even tougher than he is."

Why is action empathy any less deep and meaningful than the verbally intimate moments shared among girls and young women? Why should John and Hal, shirtless, bending over John's motorcycle, attempting to adjust the throttle while intermittently slapping each other on the back and spraying water on each other's heads be projecting a model of friendship any less meaningful than Amy and Ellen working out together at the all-women's gym and discussing Andrea's difficulty telling her new boyfriend that she's not yet ready for sex?

So it seems boys may follow their own formula for friendship: start with action and energy, throw in loyalty, laughter, and "doing together." Add covert verbal expressions of caring, earnestness, and hidden physical touching—and you get a good friend. This formula may differ completely from that for a girl's friendship, but it may be no less real or intimate.

My most striking personal encounter with a researcher's blind spots toward boy friendships occurred when I saw the movie *Stand by Me*. I went to this movie with a female researcher. In the literature of books and motion pictures that explore friendships among boys, this 1986 film, in my estimation, is one of the more genuine and realistic works. Four boys embark on an adventure to find the body of a missing boy. The boys face external dangers as well as internal ones. They talk about the death of a brother, a teacher's betrayal, and their fears for the future. They comfort each other, protect each other, and end up closer than ever.

The woman colleague with whom I viewed this film was startled, and somewhat repelled, by the boys' friendships in the movie. She was amazed at the way these self-described best friends addressed one another with insults and taunts. (Granted, I too was impressed by the number and variety of derogatory names that these boys threw at one another.) However, she was particularly struck by the line "Finding new and preferably disgusting ways to degrade one's mother was always held in high regard." She was further aghast at how often these so-called best friends *physically* insulted each other by dunking each other in a muddy swamp, putting each other in head holds, or displaying a wide repertoire of playful slaps, kicks, and punches. In short, she seemed to feel that this movie, with these boys, was the predecessor of *Lord of the Flies*.

I didn't argue with her. But the very behaviors that repelled her about the boys were also what made the movie a realistic depiction of how many a twelve-year-old interacts. I saw their interactions in a completely different light. I came away with a warm feeling for the friendship between these boys. Judging from the last line of the movie—"I never had friends like the ones I had when I was twelve"—the writer clearly felt this as well. I was moved by the support these boys gave one another and the warmth that existed between them. The name-calling, insults, and physical roughhousing were part of the way they expressed their feelings for one another—in "action mode." I saw affection underneath the physicality.

We have to take the friendships between boys—and the intimacy they provide—on their own merit. Boys won't usually walk arm in arm or say, "I love you," but they have found compensatory strategies that work for them and are understood by them. Certainly, we must try to understand them too.

As stated earlier, perhaps one of the most stubborn blind spots obstructing our view of boys' friendships is society's tendency to see boys as essentially "toxic" or dangerous. As a result, some parents worry about the possibly pernicious influence of other boys on their sons instead of seeing boys' friendships as constructive, healing influences. Parents fret when their boy learns his first swear words or first karate kicks in elementary school. When he becomes an adolescent, they worry that older boys will pressure him to take drugs, have sex, drive drunk, dive off a quarry cliff, lie down on railroad tracks, or engage in the other incredibly risky behaviors that we tend to associate with teenage boys. There is an unfortunate tendency for people to regard any group of boys over the age of ten as a "gang"—as antisocial until proven otherwise.

While a few boys do get in with the wrong crowd, Thomas Berndt, of Purdue University, found that, overall, boys exert a healthy, positive influence on one another. Berndt concluded that boys with healthy friendships are actually *less* likely to engage in risky behaviors and more likely to do well in school. Boys actually protect one another through their friendships.

THE CODE OF BOYS' FRIENDSHIPS

So what exactly is the boy code of friendship? Observers may not see it, but boys understand it. As we have discussed, the themes of friendship in my "Listening to Boys' Voices" study focused on the activities boys enjoy together, the conversations they share, the way they deal with one another's sadness and disappointments, the way they work through conflict and competition, and remain loyal by "being there." It appears that talking is not the only thing that brings these boys close. As sixteen-year-old Phil puts it, "We talk, but it's not like we sit down and have a conversation. We talk while we're doing something else. We always back each other up. We always stick together. My friends would do anything to help me out." So a primary part of the boy friendship is also just finding someone whom you trust enough to be around him. As Shawn put it, his friends "know me for who I am and accept me." Friendship is a place to let down the mask, or at least to let it slip a little bit. With a friend, a boy can show his vulnerabilities and not be shamed for them. And yes, boys expect a certain amount of good-natured teasing, insults, and playful abuse from their friends. In their games, boys generally learn not to take arguments too personally. They like resorting to a rule book or applying a principle to decide an argument in part because it's fast and fair. In fact, that well-developed sense of fairness is one way boys take care of one another.

Boys and men have had to learn to walk a fine line: to have intimacy without sentimentality, closeness without long conversations, empathy without words. Once we can read this code of boy's friendships, we can see that boys on a soccer field are engaged in sociable activity, building friendships that matter.

As I stressed earlier, if we want to raise boys who are empathic to us, we must first show them our empathy. We need to respect boys' friendships. They serve boys well and are vitally important to them. Given the amount of shame society heaps on boys when they attempt any sort of closeness, the depth they achieve in their friendships is worthy of our praise and recognition.

PLATONIC BUT DEEP: BOYS' FRIENDSHIPS WITH GIRLS

One of today's best-kept secrets is that many adolescent boys and girls are great friends—deeply yet nonromantically involved with one another. In my interviews with boys, I have found that almost all of them report having girls as friends, important and special friends in their social network. For many boys, intimate but nonsexual friendships with girls often replenish and restimulate the "lost half" of the feeling selves they buried when they experienced the trauma of prematurely separating from their mothers. These platonic girl-boy connections help boys regain access to long-forgotten and repressed aspects of themselves, and gives them the opportunity to expand emotionally. It seems impossible to overestimate the significance of these deeply platonic boy-girl connections.

JULIAN AND ALYSSA

On Wednesday after soccer practice, Julian heard the bad news. His parents sat him down and told him they were getting a divorce. Julian was devastated. When he told his "shameful secret" to John Simpkins, a trusted school adviser, Mr. Simpkins suggested he join a time-limited psychotherapy group with other ninth-graders who were struggling with similar problems. Julian, who did not like the idea of sitting around and talking about his feelings with "a bunch of losers," decided he was in so much pain he would try anything. One Saturday morning he found himself in the school cafeteria attending a Rap About Home Group with three boys, three girls, and the school guidance counselor. Nervous about talking about his problem in front of girls, he relaxed when he suddenly saw Alyssa Garrity, his neighbor from across the street who used to be his best buddy in his preschool days.

"In preschool we were so close we even had our birthday parties together, but then, you know, you start doing things with the guys, she took ballet, I tried out for football, and before you knew it, it's just 'Hi, how you doin'?' every few months," Julian told me. "When I first saw her again in my freshman English class this fall, I had this very weird feeling deep inside me. She felt like a sister or cousin, someone I had missed without even knowing it. In the group, I found there was something different about her, especially the way she could talk about things. She could apply words to the pain I always felt in my gut. We started to spend time together as friends. We'd talk on the phone for hours, especially after one of our folks drove us crazy. It was like something from way back. Something deep was coming back. She was helping me to talk and loosen up. I think I was helping her too, because sometimes I thought she was thinking about things too much. She'd obsess and then I'd say, let's go out for ice cream. I even taught her to play 21 in basketball. It seemed to cheer her up. I really depended on that friendship."

BOYS AND GIRLS: TWO HALVES OF ONE WHOLE

Boys' friendships with girls help boys come out from behind the mask and experience feelings and activities traditionally forbidden by the old Boy Code. As we've seen, we live in a society in which all of the essential qualities we would value in one ideal child get split down the middle by gender. As Carol Gilligan reported, boys grow up with an emphasis on values of fairness and justice, while girls grow up with an emphasis on caring and nurturing. Historically, each gender has had the opportunity to live out only half of what a healthy person might be.

While girls have recently been encouraged to express a wider range of previously unacceptable behaviors, we continue to keep boys in the tight straitjackets of nineteenth-century models of masculinity. The capacity for boys to create and nurture friendships with girls provides them with the chance to express the "other half" of themselves. It liberates them from outdated restrictions and creates possibilities for them to emerge from behind their false masks of self-sufficiency.

Although boys are frightened of connection with girls, they search for it desperately. They fear rejection and vulnerability, perhaps even more than girls do. "Most of my friends are guys," explains fourteen-year-old

Brian, "but I like this one girl, Rachel. She's really cool. But, you know, if I try to hang with her and then she's not into it, people might start saying like, 'Brian is such a loser,' and then I'd feel like a total jerk."

Boys carry around the wounds from the first premature separation from their mothers, when they learned that being a man meant scorning all things feminine. Being a man meant going it alone. When boys reconnect with girls, old fears and unhealed wounds are awakened. Afraid to express their pent-up yearnings, they fear they will get washed away in a flood of neediness. Yet when boys do connect with girls, they find they begin to feel whole again.

Boy-girl friendships are profoundly meaningful and emotional center-pieces to teenage boys' lives. They provide boys with opportunities to express feelings again. They also offer a new chance to reunite with the world of female nurturance from which they were thrust out prematurely and traumatically as young boys.

A DEVELOPMENT PROCESS—RECONNECTION TAKES TIME

There is, however, a substantial variation—often of a developmental nature—as to precisely what these cross-gender friendships are all about. For many boys, especially boys younger than fourteen years of age, girls as friends means sharing respectful, fun-oriented experiences that gener-ally involve only limited talking, with this talking focused primarily on shared interests and struggles with parents. For other boys, usually older, having a girl as a friend offers an opportunity for intimate verbal connec-tion and deep emotional support freed from the struggles of romantic demands and sexual nuances.

Ten-year-old Robert has one good friend, Marianne. They share a level of familiarity that allows them to just hang out and do things together without always talking. "We both like watching fun movies, so she comes over and watches them a lot. We like the same type of music. She is just one of the guys, basically."

Some boys, however, engage in long-drawn-out, feeling-centered con-versations. Sixteen-year-old Peter says his conversations with male friends tend to stay focused on one subject, while, with a longtime female friend, Eliza, he feels freer to let his conversation wander. "Eliza will call me two or three times a night and neither of us will have anything specific to say. She'll just start talking about something and I will just start talking about something and the two of us are just rambling on the spot. With Greg, I wouldn't just call him and say, 'Hey, what's up?' But with Eliza, I call and say, 'Hey, I'm bored.' "

In essence, as a boy grows older and feels more and more constricted by society's old rules about masculinity, he may increasingly turn to girls for friendship, to experience at least fleeting moments of liberation when it's safe to break the rules and just be himself.

A WHOLE NEW WORLD: A DIFFERENT KIND OF FRIENDSHIP

After spending years in same-sex play groups, getting used to a girl's style takes some time. Some boys still talk about how they aren't quite as comfortable and relaxed around girls as they are around boys. Fifteen-year-old Dwayne says: "It's not so much when I talk to girls I feel nervous or anything, but it's just personally I feel that you can open up more to another boy than to a girl. Sometimes you feel a little uncomfortable with some of the things you'd share with one of your male friends."

Michael realized that he needs to spend more time in conversation to maintain friendships with girls. "I guess it's a lot of friendship maintenance with friends who are girls. It's always a matter of having to call them up and being like, 'Hey, how's it going' or else they get mad at you."

While at first this seemed to him to be a chore—he had to consciously remember to do it if he wanted girls as friends—the results were obviously worth it to him, since now he counts several girls among his closest friends and appreciates their different perspective on life. Having made the effort to cross the gender line, he is able to engage rather easily in conversations that would typically be called feminine. "With girls we do more talking and sharing about each other's problems. We comfort each other." Some boys, like Justin, who were defensive at first about friendships with girls, soon came to understand the benefits. "Sometimes I think girls aren't on the intellectual level that I perceive myself to be, so they can understand my emotions more than my thoughts. But that's not always the case. Maybe I open up to them more because they're more emotion-centered and observation-centered. If I say I feel really burdened with school or something, they will be a lot more likely to respond with some insight." Justin's first instinct is to dismiss girls' skills at helping him handle his feelings and to view that particular skill as a sign of their intellectual inferiority. Yet he lets himself wonder about his knee-jerk reaction and admit that yes, girls are damn good at understanding him and perhaps that's a skill to be valued. As Alex remarks: "They will look at a situation a bit differently. You get a different reaction from girls."

Other boys are more clear that their friends who are girls are a huge benefit. Sixteen-year-old Patrick says: "Over the past few years, I've developed friendships with girls. Girls give you a different point of view than a guy. They sometimes can be more sensitive with advice. When a guy gives you advice you get one half of the picture and when a girl gives you advice you get the other half of the picture. When you get advice from both sides you get the whole picture."

Another sixteen-year-old, Chen, counts Liz as his best friend. "We talk to each other about anything and everything. She is a really good friend. I can tell girls all my feelings, feelings I can't tell my guy friends about—girls have no problem with that. I guess I probably rely more on my friends who are girls."

Those parents who become aware of the new friendships between boys and girls are impressed and respectful of these new gender arrangements. Cynthia Reeves is proud of her thirteen-year-old son Greg's circle of friends. "I can't speak highly enough about them. I'm especially pleased he has such close friends who are girls, girls who are just like sisters to him."

Cynthia did not have those kinds of friendships with boys when she was young. "There is a very different way that they have of relating with each other than when I was growing up. Much of it is casual and warm. They will hug each other. His friend Nina will run up and give him a hug and a kiss after a soccer game. They will all come over here and all watch a movie together. It's nice to observe, because they have these comfortable relationships between the sexes."

Several parents I spoke with told me about how teens today have coed sleepovers that are chaperoned by parents and are completely platonic. One father said, "When Anders first told me he was invited to a sleepover at a girl's house, I flipped. I thought sure this was some sort of sex-fest. I told him absolutely not, there was no way he was going. He's only fifteen. But then I started talking to some other parents and found out they've sent their kids and it's all platonic. Hard to believe? It never would have happened when I was a kid," he concludes, shaking his head.

These boy-girl friendships allow boys to be more free about emotions and feelings. Without outside society intruding and without other boys around to challenge or shame them, boys feel liberated to verbally uncover that part of them that is tender, caring, and loving. They can, as Michael says, just comfort each other. One of the things that make boy-girl friendships emotionally nurturing for many boys is that these relationships tend to create unique *private spaces* where the Boy Code is not in force, where boys feel able to be more honest about who they really are and what they are truly feeling. In their one-on-one relationships with girls, boys frequently feel comfortable revealing their true playful, connective, empathic personalities.

It is important that boys and girls recognize what they are both getting from these friendships. In boy-girl friendships, each sex gets to see the fragility of the other. This is what Judy Jordan at Harvard calls "gender empathy." Girls begin to see through boys' bluster and recognize boys' deep fears and vulnerabilities. Boys begin to see girls as less threatening, and admire their ability to communicate emotionally. These gender-empathy friendships become a blueprint for adult heterosexual love relationships.

WHEN LOVE BLOOMS

While the majority of adolescent boy-girl platonic friendships remain just that, they may also create the subconscious foundation for later heterosexual love relationships. In the "Listening to Boys' Voices" study, I discovered a definite developmental age-related pattern to the maturity and depth of these boy-girl romances that followed these new models of cross-gender friendships.

Specifically, I discovered that boys take great comfort in romantic relationships, but as with platonic connections, these dating relationships vary in scope. Young boys, in particular, are unsure of themselves in romantic situations. And sometimes they find themselves confused or simply depleted by the need some girls have for conversation and connection before establishing intimacy. Fourteen-year-old Tony broke up with a girlfriend after two years because, he says, "I was getting exhausted. I couldn't handle it. I would tell her I needed to go and she just kept telling me to hang on a little longer."

Older boys begin to be able to meet girls halfway by engaging in certain activities with them, but also by valuing their female partners' ability to talk about feelings and provide emotional support. Justin finds his girlfriend Theresa's nurturing style very comforting, an important counterpart to the interactions he has with his male friends. "I talk to her every night and basically everything that goes on in my life we talk about. If something bad happens, we have a discussion about it. It lets you share stuff that happens with someone who isn't going to be like, 'Oh yeah, whatever,' but is going to understand where you're coming from. I wouldn't talk to my guy friends about the stuff I tell Theresa."

Theresa meets many of Justin's emotional needs. In fact, Justin told me that dating her last year helped him out of a period of teenage blues. Her care for him gave him some emotional grounding that he was missing before. He struggled to explain to me why she's so important to him: "It's just having a person who you know is always thinking about you. Having someone there who cares about you and is there for you all the time. Friends come and go but your girlfriend is always there for you."

Here, of course, we may well be seeing the shadow, the echoes, of the earlier prematurely lost connection with the primary nurturant mother showing itself in a newly disguised adolescent form. Such a link may also help to account for the "sexual" or love-related power some teenage girls appear to have over boys. One study, by Thorne and Michaelieu, found that boys' self-esteem is most threatened by failing to receive love from a girl they like. Boys, then, are not self-sufficient loners but, rather, yearners for connection, seeking security lest the early trauma of premature loss reemerge.

As our boys begin to form deep relationships with girls, parents can nurture these relationships by supporting them. We must try to provide safe spaces for our sons' intimate platonic connections and not sexualize their meaning. Try to talk to your boy in a nonintrusive way. Invite the girl as a friend to your home, on an excursion, etc. Fathers should avoid the temptation to suggest the beginnings of a sexual relationship if their sons are clearly not in that type of companionship. Mothers should be wary of a natural jealousy that their little boys are going to other females for nurturing and support.

The task for all of us, in the end, is to break out of our stereotypes, to look for ways in which we can expand our abilities to be intimate with one another. Boys should learn how to express vulnerable feelings in front of others and show physical affection for one another. By the same token, girls ideally should learn about action empathy, nonverbal bonding, the affectionate insult, and the camaraderie that emerges from competitive games.

John Bednall, writing about education in single-sex schools, calls for a "bilinguality" between genders; in other words, teaching each gender to speak the language of the other. Education for boys should teach them a second language of love and friendship. As Bednall explains, "It will be the language which enables them to enter intimately and respectfully into dialogue with females, to learn from that dialogue and to see the feminine perspective as enriching and relevant to their growth as complete males. But they will not forsake their own masculine language. Rather they will learn to be bilingual in gender, able to hear and speak the feminine with the same empathy and comfort as they speak and hear the masculine."

I believe that when we can all speak a boy's nonverbal language of intimacy, he will feel more respected. When we can help a boy develop his verbal expressions of intimacy in a nonshaming culture, he will grow up healthier. When we can value action as much as talk, we will be stretching our gender values. When we can all hear and speak both languages, our relationships with each other will be richer and more satisfying.

—9—

BEING "DIFFERENT": BEING GAY

*"I thought they would disown me. I thought they'd tell me
I wasn't a member of the family anymore."*
—*Robert, age fourteen*

"I always knew I was different from the other guys," seventeen-year-old Bill explained to me. "Whenever I went out to the movies with friends, most of the other guys were just dying for a cute girl to sit next to them. Nobody else seemed to realize it, but I was really hoping a good-looking guy would sit next to me. I don't think anybody had any idea what I was going through."

Eighteen-year-old David reported a similar, even earlier memory. "When I was about ten years old, I went to see the school play put on by kids from another nearby school. It was scenes from the musical *Oliver.* As soon as I saw the boy playing the lead role of Oliver, as soon as I heard him sing about seeking love, about finding himself, I just couldn't keep my eyes off of him. For months, all I could think about was that little boy. I longed to meet him. I think I wanted to hold him, to have him as my friend. It was such a lonely, sad feeling. I remember thinking there was probably nobody else in the whole world who felt like I did."

Sixteen-year-old Nigel told another story of isolation and loneliness: "I knew I was different ever since I was about twelve. I didn't know I was actually gay, but I knew how good it felt to spend time with other guys—

and I always dreamed about holding one of them really close to me. But it was really hard. All the guys in my class made fun of me. They seemed to know something was up, calling me names and everything. I knew I couldn't tell my parents because they're Baptist—they're very religious people. I figured they would have me sent away, maybe put me in a mental hospital. I felt like I was the only person I knew who felt this way, so I tried really hard to repress my feelings. It actually made me just want to kill myself."

Nineteen-year-old Jackson told me a slightly different story. "For a long time I always felt pretty good about myself. I was captain of our high school soccer team, pretty high up in my class, and really popular with just about everybody. At the end of my junior year, I won the 'best-looking' and 'most likely to succeed' awards. But then I started drinking. At first I thought I was just being cool—you know, one of the guys—but then I knew that I was drinking because I *didn't* feel like just one of the guys. It took me a long time to realize it, but for three years I'd had a crush on this other kid on the soccer team. I guess I was really in love with him. If other people found this out, I thought they'd definitely stop liking me. I've never really acted like a stereotypical gay person, so nobody's ever suspected anything. I thought that if I told my friends about falling in love with another guy, they'd start calling me 'faggot' and stop hanging out with me. I thought that maybe I wasn't gay anyway. So instead of telling my friends or doing anything else about it, I just started to drink a real lot."

Among our diverse male population, among our "real men" of all religions, nationalities, racial and ethnic backgrounds, about 5 to 10 percent will discover as young or adolescent boys or during early adulthood that they are homosexual. Being homosexual, or gay, means, of course, that a boy, when he grows into manhood, will primarily feel attracted, in a romantic sense, to other men. Rather than falling in love with women and longing for a woman as a spouse, gay men fall in love with other men and hope to find a man with whom to share their adult lives. And just as heterosexual, or straight, boys do not "decide" they are going to be heterosexual and, as adults, do not "choose" a heterosexual lifestyle, homosexual boys do not "decide" to be gay and, as adults, do not "choose" to live a homosexual existence. Based on my years of experience counseling adolescents and adults, I have come to believe that being straight or being gay, for boys and girls, and for men and women, is something that each of us *discovers* about ourselves. It is just a natural part of who each one of us is.

While being homosexual may lead boys, as they're growing up, to sense that they are somehow "different" from other boys of the same age, we now know that most boys who learn they're homosexual—if given the same love, support, and empathy we give to heterosexual boys—are equally likely to become happy, healthy, successful men. Yet during adolescence when most young people begin to question their sexual identity, many homosexual boys do not feel comfortable speaking to either their peers or their parents about their fears and confusions. At this age boys feel that they must keep their feelings secret, and often sense there is nobody willing to talk to them in a safe and confidential way about what they are experiencing. Some boys in this situation are harassed by peers, family members, or teachers and administrators at school. Many of them are afraid of what would happen if their closest friends or family knew what they were really going through. Almost all of them intensely fear rejection.

Fortunately in some schools and communities there are now special awareness programs that teach teenage kids about gay and lesbian issues. Some states, such as Massachusetts, have a statewide task force dedicated to developing social and educational programs specifically tailored for gay adolescents. In some school systems, there are after-school discussion groups for students who are gay or who wonder whether they might be. Some of these groups are led by teachers who themselves are gay and stand as role models for their students. Some are led by empathic parents who want to help students struggling with these issues.

But probably in most school systems and in most communities there are no special programs, no task forces, no after-school discussion groups, and certainly no openly gay teachers. Either these school systems or communities do not have the resources to provide such programs or, more likely, they haven't yet seen the need for them. Regrettably, in many communities, there is still a stigma attached to being homosexual, and feelings of bitterness, even pure hatred, are still directed toward gay people. Many young people who are gay (or heterosexual but perceived as gay) report receiving threats of violence or actually getting beaten up, sometimes severely. For the adolescent boy who begins to wonder whether he might be homosexual, living in this kind of community is inordinately difficult.

"I felt like I had nowhere to turn," recalls Eric, now a freshman at Harvard, "I grew up in a small town in Iowa where people probably didn't even know how to pronounce 'homosexual.' When I first thought I was gay at about age thirteen, I just started to go crazy. There was only one person in our whole town who was thought to be gay—this guy who worked at the local video store—and he was ridiculed by everyone beyond belief. I didn't dare tell my parents about what I was feeling, and I figured I couldn't talk about it with any of my teachers, since they would probably just turn around and tell my parents. At our town library, there were no books about gay people. I really thought I was the only guy in my whole school who had these kinds of feelings. There was just nobody I could talk to about it and nowhere to go for the support I needed. I remember coming home from school each day, going into my room, and just crying by myself for hours at a time. It was a really traumatic time for me."

The profound feelings of isolation, fear, shame, and self-hatred that boys like Eric feel when they think or know that they are homosexual—especially when they sense there is no place they can go for nonjudgmental love, encouragement, and support—lead many of them to seek out their own solutions to the pain they feel. They may run away from home, get involved in drugs or drinking, misbehave at school, get involved in fights, engage in promiscuous sexual relationships, fall into a depression, or, worst of all, contemplate or commit suicide.

The suicide rate for gay teens is particularly distressing and, in my opinion, cannot be ignored. According to one recent study, gay youths account for up to *30 percent* of all teenage suicides. And in another study of gay and bisexual adolescent males, nearly *one third* of them reported that they had attempted suicide at least once.

When we hear these staggering statistics, when we begin to appreciate how lonely and frightened so many gay youths feel, some of us may be quick to conclude that being homosexual must be the primary cause of these problems. This kind of knee-jerk assumption—the assumption that if these adolescents are facing such tough problems, the problems must be caused by their sexual orientation—is perhaps only natural. But what I have come to understand—and what I tell parents who ask me—is that these problems are caused not by homosexuality but rather by society's *misunderstanding* of homosexuality. The stereotypes and stigma that burden gay people—which I have come to believe are not that different from the stereotypes and stigma attached to other minorities such as Jews, African Americans, and Asians—lead many adults to develop irrational fears about gay people and even to hate them for no rational reason. I have found that this homophobia—not homosexuality itself—is what makes the lives of gay people so difficult.

If we want to help boys when they are uncertain of their sexuality, if we want to show them that we love them no matter what they discover about themselves, if we want them to feel positive about who they are as young people and as adults, I believe that the most helpful thing we can do is to teach all of our boys, gay or not gay, that homosexuality is nothing to fear and nothing to hate. We need to help our sons, in particular, to puncture old myths about homosexuality and teach them that no matter what their sexual orientation may be, they can be successful, strong, happy, "real" men.

While teaching their sons these truths feels difficult for some parents because they themselves have fears and doubts about homosexuality, failing to impart these messages to boys can place our sons in serious psychological if not physical danger. I will never forget the words of Susan Wallace, mother of Jessicah, age twelve, and Alex, her only son who hanged himself at the age of fifteen: "I just wished Alex had told us what he was going through. If he had, I would have told him that his father and I loved him very much. And Jessicah loved him too. We would have loved him no matter what. As long as he was happy, we would have been so happy too."

HOMOSEXUALITY: A NORMAL VARIATION OF HUMAN SEXUALITY

For generations, experts in psychology and psychotherapy did not entirely understand homosexuality. During times when being openly gay was extremely difficult if not impossible, it must have been quite challenging, too, for psychologists and psychiatrists to get to know and fully understand gay men and lesbians. Because they were largely ignorant about what it meant to grow up as a gay person or to live adult life as a gay man or woman, psychologists and psychiatrists for years made assumptions about homosexuality based on very limited information or knowledge. Many of these assumptions, with the new psychological and biological research we now have, have been shown to be incorrect.

Based on numerous studies by top scientists in the United States and across the globe, we now know, first and perhaps most important, that homosexuality is not a psychological "disorder" or "disease." Although, as early as 1935, Freud himself argued that being homosexual "cannot be classified as an illness," for years most traditional psychoanalysts, based on the core belief that what is "healthy" is whatever is most "socially adaptive," decided that since being heterosexual was more common or "normal," homosexuals were "abnormal" and should be "cured." But most mental health professionals (including less conservative psychotherapists) began several decades ago to revise their opinions about homosexuality, and by 1980 homosexuality was deleted from the *Diagnostic and Statistical Manual* of the American Psychiatric Association when psychiatrists decided it could no longer be seen as a behavior disorder. Today, even the most conservative psychoanalysts are beginning to accept that homosexuality is a normal part of human life and that being gay is *not* something that mental health professionals should attempt to change (or that they *can* change).

There are probably two major factors that brought about this critical shift in how the world's scientific community looks at homosexuality— and thus at how we must look at what boys and young men should be taught about being gay. The first factor has to do with science and with what we have learned about homosexuality. The second factor has to do with society and sociology, with what we are learning from and about gay people as they become more open and fully integrated into society. While scientists have not yet determined the genesis of homosexuality in a definitive way, there is broad consensus that homosexuality is "constitutional"—in other words, that being gay, like being straight, is a natural, unchangeable part of who a person is inside. This is very important because it suggests, among other things, that in raising our sons, there is nothing we as parents can do or not do that will somehow cause our child to "become" either homosexual or heterosexual. While environmental factors, such as parenting, can of course influence the developmental experience of boys both gay and straight, they seem to have relatively little impact on what his genuine sexual orientation will ultimately be—that is, on whether as an adult he will feel primarily drawn to a man or a woman as the healthy object of his love and affection.

These scientific findings, as I'll explain a bit more later, are joined by society's changing attitudes about homosexuality in general. As more and more men and women "come out" and share the ups and downs of their lives as homosexuals not only with one another but also with their heterosexual friends, families and co-workers, many of the prejudices we've felt about homosexuality have begun to evaporate. Many of us have come to know gay people in professional and business settings: perhaps our family physician, political representative, postman, plumber, priest, accountant, lawyer, or nursery school teacher is openly gay. Some of us have family members or friends who are homosexual: our brother, sister, mother, father, aunt, uncle, son, daughter, best friend, college roommate, or neighbor might happen to be gay. Others of us have not yet become close to a person we know to be gay, but have learned of a celebrity who is openly gay—such as Ellen DeGeneres or Elton John—or who openly supports gay people—such as Whoopi Goldberg, Richard Gere, or Elizabeth Taylor. Throughout the world, it seems, more and more people are learning not only to tolerate but to accept and embrace gay men and women. In fact, in a recent study of over seventy-six societies from around the globe, researchers Clellan Ford and Frank Beach discovered that a majority of these societies considered homosexuality either socially acceptable or normal. Today even the Catholic Church is offering words of support—in a recent press release the National Conference of Catholic Bishops encouraged parents to show love to their gay sons and daughters and to accept that "generally, homosexual orientation is experienced as a given, and not as something freely chosen."

Indeed as we learn that being gay probably has much more to do with a biological given than with a psychological development or choice, and as we get to know and become friends with gay people from all walks of life, I believe we also need to begin to change what we are teaching young people about what it means to be gay. In my work with parents, I've learned that most of them, even if at first they have to struggle, sincerely want to give their full love and support to their sons whether they turn out to be gay or straight. When they believe their boy might be gay or when he himself tells them that he is gay, most of the parents I advise find it best not to dwell on how they might possibly be able to change him. Instead, once they feel ready, parents usually discover it's more helpful simply to focus on listening to what their son is saying about his relationships, on giving him their full empathy, and on helping him, as best as they can, to grow into an emotionally strong, confident, masculine young man, to feel proud and good about who he really is—gay or straight.

WHY IS OUR SON GAY?: THE ROOTS OF HOMOSEXUALITY

In discussing what makes people either gay or straight, perhaps the best place to start is by reviewing what we now know are *not* the root causes of

sexual orientation. One misconception that has now been largely disman-
tled is that homosexuality is usually caused by some sort of developmental disturbance or pathology—that boys become gay because they suffered
from some kind of mental or psychological disease. This misconception is
understandable because for years many of the gay men who actually went
to see psychotherapists probably had in fact been abused, endured trauma,
or suffered from severe emotional distress. Many of the therapists who
counseled these men logically assumed that these kinds of disturbances
were what had led their patients to become gay. But what the therapists did
not realize, and what we now know to be true, is that in most cases it was
not the disturbances that led to the sexual orientation, but rather the sexual
orientation that, indirectly, because of society's attitudes toward homosexuality, was most probably the cause of many of these disturbances.

Specifically, because of the historical bias against homosexuals in
many societies, for years boys who were gay—or who were perceived as
"acting gay"—were mistreated by their peers and by society in general.
Because they felt hated, because they felt shame about who they really
were, these boys—only some of whom were actually gay—became susceptible not only to abuse and trauma but to a whole gamut of emotional
and psychological disorders. Many of these disorders—such as anxiety,
depression, and substance abuse—only got worse when men went for psychotherapy because the therapists, far from helping these men accept and
feel good about who they really were, instead tried to push them to dis-
avow their genuine experience, to try to "become" heterosexual when in
reality they could only feel happy and fulfilled—in fact could only really
be—homosexual.

Another misconception that has been largely removed is that somehow the way a boy's mother and father behave and relate to their son can
cause the boy to become homosexual. Indeed traditional psychoanalytic
theory linked homosexuality in men largely to how a boy's mother and
father interacted with him as a young child. Psychoanalysts probed the
early-childhood experiences of their gay patients to uncover whether the
boy, for example, had a domineering mother who suffocated his masculinity or a weak or hostile father who thwarted the boy's attempt to separate
from this overpowering mother. Based on the views of these psychoanalysts, many mental health professionals, and thus the general public,
assumed that a mother, if she played with her son too much, involved him
in "feminine" behavior, or simply loved or depended on him too much,

could somehow make him gay. While perhaps some psychoanalysts or other therapists still rely on these kinds of factors to explain homosexuality, the new predominant view is that *these early child-parent interactions have little effect on whether a boy is gay or straight.* Though they may very well affect how secure and self-confident a boy comes to feel about himself and his sexuality and how successful and satisfied he will be in his adult romantic relationships, there is simply no evidence that these childhood experiences can somehow make a genuinely gay boy become straight or a straight boy become gay.

As scientists explore the origins of human sexuality, it is becoming more and more clear that people are probably born with a predominant orientation toward either the opposite sex or the same sex. While environmental factors like parenting and education may influence how quickly and successfully a person accepts and acts upon this inborn sexuality, he or she does not seem to be able to change or erase it. Thus although outside influences, such as a passive father, dominating mother, or a mean older brother, may lead a boy who is born gay, for example, to manifest his homosexuality sooner or more intensely than most other gay people normally would—or instead to try to ignore and suppress his sexuality altogether—none of these influences, in reality, actually make the boy become either more homosexual or more heterosexual.

We now have evidence that sexual orientation is often (although perhaps not absolutely) hereditary. For instance, research has been done on twins to see whether if one twin is homosexual, the other one will be too. In one study, Professor Kallman investigated eighty-five gay men, each of whom had either an identical, or monozygotic, twin (a twin who comes from the same egg and is genetically identical with the other twin) or a fraternal, or dizygotic, twin (a twin who comes from a separate egg and has only some genetic similarities to the other twin). Kallman found that in identical twins, if one twin was gay, so too was the other. The concordance was 100 percent. By contrast, in fraternal twins, if one twin was homosexual, only 11.5 percent of the other twins were also gay. In subsequent twin studies, high (although not perfect) concordance rates for homosexuality in identical twins was shown again and again.

In a second kind of study, researchers observed a pair of identical twins who were separated at birth and raised apart, without seeing each other, in two entirely different families. In one early such study, both of these twins, even though they were raised separately, were found to be homosexual. This was a critically important finding because it helped put to rest the possibility that environmental factors were primarily at work among the twins investigated in the earlier studies who lived together. Notably, two additional sets of identical twins who were reared separately were recently studied and a significant concordance for homosexuality was shown again—in one pair, both twins were exclusively homosexual, and in the other pair, one was exclusively homosexual and the other married a woman but had adult homosexual experiences. While it must be emphasized that these twin studies do not prove that homosexuality is 100 percent inborn, they do provide ample evidence that sexual orientation is heavily influenced by heredity.

Some scientists believe that a hereditary or biological basis for homosexuality can also be established by looking at the typical play styles of children who, when they become adults, identify as homosexuals. By linking these play styles to what we now know from animal and human studies about testosterone and other hormones, some researchers are gathering impressive evidence suggesting that the presence or absence of these hormones at critical times before or following birth or during early childhood may play a powerful role in determining (or explaining) not only how children play with one another but also the child's sexual orientation. While this research is complex and difficult to summarize accurately, what it basically shows is that in their early years many boys who grow up to be homosexual tend to avoid the rough-and-tumble play we now know to be induced, in part at least, by the interplay of testosterone and other male hormones in young boys. This difference between how some "pre-homosexual" and "pre-heterosexual" boys play appears to exist in boys from different countries and cultures. (Although, as I will explain later, having a different play style does *not* necessarily mean that a boy will become homosexual.) Likewise, a large percentage of female homosexuals report that, as girls, they engaged in more rough-and-tumble play than the other girls. By coupling these findings with what we are learning about the production of hormones in the brain and about how the presence of these hormones influences sexual development in general, scientists are beginning to show that hormones and other similar biological factors probably play a significant role in shaping sexual orientation too.

Finally, scientists are beginning to examine whether the brains of gay people are somehow wired differently from those of heterosexual people. In one recent study that garnered significant public attention, Professor

Simon LeVay showed that the volume of certain nuclei taken from the hypothalamus (the part of the brain that helps control hormone production, sexuality, and the emotions) was larger in heterosexual men than in either homosexual men or heterosexual women. It is widely thought that LeVay's study, standing alone, does not provide definitive evidence that there are major structural or functional differences between the brains of homosexual and heterosexual men and women. But his study is important in that it strongly suggests that these kinds of differences may exist, and has thus helped open the door for further research on how biology influences development of the brain and on how this, in turn, may affect our sexual orientation and behavior.

When we look at the research available to us today, what seems to be clear is that biology plays a significant role in shaping the sexuality of human beings. The research we have on identical twins, on the powerful early influence of hormones and on possible brain-based differences all suggest that our sexual orientation—while it may not be as genetically inevitable as, say, the color of one's eyes—is determined substantially by biological processes. There may even be evidence, as a matter of evolutionary biology, that homosexuality came about as an important and positive adaptive trait for human beings. Evolutionary biologist E. O. Wilson, for instance, believes that homosexuality may be a "normal" trait that, in his phrase, "evolved as an important element of early human social organization. Homosexuals may be the genetic carriers of some of mankind's rare altruistic impulses." Whether or not we agree with Professor Wilson's argument that gay people have evolved biologically to be more "altruistic" than nongay people, what does seem irrefutable is that homosexuality has been part of human life since the beginning of mankind, that gay boys exist in all countries and cultures, and that gay people, if raised in homes full of love and caring, can become adults who lead healthy, normal, fulfilling lives and make as important contributions to society as heterosexual people.

IF MY SON SEEMS GAY, WHAT SHOULD I DO?

"I'm very concerned," one parent recently told a colleague of mine. "My six-year-old Timmy still prefers playing with girls. He hates to get his hands dirty and refuses to play with the other boys in the neighborhood."

"Maybe right now Timmy is happier playing with the other girls. There is nothing wrong with this. There are always some boys who are less interested in playing rough, just as there are some girls who easily get bored with quiet game playing and want to join up with the boys," my colleague explained.

"Yes," Timmy's mother began, now blushing, "but I worry that maybe Timmy is going to end up homosexual, you know, gay or something."

Given society's lingering fears and doubts about homosexuality, given its abundant antigay anxieties or homophobia, it is not surprising that many parents become upset or worried when they think their boy may be homosexual. Parents want to do everything they can to assure the happiness of their children and many of them feel concerned that being homosexual will lead their boy to suffer as an adult more than he would if he were heterosexual. As a clinician who works primarily with adolescents and adults, I have frequently been approached by one or both parents of an adolescent boy who they suspect might be gay. Some parents notice their boy is interested in what society tells us are more "feminine" activities, such as reading fashion magazines, cooking, or singing. Others are surprised when they see their son showing affection to another boy or gazing at other boys in a way that might reflect a romantic attraction. And in some cases, parents of older teenage boys have discovered that their sons have secretly purchased gay pornography or actually caught their boy engaged in sexual play with other male friends. Colleagues of mine who work primarily with younger boys are usually approached by parents—and these parents develop questions about homosexuality—when their boys spend more time with girls, consistently avoid participating in rough-and-tumble games, seem overly attached to mother, or manifest the kind of gentleness, quietness, sweetness, or similar qualities generally thought to be more typical of girls.

When parents approach me or my colleagues with these kinds of concerns, we have learned that the most effective way to help is through two critical steps.

First, what almost all parents seem to appreciate and benefit from enormously is learning everything there is to know about gender and homosexuality. As I will explain in greater detail, people often make assumptions about sexual orientation when in many instances what is truly at issue is gender roles and society's attitudes toward those roles. In many cases the so-called effeminate behavior of a boy has little or nothing to do with homosexuality and far more to do with the boy's interest in staying connected and relating to his mother, in winning the love and attention of his father, or in just being the kind of boy that he happens to be.

Second, once parents separate and distinguish issues relating to gender from issues relating to sexual orientation, I then suggest they address what they themselves are experiencing emotionally and how their feelings are affecting the way they are treating their son. Too often, therapists focus all of their attention on the boy, and forget to listen to what his parents are going through as well. If it turns out that their son is in fact gay, I often encourage parents to try to meet with other parents of a gay child. If they do not know any such parents or do not feel comfortable approaching them—which is often the case—many find they gain great benefit from going to a local meeting of Parents and Friends of Lesbians and Gays, or P-FLAG, a national organization that provides guidance and support to the friends and families of gay people.

My starting place with parents is usually to share the research we now have about homosexuality and to help them see that they are not the cause of their son's sexual orientation whether he is gay or straight. I review the findings that point to the role of biology in determining sexual orientation and emphasize that in young and adolescent boys, acting effeminate or tending toward "girl-like" play activities are hardly absolute predictors of homosexuality. Though it is true that a fair number of gay men report that, as young people, they preferred more quiet play activities over the typical rough play of most boys, other gay men do not recall this tendency. To make things even more complex, there are plenty of heterosexual men who also remember preferring gentle games over more rigorous "masculine" boy play. Likewise, just as some of the adolescent boys who exhibit "feminine" behavior are homosexual, many of them, it ends up, are not. And while some adolescent boys who date and have sexual intimacy with girls later realize they are homosexual, some adolescent boys who engage in homosexual behavior discover they are heterosexual when they become adults.

When we try to link boys' early behaviors with their adult sexual orientation, we are often trying to see a cause-and-effect phenomenon when all of science is telling us that there is none. Boys who love sports, enjoy play fighting, and act tough or macho may, as adults, find they are exclusively and happily homosexual. Boys who prefer the nurturing realm of their mothers, who don't like rough play, who relish the same activities as most girls do, may, as adults, be exclusively and happily heterosexual.

When we encourage our "effeminate" sons to toughen up and "act more like a man," we are probably doing little that will either increase or decrease a boy's chances of being homosexual. If anything, we are simply engaging in classic gender straitjacketing and thus making our sons feel shame about who they are and what they most enjoy doing.

For instance, almost twelve years ago I was approached for help by thirty-five-year-old Jackie Jefferson, the mother of Kenny, a fifteen-year-old boy whose peers were constantly teasing him about the kinds of fancy silk shirts he liked wearing and calling him a "sissy" and "faggot." Jackie asked if I would meet with her and Kenny and try to help him with his "sexuality issues." In our first meetings together, we worked exclusively on how hard it was for Kenny to deal with the harassment at school, and how difficult it was for Jackie to see her son mistreated in this way. Kenny spoke a lot about how tired he was of being called names, and Jackie expressed how powerless she felt, how she didn't know what she could do to support her son. The sessions seemed to be helpful to both mother and son.

After several weeks of meeting together and sharing their struggles with me, Kenny and his mom both announced that things were going better and opted to terminate the therapy. In the end, we never discussed issues relating to sexual orientation because the heart of what both Kenny and his mother were actually coping with, it turned out, was gender straitjacketing—the Boy Code and the shame that gets thrust on boys who do not abide by it. In our sessions Kenny never raised any thoughts or feelings about loving other boys or feeling attracted to them. He spoke only about being teased for some of his personality traits and personal interests.

Kenny, it now turns out, is heterosexual. Just recently, I happened to meet his mother at a local store. She shared not only pictures of a handsome, happy-looking twenty-seven-year-old young man but also shots of Kenny with his wife, Amy, and their newborn daughter, Crystal.

Kenny's story shows how one parent who feared her son was dealing with issues related to sexual orientation was actually coping with society's ideas about gender. Of course, the opposite happens too. Because we as a society tend to equate being "effeminate" with being "gay," some parents fail to notice when a boy who may appear to be classically "masculine" is actually struggling with his sexual identity.

For instance, I was recently approached by Dennis and Sharon Cotton who wanted me to meet with their son, Owen, who, they confessed, "seems like he might be depressed." Seventeen-year-old Owen "looks very thin to us," they told me, "and he spends too much time every day just sulking in his room." When I began my sessions with Owen, the source of his depression was mysterious. He was a tall, well-built young man and looked more like a college football player than like the emaciated teenager his parents led me to believe would walk through my door.

"Your parents sent you here because they're afraid that you are losing weight, maybe not doing so well emotionally."

"Yeah," Owen began, "I stopped going to lacrosse practice and I just haven't been that hungry lately."

"Why did you stop going to lacrosse—did something go wrong in one of the games? Are you having problems getting along with some of your teammates or with the coach?"

"No, not really. I was actually voted most valuable player for the last two years and I get along great with everybody. I just don't feel like going anymore."

While it took weeks before Owen felt comfortable enough to open up, it turns out that what was getting him down was not a problem doing well at lacrosse, "fitting in" with his peers, or getting teased for being effeminate the way Kenny once was. Owen was depressed—and anorexic, I soon realized—because he was struggling all alone with how much longing he felt for some of his teammates, longing that was not just for friendship, but for something much more intimate, for something romantic, something sexual. He felt it when he was in the locker room with the other boys, when they won a match and joined in a teamwide hug, when they went drinking together and some of the other boys "started acting affectionate." Owen, after weeks of talking to me, discovered that winning the love and affection of other young men was what he really needed to be happy. Owen, it turned out, was gay.

SHADES OF GRAY: BISEXUALITY, SEXUAL EXPERIMENTATION, AND BOYS' CONFUSION

When a boy first confronts the issue of whether he is homosexual, often the answer may not come easily to him. Though part of his uncertainty may come from his fears and anxieties about what it would be like to lead life as a gay person, it may also arise from his confusion about whether he is homosexual at all. It might be intellectually convenient for us to assume that any given human being is either 100 percent homosexual or 100 percent heterosexual, that it's all just a matter of deciding which category one falls into. But there is every reason to believe that homosexuality and heterosexuality are not absolutes, that substantial gray areas exist. Not everybody is 100 percent homosexual or 100 percent heterosexual. In addition to people who are "bisexual"—who feel a strong romantic pull toward people of both sexes—there are many gay people who sometimes have heterosexual feelings or experiences, and many straight people who sometimes have homosexual feelings or experiences.

Indeed, if we accept that homosexuals, by definition, are *predominantly* attracted to people of the same sex, it is implicit that some homosexuals—or perhaps some small part of almost every homosexual—feels attracted to a certain extent to people of the opposite sex. Likewise, if we accept that heterosexuals, by definition, are *predominantly* attracted to the other gender, it must also be true that some heterosexuals—or some small part of almost every heterosexual—feels drawn in one way or another to members of the same sex. Determining our sexual orientation, at the end of the day, is not about finding simple black and white answers. Our sexual identity is almost always complex, unclear, confusing. And if it's difficult for us as adults to discover our genuine sexual orientation, our prepubescent or adolescent boys must experience substantial apprehension, ambivalence, and uncertainty.

A big part of the confusion that many people experience stems from the widely held belief that one's sexual orientation can be determined simply by looking at what sexual acts one chooses to carry out. This is misguided because being gay or straight, in reality, has to do mostly with what a person *feels* rather than with what he or she does at any given time. Just as a heterosexual person is not less heterosexual because he or she does not actually have sex with people of the opposite sex, a homosexual person is not less homosexual because he or she hasn't actually had sexual experiences with somebody of the same gender. The reason this becomes so puzzling for a boy (and often for his parents) is that in many cases a boy may *do* one thing, but *feel* another. When this happens, he is bound to become unsure about his true sexual orientation.

Take, for instance, Scott Schindler, a seventeen-year-old whose mother, Arlene, discovered that he and Benson Hawthorne, another teenager who lived just blocks away from the Schindlers, had been getting together in the afternoons, drinking beer, and then masturbating each other. Several years ago Arlene came to my office for a preliminary meeting. She came without

Scott and implored me to "do whatever it takes to get Scott to stop this inappropriate behavior."

While I explained to Arlene that I would be happy to help Scott examine the feelings he was experiencing, I emphasized that I was not willing to try to change Scott from being whoever he truly was. "If your son is gay—which it's not at all clear he is—I'm not willing to try to make him become straight."

"That's all right," she replied, "I just want Scott to work through this because neither I nor my husband, David, know what to make of it. David and I just want Scott to have someone to talk to so that he can figure things out. And I admit that I don't want Scott to continue these encounters with Benson."

"If Scott agrees that meeting with me would be a good thing, then I'd be happy to try to see him," I replied.

At the meetings with Scott, he at first seemed nervous and not terribly interested in talking to me. But as we developed a rapport, he began to open up and share what his life was like. He spoke to me about what he enjoyed and didn't enjoy about school, about girls he had tried to date, about his relatively moderate consumption of alcohol, and about who his closest friends were. In our third meeting, Scott initiated a discussion about Benson: "I know why my mother sent me to see you. She caught me and Benson fooling around and now she's all freaked out about it."

"Are you feeling worried about it too?" I asked.

"Not really," Scott replied. "I mean, we've only done it a couple of times and it's no big deal."

"So you feel positively about your experiences with Benson—you haven't felt down about it at all?"

"Well," Scott confessed, "the first time we got together and fooled around, I thought I might be gay. I felt really weird about it. But the truth is, when I hang with Benson and we do stuff together, it's fun and everything, but I'm definitely into girls. I mean, I'm thinking about girls when he and I are together."

While at first I wondered whether Scott might have been unintentionally suppressing the truth—that perhaps he might actually be gay—it turned out, after weeks of meeting together, that Scott primarily felt attracted to girls. While he had explored touching Benson's body and had let Benson touch him, the experimentation had more to do with a general need Scott felt to let out his "sexual energy" than with a true physical attraction to Benson. All of Scott's fantasies were about women. When the junior prom came along, Scott unequivocally decided to take Sharon, a classmate he had "had his eye on" for several months. Scott's encounters with Benson stopped prior to the end of his junior year and, the last I heard, Scott was living happily with a woman he'd been dating for several years. Scott, as far as I can tell, is heterosexual.

When I remember my work with Scott, it's hard not to think too of Samson Kim, a thirty-two-year-old patient of mine who worked as a radiologist at a local hospital. Samson came to me while he was still seeing Susan, his live-in girlfriend of six years. For his entire life, Samson had had sexual relationships exclusively with women. He enjoyed the feeling of being with women, he explained, "but I never feel entirely complete—I always feel like something is missing."

As a teenager and a young man, Samson recalled feeling "a real pull" toward other men. "I guess I've never been ready to admit this before," Samson added, "but when I think back on it, I've only really fallen in love with guys. I've loved many women—I've loved them dearly—but I've never really been *in love* with them, I haven't really yearned for them the way I have for some of my guy friends."

"Did you ever tell any of these men how you felt?"

"I tried to," Samson began, "but I always got too afraid. Besides, I figured that since I seemed to like sex with women, I probably wasn't gay. I figured I just felt 'warmly' towards these guys—but that I was basically straight."

Samson was propelled to come see me after he met Jason, a handsome, talented heart surgeon who worked at the same hospital as Samson did. Samson's feelings for Jason were so overwhelming that he felt he could no longer simply hide them away. What emerged in our sessions together was that Samson was in fact gay. Because he was a sincere, loving man who cared deeply for the women he had dated, he had experienced a series of important sexual relationships with these women. But when it came down to his real core self, to what truly gave him the greatest joy and satisfaction, Samson longed for men. Samson ended up forming a committed partnership with Jason, while continuing a close friendship with his former girlfriend.

As we think about how to help boys who feel confused about their sexual orientation, Scott's and Samson's personal stories are important in that they reflect how common it is for people to engage in sexual relationships that do not actually follow their genuine longings. These relationships, in some cases, can last a lifetime. If for some people this results in only a small sense of loss, for others it pushes them to seek secret outside relationships, become anxious or depressed, or suffer other acute physical or psychological problems, such as migraine headaches, insomnia, eating disorders, or substance abuse. It is generally exceedingly painful and unhealthy when human beings suppress their true yearnings. Thus while it is not at all uncommon for a homosexual man to get married and embark on a life in which the world thinks of him as heterosexual, it would be highly unusual if he was completely happy and fulfilled in living that life. By the same token, if a heterosexual man falls into a primary sexual relationship with another man even though his essential yearnings are for women, it would be unlikely he would feel entirely satisfied and whole in that same-sex relationship.

When parents ask me how to address the confusion boys may feel about their sexual orientation, I encourage them to help their boys talk not only about whom they are attracted to or involved with sexually, but also who their sons like—or love. Our boys can only come to the truth about their sexual orientation by examining what the truth is about who they yearn to love—not simply by looking at who they are dating or experimenting with sexually. Because sexual orientation is truly about what is in *our hearts,* we can help our boys most by encouraging them to be honest with us and themselves about where their true passion lies, who they truly love, and what they really want.

WHAT DO I SAY WHEN HE TELLS ME HE'S GAY?

For a teenage boy who discovers he's gay, perhaps one of the most difficult steps he may have in accepting his own sexuality is mustering the courage to tell his closest friends and family. Because society still has not universally accepted homosexuality, because the gay teenager cannot ignore the hateful homophobic messages he hears around him, he is bound not only to suffer extremely low self-esteem but also to become exceedingly nervous about how others might respond to his revelation. When he first comes to realize that his primary sexual attraction is toward other males, he may decide to suppress his own feelings in the hope they'll go away. He might turn inward, try to cover any outward signs of his orientation, or engage in acts of self-destruction. The fear that his closest friends and family will reject him is often overwhelming. Telling his parents is especially terrifying, since these are the people he depends on the most—not only for love and approval, but for the very home he returns to each day.

"I thought they would disown me," fourteen-year-old Robert told me. "I thought they'd tell me I wasn't a member of the family anymore."

"Just before I was going to tell them," Peter recalls, "I drove my bike to this bridge on the Charles River. I got off my bike and stared out at the river for what seemed like hours. I really thought it might be better to just end everything right there and then, to just plunge into the river. It seemed like it would be easier than having to tell my parents."

"I didn't find it in me to tell my dad until he got cancer," Jerome explained. "When he got sick and we knew he was going to die, I wanted him to know who I *really* was. I was almost eighteen years old, an honors student, and headed for Bates on a scholarship—and I was totally in love with Skip Thompson, another guy in my high school class. Dad knew Skip and liked him a lot. I didn't want Dad to die without knowing how happy I was and how close Skip and I had become."

Richard remembers how tough it was to tell his mother that he was gay: "When I came home from school in tears one afternoon, my mom asked me what was wrong. The truth was that I couldn't take it anymore. I knew that I was gay and I hadn't told the two people I loved the most in the whole wide world. My mom is this really great social worker and my dad's a minister who everyone just loves. They both are really cool about gay issues, but I knew they'd be disappointed if it was *me* who ended up being gay.

"But when I saw my mom that afternoon," Richard continued, "I just couldn't hold back the tears. When she saw how hard I was crying, she seemed to know just what to do. She sat me down in our living room, put her arm around me, and told me how much she loved me. When I told her 'Mom, I'm gay,' I just started crying uncontrollably. I guess I was afraid she'd tell me to leave the house or something. Instead she just held me tight and said, 'We love you so much, Richard. We'll always love you no matter what. We're very proud of you.' "

While there's no one perfect way of responding to a teenage boy when he first tells us that he's gay, perhaps there's nothing more important than reminding him, as Richard's mother did, that we love and cherish him, that we're proud of who he is, that nothing will change in our relationship with him. What a boy fears most is that we will in some way try to shame him, punish him, or send him away. In my opinion, responding in any of these ways would be terribly misguided, since it would be highly likely to traumatize him, to hurt him in a way that he might never be able to forget or forgive.

"I haven't spoken with my parents in ten years," Evan told me despondently, "because when I told them I was gay, they kicked me out of the house. I was only fifteen years old and had nowhere to go. I ended up staying with friends of mine who understood what I was going through. When my parents let me move back home a few months later, things were never the same. My father never talked to me and my mother told me over and over again that in her mind I was just a 'boarder,' that I was no longer her son. I never got over this and felt bad about myself for years. The only way I could cope was to stop seeing my parents at all."

"My parents are old now," Evan explained, "and sometimes they leave a message on my answering machine begging for me to come home to see them. But as much as they want to see me now, I just can't get myself to do it. Whenever the holidays come around, it hurts a lot."

While it might be easy to think of Evan's parents as having been thoughtless or uncaring, the reality is that they probably believed that if they withheld their love and affection from their son, somehow he would "decide" he was no longer homosexual. But sexual orientation is constitutional—an essential part of who each of us is—and is not a "decision" that we can control or that can be changed by or for our parents. Especially because a boy may be in an extremely tenuous emotional state by the time he finds the courage to discuss his sexuality, I believe it is critically important to convey to him, as soon as he shares his feelings, that he is still loved through and through, that his sexual orientation will not in any way diminish how much he is admired and respected. These are the things a boy needs most to hear.

To refrain from saying them is to risk placing a boy in serious emotional—even physical—jeopardy. And to risk losing him, in one way or another. But if instead a boy is given the love and support he so desperately needs at this crucial time, if he is assured that his sexual orientation will never change the way he is thought of or how much he is cared about, we are then doing the best thing we can do to restore his sense of self-worth, preserve his faith that we can be trusted with even his most challenging feelings and struggles, and ensure that his adult romantic relationships—whether he ends up being either gay or straight—will be as happy, healthy, and fulfilling as possible.

Only then will he be clear that being a "real boy" or becoming a healthy masculine adult—contrary to the myth of boyhood culture—has no relationship whatsoever to whether one is gay or straight.

SOME THOUGHTS ON BOYS AND AIDS

When we broach issues of sex and sexuality with our sons, we cannot help being also concerned about AIDS.

As distressing as it is for us to face it, acquired immune deficiency syndrome, or AIDS, is an extremely serious health crisis affecting millions of young people around the globe. I firmly believe that as reluctant as some parents and some schools may once have been to teach children about sex and sexuality, especially about homosexuality, the reality of AIDS, the reality that it complicates, unravels, and even ends human life, makes teaching our kids about these issues absolutely critical. We must speak to them, and speak to them frankly.

The worldwide impact of AIDS has been absolutely devastating. As of December 1997, an estimated 30.6 million people worldwide—29.5 million adults and 1.1 million children younger than fifteen years—were living with the HIV virus or with full-blown AIDS. Through 1997, cumulative HIV/AIDS-associated deaths worldwide amounted to approximately 11.7 million—9 million adults and 2.7 million children. And since the beginning of the HIV/AIDS epidemic, approximately 8.2 million children younger than fifteen years have been orphaned worldwide because of the premature deaths of HIV-infected parents.

Statistics relating specifically to the United States are also staggering. As of June 1997, in the United States, 612,078 cases of full-blown AIDS had been reported to the Centers for Disease Control and Prevention. Of these, 511,934 (84 percent) were males aged thirteen or older, 92,242 (15 percent) were females aged thirteen or older, and 7,902 (1 percent) were children under age thirteen.

While by now we all know that the HIV virus is blind to sexual orientation—it infects gay people and straight people alike—in the United States the largest number of men with AIDS contracted it through homosexual sex. According to a 1996 study of men in the United States diagnosed with AIDS, male-to-male sexual contact accounted for the largest proportion of cases (50 percent), followed by injection drug use (23 percent).

But lest any of us conclude that AIDS in the United States is essentially a "gay disease," I should emphasize that the transmission of HIV by *heterosexuals* now accounts for an increasing proportion of AIDS cases in the United States. From 1988 to 1995 the proportion of U.S. AIDS cases attributed to heterosexual contact each year grew from 4.8 percent to 17.7 percent. And AIDS is now the second leading cause of death in the United States among people aged twenty-five to forty-four.

All of these statistics point to an unassailable fact—we *do* need to be worried about our children and what they learn about AIDS. Addressing the reality that many adults still hesitate to talk to their children about sexuality and AIDS, Surgeon General Antonia Coello Novello wrote in the 1993 Surgeon General's Report on AIDS and HIV: "Yes, it is painful to think about the temptations and the dangers they face every day. But sex and drugs are facts of life; we can no longer ignore them than we can death itself. We must prepare our children to face the reality of AIDS in their lives."

Indeed, since 1 in 5 of all reported AIDS cases is diagnosed in the twenty- to twenty-nine-year age group, and since we know that the median incubation period between HIV infection and AIDS diagnosis is nearly ten years, it's now clear that *most of those people in their twenties who are diagnosed with AIDS were probably teenagers when they first became infected.* This means, simply enough, that scores of our teenage sons and daughters are being infected with HIV each year and that by the time they reach their twenties many of them may develop the symptoms of AIDS.

As we've learned in this chapter, many boys feel afraid to talk about their sexuality. If they're gay, many of them are terrified about how their parents, friends, teachers, and others might respond. They fear rejection, even abandonment. And so they go silent. And so we never speak to them about what they're feeling inside themselves.

But if colluding in our sons' silence, if "just letting things work themselves out," might once have been an acceptable option, I simply don't see how it can be anymore. We not only owe it to our sons, and to our daughters, to talk openly about the fears and concerns they have about being sexually active and about whether they're gay or straight, but now we owe it to them to explain what AIDS is all about for homosexuals and heterosexuals, how it is contracted, and what you have to do to make absolutely sure you'll never be infected in the first place. Taking the necessary precautions is easy. Talking about it may be less so. But I believe we simply must overcome our qualms about discussing this.

It's nothing less than a matter of life and death.

_1O_

SCHOOLS:

THE BLACKBOARD JUMBLE

"Girls have an easier time opening up and communicating than guys do. . . . Many guys are afraid to speak up because they don't want to look stupid."—Kevin, age fourteen

SCHOOL: A WHOLE NEW WORLD

It was the first day of third grade for Alexander. He rushed out to the bus stop ten minutes early, dragging his mother and father with him. He chatted happily with the other kids at the bus stop and, when the bus arrived, climbed aboard without hesitation—with only a perfunctory good-bye peck on his parents' cheeks. He strutted down the aisle and plunked down into a seat next to a child his parents didn't recognize. Both mother and father waved as the bus pulled away, but Alexander was so engrossed in conversation with his unknown seatmate that he didn't return the wave. "What a difference from his first day of kindergarten!" his mother remarked to the father as they watched the bus disappear. "I felt like I was abandoning him then. Now, I feel like he's abandoned us!" That afternoon, his mother asked Alexander who the kid was he had sat next to. "Oh, just a guy I know from last year," replied Alex and headed toward the door. "Where are you going?" his mother asked. "Nowhere," Alex said. "Don't worry."

As every parent quickly learns, school is about a great deal more than learning to read and write and do math. School represents a whole new world, the place where our sons will wrestle with many of the most important social, emotional, and psychological challenges of boyhood. It is where a boy will expand his knowledge, forge relationships, explore his abilities and limitations, and—we fervently hope—build a strong sense of self-esteem.

For parents, the prospect of this new world of school is exciting, because they wish to see their children grow and succeed. It is also a matter of some concern because they know they will now be sharing the task of raising their child with the professionals: teachers, administrators, guidance counselors, and other school staff. From the ages of six to eighteen, our boys will spend the great majority of their waking hours at school. In any given week, a boy may see more of his math teacher than he will of his father or mother. He may spend more time on the school playing field than in the family living room. Especially in today's busy and overstretched families—in which both parents often work long hours or where there is only one parent—school may become the arena where a boy works through many of the challenges of growing up male.

Because of the tremendously important role that school plays in a boy's life, I think that parents of a boy should be asking, "Does my son's school have a sufficient understanding of the emotional challenges boys face in becoming confident, successful men? Do the school's teachers and administrators know about the Boy Code? Do they understand the mask? Are they sympathetic to boys? Does the school teach subject matters and use classroom materials that interest my boy? Does it use approaches to teaching that will stimulate him and make him eager to learn? Is the school a place where my son feels safe, happy, and engaged, a place where he'd like to be?"

I believe that much too often, the answer to these questions is *No.* Our schools, in general, are not sufficiently hospitable environments for boys and are not doing what they could to address boys' unique social, academic, and emotional needs. Today's typical coeducational schools have teachers and administrators who, though they don't intend it, are often not particularly empathic to boys; they use curricula, classroom materials, and teaching methods that do not respond to how boys learn; and many of these schools are hardly places most of our boys long to spend time. Put simply, I believe most of our schools are failing our boys.

They are failing them in at least four major ways. First, they simply do not appear to be doing a good job at noticing the problems many boys are having in certain academic subjects—namely, reading and writing. As a result, many boys are doing extremely poorly in these areas—less well than girls—and their self-esteem as learners is plummeting.

Second, our schools and their teachers tend to be poorly versed in the specific social and emotional needs of our sons, and so they often handle these needs inappropriately or inadequately. Many of the specific difficulties boys face that we've discussed in this book—the old rigid Boy Code, the mask, the vicious cycle of shame and hardening—are poorly understood or completely ignored by many schools.

Third, a good number of our schools are not environments that are either warm or friendly toward boys. Especially when boys misbehave, rather than probing behind the misconduct to discover their genuine emotional needs, there's a prevalent tendency to interpret their behavior solely as a discipline problem. Because the myth of boys' toxicity is still deeply entrenched within many school systems, teachers and school administrators are often permitted to become hostile toward boys—and so they may push our sons even further toward academic failure, low self-esteem, conduct disorders, and a host of other emotional and behavioral problems.

Fourth, our schools generally do not have curricula and teaching methods designed to meet boys' specific needs and interests. To date most coeducational schools have done little to investigate how they can make the classroom experience stimulating for boys. They have not developed boy-specific classroom materials. They have not been creative about making the materials they already have interesting for boys. They have not addressed boys' unique learning styles and developed teaching methods that take them into account. And most of our elementary and middle schools have a dearth of male teachers. This sends an early and faulty message to our boys—that education and learning are primarily for girls and women.

It is understandable that parents put a lot of faith and trust in schools and the people who run them. Depending on how curricula are structured, how classrooms are run, and what essential attitudes about boys prevail, a school can positively shape our boys and their behavioral development. On the other hand, it can confuse them and lead them terribly astray. Research shows that being part of a school that addresses who a boy really is and what he really needs can make a major difference in helping the boy not only to do well academically but to feel positively about himself and develop a strong healthy sense of his masculinity. A positive school experience, in short, can bolster a boy's self-esteem.

By contrast, attending a school that does not address boys' specific concerns can affect whether our sons will fully realize their academic potential, whether they will succeed at nonacademic activities such as sports and the arts, and whether they will find their way to a fulfilling social life. Worse, a difficult school experience may cause our sons to act out in class, suffer depression, become involved with drugs or alcohol, engage in inappropriate or unsafe sexual activities, or become either victims or perpetrators of violence. The quality of our schools may make all the difference for the academic and emotional success of our boys.

Many of the schools I visit are trying hard to do well. Many teachers and administrators care greatly about boys. But often because of a lack of resources or of sufficient and/or appropriate training and understanding, a lot of our schools simply don't know how to handle the specific challenges of teaching and supervising boys. They can be hindered in their efforts when they aren't completely knowledgeable about boys, especially when they confuse the psychology of boys with that of girls. That is the subject of this chapter. While it may still seem like a "man's world" from the perspective of power and wealth in adult society, in our schools boys on the whole are failing.

THE BLACKBOARD JUMBLE: HOW ARE SCHOOLS FAILING BOYS AS STUDENTS?

There has been a great deal of discussion in the past few years about the relative performance of boys and girls in the classroom. We have been told that schools shortchange girls, fail in providing gender equity and fairness, and actually hinder women's intellectual advancement in society. While these objections have largely been substantiated, I believe that in the heat of the debate about girls we have failed to analyze how boys are doing in our public coeducational schools. In fact, many boys are not performing well.

One of the reasons that boys are assumed to be doing well in school is that many of our most brilliant academic stars are boys, especially in math and science. According to one well-regarded study conducted by educational researchers at the University of Chicago, boys outnumbered girls by about 3 to 1 in the top 10 percent of math and science performers. In the top 1 percent, boys outnumbered girls by 7 to 1. In some science and vocational aptitude tests, no girls scored in the top 3 percent. These few boys are the academic superstars, and our focus on them has, I believe, skewed our perception of how boys are doing in general.

According to the same University of Chicago study, there is a new gender gap with a predominant number of boys falling to the *bottom* of the heap. The study, which combined results of six major surveys of educational achievement spanning thirty years and involving thousands of children, showed that especially in relation to reading and writing skills—those most basic to functioning in our society—boys are in deep trouble. For reading comprehension, perceptual speed, or word association memory, boys outnumbered girls at the bottom of the scales by a margin of 2 to 1, and many *fewer boys* than girls scored in the top 10 percent of the groups.

Another report, entitled *The Condition of Education 1997,* issued by the U.S. Department of Education, confirms the University of Chicago findings. At all age levels, it states, "females continue to outscore males in reading proficiency." This deficiency is particularly disturbing because, as the report itself stressed, reading is a skill that is absolutely critical not only to the boy's progress as a student but also to his overall lot in life.

In addition to their problems with reading, boys are equally dogged by difficulties in learning how to write. The University of Chicago study found such large differences in boys' and girls' writing skills that Larry Hedges, who led the study, concluded that "males are, on average, at a *rather profound disadvantage* in the performance of this basic skill." The Department of Education report confirms this, stating that for the last thirteen years females of all ages "have outscored males in writing proficiency." The report characterizes writing as a fundamental skill we need to have not only to learn how to probe and understand ideas and information but also to motivate others to do so. It also explains that a deficiency in writing skills is likely to undermine one's academic success as well as one's prospects for a meaningful career.

From these statistics, you might be tempted to conclude that girls are "naturally" good at reading and writing, boys "naturally" good at math and science. But, over the years, girls have steadily improved their performance in math and science. So, although they are still underrepresented in the very top echelon of performers, they are making steady progress. The same cannot be said of boys and reading.

Secretary of Education Richard Riley spoke to Congress in 1997 about these basic reading and writing skills as being "make or break" points not only in children's education or career achievement but also in their later life choices. In Riley's words: "Teachers will tell you that . . . [poor readers] . . . often get down on themselves . . . become frustrated, and often head down the road to truancy and dropping out." Then things can get worse: "Some . . . begin to make the wrong choices about drugs."

Boys' weakness in the basic skills of reading and writing contributes to a variety of problems at school. For example, eighth-grade boys are 50 percent more likely to be held back a grade than girls. And, by high school, two thirds of all "special education students" are boys. Statistics also reveal that in general boys have a greater difficulty "adjusting" to school life, and constitute 71 percent of school suspensions.

What's more, the percentage of boys who attend college has dropped dramatically. Twenty years ago more boys went to college than girls. Today, only 58 percent of male high school graduates make it to college, as compared with 67 percent of females. Women earn approximately 55 percent of all bachelor's degrees granted today, and the percentage continues to grow.

Overwhelmingly, recent research indicates that girls not only feel more confident about themselves as learners but also show more vigor in the steps they take toward developing meaningful careers. For instance, when eighth-grade students are asked about their futures, girls are twice as likely as boys to aspire to a career in management, the professions, or business. A 1993 U.S. Department of Education study found that among high school seniors, fewer boys than girls expect to pursue graduate studies, law, or medical school. Fifty-nine percent of all master's degree candidates are now women, with males' percentages in graduate and doctoral training shrinking each year.

These statistics show that *there are many more boys at the lowest rungs of the ladder of academic achievement than we had ever imagined or been led to believe.* The reality is that although there is an attention-getting handful of star performers, many boys muddle along in the mediocre middle, getting by as "average" students, and that the bottom of the class actually contains a majority of boys rather than girls. And, although the issue of girls and their lagging performance in math and science is now well acknowledged by the U.S. Department of Education as well as by numerous private educational foundations, and targeted as an area for research and program funding, *the problem of boys and their poor reading and writing performance has received little or no attention whatsoever.*

BOYS' POOR PERFORMANCE IS A GLOBAL ISSUE

This pattern of academic "boy problems" is not confined to the United States. It exists across Western Europe and Australia as well. In England and Wales, girls uniformly score higher than boys in standardized tests conducted at ages five, seven, nine, and eleven. While boys still show some advantage in mathematics scores in the teen years, the major standard achievement measure for sixteen-year-olds (the GCSES) shows that 48 percent of girls—versus 39 percent of boys—receive the highest grades in five or more subjects.

When poverty is factored in, the discrepancy between boys and girls doubles in favor of the girls. In the European Union, more girls complete secondary education, and in most West European countries, they stay on longer in all forms of postsecondary schooling. In New South Wales, Australia, a study found that the majority of "special"- and "support"-class occupants were boys, a finding that sparked a major educational debate. It was also shown that boys performed less well than girls in literacy tests, had lower scores on entrance exams for higher education, and left school earlier than girls.

POOR PERFORMANCE LEADS TO A CRISIS IN SELF-ESTEEM AS LEARNERS

Behind these disturbing statistics lies what I believe is an irrefutable yet underdiscussed reality: boys have a significant problem with their self-esteem as students.

Several well-publicized large-scale surveys have shown a crisis of low self-esteem among adolescent girls. They've revealed that when girls don't feel confident about themselves at school, their unique voices become suppressed and they begin to suffer emotionally and academically. While the attention these studies have garnered is commendable, I worry that they've led us to conclude that if girls are in trouble, boys must be doing fine, that if girls have low self-esteem, boys must feel confident about themselves as students.

I believe that another reason we have failed to recognize boys' low self-esteem is that some of the surveys used to assess self-esteem are not designed to generate accurate results for boys. They ask very direct questions about self-esteem, such as "Do you feel that you're good at math?" or "How would you rate your reading abilities?" Boys, more than girls, have a tendency to answer such questions in the way they think they are "supposed to." In other words, boys know the answers that will make them sound self-confident—as dictated by the Boy Code—and are quick to respond accordingly.

In one study by Editha Notleman at the National Institute of Mental Health, for example, boys and girls were asked to rate themselves on how well they functioned academically during transitional periods in adolescence. Their teachers were also asked to rate their performance. The largest discrepancies between the students' responses and those of the teachers were always found with the boys. The boys tended to inflate their scores, to brag and "puff" them up, perhaps because they were ashamed of their weaknesses as learners. The girls' self-ratings, in contrast, were much closer to those of their teachers' assessments. But there are many ways to measure self-esteem, some of which overcome the tendency of boys to brag and overstate their strengths. The Self-Concept as Learner Scale, developed by William Purkey at the University of North Carolina, uses indirect measures to pick up on students' sense of self-image—i.e., on how well they feel they are doing within the school environment.

When Purkey gave his test to a wide range of students—gifted and average, urban and rural—in grades six, seven, and eight, he discovered two important facts. First, he learned that for all students—boys and girls alike—this measure of self-esteem lowers as kids move into mid-adolescence, from sixth to eighth grade. But he also reported that "significant differences were found between male and female students." Across all grade levels and in all categories, girls scored higher than boys. Put simply, Purkey showed that *boys' self-esteem as learners is more at risk than that of girls.*

Joan Finger, one of Purkey's graduate students, created a similar study to look at African American middle school students. She discovered no significant differences in self-esteem between African American and Caucasian boys. However, she found that African American males had "generally lower" scores in self-esteem than African American females. In other words, self-esteem seems to be more an issue of gender than it is of race.

Purkey's results differ from those of a widely publicized report called *Shortchanging Girls* by the American Association of University Women. That report argued that girls have relatively lower self-esteem than boys, while Purkey's findings show that girls, not boys, are the ones who think of themselves as smart enough to succeed. Purkey believes that the disparity comes as a result of boys' tendency toward braggadocio. In his phrase, "boys tend to brag more to impress their friends," while girls "brag less and *do better in school.*" Boys, he stresses, are simply using bragging as "a shield to hide a deep-seated lack of confidence." This shield, of course, is what I call the mask, the emotional defense mechanism boys use to hide their shame.

Purkey's findings fit with those of my own work. I tested a group of boys for their performance on the Coopersmith Self-Esteem Inventory, a series of questions designed to measure a child's self-esteem. What I discovered is that, though the boys in my group were functioning quite well on the outside, and their measures of self-esteem were generally at least average, many of them were giving what are known as "false-positive" responses. A false-positive response is one where the child thinks he is answering a question in a way that reflects his high self-esteem, but his answer in fact reflects that the child's genuine feelings are different. When a child gives several false-positive answers on this test of self-esteem, the researcher knows that the child is not able, for one reason or another, to give sincere responses. Indeed, the false-positive scale is actually referred to as the "lie measure."

Although the boys in my study showed average self-esteem—neither terribly "high" nor terribly "low"—not only did many of them give false-positive responses, but the extent to which they gave such false-positive or defensive responses significantly grew as the boys got older. On a scale from 1 to 8 (where 1 suggests *genuine responses* and 8 suggests *false-positive* ones), the boys "scored" higher and higher over time. Specifically, boys from grades seven through nine scored between 1.53 and 1.95; boys in the tenth grade scored at 2.45; those in the eleventh grade received 3.0; and the twelfth-graders scored a 5.0.

These findings suggest that as boys move through adolescence, they are more and more prone to distort the extent to which they truly feel confident about their masculinity. In other words, as they move through adolescence, they feel an increasing need to *say* they conform to society's ideal of "masculine" self-confidence (even though inside themselves they may not feel confident at all).

This escalating masking of a boy's real feelings is consistent with the research of Professor Notleman at NIMH. He studied young teens as they made the transition to secondary schools, assessing what they perceived about their competence and self-esteem as compared with what their teachers felt about them. "Boys," Notleman found, "consistently rated themselves more competent . . . than they were rated by their teachers." His findings, like my own, imply that boys resort to bravado to cover over the shame they would experience if they actually showed their fears about not measuring up. Rather than realizing or expressing their feelings of insecurity, boys "whistle a happy tune." This confident tune may fool many adults, and the boys themselves—at least for a while.

These studies also suggest that the longer boys are out there in society—in other words, the more they're influenced by society's ambivalent feelings about gender roles and masculinity—the more they feel they have to hide their own confusion by "making believe" they feel good about themselves when they don't, and by pretending that everything is fine, when perhaps it is not so fine. As the years pass, the mask for many boys becomes tighter and tighter.

So, while it's not always easy to detect, adolescent boys, *just like adolescent girls,* are suffering from a crisis in self-esteem that seriously threatens their capacity to learn, achieve, and feel successful.

THE SYSTEM DOES NOT ALWAYS FIT OUR BOYS: THE EMOTIONAL DISCONNECT BETWEEN TEACHERS AND BOYS

To remedy this predicament, the solution, of course, is not to stop focusing on girls but to begin focusing more effectively on boys as well. This will not be easy, because I believe that *the very structure of most coeducational schools tends unwittingly to favor female students,* that teachers have become well sensitized to girls' voices—sometimes at the expense of their ability to recognize boys' voices—and that many educators do not understand boys' characteristic learning styles. Many coeducational schools, I believe, have evolved—due to a variety of societal, cultural, and historical factors—into institutions that are better at satisfying the needs of girls than those of boys. Or these schools have evolved into environments that are essentially "gender-blind." Either way, too many schools are failing to address boys' unique social and emotional needs and are not providing the kinds of classroom activities and approaches that will help most boys to thrive.

In a recent study entitled *The Influence of School Climate on Gender Differences in Achievement and Engagement of Young Adolescents,* Valerie Lee and her associates at the University of Michigan analyzed data on the educational progress of more than nine thousand eighth-grade students. They found that the impact of a student's gender on his or her academic performance was inconsistent—boys did better in some areas and girls did better in others. Their more striking discovery, however, was that eighth-grade girls were more engaged academically than boys, evidenced better study habits and better attendance, were more likely to successfully complete their homework, and generally had a more positive set of academically oriented behaviors. Thus, though girls, as we've seen, may perform below boys in certain limited areas (generally math and science), it seems they are better adjusted to schools than boys are. But is it that girls are better adjusted to schools or that schools are better adjusted to girls?

Consider this example. I was recently asked to consult at a highly ranked suburban public elementary school where the teachers had received compulsory retraining in gender equity. The teachers had become especially vigilant, even obsessive, about making sure that the voices of girls in their classes received ample attention. On several occasions I had observed the fourth-grade class of Ms. Callahan. She was particularly skillful, modern, and warm in her approach, universally beloved by the students. I have every reason to believe that Ms. Callahan was a teacher who would want both boys and girls to derive all they could from the classroom experience.

On this visit, some boys and girls who had been organized into "teams" were working together on a writing project about friendship. Adult volunteers were consultants for these teams and were helping them with their computer skills. I was surprised to see that instead of focusing on the writing project, Ms. Callahan's attention was almost entirely taken up by disciplining the boys. Several lively boys were making a commotion in one corner near the computer. Ms. Callahan cautioned them about making too much noise, and told them to return to their desks and wait their turns.

With long faces, the boys meandered across the room and slumped into their seats. A moment later one of the boys could not resist calling out about something. Ms. Callahan gave him a stern second warning. "I don't want to have to caution you again," Ms. Callahan said. "If I do, you're heading for the principal's office."

I had observed this class before, and now I noticed that two of the more creative male students—Robert and Shawn—were not in evidence. I asked Ms. Callahan if they were sick that day.

"No," she explained. "Robert is too excitable for the group process. He's working on an entirely different project." She pointed him out—sitting alone on the floor, tucked out of view, banished from the team endeavor.

"And where's Shawn?" I inquired.

"He was telling inappropriate jokes about Albert Einstein earlier in the day and distracting the entire class. So, he's sitting outside working on his spelling." Ms. Callahan sighed. "Some kids just seem unable to fit into this more quiet team-based teaching."

I wish I had asked her what those jokes about Albert Einstein were, but I was too concerned about her attitude toward these boys. She clearly felt that they could not "fit in" and that they were "unable" to participate appropriately, when I knew (as she did) that these were bright boys with a lot to offer. Although I doubt that Ms. Callahan would agree, I think the prevailing method in class that day was structured around the way girl students prefer to work, and that boys were at a disadvantage.

This unintentional disconnect between teachers and boys can grow more intense as boys approach adolescence. In elementary school, most teachers find it relatively easy to see their male students for what they are—little boys with weaknesses and vulnerabilities. But when a boy takes on the physical characteristics of a man—when stubble begins to appear on the upper lip and he starts to tower over the teacher—it can become very difficult for a teacher to remember that there is still a little boy inside that mature male body. All the teacher's personal feelings about men and masculinity now come into play, and he or she may be less effective at focusing on what the boy needs from that teacher to learn. The teacher may not have been taught about the Boy Code or the mask; he or she may not fully understand the societal pressures that make boys feel they need to act strong, tough, and aggressive, and so the teacher may be unable to see the boy's genuine vulnerability and thus even feel intimidated or, in some cases, physically threatened by him.

These attitudes toward boys as learners are not confined to teachers. Girls themselves, encouraged by the school environment itself and picking up on their teachers' attitudes, may unwittingly contribute to boys' difficulties. As one eleven-year-old girl recently explained to me: "Boys mess everything up. They act goofy and we don't want them in our groups."

Obviously, boys quickly sense these anti-boy attitudes. Fourteen-year-old Kevin explained to me how many boys at school fear getting involved: "I know that in many classes girls are supposedly intimidated by guys. But I think the *opposite* is true. Girls have an easier time opening up and communicating than guys do. . . . Many guys are afraid to speak up because they don't want to look stupid."

Jacob, an eighth-grade student now in an all-boys school talked about the effect of not having girls in his classes: "When girls are around, you can't help acting different. *The good thing here is that you can say what-*

ever you want in class and not feel stupid. We also say exactly what we mean to each other. That's really important. It's also nice not to care about how you look at school. It's fun to see girls out of school or on the weekends, but I just don't think I would feel like myself if there were girls in school."

Though younger boys may be less able to articulate the effects of girls' attitudes toward them, of course they respond to them too. For example, Randy came into first grade as a strong reader. But, when Ms. Cohen organized the class into six reading groups, she decided Randy wasn't quite strong enough to join the top group, consisting of three girls. After about six weeks, however, Randy had improved enough in his reading that the teacher felt he could join them. Randy was very excited; the girls were not. They did not welcome Randy. In fact, Laura, the girl acknowledged by everyone as the best reader in class and leader of the top group, was overtly hostile to Randy. If he made a mistake while reading aloud, she would stifle a giggle or roll her eyes. When it came to choosing a book for the group to read, Laura would always prevail, vetoing Randy's choice and gaining support from the other girls for her own.

It was tough for Randy to deal with reading at the higher level, tougher for him to be the only boy in a group of three girls, even tougher to deal with Laura's derision and hostility. But I believe most of his stress could have been relieved if the teacher, Ms. Cohen, had chosen to intervene. But she too saw Randy's elevation to the top reading group as a privilege—he was taking a position that she believed was "naturally" occupied by girls. And, in fact, the statistics about reading and writing performance support her belief. The treatment of Randy was, in effect, very similar to the treatment a girl might get if she were to join an all-boy sports team. He was rejected and made to feel unwelcome. In my opinion, such gender-based animosity should never be tolerated.

GENDER STEREOTYPING IN THE CLASSROOM

The gender stereotyping that leads up to the way that Randy was mistreated begins as early as kindergarten, and by the time kids reach middle school it often becomes virtually sanctioned. Based on many of the myths about boys that we've discussed—especially the myths that there's just one way boys will behave ("boys will be boys") and that boys are somehow wired to be rambunctious, socially immature misfeasors ("boys are toxic")—many teachers may develop rigid or misguided ideas about how to deal with the boys in their classrooms.

Like anybody else in society, teachers tend to place boys in gender straitjackets and thus restrict boys when they attempt to break out of them. Consider, for example, what happened when Linda Bakken, an educational psychologist at Wichita State University, recently visited a kindergarten classroom. When a little boy dressed up as a woman, complete with necklace and handbag, the teacher angrily chided him. "Little boys shouldn't be playing with necklaces," she said, and pulled him away from the girls' area.

A friend of one of my colleagues recently told me of how a budding friendship between my colleague's daughter and our mutual friend's son was almost destroyed in first grade when a teacher at their school sarcastically remarked: "Adam, it looks like your *girlfriend,* Sarah, wants to sit next to you."

By looking at boys in a narrow way and failing to recognize the gentle, creative, empathic sides of many boys, I believe that some teachers— though they may not consciously intend it—can seriously encumber the emotional and scholastic development of boys in their classes who do not necessarily comply with society's old stereotyped gender rules about how they should behave, learn, and grow. Unwitting as it may be, many teachers strictly enforce the Boy Code and suppress any boys who try to buck it.

In addition, many educators simply cast boys as the "bad guys," pointing to our sons as the source of many of the serious problems girls have recently faced at school. And so rather than doing what's necessary to address boys' unique behaviors, concerns, and dreams, there's actually a prevalent tendency in the educational establishment to ignore these needs. Boys are allowed, in effect, to "sink or swim." When they clash with teachers, administrators, or other students, they're often seen as troublemakers or problem cases. Based on the "myth of toxicity," boys at school are often perceived as "little (testosterone-driven) monsters" whose "aggression" must be controlled and disciplined rather than as vulnerable little boys who must be nurtured and encouraged. This, of course, makes it hard for us to see new, helpful, creative solutions to schooling them.

While it's true that some boys may raise serious safety and discipline concerns, I am convinced that most simply aren't getting the right kind (or amount) of attention and instruction. Consider, for instance, Julia Winslow, a teacher who has taught social studies in her town's middle school for eight years. "When I first started teaching," she said, "I was determined to be different from the teachers I had when I was young. I wanted to really listen to kids, really respect them, not ever speak down to them or get harsh with them."

The reality, Julia laments, had not matched her hopes. "There are days when I feel really pleased with what's gone on in my classroom. The kids have built a castle to learn about medieval times, or we've had a really good discussion about some current event. But a lot of times I'm just a referee, or a circus trainer for twenty-eight seals. I'm barking orders, throwing fish, handing out reprimands. No one is getting what they really need."

Julia feels that boys in her classes often pay the biggest price. "I'm constantly yelling at the boys. No matter how much bluster they have, I know it hurts when I snap at them. A lot of times I'm sure there's some underlying reason for their misbehavior, but I don't have the time or energy to deal with it."

"What about the girls?" I asked.

"The girls tend to take care of themselves more. The boys usually need more help with the work, but I can't be ten places at once. So I'm always just trying to get through the day by telling this one to wait, this one to be quiet, this one to quit doing such-and-such to that one."

"It sounds like it's been somewhat tough for you," I suggested.

"Well, I had one boy last year that I couldn't deal with at all. He could never keep up with the rest of the class. Every time I looked up, he was pulling some girl's hair or punching some kid. I recommended that he be put into the special ed class. After he left, I felt terrible. He wasn't one of the brightest kids, but he probably could have made it on the regular track if I just had more help or more patience or something. My decision to send him to special ed may affect him forever. I don't feel so great about it."

But if Julia laments the difficulties she has in addressing the needs of some boys, some educators actually target boys as the source of all our problems and blame them for the difficulties girls are currently having. For instance, I recently received a copy of a newsletter for parents from a sophisticated coed middle school that ran an article entitled "Girls Speak Out/Boys Share *Star Wars*." The newsletter explained that the issue would include two subjects because the boys and girls couldn't agree on just one—the boys wanted to focus on *Star Wars* while the girls wanted to write about women's rights. Accordingly, one half of the newsletter would be about *Star Wars*, the other half about what it means to be young women.

"The girls of this school," the newsletter read, "are the *good part* of the future." The inescapable implication, of course, was that boys are the *bad* part of the future, as represented by their obsession with silly movies like *Star Wars*. One of the articles in the section on girls was headlined WHY IT'S FANTASTIC TO BE A FEMALE. Nothing wrong with that, if it had simply cataloged girls' positive traits. But this article stated girls' attributes in contrast to those of boys. Here they are:

- Females are superior at nonverbal communication.
- Males appear to be more active and athletic . . . but females are actually more active athletes.
- Except for muscles and skeleton the female body is stronger than the male's in every way.

And on it went. Harmless fun, you might say. But if boys were degrading girls in this way, would we be laughing? Would we ever tolerate a school newsletter that pronounced that "the boys are the good part of our school's future"?

The reality is that in our thoughtful efforts to help girls find their voice in the classroom, we've unintentionally allowed potent anti-boy sentiment to creep into our schools. As a result, many of our educational institutions have been frightfully slow to respond to the genuine emotional and academic needs of our sons.

A DIFFERENT DRUMMER: BOYS' CHARACTERISTIC LEARNING STYLES

And if many of our schools do not embrace boys in an empathic way and inadequately address boys' unique emotional issues as students, I believe that many also fail to recognize that many boys may actually learn differently than girls do and thus need to be taught differently too. Research confirms these differences.

For example, Richard Hawley of the University School in Cleveland has posited that there are differential "tempos" in learning between the genders. Former chair of the International Coalition of Boys Schools, Hawley has cautioned his fellow educators that boys and girls learn at different paces and with different styles. "Gender-based variations in tempo and pattern of learning can be identified from the pre-kindergarten through the high school years. Primary school girls generally demonstrate reading and writing proficiency earlier than boys do. . . . Females reach the peak of their pubertal growth spurt a year or two sooner than boys. Each gender-based physiological difference is accompanied by distinctive psychological and social adjustments. Boys develop language skills . . . large and small scale muscle proficiencies at a developmentally different *tempo* from girls."

Hawley's observations are important because they suggest that if a school is to provide a successful instructional environment for boys, that school must stay in touch with the unique "tempo" and learning style of each boy. Teachers and administrators need to be cognizant of the developmental level of the boys at their schools, making sure that the activities selected for boys are appropriate given the level. *If the tempo is off, boys can be led to academic failure and low self-esteem.*

The specific learning style of a boy may also require a teacher's careful attention. For instance, I've observed some boys who are so resistant to reading books in class that they'll literally toss them aside to pursue more hands-on activities. Yet some of these same boys have been appropriately motivated to read by letting them use a computer, which allows them to have fun scrolling through the pages using the keyboard or mouse.

I've also seen boys who, though they were known to be "lazy readers," became very active, proficient readers when given reading matter on subjects (such as sports, adventure stories, murder mysteries) that actually interested them. In a fascinating study, Donald Portoff, a professor of reading at the State University in Allendale, Michigan, recently found a correlation between boys' low reading skills and their association of reading with "feminine" skills. There's little question that introducing texts with boy-specific interests would help boys to develop stronger reading skills.

Many classes simply aren't taught in a way that boys find captivating. As one high school teacher stressed, "If boys aren't really engaged, they're discipline problems—the key is keeping them engaged."

Maryland psychologist Gloria Van Derhorst explains a similar concept, stressing that schools often don't sufficiently embrace what she calls "high-energy kids." According to Van Derhorst: "Traditionally classrooms are not organized to suit high-energy learners. . . . In most classrooms, students are discouraged from getting out of their seats and are forced to learn by listening. This frustrates students who can learn better when they visualize concepts and physically move around." Though Van Derhorst is not referring to students of just one gender, clearly many of the squirming scholars she's talking about are boys.

Some research suggests that, whereas many girls may prefer to learn by watching or listening, boys generally prefer to learn by doing, by engaging in some action-oriented task. In learning environments biased against their strengths, boys may get turned off or begin to become frustrated, attempting now to get their needs met by seeking negative attention—or, we might say, through unwitting protest against this educational gender straitjacket that hems them in. This last-ditch rebellion completes the circle of failure, for now these boys are labeled as "conduct disordered" or "troublemakers" or diagnosed with "hyperactivity." Once again, boys' needs—and their protests against being negatively stereotyped—are misunderstood.

Sometimes the straitjacket can take the form of the school's physical surroundings. Five-year-old Eric, for example, had attended a coed preschool before enrolling in a progressive kindergarten. The teachers at his new school had observed Eric at his preschool and found him to be an appealing boy, willing to engage in any task set before him. But they also noticed a worryingly "numb" manner about him, especially when he was required to join in group activities that involved small-muscle activities—he had been so uninterested in a puppet show at his preschool that he seemed entirely disengaged and almost frightened. At his new school the teachers encouraged Eric to take part in far more active pursuits, such as working in the class garden, shoveling soil and mulch and pushing around a junior-sized wheelbarrow. His teacher remarks that "being able to move so freely and so often in the course of the school day has seemed to liberate Eric from his former still and tentative condition."

As well documented as the characteristics of boys' learning styles may be, many educators seem not to take them into account in their attitudes toward boys in the classroom. This was impressed upon me when I conducted my seminar on "Understanding Boys" at a well-respected graduate school of education. I asked the group of master public school teachers to describe boys' learning styles to me. I implored them to put aside "political correctness," external expectations, and worries about gender equity, and to speak only from their hearts and their educational experience in talking about boys in the classroom. Here are some of the comments they made:

"Younger boys are more literal and concrete than girls."

"Younger boys engage in more open rebellion than girls."

"Boys are often poor auditory [listening] learners and better kinesthetic [action-oriented] ones."

"Boys engage in much more physical stimulation for persuasion, may get into more open conflicts and tend 'to punch' their way out."

"Boys may show their affection through action or bumping into you."

"In order to assimilate new ideas, boys may need the freedom to play them out with games and self-imposed rules."

"Boys put forward a storm of 'intellectual bravado,' behind which they seem very unsure, but need the bluster to prove their points."

What I find interesting about these comments is that they were quite perceptive and accurate; these teachers had a pretty clear picture of boys. But it's *how* they talked about the differences—as positives or negatives—that made all the difference. When considered with empathy, these characteristics can be seen as the positive attributes of boys. If described less lovingly and with less empathy, however, they might sound rather like this: learning difficulties, conduct disturbance, physical aggressiveness, inattention syndrome and hyperactivity, perhaps even the code words "attention deficit disorder."

What I find tragic is that by failing to understand and appreciate each boy's unique tempo and characteristic learning style in an empathic way, we make it hard for him to feel confident about himself and flourish as a student. Moreover, when he subsequently withdraws from classroom activities or begins to rebel or act out, we often deal him a second blow by interpreting his natural response as the sign of a "learning disability" or so-called hyperactivity when in reality it's shame, boredom, or restlessness.

Fortunately, some educators "get it." Some educators understand that boys may learn differently than girls and that if boys' unique needs are properly addressed, boys will be able to catch up in areas like reading and writing and rediscover their confidence as learners. Lest we doubt this, here's a story from a school in England where two teachers recently got together and changed things for boys.

DEAD POETS' SOCIETY: TURNING THINGS AROUND FOR BOYS

"People think that boys like you won't be able to understand writers such as the Romantic poets. Well, you're going to prove them wrong. Do you understand?" Mr. Jeckells, a teacher at Kings' School in Winchester, England, addresses a classroom full of boys.

Just two years earlier the head teacher at the school, Ray Bradbury, had analyzed the results of his students' scores on the GCSE, a standardized test that rates students from A to F in various subject matters: 78 percent of girls at the school gained five or more A–C, but the boys trailed behind with only 56 percent. Boys scored particularly poorly in English— in that subject, 27 percent fewer boys than girls gained grades A–C. Mr. Bradbury was unhappy about the enormous disparity between girls' and boys' academic performance. While he understood that some boys were doing well, he realized—as we've discussed above—that the largest portion of the kids at the bottom of the class were boys. And he decided to do something about it.

Since he recognized that some boys were already doing relatively well, he decided against segregating these boys from girls at the same academic level. But he decided to place the boys who were doing significantly less well in an all-boys class of their own.

"The most vital ingredient in the scheme's success was finding the right teacher for this group," says Bradbury. "So I chose Rob Jeckells . . . who is involved with sport, and someone to whom the boys relate very easily. We consciously planned the teaching methodology. The class is didactic and teacher-fronted. It involves sharp questions and answers and constantly checking understanding. Discipline is clear-cut—if homework isn't presented, it is completed in a detention. There is no discussion."

While some of the boys (and their parents) resisted the approach at first, Mr. Jeckells seemed to know that speaking the truth would disarm them:

"I presented the boys with the statistical evidence, which showed they were in danger of underachieving, and made clear what I expected of them. When they saw themselves as being part of a pilot scheme which was meeting their educational needs, their attitudes changed and their motivation doubled. Also, the head has dropped in on the group frequently, sometimes with visiting advisers. Now, the boys have a sense of pride. They feel they are special."

Mr. Jeckells quickly developed a keen understanding of why his all-boys class was working well:

"In a single-sex class, you can create a team atmosphere where the boys support one another. But when girls are present, boys are loath to express opinions for fear of appearing sissy—their instinct is to stay aloof and macho. If it's all boys together, then it's much easier to break down inhibitions. . . . Also, I can choose course material that appeals to boys. Members of my group are football-mad. . . . In the mixed groups, they would be turned off by *Jane Eyre,* whereas I can pick texts such as *Silas Marner* and *The War Poets,* which they feel are more relevant to them."

One of the boys in his class seems to agree:

"I like English now," the boy explains, "because there is less pressure in the classroom. Previously, if you made a comment, the other boys would make fun of you just to make you look silly in front of the girls. Now, we support each other. We are all working hard to show that we can be just as successful as the other groups."

According to the school, after just two years, Mr. Jeckells's all-boys approach already seems to be successful. Among those boys at the same academic level last year, only 7 out of 25 gained a C or better in English literature. Yet based on recent mock examinations, Mr. Jeckells believes 25 of the 34 in his all-boys group will gain a C grade or better. Perhaps even more impressive, while two years ago the school had had a 22 percent disparity between boys and girls gaining five or more A–C grades, last year there was just a 1 percent difference.

Colleagues of Mr. Jeckells are so encouraged by these results that apparently similar all-boys classes are now being set up for mathematics and science.

FINDING THE RIGHT FIT FOR BOYS: HOW TO GUY-IFY A SCHOOL

Indeed, boys will thrive at school if there is a pervasive sense that they are welcome, that they are liked, and that who they *really* are—and how they *really* enjoy learning—will be embraced in a genuine way by their teachers. In the national longitudinal study on adolescent health, *Protecting Adolescents from Harm 1997,* researchers demonstrated that the largest major factor protecting young people from emotional distress, drug abuse, and violence—other than the closeness they were able to achieve within their families—was "perceived school connectedness."

The more a boy feels warmly toward his school, connected, understood, and treated fairly, the less likely he is to become suicidal, abuse drugs and alcohol, become addicted to nicotine, or engage in impulsive sexual activities. A boy does best when he feels cared for and understood by his teachers and when he senses that they have high hopes for him academically. By designing an inviting educational experience for boys, schools can help them boost not only their academic performance and self-esteem but also their hopefulness about the opportunities ahead of them.

Just as we've implemented specific measures to help girls benefit maximally from their school experiences, there's a lot we can do to create school connectedness and help boys succeed at school. Most critically, I believe we must make absolutely sure that for every boy there is a "good fit" between what makes him thrive as an individual and what his school actually provides for him. For instance, if a boy learns best by reading quietly by himself for a certain length of time—say, half an hour—and then taking breaks in which he engages in vigorous physical activity, such as running or playing a sport, ideally his school will not require him to attend four hours of classes in which he is given no time to read by himself and no time for motor activities. If another boy learns best by working in small groups in which the students teach one another through shared lessons and activities and where no one student is ever put on the spot to come up with the right answers, ideally the boy is not placed in classrooms with huge numbers of students and then grilled by a teacher using the Socratic method.

So many of us have memories of teachers or classroom experiences that left us feeling understimulated or shortchanged. When I asked Barry Rosenman, thirty-five, about his elementary educational experience, he immediately recalled Mrs. Ramedi, his first-grade teacher.

"Mrs. Ramedi hated me!" Barry exclaimed. "And I hated her!"

I asked him why.

"I grew up in a supportive environment," Barry continued. "My mother stayed at home full-time, and she was devoted to all three of us kids. On nice days she encouraged me and my brother and sister to play energetic games outside, or go explore the brook near our house for tadpoles. When I came home covered in mud, my mother shook her head a little, but she wasn't disapproving. She wanted me to be adventurous.

"On rainy days, she'd set up her college microscope in the kitchen so we could discover what salt and sugar and pond water looked like. She had a recipe for cookies where you could make a figure and fill it in with candy that melted in the oven to look like stained glass. By the time I started going to school all day for first grade, I was used to trying things out, running around whenever I needed to, and everything being hands-on.

"That definitely wasn't Mrs. Ramedi's style," Barry continued. "I guess it couldn't be with twenty-five or thirty first-graders. She had us sitting quietly in rows, filling out those dittos they used to have before Xerox machines came in. I'd finish a ditto in ten seconds, then be expected to sit there in silence for it seemed like hours. I was bored to death."

Barry rebelled. "I'd make little squeaking sounds while the other kids were finishing their dittos, getting louder and louder until she heard me. I'd throw paper airplanes. I'd fidget. One time she left the room for a minute, and when she came back, she found me standing on top of my desk and screaming as loud as I could. That didn't go over real well!"

In November, Barry's parents had him switched into a different first-grade classroom. "My parents thought I was a bit mischievous, but they knew the problem wasn't just me. My new teacher gave me more challenging work, and I settled down a lot more after that."

As Barry's recollections demonstrate, there are ways in which schools can either respond or fail to respond to a boy's specific needs. Barry needed to be creatively challenged, to engage in action-oriented tasks, to experience a continuation of the stimulating educational environment his mother had created for him at home. Thrust instead into a first-grade classroom that left him feeling bored and restless, Barry acted out. He was lucky that—instead of being placed in a special education class as a "disturbed" child or being misdiagnosed as "hyperactive"—he found his way into another classroom with a teacher who was better attuned to what he needed most to succeed: creative, high-energy, hands-on learning activities.

Listen to my interview, in a similar vein, with two concerned parents who struggled with the educational environment in which their son was initially placed. After explaining to me that they had tried to raise their son and daughter without abiding by the narrow gender roles imposed on them as children, Regina and Donald Lincoln acknowledged that they had communicated distinct expectations to each child. "Without being conscious of it, I know I've been more protective toward my daughter, and I've encouraged my son's independence more," Regina Lincoln admitted. "Both of my children are bright and creative. But Corey is much more quirky and exploratory, Marissa is much more diligent and deliberate."

The Lincolns found that their son's learning style did not fit well with the neighborhood's public school. "No matter what the assignment was, Corey wanted to change it or abandon it altogether. While Marissa was enjoying filling out endless worksheets, Corey was bored to tears. When his teachers started complaining about his wildness in class, we quickly figured out he just couldn't stand the tedium."

The Lincolns transferred Corey, who is now eleven, to an arts-centered experimental school. "I like school much better now," Corey told me. "We get to make spaceships out of clay, and play drums, and play around a lot more." While his new school has the same amount of recess each day, Corey experiences the curriculum as a medium for self-expression.

The Lincolns are pleased with their decision. "I question whether the structure of Marissa's school is ideal for her. But in Corey's case, it was imperative that we get him out of there if we wanted him to flourish."

Boys, just like girls, do best in schools that give them the chance to participate in learning activities that correspond to their personal interests and competencies, enabling them to sound their authentic voices and thrive as individuals. It's important that boys feel at home in the school environment and that they find the teacher and the activities he or she organizes sufficiently appealing. Indeed the studies on self-esteem by Professor William Purkey also demonstrated that when classrooms are specifically made to be inviting for boys, their problems of lower self-esteem were significantly abated.

WHO'S GOT THE PROBLEM PAYING ATTENTION? THE BOYS OR US?

When schools fail to attune themselves to boys' unique ways of learning and don't truly address our sons' needs, the consequences can be devastating.

In some schools a boy with ordinary exuberance may be "punished" by being placed in classes intended for learning-disabled children or sent regularly to a detention room where he sits unattended for several periods, losing valuable classroom time. For this unlucky boy, this may mark the beginning of a life relegated to second-class economic and intellectual citizenship, invite dangerously diminished self-esteem, and significantly increase the likelihood that he'll later be misdiagnosed with attention deficit disorder or some other psychiatric disturbance. Even for boys who escape these more dire fates, being at the "wrong" school can mean twelve years of feeling like a square peg in a round hole, of squirming with excess energy that is suppressed rather than harnessed, and of doing worse academically and emotionally than they would in schools that meet their individual needs and abilities.

GABRIEL: WHEN AN ACTIVE BOY IS DIAGNOSED AS "HYPERACTIVE"

Gabriel Bauer-Brown was in the third grade when his teacher first labeled him with attention deficit disorder, or ADD.

"She told us he spoke out of turn, got too rough on the playground, and disrupted class," his dad, Perry, remembers. "She said he could never focus on his work, so it must be ADD."

At her suggestion, the Bauer-Browns sought help from their pediatrician, who immediately prescribed Ritalin. Perry was nervous about the drug. "I didn't like the idea, but if it worked, it would be worth it. If my kid needed Ritalin to be able to do all right in school, then that was just what we would have to do."

On Ritalin, Gabriel changed. Instead of acting out, he became sullen and unresponsive. "It was as if the Ritalin had carried him away to some other planet," Perry says. "He wasn't making a lot of noise in class, but he wasn't concentrating on his schoolwork any better either. And at home, he was spacey and much less communicative than he used to be."

The Bauer-Browns decided to take Gabriel off Ritalin and pursue professional counseling for him. At first, Gabriel saw a school social worker. Then, after several months, the Bauer-Browns met with a therapist who specialized in child psychology. "What the therapist told us felt shocking at first, but later we had to admit we had suspected it all along," Perry told me.

"We adopted Gabriel when he was almost a year old. We got him from an orphanage in Brazil where we knew conditions were pretty awful. The therapist said she believed Gabriel had been seriously neglected there. She said we had done the right thing about taking him off Ritalin, and that therapy could help him express his pain in more constructive ways than those outbursts he used to have."

Progress has been gradual but continual, Perry now says. "He has a really strong bond with his therapist, and he's becoming more and more secure and confident. His teacher was right that he needed help, but Ritalin wasn't it."

For most any psychologist who works with boys or men, Gabriel's story is painfully familiar. In the United States boys are up to ten times more likely than girls to be diagnosed with attention deficit disorder—a severe enough disturbance to require extensive counseling and potent medications. Of the more than one million children taking Ritalin (a powerful stimulant medication for ADD), three quarters of them are boys. According to a recent study, three times more boys than girls are enrolled in special education programs, with close to 70 percent of all high school "special classes" populated by boys. Many of the boys sent to these "special" classes and programs are boys diagnosed with ADD.

As a clinical psychologist who has seen the severe damage done in *missing* a *legitimate* case of ADD in childhood and the miraculous effects of appropriate treatments—psychological and medical—in both children and adults, naturally I would urge against a simpleminded attack on the legitimacy of ADD or its necessary treatment. Even the great gender disparity—almost ten males to every female—is not without sophisticated biological underpinnings. However, one cannot help being concerned by the sheer number of diagnosed cases, the frequency of diagnoses initiated by overwhelmed classroom teachers and children's guidance counselors, and the possibility that many mild to moderate cases of ADD are a normal variant of boys' temperament that could be corrected by a properly trained, attentive adult. Many of these cases probably wouldn't even come about in a classroom that was thoughtfully designed for typical boys' temperaments—one that kept them motivated and energized with a variety of interesting learning activities and paced these activities according to their unique learning tempos, one in which the teacher understood that so much of boys' outward agitation and rowdiness is often just masked emotional pain.

Indeed I believe that much of the behavior we label as "attention deficit disorder" is actually just the externalization, through action, of boyhood emotions. After all, action is often boys' only way of saying "Look at me," "Give me love and attention," or "Please, I need your help!" When boys act out, I believe that—more often than not—they're looking for understanding and empathy rather than diagnoses and medication. They are telling us, in essence, "I feel too ashamed to talk to you directly about what's going wrong, so I am going to use my behavior to let you know indirectly."

The official name for the disorder with which so many boys are diagnosed is actually "attention deficit and hyperactivity disorder" or ADHD (ADD for short), and it includes several scientific categories of subclassification necessary for a diagnosis. But the behaviors to be identified are so close on the continuum to those often manifested by emotionally healthy boys that the capacity to distinguish serious learning disabilities from a boy's ordinary boisterousness is difficult at best, even for a trained professional.

In theory, the typical ADHD boy will have problems sustaining attention or concentrating, sitting still in class, or waiting his turn. He may yell out impulsively, talk too much, act disorganized or distracted, be forgetful.

He may wriggle in his seat or abandon it for almost incessant movement, and the interruption of others may be common.

I think you can begin to see how the line between pathological hyperactivity and a boy's normal rough play is often hard to ascertain. The decision about how to diagnose him—and how to solve the behavior problems he's exhibiting—is influenced by the school he attends, the attitude of his teacher, the ethos of his classroom, and the perspective of his parents. For example, a school that has a more tolerant and less rigid milieu that harnesses extra energy may be much less likely to tag Johnny with a diagnosis than an overcrowded class with strict "Sit in your seat" rules and negative attitudes toward boys' rambunctiousness. These factors may make all the difference in the world not only in whether he is seen as "dysfunctional" or normal but also—even if he is appropriately diagnosed with a mild to moderate form of hyperactivity or learning disability—in whether his situation will be redressed appropriately. Will he be treated with pills and pushed into a special classroom, or will his caregivers try creative nonpharmacological interventions, such as placing him in an "open classroom" in which he can participate in hands-on activities or establishing a regimen of counseling sessions on a regular basis? Depending on how he is treated for ADD, the boy could end up either suffering years of psychological problems or, if the approach is a healthy one, enjoying a life full of creative energy and success.

MARTY WOLT: ICONOCLASTIC OR "DYSFUNCTIONAL" LEARNER

Marty Wolt had been tagged with the ADD label when he was a teenager. His mom, Beth, did not believe her son had ADD, but had to fight the educational establishment to have Marty treated as a "normal" boy. Marty was the kind of boy who typically ends up with the "disabled" label. He talked incessantly in preschool. In elementary school he followed kids around, acted rowdily, and incited classmates to act up. Teachers and school authorities told Beth that her son was "sick" and in need of medication, such as Ritalin.

Beth resisted the diagnosis and the treatment. She volunteered to be in the classroom to help calm Marty down. She had him transferred to more creative educational settings with more flexible teachers. She found a sympathetic guidance counselor who was willing to talk with and listen to her son. She fought so that Marty could maintain his own eccentric form of boyishness without being branded as disabled.

To Marty, having the sympathetic ear of supportive adults, made all the difference in the world. Of one of his guidance counselors, he said, "She heard me. I like it when somebody is listening. Who doesn't?"

Marty's story turned out a success. He's about to graduate from high school, hoping to head for college. He gets good grades, works part-time, and has begun writing plays as a hobby—plays about adults who can't listen to kids. No one, not even his mother, denies that his behavior was extreme at times. A diagnosis of ADD and medication might even have been justified. Indeed, many boys who are labeled as having ADD are less disruptive than Marty.

Although Marty wasn't one of them, 5.4 million U.S. children were classified as "disabled" in 1995. ADD was the fastest-growing category, its ranks having doubled from 1990 to 1995. And remember that more than nine out of ten children diagnosed with ADD are boys!

I believe it's important that we as parents make sure our boys are not branded as "abnormal" and slapped with the ADD label before we're absolutely sure it's the case. As psychologist Diane McGuinness at the University of South Florida warns, many school systems to a large extent have "pathologized what is simply normal for boys." Though ADD is a genuine neurobehavioral disorder, and research shows that it does occur in boys more often than in girls, I believe society's response to this boyhood quandary has actually exacerbated the problem. In some cases we've misdiagnosed boys as being *hyper*active who are simply *very* active. In other cases, where there is a pathology that looks like ADD, the boy is actually exhibiting the symptoms of depression. Some boys, properly diagnosed as ADD cases, are overmedicated. Other boys, who clearly are ADD cases, are branded as troublemakers and receive punishment rather than treatment. Both the sheer numbers of boys identified with "hyperactivity" and the distinctly unempathic ways many of these boys are responded to must give us pause to rethink the ADD dilemma.

Although genuine hyperactivity exists and deserves our every effort at a nonstigmatizing treatment, one can justifiably suspect that much of what is called ADD is closer to MDD—male deficit disorder—with the deficiency lying not in our sons but within society's inability to correctly perceive boys' inner needs, yearnings, and pain. We tend to label and treat, rather than *listen.* Indeed, it is quite possible that the upsurge in "hyperactive" behavior in boys, especially younger boys in the early elementary grades, is a symptom of the trauma of separation we have spoken of and a protest against being fitted for the emotionally limiting gender straitjacket that awaits them.

As we create more classroom and learning environments in sync with boys' academic "tempos" that allow boys' genuine voices to emerge, we may expect to see fewer cases of pseudo-hyperactivity, better interventions when the disorder is really present, and greater success in attending to our sons' struggles for recognition, love, and achievement.

LESSONS FROM SINGLE-SEX SCHOOLS

As we try to guy-ify our coed schools and make them a better fit for boys, it's helpful to look to what all-boys schools do in order to succeed with boys. I know that most boys will not attend an all-boys school, nor do I advocate that they should. But, having had the opportunity to consult to a large cross section of single-sex day schools for boys throughout the United States, I have found that many of them, because they're specifically geared for boys, do a good job of creating an educational environment in which boys can triumph academically and emotionally. I have worked with many of these schools to help them develop an intramural culture that is empathic to boys, one that is sensitive to how the shame-based hardening process comes about and how boys use a mask to conceal inner struggles and uncertainties. Many of these schools have become comfortable learning spheres for the rough-and-tumble world of boys and some have thoughtfully addressed gender stereotyping in terms of how it restricts boys emotionally, academically, and professionally. Contrary to the myth that all-boys schools are dangerous, toxic breeding grounds of misogyny and aggression, I have found that many of them cultivate boys who have positive attitudes toward girls and women and who may feel as at ease being gentle and sensitive as they do gearing up for a rugby match.

For almost a decade psychologists and educators have recommended all-girls schools as institutions that help shelter girls from the uninviting atmosphere of coeducational schools where they must compete with boys and overcome anti-girl bias. Girls' schools have been widely reported as bolstering girls' academic achievement, empowering them to feel more confident about who they are and what they're capable of. The time has come, I believe, to look at whether the same is true for boys and, if so, to see what can be learned from these schools and apply it as best as possible within coeducational environments.

Though we've grown comfortable with and thrown our support toward all girls' schools, all my research suggests that, in America at least, we have not yet accepted a similar approach for boys. For instance, we look askance at all-boy remediation environments for students with legitimate learning disabilities and diminished self-esteem, and even challenge traditional all-boy social organizations such as the Boy Scouts. And, regrettably, the federal courts have rejected well-intentioned efforts to develop special all-boy academies to help young African American boys improve their English-language skills, viewing these "separate but equal" arrangements as patently unconstitutional. There is almost a sense that while we plan Take Our Daughters to Work Day and support women's colleges and affinity groups, we are Taking Our Boys to the Psychiatrist, forcibly integrating them into coeducational environments focused on meeting girls' needs, and denying them any all-male bonding environments short of the bench outside the principal's office or the defendant's seat in front of the arraignment judge on the way to jail. I wonder what has gotten in our way of examining the alternative of the all-boys schools for our sons, or of applying the lessons of all-boys schools to make our coed institutions more hospitable to boys.

Fortunately, recent research suggests that some boys' schools may provide just this kind of protective environment. In 1997 Diane Hulse, head of the Middle School at Collegiate School in New York City, completed comparative research on boys in the fifth through eighth grades at two premier independent schools—one coeducational, the other just for boys. Utilizing a broad array of empirical testing measures, Hulse showed that boys in the all-boys school seemed less defensive and less susceptible to peer pressure, more comfortable with their "aggression" as well as their relationships with girls, and more egalitarian in their attitudes about male and female roles than their counterparts in the coeducational institution.

These findings, in my view, imply several things. First, much as Richard Hawley would probably argue, students at an all-boys school are likely taught in a manner that recognizes and encourages their unique learning styles and tempos. Such schools are more flexible and less defensive in attitude, in comparison to institutions that seek to fit boys into a rigid traditional coeducational curriculum that ignores individual learning styles and paces. Even more important, I believe, these findings suggest that at a well-run boys' school a peer culture evolves in which boys feel more comfortable about themselves, are more confident about their abilities, and therefore do better in their class work. Especially for boys ages ten and older, with no girls around there are fewer reasons to feel they must brag, tease, and bluster. In the absence of girls, boys don't feel as competitive—or as vulnerable—and thus tend to be less tough on one another. They do less to shame their compatriots. All in all, they each tend to feel more self-confident and less dependent on a mask of bravado to cover their insecurities.

In coed environments, by contrast, many boys fear that teachers or other students will ridicule them if they behave in certain ways that might not be seen as fully "masculine." They may become anxious about discussing emotions evoked by a story or a poem, avoid answering teachers' questions so as not to look "stupid" by making a mistake or appearing effeminate by getting it right, and steer away from subjects thought of as "feminine." When boys get to school, gender stereotypes are often vigorously enforced by students and teachers alike, and boys feel obligated to conform to them. This gender straitjacketing disrupts boys' educational experience. It leads them to "overcompensate" by being disruptive in the classroom, harassing other students, or intentionally "acting dumb" in courses like English and social studies where showing even a scintilla of passion or intelligence may lead others to condemn them.

To be fair, as these results from Hulse's study are based on observations at only two schools, they probably require further corroboration. But even if we cannot come to conclusions about the advantages of all-boys schools with scientific certainty, I believe this study provides compelling initial evidence that, at least for some boys, being at an all-boys school provides important benefits.

Of course, the vast majority of boys—just as the vast majority of girls—will continue to receive their education in some type of coeducational environment. Our solution cannot and probably should not be to make all of our schools separate-sex schools. But I believe that we must try to apply the positive things we're learning about boys' schools to how boys are taught and treated in coeducational schools. For instance, just as some public schools have set up special "girls only" programs in math and science—a kind of single-gender academy within the coed environment—I believe that similar experiments for boys, especially in areas of reading and writing, have tremendous promise.

To cite one successful example of this concept, I should share the story of Jean Ellerbe, a teacher in a coed public school, who serendipitously ended up teaching an all-boys English class. By chance, all the students in her high school freshman English class in one semester were boys. At first it upset her and she tried to force the school to dissolve it, but slowly she came to realize the unique possibilities it offered. While in her coed English classes girls were more motivated and articulate, in the single-sex class the boys appeared to her "more at ease" and "not as embarrassed to speak up." The class, however, was looser and rowdier, something it took her a while to appreciate and value along with her boys. As one of the boys in her all-guy class commented to her: "Sometimes it can get a little rowdy with all guys, but it's easier for them to say what they want to say. If girls were there, you'd be scared of looking stupid."

Indeed, as this comment reflects, even in a traditional coed school, boys placed in an all-male class that is empathic to boys' typical learning styles and tempos may feel freed to take off their armor and sound their authentic voices. Among the boys I interviewed who either attended an all-boys school or had the chance to take key subjects in a single-sex class within a coed environment, many confirmed the freedom they felt to shed their masks.

Seventeen-year-old Liam explained: "When I'm in a class with girls, sometimes I feel that for girls to like me, I have to be cool. And being smart isn't cool. The guys who everybody considers the most cool don't do that well academically. They never raise their hands in class."

"But in an all-boys class, I can really concentrate on academics," Liam continued. "I don't have to feel uncomfortable about how I am perceived by the girls in the class, and I don't have to worry that they think I'm a geek or a dork or something like that. Now I work hard, and I am definitely doing my best. I feel good when I get a good grade."

When I talked with Toby, a bright-eyed fifteen-year-old dressed in a wrinkled shirt and jeans who attends an all-boys school, he described a number of benefits to receiving an education in a single-sex institution. "Academically, I've been able to strive because there haven't been girls around to impress or anything. In class I can raise my hand and say whatever I want to say, because I am not going to be embarrassed by talking around girls. You don't have to worry about the normal things, like how your clothes look, or ironing. It's just a lot easier to work with no girls around. I can see girls on weekends, but I'm not distracted by their presence at school. At a boys' school, I can just go out there and take chances, I guess. I can be the best student that I could be."

Toby also observed teachers bonding with male students more when girls are absent from the environment. "Teachers, especially women teachers, always like girls better. Here you get to be closer to your teachers [male and female] even if you're a boy."

He contrasted his current experience with his earlier years in a coed school. "I think people expect girls to be smarter. So it's hard for a guy to excel academically, just because of the situation they are in. When I was in a coed school, a lot of little things would embarrass me, like answering a question wrong in class or making a mistake on the athletic field or having one of my friends make a wisecrack about me in front of other kids."

Teachers and administrators corroborate what these boys are saying. For instance, two formerly single-sex schools that merged into coeducation years ago, St. Stephen's/St. Agnes School in Alexandria, Virginia, have experimented with keeping some math and science classes segregated by gender. The results have been positive. "All of the advantages we see benefit both boys *and* girls," one administrator commented. "Teachers can tailor the way they teach their classes—the amount of group work and the amount of individual learning."

The experiment that these two schools implemented is a good example of the kind of creative problem-solving I believe is critical when it comes to developing successful schools for boys. Even when its resources are tight, a school—public or private—can implement innovative programs and approaches to help boys thrive emotionally and academically. What I find sad is schools not taking this extra step, when they simply rest on their laurels. For I believe it's just this kind of complacency that has led so many boys to rebel in the classroom and that has triggered our schools' epidemic overdiagnosis of behavioral disorders in young and adolescent boys.

PRESCRIPTION: HOW PARENTS CAN HELP CREATE SCHOOLS FOR BOYS' VOICES

To alleviate the negative impact of gender stereotyping and anti-boy bias, I urge parents to take several steps:

Praise your boys' school achievements. Just as it's vitally important to affirm girls' unique talents and strengths, I believe boys—as tough, invulnerable, and confident as they may seem on the outside—desperately need to hear our words of praise and encouragement about what they're doing well at in school. We need to reinforce *all* their successes at school—not just those typically thought of as "masculine." A kindergarten boy who successfully mixes together the ingredients for cookies in the kitchen play area yearns for and deserves a compliment just as much as the one who builds a four-foot tower with building blocks. The boy who writes the best essay on Chaucer merits praise as much as the one who aced his geometry exam.

You simply can't give your boy too much positive reinforcement. When parents or teachers see a boy's mask go up—when our sons begin to act tough and self-reliant—there's a tendency to want to respond in the same way. We often feel we're going to humiliate the boy in some way if we don't reflect back the same kind of cool, dispassionate attitude. While it's important not to pressure your boy to discuss things if he's not yet up to it, you should not feel you need to match his macho stoicism with your own. Instead, try to contradict his masked insecurities by giving him lots of love, support, and affirmation. When he comes home from school and grunts when you ask him how his test went, tell him that no matter what grade he got, you believe in him.

Look for opportunities to be specific in your words of approbation. For instance, if you read a story he wrote and you notice he's got an impressive authorial flair, tell him how much fun it was to read his story. If he completes a scientific experiment for his biology class and prepares a report with handsome graphics in it, tell him what a great job he did in putting together the report and that you especially noticed the neat graphics. Even if he shrugs off your positive comments, continue to share them with him. It's this kind of consistent warm praise that goes a long way in helping your boy endure the many less positive messages he's bound to receive at school.

Get involved, stay involved. Observe and monitor the progress of boys in your particular school system. How are boys faring? Do the teachers and administrators have a modern understanding of boys' dilemmas in our society and understand how those dilemmas affect boys within a learning environment? Call meetings, sponsor workshops, attend after-school programs, and make sure that the school is evaluating itself regularly and is being creative about developing approaches for boys that work. Demand that schools recognize your boy's unique learning style and pace. If he needs extra help in English, make sure he's getting it. If he learns writing best by using an interactive computer program (rather than copying paragraphs from a textbook), lobby for him to get sufficient time with the computer. If he has a hard time sticking with any one activity for more than a certain length of time, make sure he's given all sorts of projects to work on.

Observe and monitor his emotional life. Third, in addition to monitoring how well he's doing based on report cards and other similar evaluations, try to keep an eye on how *you* think your son is faring emotionally at school. Try your best to create safe spaces for him at home and advocate that his school do the same. Ideally no boy should have to spend an entire school day without having anywhere he can go to express his vulnerable emotions free from attack or ridicule. As often as possible, when your boy comes home after school, ask him what he likes about school and what he doesn't like so much about it. Inquire who his best friends are. Ask him what teachers he prefers. If he doesn't open up right away, tell him about your own school experiences. Talk about the exam you forgot to study for. Tell him about how some of the other kids drove you crazy. Tell the story about that fifth-grade teacher you couldn't stand. By showing your own vulnerability, your boy may grow comfortable showing his own. And by finding out what he's truly feeling about school, you can do your best not only to confirm that he's being treated properly but also to discern whether he feels positively about how well he's doing as a student. If we are to redress the crisis of low self-esteem among so many of our sons, we first need to give them a place to tell us how they're feeling and what they're experiencing.

Don't let schools misjudge your boy. Fourth, if there are deficiencies in your boy's academic performance—or any shortcomings in his conduct—make sure they are not rashly treated by his school as though he's pathological. If he suffers a severe learning disability or legitimately has attention deficit disorder, obviously he should meet with a knowledgeable educational specialist, psychologist, or psychiatrist to explore appropriate options. But before any rushed judgments are made, it's important to spend as much time as possible with your son to give him the chance to open up and tell you what school is actually like for him. In so many cases, when your son reluctantly reveals his poor test result or low grade or confesses to having gotten "in trouble" at school with a student or teacher, the problem does not stem from the boy's pathology.

As discussed above, it may well be the school that is deficient, often because it hasn't created an atmosphere in which the boy can succeed. Sometimes a school is too rigid with a boy who needs a more open exploratory classroom experience. Sometimes a school doesn't address his particular pace and style of learning, going too fast or too slow, requiring too much passive listening or too many rote exercises; and sometimes, because of gender stereotypes and biases, a school either restricts him from participating in activities he genuinely finds interesting or prematurely writes him off as a troublemaker. If your boy begins to behave inappropriately at school, I strongly suggest speaking not only to his teachers but also to other parents with kids in the same school. You may very well discover that it's not just your boy who is struggling at his school or with a particular teacher there. When behavioral issues arise for your son, it's terribly important to explore all the possible factors contributing to the situation before allowing the school to dictate a quick-fix solution that may actually serve the school better than your boy.

Help shape the mission of the school. Try to ensure that your boy's school is thoughtful about the unique needs of all boys. For example, it's important for parents and teachers to interrupt situations where they see boys being put into gender straitjackets as students. If a teacher overhears one boy telling another that "poetry is for wimps," ideally that teacher will intervene and explain that not only is reading and writing poetry appropriate for boys but a good number of our most favorite poets are actually men. If a parent learns that the elective courses in a junior high school (such as tech art, chorus, drama) are designed to be gender-segregated, I hope that parent will find the courage to approach the school administrators and insist that boys and girls be made to feel equally welcome to try out these courses.

I think it's particularly helpful when parents, teachers, and school administrators meet regularly—at PTA meetings, special workshops, and so on—to study how boys are being educated to ensure that the school's curriculum is structured in a manner empathic to boys. Boys must not become a political football, the target of a backlash against the ways we fail to meet girls' rightful entitlements. Rather, boys' specific educational needs should be reviewed as closely and carefully as the needs of girls.

I also believe it's important for us to figure out when traditional schools simply are inappropriate or ineffectual for a particular boy. Less conventional academic teaching methods such as Outward Bound or other group-team activities that build on boys' physicality in a more open setting may help both to expand our view of intelligence to a larger range of skills, as Howard Gardner has so aptly argued, and to capture more of boys' interests as well. The use of media—such as videos or CD-ROMS—with fast-paced activity may capture the interest of many a boy stuck in more traditional literary text. Integrating sports activities and coaches, arts programs, and specialists may be just the ticket to spark the sagging interest of an educationally "turned off" boy or to discover the hidden talent of one of our sons buried beneath the sense of shame and failure emanating from his frustration within an all too traditional, all too rigid curriculum. Whatever the creative intervention aimed at boys—and there are many more than space allows me to mention—when we don't probe what it really takes to meet boys' needs, they, in turn, lose interest, don't perform well, and begin the downhill slide into feeling bad about themselves.

WHAT SCHOOLS AND SCHOOL SYSTEMS CAN DO

Whether or not parents prod them to do so, schools need to develop and implement innovative approaches to address boys' specific needs as students:

Boy-friendly subject matter. Just as any adult who goes into a bookstore tends to select books that mesh with his or her personal interests, it is critical that our schools teach courses that cover subject matter interesting to a wide range of boys. We all know that there is not just one kind of boy, and thus there cannot be a simple answer to what topics and what materials will stimulate every boy. But a school can be creative in developing eclectic classroom materials and covering a broad range of topics that will spark the interest of many boys (and many girls). For example, in English, this means covering poems, stories, novellas, novels, and other literature by male and female authors and on traditionally "male" and "female" topics. In a subject like history, making the class stimulating for boys might mean reading and telling stories not only about men but also from the perspective of men. It's so easy for schools to make classes interesting to our boys in this way, I believe it is truly unacceptable for them not to take this simple step.

Use teaching methods that work well for boys. As we've seen in this chapter, many boys may have different learning styles than girls do. Schools need to make sure that they're aware of this and doing something about it.

For young boys, this may mean providing lots of opportunities for hands-on learning and problem-solving and a lot of interactive teaching. So, for instance, rather than asking eight-year-olds to do math problems from a book, a teacher might instead set up a "game show" where the boys solve math problems as "contestants" on the show. Rather than reading a fable to little boys, a teacher might convey the same literature through a puppet show in which the boys have the chance to talk to and interact with the puppets during and after the show. In a class teaching poetry, instead of asking each child to read several classic poems and then write his or her own poem, the teacher might have a guest speaker come in to read his or her own poems, and then ask that guest speaker to coach the students through writing a group poem (on a boy-friendly topic) that would come to life on the classroom blackboard.

Older boys too need lots of creative opportunities as students. In an English class on Shakespeare, rather than simply assigning *Romeo and Juliet,* teachers may have much greater success asking students to act out the parts in class. In a class on economics, rather than asking students to sit quietly and write out answers to questions in a textbook, the teacher might instead assign the students to groups, give them a short period to discuss their answers, and then hold a classroom "debate" in which a designated representative from each group participates in the deliberations. For a boy who becomes restless when he's asked to sit in his chair and read history, a teacher might give him the chance to use a multimedia CD-ROM to learn the same required information. Even with very limited resources, a school can be creative about using teaching methods that keep boys interested and involved.

Respect the learning pace of every boy. There is probably nothing so humiliating as being asked to learn material before one is ready or able. As we've seen, boys often lag behind girls at school, particularly in the areas of reading and writing. I believe it is absolutely critical for schools to be sensitive to each boy's individual pace as a learner. For example, there's little use asking a boy to start writing short stories if he cannot yet complete a sentence. Likewise, there's no use asking an older boy to begin reading Homer if he cannot make his way through the simplest of texts. As a practical matter, this means that schools not only need to regularly determine where each boy is testing in every important subject area, but also to structure classes, give assignments, and test students using materials that are appropriate to their then-current level of understanding. Put simply, if some boys need more time to learn, schools need to be patient and give them that time. Otherwise, as we've discovered, they simply don't learn very well and their self-esteem as students falls dramatically.

Experiment with same-sex classes. As illustrated earlier in this chapter, some schools have discovered that especially for boys who are slower learners or who do not do well within traditional coeducational class-rooms, it may be helpful to place them in all-boys classes, at least in the subject areas where they are doing poorly. By setting up boys-only classes, schools enable teachers to focus in a positive way on the needs of the students and develop classroom materials, teaching methods, and a pace of teaching that correspond to those specific needs. Also, by removing boys from classes attended by their female counterparts, much of the pressure boys often feel to act in certain self-protective ways becomes significantly diminished and many boys come to feel freer, more confident, and better able to succeed as students. I believe this to be true despite the report recently made by the American Association of University Women entitled *Segregated by Sex: A Critical Look at Single-Sex Education for Girls,* which denied finding much improvement for girls placed in single-sex environments (after the same association, in 1992, had advocated separating girls to enhance their classroom experiences). Many educators persistently cite success with same-gender programs for both girls and boys. So I strongly suggest that schools, both public and private, continue to experiment with setting up properly supervised all-boys programs.

Hire more male teachers. It's critical that school systems make serious efforts to find more male teachers, especially at elementary schools where boys are first forming notions about gender-appropriate behavior. Although I have shown how important mothers and other women may be in helping boys to achieve healthy masculinity, if *all,* or almost all, of their role models at elementary school are women, how can we expect these little boys to see learning—and the celebration of learning—as things that men do? Imagine how many parents would be up in arms if all their girls' high school teachers were men! Why then, I wonder, do we tolerate elementary schools for our boys taught predominantly or exclusively by women? Likewise, throughout school systems, I believe it's important that men and women be hired to teach in less gender-stereotypic areas so that, for instance, not all of the science and math classes are taught by men and all of the literature and arts classes are taught by women. This will go a long way in helping boys feel more comfortable and confident about succeeding in areas—whether it's learning how to write haiku or figuring out how to sew a hem—where normally they would fear ridicule or failure.

Set up mentoring programs. Boys benefit enormously from having mentors who are sympathetic to them as learners and who can serve as models for what it's possible to achieve. Because of all the ways in which our schools continue to be weak in recognizing boys' unique emotional and scholastic needs, I believe that mentoring programs are of special importance to boys. I've spoken just above about the significance of having more male teachers in our schools. But let me emphasize that a boy's mentor can of course be male or female, an adult (such as a teacher, guidance counselor, or school administrator), or even an older student. What's most important is that the mentor be interested in the boy's growth and development and, ideally, that he or she have personal interests that are relatively compatible with those of the boy (so that, for instance, a boy who loves football is not paired with a teacher who abhors all sports).

The mentor, in my opinion, can do several things for the boy. First, he or she can simply check in with the boy on a regular basis—at least once per week—to see how things are going for him emotionally and academically. To help the mentor, the school might prepare a list of questions the mentor should consistently ask, such as: How is your English class going? What homework are you getting? Can you show me how you did on it? What's going on with the other students in the class? Are they good people? Who do you spend time with? What's the teacher like? Do you enjoy being in the class with that teacher? In effect, the questions should be designed to elicit not only how the boy is doing scholastically, but also how things are going for him emotionally.

Second, the mentor should offer to help him, to the extent possible, in those classes and subject matters where the boy is doing less well. Helping him may mean tackling areas where the boy actually needs to be coached. But it may also mean finding out who his teacher is, contacting that teacher, and making sure that he or she is aware of the boy's needs and working with him or her to address them creatively.

Finally, the mentor should simply become a devoted buddy to the boy. By knowing he's got an older friend who cares about his social and academic progress, the boy will feel greater confidence in all his interactions and activities at school. Especially for boys who at home may not be getting the kind of intimate caring attention they ideally should be—for instance, boys with two parents who work long hours or with a single overworked parent—having a mentor who is empathic to them and "watching out" for their ongoing emotional and academic needs is of immense value and can make a hugely positive impact on these boys' achievements at school.

Provide safe "guy spaces." Finally, just as schools have attempted to create a comfortable environment in which girls can have their own voice as learners and feel free to express their thoughts and opinions in an open genuine way, schools must take appropriate steps to ensure that boys can do the same and feel they have a safe haven at school where they can express vulnerable emotions. Creating such safe "guy spaces" helps undo some of the shame-based hardening, loosening the straitjackets of gender and allowing boys to connect again—not only with the excitement of their minds but with the genuine depth of their hearts and souls.

This involves several steps. First, for boys of all ages, schools need to set up the school schedule with times and places at school where boys feel free to be themselves, free of normal classroom constrictions. For younger boys, for instance, this may mean making sure that there are enough breaks each day during which boys can enjoy uninhibited play and engage in the gross motor activities that may come naturally to them. Some schools have successfully experimented with shifting the time in which boys go to gym class so that it's not always at the end of the day. For older boys, providing "guy spaces" may mean setting up indoor and outdoor study halls—ideally supervised by adult mentors of the kind I described above—where boys can talk, romp, dish, and rumble to their hearts' desire. Some schools have found that setting up the indoor space as a "quiet space" and the outdoor space as a freer space allows boys, depending on their individual propensities, to choose the kind of space that most suits them. These study halls can happen once or several times a day, depending on the resources of the school and how effective the particular school finds them. What is most important is giving boys the chance to enjoy the kinds of less restricted action-oriented behavior that, as we've seen throughout this book, helps many of them to flourish emotionally and intellectually.

In addition, I believe schools should make absolutely sure that boys always feel they have a place to go at school where they can—and where they *will*—discuss their inner emotional lives with girls and other boys and with teachers and other adults. These "safe spaces" can be single-gender or coed, supervised closely by an adult, or set up as "kids only" centers along the lines of the peer support groups we discussed in the chapter on adolescence. It simply is not enough for schools to assume that boys will get their emotional needs taken care of at home. In my opinion, it's not fair to boys or their parents for two basic reasons. First, many parents are already doing the best they can, given their other obligations, and simply cannot "do it all" without the help of their sons' schools. Second, some parents are not available to their boys for any emotional support. They may be either physically or emotionally absent, or both.

So schools have an obligation, I think, to pick up the emotional ball and run with it. It doesn't take a lot of extra funding or personnel to set up effective peer support groups, "social centers," discussions groups, and so on. I believe that every school should ask itself: "If a student in our school is unhappy about something in his or her life, school-related or otherwise, would that student have a place he or she would *want* to go to talk about that unhappiness?" If the answer to that question is "No," the school probably has not yet met its responsibilities.

So as our boys traverse the blackboard jumble, I firmly believe that schools need to address their ongoing emotional needs in an honest, consistent, dedicated way. Only then will a boy and his parents be able to trust that the many hours of time he will end up spending at school will most likely be enriching and enjoyable, hours well spent that will lead him to grow up into a happy, intellectually curious, emotionally fulfilled, and successful young man.

_11_

SPORTS: PLAY

AND TRANSFORMATION

"There's this real warm feeling you get. I don't know how to
explain it. Like we're all in something together, and it's even
OK to lose."—Martin, age thirteen

THE PARADOX OF SPORTS: THE DOING AND UNDOING OF THE BOY CODE

One of the oldest forms of recreation known to humankind, sports are the one arena in which many of society's traditional strictures about masculinity are often loosened, allowing boys to experience parts of themselves they rarely experience elsewhere. At their best, sports provide boys with an opportunity for play in a free atmosphere so that they can be themselves and express a full range of emotions—from the exhilaration of a last-minute goal to the acute disappointment of being defeated by the opposing team, from the joy of being the one to pull off an unexpected play to the embarrassment of fumbling the ball in the last quarter of the game.

Sports provide boys with a theater for the unfettered expression of their feelings, a place where it's OK to be spirited, emotive, passionate. As twelve-year-old Max told me, "During school we have to be quiet and raise our hands to talk. It's boring and sometimes I feel like there's nobody to talk to. I love doing sports after school because we can all be together. We get to run fast, shout things out, scream, whatever. It lets me be *me.*"

For many boys, sports are a form of intimacy and a way to be honest. By temporarily freeing boys from the Boy Code—especially from the rules that say boys shouldn't express feelings, show affection, or expose their yearning for connection—sports can become one of the most important activities through which our sons, as their genuine selves, can relate closely with girls and other boys.

But just as much as they can offer a break from the Boy Code, a chance for openness, expression, and intimacy, sports can also push boys back to loneliness, shame, and vicious competition. "It's rough out there," one high school football player recently told me. "Some guys play hard just the way they should. But other guys just seem like they're out to get you—you know, they just try to demolish you." Thus sports can also be a place where boys show unbridled aggression, let out inappropriate feelings of anger and frustration, and actually hurt other boys.

And then sports can thrust boys into a cult of competition, the goal of winning at any cost, a quest for narcissistic glory at the expense of others. They cause some boys—especially those who are not interested in sports or who are not skilled at playing them—to feel left out, unworthy, ashamed.

I firmly believe that the positive benefits to boys dim when sports cease to be play. D. W. Winnicott, the distinguished English psychoanalyst, observed that for children, play is at the heart of healthy, integrated development. His words are especially pertinent to boys whose inner selves are too often suppressed: "[P]laying shows that . . . [the] child is capable . . . of developing a personal way of life . . . eventually becoming a *whole being* . . . welcomed by the world at large."

Sheer competition among boys rarely builds character and does little to bring boys closer to one another. But sports, when they are play, can be a tremendously good thing for boys. The late commissioner of baseball and Renaissance scholar A. Bartlett Giamatti spoke of sports as: "that aspiration . . . to be taken out of the self . . . for a moment in touch . . . with a joy . . . free of all constraint. It is a sensation not of winning, but of fully playing." When sports are kept in proper perspective—when we see sports primarily as a chance for boys to come together for joyful, spirited, high-energy *play*—they can help boys discover new competencies, buttress their feelings of self-worth, and reunite them with their authentic voices, enabling them to express the deepest stirrings of emotion in their hearts, widening their circle of connections.

SPORTS AS TRANSFORMATION

Indeed I believe that with the right attitude and the right coach, sports are transformational for boys. When the Boy Code is relaxed and the mask can come off, our sons can go from being reserved, detached, and hardened to being expressive, affectionate, resilient. Sports transform boys in this way. Sports open them up, give them a new élan, a new authenticity. And they simply make many boys into far happier, far more fulfilled human beings.

Listen, for instance, to Tom and Phillip Marson, brothers aged thirteen and fifteen, who tell us how sports can turn things around for boys.

"There used to be nothing to do around here," Tom told me, referring to the small, economically depressed town where he and his brother live.

"There was like just one bowling alley, and it was closed on weekends. We had nothing to do, especially during the summer," Phillip agreed.

"Not quite a year ago," Tom explained, "three of our best friends died of an OD."

Indeed, the autumn before, three teenage boys in the same sleepy town had all drunk themselves into oblivion and then overdosed on a lethal cocktail of various barbiturates. Sure, the town had always had its problems—high unemployment, poorly funded schools, and many broken families. But this was different. Three boys, the oldest only sixteen, were gone forever.

The mood in town was sullen the summer following the deaths, and Tom and Phillip were resolved to change things. "We went to the mayor and to the priest at our church, and we asked if we could set up a regular sports program for kids around here," Phillip explained.

"A softball league," Tom added.

"What a great idea," I told the boys.

"Yeah. At first we were just ten guys," said Tom.

"But then, like, everybody wanted to sign up—girls too," explained Phillip. "Now there are too many kids who want to play. More than a hundred. But the state government offered to help with some money and coaches."

"So it is making a difference, to have this new league?" I asked the boys.

"Hell, yeah," Phillip replied. "Now we've got a schedule. We've got something to do."

"I'm not sure I'd be here anymore if it wasn't for the league," added Tom. "For a long time I couldn't deal with things. Now I've got a place to go."

Tom and Phillip show us there are many ways in which sports can change things for boys, and I have found that there are at least four major areas in which sports are often transformational for boys: they free boys up to express a broad array of emotions; they allow boys to show their love and affection in a shame-free environment; they boost self-esteem; and they teach boys how to be flexible in difficult situations, how to deal with losing and loss in general. Because each of these areas has been so under-explored in the literature available to parents, I would like to discuss each of them in turn.

SPORTS AND TRANSFORMATION: EMOTIONAL EXPRESSION

The first area of transformation is that of emotional expression. Sports can be a forum where boys learn how to deal openly with feelings of failure, shame, sadness, and the simple realities of human limitations.

Whether it's football, basketball, baseball, or golf, almost all sports provoke tremendous swings of emotion, highs and lows. Sometimes our victories and defeats are personal—for instance, when we win a game of one-on-one tennis, fall down when we're skiing, or score substantially below par in a round of golf; and sometimes they are communal—a basketball team's defense gets clumsy in the third quarter, a baseball team rallies to hit a string of home runs in the final inning of a home game. But whether we experience them individually or as a team, these ups and downs encompass a plethora of emotions: joy, despair, pride, embarrassment, anger, triumph, humility. Sports help boys handle these feelings, much in the way that fathers, as we saw in Chapter 6, teach young boys how to handle intense emotions through rough-and-tumble play.

Indeed on the court and in the field, boys—if they are not discouraged from doing so—often seem impressively capable of sharing these kinds of feelings, free of the masks they usually feel pressured to wear:

"Normally, I would never cry in front of my friends," explains Josh, the seventeen-year-old quarterback of his high school football team, "but when we lose a game—especially if it's really close—I've seen a lot of guys cry. Sometimes you just can't hold it back."

"We almost made it to the state finals," said fifteen-year-old Peter, lamenting his track team's recent lost match to another local team. "At our last meet, when we lost in pole vaulting and then in the five-hundred-meter run, our captain was so fed up he just got all choked up and started to cry."

"Football's a pretty rough sport," seventeen-year-old Willis explained, "and a few weeks ago one of our guys got really badly injured and they had to take him away in an ambulance. There was this really long time-out, so our whole team got together, went into a huddle, and started praying for him. Some of the guys were really shaken up by it."

For many boys, sports is the one place where they sense it's all right to show what they really feel and who they really are. Because the source of their feelings is external and obvious—a missed goal, a great shot, a huge win, a narrow loss—the shame they usually experience if they show these feelings can sometimes fall away. Especially with a coach who does not humiliate them for their mistakes and who instead encourages them despite how they perform, boys can come to feel less inhibited, freed to share their feelings honestly, without fear of embarrassment. Sports help boys break out from behind the silence of the mask, and allow them to assert sides of themselves they ordinarily feel pressured to hide.

SPORTS AND TRANSFORMATION: FRIENDSHIP AND AFFECTION—TEACHING CONNECTIONS

Through sports boys can also transform themselves by ending their isolation and discovering comfortable ways to share the caring and affection they feel for their peers. And in this sharing, sports may lead boys toward friendships with girls and other boys, friendships with their own physical vocabulary and their own disciplines of love.

Lionel, the sixteen-year-old captain of his highly touted high school basketball team, spoke to me about the kind of sharing he appreciates from his teammates. "When we win, we just get all together in a group huddle and start hugging each other, patting each other on the back. When we won against this undefeated team the other day, one guy on my team came up behind me and just grabbed me. For a second I thought he was going to tackle me. But actually he was just giving me this huge hug. He couldn't believe we won!"

For some boys, sports offer opportunities for emotional closeness too often lacking in other areas of their lives. Sports allow boys to feel a dedication to others, to experience feelings of love and commonality within comfortable bounds. In fact, boys often feel more comfortable caring about and nurturing one another in the context of playing sports than in almost any other area of life—so long as the caring and nurturing is expressed in the team concept and channeled toward a task, toward the external goals of the game. Because they feel that they are part of a higher mission beyond the self, boys feel a kinship and a freedom to show affection that they don't tend to feel comfortable about in other contexts. Boys show these feelings sometimes by using words—"Nice going," "Don't worry about it," "Hey, are you all right?"—and perhaps most often through physical gestures, such as a pat on the back, an embrace, a congratulatory slap on the buttocks, or thumbs up. For many boys, their most affectionate, intimate experiences take place when they are part of a group with a clear common objective, to which deep feelings can legitimately be linked.

In Mark Harris's baseball novel *Bang the Drum Slowly,* one ballplayer expresses his feelings this way: "[Y]ou felt warm toward them, and you looked at them, and them at you, and you were both alive, and you might as well have said, 'Ain't it something? Being alive, I mean! Ain't it really a great thing at that?' And if they would of been a girl you would of kissed them, though you never said such a thing out loud but only went on about your business."

SPORTS AND TRANSFORMATION: A BOOST IN SELF-ESTEEM—A SENSE OF MASTERY

When coaches and parents work hard to make sure that participating in sports does not become an emotionally damaging experience, the activity can also transform boys by offering them a chance to excel at something that comes naturally to many of them, to achieve a newfound sense of *mastery,* and thus to boost their self-esteem. Especially for boys who find it difficult to do well academically, sports may be one of the few contexts in which they receive praise. In team sports, boys may be able to feel a sense of success by making small contributions to the team's victories—a good pass, a nice save, a skillful tackle. Even when they're on the bench playing a very minor role in a particular game, boys can often derive a sense of vicarious pride and accomplishment through the athletic prowess and success of teammates.

SEAN: SELF-ESTEEM THROUGH HOCKEY

"I felt like there was nothing I could do the best," Sean said. His older brother, Nick, was an outstanding artist who had won statewide competitions with his drawings. His oldest sister, Maura, had frequently impressed her parents and grandparents at her dance recitals. And Christina, the sister closest to Sean in age, was a top flutist in her junior high school band. Meanwhile Sean was just struggling in school and, by the age of thirteen was beginning to be angry and defiant at home, too.

While Sean's parents had always been convinced he was a bright child, Sean's performance at school was consistently mediocre. One of Sean's sixth-grade teachers was particularly perceptive. "She told us Sean simply wasn't trying that hard," his mother, Lynn O'Hanley, remembered. "He would be the first in the class to put down his pencil, even though he seemed capable of very good work. He was rushing through assignments. He always did his homework, but we could see that his homework was just 'anything to get it over with.' We really thought about having Sean tested for ADD, although when he was home playing with Lego blocks or something he liked, he could sit still for hours."

Sean's father, John O'Hanley, had fond memories of playing ice hockey as a boy, and suggested he introduce Sean to a sport to build his self-confidence. Mr. O'Hanley brought Sean to a series of sporting events—basketball, football, baseball, soccer, and his own childhood favorite, ice hockey—then gave Sean the opportunity to pick one to pursue. "I could see that Sean was enjoying just getting out alone with me, there aren't as many chances for that in a large family," says John. "And I could have talked his ear off—I love talking sports—but I bit my tongue, and just told a few stories about when I was a kid. I had decided not to give him any advice, but I admit I was pleased when Sean chose ice hockey."

John attended every hockey practice with Sean, cheering him on from the sidelines. "I made another pact with myself that I would never criticize Sean's mistakes, only praise his efforts," John explains. "There's all this organized coaching now, even down to the baby levels, and it's easy for parents to become little assistant coaches, but we didn't have that. My parents came to the game and cheered, that's all they ever said about hockey. I knew I couldn't go to school with him every day, but this was something we could share together."

Sean soon became one of the strongest players on his team. "On the car rides back home, Sean would go over his best plays with me. I'd get tears in my eyes just to see him look so pleased with himself," John says.

By that spring, Sean's grades had begun improving. "I'm the greatest hockey player in my family," Sean now declares. "Even better than my dad used to be when he was my age!"

"Ice hockey gave Sean a chance to try with all his might at something he loved," John observes. "I had my doubts, getting him up to practice at weird hours so he could get some ice time, and making those long drives to games in other towns. But it gave the two of us an opportunity to get closer as well, and you can't put a price on that."

As Sean's story shows, if properly mentored, boys may find that sports provide them with a chance to apply skills that come easily to them, receive praise and attention they don't get elsewhere, and thus significantly increase their feelings of self-worth.

SPORTS AND TRANSFORMATION: LESSONS IN RESILIENCE—FACING LOSS

Finally, sports also transform boys by teaching them *emotional resilience*—how to overcome the fear of being shamed, a fear that can cause boys to toughen themselves up, especially when they become adolescents. Sports teach this capacity for resilience—a healthy ability to cope with shameful feelings openly and flexibly—through the inevitable experience of *losing*. Sports bring boys face-to-face with loss and allow them to express disappointment and grief they probably would not otherwise experience.

To learn how to deal with defeat is also to come to terms with shame. One learns, as the poet A. E. Housman put it, that glory "withers quicker than the rose." Unfortunately, parents and mentors may too often fail to teach sons about bearing such loss so that it then becomes something feared and is seen as catastrophic.

If sports were only about glorious victory and humiliating one's opponents (or one's less capable teammates), they would not help a boy to confront his fears and vulnerabilities. They would not transform him. But sports in fact do involve loss. And sports do transform boys because of this.

"It's not so bad," sixteen-year-old Martin told me when I asked him how he feels when his soccer team loses a game. "We get depressed sometimes . . . and if we play an 'away game' and lose, everybody is really quiet on the bus ride home. But there's this real warm feeling you get. I don't know how to explain it. Like we're all in something together, and it's even OK to lose."

"There's nothing like winning," explained Hamilton, Martin's seventeen-year-old teammate. "Losing sucks and you feel like you're a complete dork. But on the team, nobody ever blames you because they know they could screw things up the next time. . . . Losing is just part of the game. It's part of being on the team, so you learn how to deal with it."

"It makes you humble," adds seventeen-year-old Benson.

And sixteen-year-old Arthur opines: "It's better than failing a test at school or something."

"Why is that?" I asked.

"Well, on a test you're all alone and if you do bad, you're probably not gonna tell anyone. You're just gonna sulk and try not to show it. But when you lose a match, it's like, OK, everybody knows—and it's all of us losing together. There's no hiding it, and you just deal with it with all the other guys."

As these boys' comments reflect, sports provide a community of support that somehow makes the disappointment of losing seem more bearable. In fact, I have found that if boys are coached properly, they may also discover, as did one high school football team I know, that this community includes not only their teammates and fans but their opponents as well.

THE HAWKS: LEARNING FROM LOSING

The Hawks are a talented group of high school football players from a middle-class suburb of a large northeastern city. Not only do these boys know how to play football but many of them excel academically too. Six feet tall, built like a linebacker, Coach Paul Santanello boasts cheerfully about his team: "If you make it through a season with me and the team, I'd say you've also got a good 99.9999% chance you're headed for college."

"That's wonderful," I tell Paul, who seems to me he not only knows how to prepare his team athletically but also has a real knack for understanding the psychology behind sports.

"I know how to get them psyched up for a game," he explains to me, "and I know what to tell them about winning and losing."

"What do you mean?" I ask.

"Well, for example, about a month ago, we had to play against one of the city teams. So, before the other team arrived, I told the kids on my team a few key things. Number one, that the other team came from a school with different resources than our school has. So, no laughing or teasing them about their tattered uniforms, their broken helmets, or whatever. Number two, that this was one of the top teams in the state, so be prepared, and do the best you can. And number three, if you lose, don't say anything bad to the other side—just shake hands with them and tell them that they played great."

"Sounds like superb advice," I tell Paul.

"Well, I don't know about that. But when the game came around, the boys really handled themselves pretty well. They gave one hundred percent, did their best, although they got completely whomped by the other team. But nobody on my team said anything wrong to the other guys. There was complete respect, and when the game was over, my guys went over and congratulated the other team."

"That's really something."

"My guys were so blown away by the other team," Paul adds with a smile, "that they asked me if they could do some Saturday scrimmages against them. We've been doing these Saturday-morning things now for six weeks, and the kids seem to like them."

"Sounds like a good opportunity for the boys."

"Yeah, and not only that," Paul says proudly. "I now hear that guys on my team are starting to help some of the guys on the other team actually write their college admissions essays. You know, they've actually become friends and are helping each other out. So, I'd say the kids on my team have learned a lot since losing that first game!"

As the story of the Hawks reflects, good sports are about learning from loss, especially about the recognition of limits. Unlike what happens in much of the rest of life, in sports the limits are obvious and the consequences for ignoring them are tangible and immediate. As Phillip Isenberg, Harvard Medical School psychiatrist and former Harvard football-team captain, has pointed out, sports teach people that they have to live within the limits of the game and of their bodies, to realize their *relative* talents. No matter what one's skill level, there's almost always someone stronger, faster, or better coordinated. No matter how hard one tries to win, there's also the role of chance—the injured star player, the distracting fan, the wind that carries the ball. And no matter how unfair, losing is simply reality.

And so this is the fourth important way in which sports transform boys. Sports take boys who thought they would always have to cover up their feelings of loss and vulnerability and show these boys that losing, and the pain that goes with it, are part of life, that one can be honest about one's disappointments, and that all one can do is just get up again, head back into the field, and continue to do one's best.

THE EMOTIONAL IMPORTANCE OF THE COACH:
A ROLE MODEL FOR ONE'S PERSONAL BEST

My research shows that so much of what distinguishes what is good and "transformative" about sports from what is bad and destructive is what attitudes prevail among the people a boy plays with, and how he is treated when he succeeds or fails in playing; and crucial to each of these factors is the coach. The coach and the emotional environment he or she creates within the team are essential to developing boys' sense of self-esteem and of connection to others. It is the role of the coach to encourage boys to play cooperatively while nudging them away from attitudes that may make them self-serving, overly aggressive, or even reckless.

The coach may be an employee at the local school, a parent volunteering for an after-school program, or an older sibling leading younger kids in athletic play. When I refer to the coach, I mean anybody who supervises boys playing sports. So much of a boy's experience with sports, I believe, depends on the coach: how aware and sensitive he or she is, whether he or she mentors the boy, how the coach deals with a boy's strengths and weaknesses, his successes and failures.

A coach is an emotionally important figure in a boy's life. When he or she cheers on boys at all skill levels, models a sense of fairness, and exudes a sense of levity, fun, and fair play that transcends winning or losing, a coach can make playing sports the immensely positive transformative learning experience I've been speaking of. With the right coach, a boy is transformed from an isolated competitor into a bonded teammate, from someone who simply wants to beat the other guy to someone purely striving to do his personal best.

A coach who ensures that sports are an inclusive activity—one who cheerfully embraces boys at all different skill levels (and who makes sure the other boys do too)—can help each boy feel that he is able, skilled, and important, that he really matters to the team. This kind of coaching helps a boy not only to overcome his sense of loneliness and isolation—substituting connection for more removed autonomy—but also to boost his feelings of self-esteem. By contrast, a coach who derides or humiliates boys when they make mistakes, who pushes boys beyond their natural skill levels, or who offers words of encouragement only when the boys actually win, may cause our sons to feel ashamed, harden themselves in the ways we've already discussed, and hide behind a mask of false self-confidence.

Likewise, a coach who teaches the value of balanced disciplined effort—"a personal best"—rather than stressing fierce competition and winning as the crux of a game, can play a vital mentoring role that encourages boys to see sports as an opportunity for physical and emotional self-transformation rather than as an outright test of his masculinity.

"Mr. Hanks is a great coach," one fifteen-year-old reported about the coach of his high school football team. "Before we begin scrimmaging, he leads our team through an hour of calisthenics. We have to do about one hundred sit-ups, push-ups, deep knee-bends, jumping jacks, and a whole bunch of exercises. But Coach Hanks doesn't just shout out orders at us. He's yelling out what to do while he's doing it too! He's real demanding, but he puts himself through the training with us."

Another boy of the same age offered a similar sentiment about Mr. Hanks: "He's great because he pushes you hard but has a good attitude about it. Like he tells us that if we don't feel up to practice one day, we have to show up, but we can tell him we're tired and, for that day, he'll give us a lighter, separate routine to do. Some coaches would just yell at you or push you harder. Mr. Hanks is realistic. He never tries to harass you or make you feel bad if you can't do something. He just seems to want to help us do the best we can."

Coaches can convey a moral stance, one that is not rigid, punitive, or unyielding, but rather derives from establishing a loving sense of connection with the boys and acting as an important adult role model. As one boy told me about his soccer coach, "His golden rule is don't ever tell anybody what they can or can't do—just smile and show them what *you* can do. Nobody's perfect and the only thing you can really control is your own game. Our coach is always real nice and friendly, sort of like a camp counselor or something. He tells us that if you do good, other people will be inspired and then they'll do good too."

"What's great about Mr. Schroeder," said another boy about the same coach, "is that when we win a match, he takes us out for doughnuts and we celebrate. And when we lose a match, we still go out for doughnuts—we're just a little less rowdy."

As the boy's mentor, the coach is in many respects a stand-in for mother and father. Even a boy with two very loving parents may find his afternoons filled with the voice of his coach rather than the voices of his parents. Especially for the adolescent boy who may find himself somewhat distanced or detached from his parents at times, the coach may be one of the few adults to whom he will look for guidance, support, and encouragement.

"Mr. Jensen helped me through some hard times," offered seventeen-year-old Glenn about his basketball coach. "I had to go through a bunch of surgeries to correct my eyesight. I had a lot of problems seeing, and kids made fun of me because one of my eyes looked funny. Coach Jensen told the other kids that anybody that made fun of me would be kicked off the team and that a lot of pro players had eye problems too. He let me play in a lot of games and didn't yell at me when I fouled. Everybody loves Mr. Jensen. He's just a great guy."

A coach has a unique opportunity to help boys feel good about themselves. By setting up sports in such a way that boys can achieve personal mastery, by staying away from shaming words, and by inspiring all boys—no matter what their relative skill levels—to feel they can develop athletic skills and contribute to the team, coaches help boys to avoid seeing sports as a cult of competition or narcissistic aggrandizement; and instead make sports a place for personal growth.

COACHES WHO TEACH SHAME

But, regrettably, not all coaches have a positive, nurturing attitude, and many have limited interest in structuring sports creatively to embrace boys' varying degrees of skill. Far from helping and reassuring the boys they mentor, some coaches instead resort to shame, exhorting boys to "play with your pain," "get your butt going," and not "act like a girl." Eighteen-year-old Michael D'Amico recalled one such traumatizing lacrosse coach: "He acted like an army officer or something—a total drill sergeant. He would shout out your last name and then just tell you off, like 'D'Amico—you're doing push-ups like a little sissy. Now get your ass in gear!' or 'D'Amico—what the hell are you doing? Can't you see the damn goal? Which side are you playing for anyway?' "

A coach who manipulates his players to win at any cost, or models unrestrained anger, communicates the soul-denying harshness of sheer competition, where the essential element of play within sports has been removed, and with it much of the chance for personal growth. Parents need to know their sons' coaches, and to make sure they are men or women who see sports as play, who project the kind of warmth and understanding that enables boys to cope with winning and losing, and who encourage boys no matter what their relative skill level. Just as parents should not put up with teachers who shame their sons, parents should be sure their sons are mentored in sports by nurturing, empathic people.

WHEN THE BOY CODE COMES BACK INTO FORCE—THE RETURN OF SHAME AND HARDENING

Yet even in the presence of a thoughtful coach, boys can become prone to following the old Boy Code rules that equate masculinity and "being a man" with athletic competence and success. These rules lead some boys who do well athletically to humiliate, even condemn, boys who do less well.

I believe these Boy Code rules come back into force most often when boys are prodded into believing that performing well or winning—rather than playing for the fun of it—is the be-all and end-all of the game. When playing sports becomes about winning at any cost—and about humiliating anyone who loses or who contributes to your own loss—boys feel pressured not only to put on their emotional armor and act tough but to tease or rebuke other boys for showing any weakness or vulnerability.

Thus as much as sports can create a positive space where boys are comfortable expressing their feelings, show their affection more freely, develop enhanced senses of self-esteem, and learn together about loss in a constructive way—the transformative experience of sports—they can also thrust boys into a universe of shame and humiliation where they come to feel very anxious about doing well yet know their feelings must be buried even deeper. Just about any parent who has sat through a high school baseball game has heard the cries of "He's no batter! He's no batter!" resounding throughout the ball field and has watched the teenage batter—instead of blushing, succumbing to tears, shouting back, or just giving up entirely—actually tighten up his face, concentrate intently on the oncoming pitches, and apparently ignore the humiliating epithets flying about him. And many parents have had to deal with a son who—less talented than some of his peers—has been put through the humiliation of being consistently picked last for gym-class teams or perhaps regularly taunted as being a "wimp," a "loser," when he's attempted in vain to succeed at a particular sport. While some of these boys may try to avoid athletic activities altogether, others harden themselves against the pain of being persistently rejected and disgraced.

TOMMY: THE LESSONS START YOUNG

The first time I observed Tommy, he seemed rather lost on the large white ice-skating rink. I was taking my daughter to her skating lesson, and I noticed one of a very few five-year-old boys taking lessons among a majority of girls. Dressed in his miniature hockey uniform, Tommy looked as if this was the last place on earth he wanted to be. Still, encouraged by the comments of his father on the sidelines, Tommy valiantly struggled to stay up on those skates, but his wobbly legs kept betraying him.

After his fourth spill—this one drawing blood from his already battered knees—Tommy sought his father's solace, near the visitors' gallery. "No more today, Dad," Tommy pleaded, "My knee really hurts!"

"Nah . . . that doesn't hurt too much," his dad replied. "C'mon, keep going—you're not going to let a bunch of girls beat you out of the competition, are you?"

The shame on Tom's face was painful to see; he didn't want the whole world to think he was a "wimp," less strong than even the girls. He barely held back his tears and slid away from his dad, back onto the ice.

And then there was a loud crash. Before he could steady himself, Tommy was smashed by two teenage girls who collided with him simultaneously from opposite sides. Tommy fell to the ice, crushed both emotionally and physically.

Tommy's father helped him up, and asked, "Are you OK, kid?"

The beleaguered little boy, looking like Mohammed Ali after too many rounds of too many fights, stammered, "I guess so."

"You're OK. You're fine," his father said. "Don't give up! *I know just what will help—keep skating—it will loosen you up.*" The little boy obediently turned around and continued skating . . . falling . . . skating . . . falling.

About a year later I arrived at the rink when I noticed that a group of about twenty boys were scrimmaging in preparation for an upcoming hockey game. Donning a bright red helmet and matching uniform fitted over pads clearly too big for his frame, there was three-foot Tommy De Santis skating with the other boys and chasing after the puck.

Within just minutes of observing the practice session, I saw an inevitable "repeat play" of what I had seen many months ago. As Tommy maneuvered the puck toward the opposing team's goal, three much larger boys rammed into him from all angles. When Tommy began to lose his balance, one of the boys helped him finish the fall, shoving little Tommy onto the ice.

If just months ago this might have left him immobilized and in tears, today Tommy got right back on to his feet, adjusted his helmet, and skated off after the boys. His skating now significantly improved, Tommy raced after the opponents with abandon. As he approached the kid who had pushed him, Tommy skated even faster. When their two bodies collided almost head-on, his opponent went flying against the side board with a forceful bang.

"Thatta boy!" I heard a man shout from the bleachers just a few feet behind me. Mr. De Santis stood up, let out a loud whoop, and threw his two fists up into the air to salute his son. As if he couldn't hear his father, Tommy kept his eyes squarely on the ice and skated off behind his teammates.

I've told the story of Tommy to many parent groups, and I've learned a lot from the reactions it receives. Some people don't see anything wrong with Tommy's experience or his dad's conduct. Tommy, they believe, will have to learn to "play rough with the big boys." They see sports as a component—even as a positive component—in helping their sons learn how to act tough and endure pain silently, be fierce, quiet, and resilient, act "masculine" in the stereotypical sense of the term. They fear what it would mean if their sons were not willing to submit to this toughening process, dreading the humiliation that would follow for them and their sons. While they may not like the sight of Tommy crashing onto the ice or the sound of his coach—in this case, his father—spurring him on to be tough and retaliate against the other boys, many parents see these things as somehow necessary, part of "growing up," of "being a boy."

Other parents are far less comfortable with the hardening aspect of sports. They see Tommy as being taught an unattractive kind of ruthlessness—as being pushed to act in a way that does not actually come naturally to him. They see Tommy's father's behavior as abhorrent. Why, they ask, would a father *encourage* his child to put up with being hurt and cheer him on when he injures others? As one mother said, "I'm proud of my son when he does well at a sport, but being proud doesn't feel worth it if he's going to have to go through all of the cruelty that goes with it." Or as another parent exclaimed, "I can understand what the boys sometimes do to each other. But the parents! I can't stand those parents shouting out the meanest, competitive things from the sidelines. Don't they realize they're hurting and embarrassing our kids?"

I have found that the majority of parents feel torn between wanting their boys to excel athletically—to be prepared for the rough aspect of sports and do whatever is necessary to be counted among the team—and wanting to protect their sons from the unnecessarily mean-spirited, cut-throat, emotionally sterile aspects of so many boys' sporting activities. Many parents appear to regret the ways in which sports toughen up their boys emotionally and often wish that sports could be a more positive, uplifting, and confidence-building experience for their sons.

As one father expressed to me, "When my son, Keith, was the last guy to strike out, I could see how bad he felt. The other boys were hardly talking to him and the coach wouldn't even look at him, let alone say something to him. Keith was trying to act relaxed about it, but I could see he was miserable. I wished I could go up to him and tell him that he was a good kid and that he actually played very well—that the pitcher on the other side just happened to be pretty damn good. But I thought that maybe that would make him feel worse. I felt like I just wanted to go up to him and give him a big hug. But I knew he would be *really* embarrassed if I did that."

Like Keith's father, many parents worry that if they step in and say or do something, they will only exacerbate their sons' feelings of shame. But it is here that, in my view, so many parents miss out on an opportunity to help change things for the better. For as natural as it is not to want to "rock the boat" or make things worse, I believe that parents can make an enormous difference in what sports are about—without further humiliating their sons—by staying persistently involved in monitoring and overseeing what kinds of attitudes prevail on the court and in the field.

In fact, I've known groups of parents who have attended referee schools, coaching workshops, and conflict-resolution seminars, and then woven together these skills into a manual that teaches a new approach to coaching boys' teams. If their involvement is regular and inconspicuous, and if healthy attitudes come to pervade the game, parents can have a tremendously positive impact on how a sport is played and experienced, helping to decrease the shame ante for the whole team and to make sports transformational as we've seen they can be.

THE UNNECESSARY BRUTALITY OF SPORTS

In addition to pushing boys to taunt and reprimand one another for their mistakes and weaknesses as athletes, society's rules about masculine behavior also sanction the sheer brutality that can sometimes creep into so many of boys' games. While some sports, such as crew, tennis, golf, do not involve such brutality, many others—football, hockey, wrestling—are surprisingly ruthless. Even soccer—normally seen as a relatively easy, fluid game, less violent, and more forgiving of weakness than sports like football or rugby—can, in the wrong hands, become terribly violent.

Listen, for instance, to seventeen-year-old James, the six-foot 145-pound designated enforcer of his high school soccer team:

"Before, if someone did something to you, for the good of the team you wouldn't retaliate. Now, if somebody gets you, you're going to get them for the pride of the team. If I got hit, and one of the younger kids on my team saw me just back down and not retaliate, that would spread through the whole time. It would be like, you're not a man."

James remembers how he almost started a fistfight with a superior player: "We both went up for a head ball and he nudged me in the back. I fell down pretty hard and that triggered something in me. So I swung around—my whole body—and I got up in his face and he said, 'What the f– are you going to do?' And I said, 'What the f– are you going to do?' And we started bumping."

James added: "It used to be the old saying that it doesn't matter whether you win or lose. I don't think anybody lives like that anymore."

THE OBSESSIVE COMPETITIVE ASPECT OF SPORTS

If cultural imperatives allow our sons to experience sports as an opportunity to exchange anger and act out hostile or violent feelings, sports can sometimes also become an arena where boys are pushed to become compulsive about doing well, making themselves strong, or beating the competition. This compulsive aspect of sports can lead boys to train themselves in an excessive way, mask or ignore serious injuries, or become overly zealous in how they play a particular sport.

PETER: OBSESSED WITH ATHLETIC SUCCESS

Peter Vincent, a senior at a highly competitive public high school, describes himself as someone who was "conceived with a purpose." His parents' marriage was failing, and they hoped a new baby would reconnect them somehow. Their first two children were already ten and fourteen, and perhaps a little one's pressing needs and endearing quality would help bridge the widening gap between the parents.

But the fact that Peter was a boy, he says, added a gender-specific tone to those expectations. "I felt the pressure to be a hero to my mother and father, even my brother and sister, from the earliest time I can remember. They wanted an academic genius and a stand-out athlete, and I've always tried with all my might to give them what they wanted."

After earning MVP awards for both football and baseball last year, Peter was forced to drop out of the football team this year after just two games. "I had hurt my knee during our first game, but I didn't want to say anything to my mother or my coach. Yeah, it hurt during the warm-up before the second game, but I just hoped it would go away. I had to keep playing, and winning, to be the MVP again this year."

Midway through the first half, Peter reinjured the same knee, and had to be carried off the field. It will be a few months before the cast comes off. "I haven't looked my mother in the eye since it happened," Peter says. "How could I have done this to her? I ruined her life! My older brother and sister are on the other side of the country. My father's been gone for years, and my mom's never been out on a date or anything since then. The only thing she had to look forward to this fall was my football season.

"My father came to see me in the hospital, but he hasn't come to see me since. He says he's busy at work, but I know he wanted me to get two MVPs again this year, or at least two letters like he did in his senior year.

"Sometimes I have images in my mind of jumping in a deep pool so my cast will make me drown," Peter admits. "Then I wouldn't have to let my parents down ever again. And I wouldn't have to worry about what college I'm going to get into, either."

As Peter's story shows, boys can be overwhelmed with a feeling that they must do well at sports, that if they don't maintain a certain level of accomplishment somehow they'll suffer an intolerable loss. Peter, of course, had already had many losses in his life—the disabling injury, his parents' divorce, the remote relationship with his father, the sense he wasn't loved for himself at his own birth. All of these disappointments made him fear what it would mean if he also lost his one last way of feeling powerful and successful—by being a top athlete.

When boys feel the pressure to do well at sports, they are capable not only of hiding injury the way Peter did, but also of actually harming their bodies. Brian's story, which follows, suggests some of the problems boys can carry into early manhood when sports become all about succeeding, when sports stop being play. Despite positive success in wrestling, Brian came away so compulsive about succeeding as a wrestler, he no longer knew when and how much to eat.

BRIAN: OBSESSED WITH HIS WEIGHT

It was not until he was a college sophomore watching a made-for-television movie about a woman with an eating disorder that Brian recognized some of his own behavior. Brian had found himself on a continual eating binge since he finished high school. He hadn't thought of himself as having a problem, because hadn't he always been able to take off weight when he needed to? And, he asked himself, wasn't it just girls who starved themselves who had a problem?

In fact, Brian had been quite successful as a high school wrestler. He didn't have the size for football or the hand-eye coordination to make the baseball team, but he liked the intellectual puzzles and the disciplined, strategic, one-on-one competition of wrestling.

Brian's coach gave him a consistent message: Stick with the daily workouts, learn the right moves, cut weight, and you will win your matches. The hardest part at first was cutting weight. In the peak of his growing years, Brian had to lose almost twenty pounds to compete in the ideal division for his height. He had then regained and relost the same ten pounds a dozen times each wrestling season.

"I used to eat a peanut butter and jelly sandwich in fifty bites, just to make the feeling of eating last as long as I could," Brian told me. "I drank gallons of water a day. Then, the day of a match I'd go into the whirlpool bath for an hour to sweat the water out. I'd do anything to have a chance at winning in the one sport I could succeed in.

"Guys who weren't athletes were nerds. They got left out of everything. They hardly had friends, let alone girlfriends. I couldn't let that happen to me."

After four wrestling seasons, Brian left for college and quit the sport. "I decided I couldn't spare the time from my studies, and at first I was relieved that I didn't have to go around thinking about how long I was going to have to stay in the whirlpool bath if I had a doughnut instead of a diet soda. But now I realize I've gone the other way—I went from being anorexic to serious problems with binge eating. Because of the craziness of wrestling, to this day I can't stop gorging myself," Brian told me. "I'm afraid I'll never be able to eat normally again, and I'll get huge."

While Brian's story may seem unusual, statistics suggest that dozens of wrestlers of high school age injure themselves every year by either binging or stopping to eat normally. Because wrestling requires boys to compete against other boys in the same height and weight class, one of the strategies coaches use to win is to make smaller boys "beef up" (by eating a lot and lifting weights) so that they'll be stronger, and make the bigger guys lose weight (by going on crash diets, doing aerobic exercise, and purging water through saunas and steam baths) so that they'll end up wrestling against smaller, weaker boys. Some of these boys suffer only minor health problems while others actually become bulimic or anorexic. Even worse, it was recently publicized that in the United States each year as many as thirty high-school-age wrestlers actually die because of eating disorders. Apparently, an intense desire to do well and to be praised for their success as athletes leads many boys to become so obsessive that they actually do harm to themselves. Finally, in an emerging new area of research, much of which is being conducted by Dr. Harrison Pope and Roberto Olivardia, my colleagues at Harvard Medical School, there is growing evidence that many men (and thus probably many boys too) are becoming increasingly obsessed with their bodies, so concerned about whether they are large and muscular enough that they become exceedingly compulsive about weight lifting, dieting, and similar activities.

But what is perhaps more common is for boys simply to overdo it when it comes to playing sports. Sixteen-year-old Scott reported that when he finally found a sport he was good at—running track—he felt he had to do just about whatever it took to succeed:

"Most days I get up between four-thirty and five in the morning to go running. I usually do about five miles and then head home. During the track season, after doing sprints with the team, I run about ten to twelve miles. Off season, I go home each afternoon, get changed, and run around ten miles. On the weekends, I go running about ten to fifteen miles a day. I've always wanted to be good at a sport. Now that I've got one I can do well at, I'm going to keep on going—maybe even try for the Boston marathon."

Seventeen-year-old Adam, who competed in boxing and wrestling and who had a black belt in karate, shared the following: "I pretty much eat, drink, and sleep with wrestling, and sometimes karate. During the wrestling season, I'm really busy at practice and doing meets. But all year round, I lift weights about three hours a day. I also watch professional wrestling as much as I can. My mother's always telling me to turn off the TV. She hates wrestling."

On the surface, these may seem to be boys who have simply become very involved with a sport. The fact that they feel devoted to a particular sport in and of itself may be something to be encouraged, since it suggests they are motivated, hardworking, and destined for success. But I believe it's important for those of us who mentor and coach boys to be vigilant about distinguishing between a boy's healthy devotion to learning a sport and an all-consuming, self-destructive obsession—a loss of balance and a lack of respect for human limitations. Ideally, playing a sport should enable a boy to develop new skills and build his self-confidence as he hones them. But when playing that sport becomes the sole source of a child's self-esteem—to the point where the child is devoting all of his waking hours to training for and performing that sport—there is some risk that the boy will end up harming himself or others.

He can hurt himself through bodily deprivation (for instance, by not eating or by continuing to work out following an injury), through exhaustion (by exercising or practicing beyond his capabilities), or by setting himself up for severe emotional distress (for instance, by allowing a limitation in his game to become an intense source of self-hate). He can hurt others by going overboard in playing a game (pushing, checking, or tackling too hard), verbally attacking team members or opponents (by cussing at rivals or "telling off" team members when they make mistakes), or by actually injuring others (for instance, by starting a fight during a hockey game or by throwing a baseball at somebody with the intention of hitting him).

These kinds of damaging behavior are rare when we teach boys that a game is a game, that sports are a kind of play. But when we allow them to think of sports as a vitally important measure of their self-worth—when they become too wrapped up in how well they perform a sport at any particular game on any particular day—boys can end up seriously injuring themselves or others. So much of what affects the sports experience for our sons is how we guide them through it and how well we supervise the other adults who do so.

SYLVIA: A MOTHER'S PLACE
I met Sylvia Stanton in her second-story walk-up apartment in San Francisco. She was a diminutive woman, then in early middle age with the look

in her soft brown eyes of a person who has seen her share of heartbreak. We were surrounded by an elderly but affectionate poodle and beautiful parrots.

"It's just the animals, Andrew, and me now," she said, with just a hint of sadness in her voice, "since Jonathan died." Her husband, a popular schoolteacher, had a family history of heart disease, and despite all efforts and precautions had died of a massive and sudden heart attack three years earlier, at age forty-nine. That was when Andrew was only twelve, but he had been bearing up well under the strain, Sylvia thought.

Andrew was a scholar-athlete who played varsity soccer, tennis, and football on his middle school teams, and continued to letter in high school. We were focusing on an incident in a special football summer camp Andrew had attended only two months after his father's death. Andrew had wanted to have the opportunity to go to this camp run by a series of well-known high school and college coaches, and his father had wanted him to go as well. Sylvia thought that it would be important not to let Jonathan's death deter Andrew from this goal, and agreed to drive him the thirty miles every day so that he could attend.

As you might imagine, the workouts at the football camp were grueling, and each day after the last scrimmage, Andrew would look more and more like a limp dishrag, ready for supper and bed. "He never complained," she said, "It's just not his nature, although that summer he clearly had diminished energy, what with the sadness we all were still feeling about his dad's untimely death."

Then, one Friday afternoon, when Sylvia arrived to bring him home, Andrew was nowhere to be found. Sylvia finally traced him to the infirmary, where he was sitting curled into a little ball, holding ice to his leg and barely choking back tears. "Come on, Mom, let's get out of here," he sighed. It wasn't until near the end of the long ride home that Sylvia pieced together the entire story.

Sylvia was incensed. It seemed that Mr. Biaggi, head coach at the camp, had been pushing Andrew quite hard. Andrew continued to do the prescribed push-ups, but he began to tear up and cry. He was still fragile from his father's death. At that point, "Mr. Big," as the boys called him, started to taunt Andrew, calling him a "girl," a "pansy" who "couldn't take it." "If you're going to be a little faggot, you can go sit on the bench," he apparently screamed in front of the other kids. Andrew refused to give in, and continued the routine. But all of a sudden he heard his ankle pop—he had sprained it the previous summer—and it seemed to be pulling out of the joint again. Andrew crimped his leg and fell to the ground.

"Stanton, what the hell is stopping you?" Coach Biaggi blared.

"I sprained my ankle, Coach—this time, I just can't finish."

"That's your choice, kid. But a man plays out the game. You can do five more. You can finish the last five push-ups, or get off the field—and don't bother coming back."

Andrew, who was not ordinarily easily intimidated, began to cry. He didn't want to be kicked out of practice, and so, despite the pain and resentment, he finished the push-ups, and then reported immediately to the infirmary.

By the time they got home, Andrew's foot was quite swollen. Sylvia took him to the pediatrician, who wrapped it and suggested that the boy skip camp for a couple of days. On the way home from the doctor's office, mother and son began to talk again. Andrew was as angry as his mother was, but he was worried about what his mom might do. Sylvia felt hurt by this, and was also pained to see Andrew injured and upset as well. She was confused about how to respond. She knew Andrew needed to navigate his own world by himself and fight his own battles. "I always try to give him space, but this was different. It went beyond Andrew's personal struggle to the whole principle of how, in just a small way, do you change the world these kids have to grow up in? Andrew is a sensitive kid, still close to me. At home, he can still put his head on my shoulder, and we cry together about his dad. OK, I know it's still different for boys in a public space, but no one should be allowed to treat someone like that, without even knowing him."

Sylvia and Andrew talked. Andrew was upset and angry at first, but then realized his mom was right. Something had to be done. Andrew reluctantly agreed to let his mother speak to the director of the camp.

Sam Donnatuck had spent many years coaching boys and young men in the sport he loved best, indeed loved more than anything else in the world—football. So Sylvia had a real task before her. But the meeting with Sam was strange—neither the struggle she expected, nor the agency for change she had dared to imagine. The head coach didn't share Sylvia's sense of outrage or horror about what had been done to her son, but he immediately agreed that Coach Biaggi had "gone overboard." Sam would talk with Coach Biaggi, and Andrew would never be treated that way again. "You've got to understand, Mrs. Stanton, that unlike your son, some boys do need a kick in the pants to get motivated. It's the nature of the business, we can't be letting them get too soft on us. We coaches are there to push them beyond what they thought they could do, and that's a lesson they can carry forward in life."

Sylvia heard this, but said, "I don't agree, Sam. I believe strongly we can motivate our boys positively, without harshness, without hurting their feelings or mistreating them."

That was the day Sylvia Stanton joined the governing board of her local boy's football association, and her son, Andrew, began the certification process to become an assistant coach for the junior division. "You've got to start somewhere, and why not here," Sylvia explained.

In telling Sylvia's story, I mean to remind us of the power parents have to step in, to make a difference in how boys experience sports. While some parents might not feel comfortable being as assertive as Sylvia was, I have found that most of us have the ability to participate in one way or another to "coach our coaches." Some parents may do this just by showing up at a game and offering encouraging remarks from the sidelines. Some may do this by attending team practices and perhaps volunteering to assist in aspects of training or coaching the team. And some may do this by being advocates for caring, thoughtful coaches—for men and women who will make our sons feel like important members of the team, who will urge these boys on in positive, confidence-building ways, and who will help them learn to accept winning or losing as an inevitable part of life.

COACHING THE COACHES: HOW PARENTS CAN ENSURE THAT SPORTS ARE TRANSFORMATIVE

Given the amazingly transformative experience that sports can be, I have found that it is critically important for parents to stay involved in their sons' athletic activities. All of the positive attributes of sports militate in favor of parents intervening to make sure that this philosophy remain in the forefront of boys' athletic activities. The overly competitive, brutal, obsessive aspects of sports—the aspects that lead boys to be injured both physically and emotionally—can be avoided if parents pay close attention to how their sons' activities are being directed.

I have found that parents can intervene in all of the following ways:

Participate directly in your son's sports activities. By doing so, you can help model the positive approach to sports discussed in this chapter.

Whether you join in as a teammate, serve as a coach, or just cheer from the sidelines in an upbeat, nonshaming way, your direct participation can make a world of difference in setting the right tone and making sure your son's experience is a good one.

Monitor your son's coaches. Even if you do not have the time or inclination to stay directly involved in your son's athletic activities, you can also help him by monitoring the coaches he plays under—what I call "coaching the coaches." Just as no parent would tolerate a schoolteacher who was doing a poor job of teaching his or her children, no parent, I believe, should tolerate a coach who isn't doing an effective job at leading boys in their sports activities.

Teach sports in the same way you would teach other areas of learning. Indeed, I believe that sports should be taught to boys with the same patience and thoughtfulness with which most other areas of learning are taught. And so boys who make mistakes or have trouble learning when they're involved in certain sports should be treated no differently than students who struggle with mastering math, reading, or writing.

Accordingly, if you are coaching boys in sports (or "coaching a coach"), make sure every boy is given patient appropriate feedback and has the chance to develop his skills at a comfortable pace. As you supervise boys playing sports, you may find it helpful to try to model yourself after a teacher you admired when you were growing up—somebody who was thoughtful and encouraging, someone who actually helped you learn and grow.

Try to remember, for instance, the kind of teacher who assigned tasks that students could actually do reasonably well if they tried, who explained why an answer was wrong (rather than berating the student who gave the incorrect response), and who helped each student—so long as that student was making a good-faith effort—to feel good about the academic progress he or she was making. Then imagine how different your experience would have been if that teacher was one who, instead, always taught students using problems that were far above their skill level, or who, every time a student offered an answer in class that was wrong, signaled that the student was a "zero" or a "loser," or who told his or her students that if they couldn't get 100 percent on all their tests or couldn't achieve straight A's, they would be considered failures. Obviously the first kind of teacher ends up helping a broad range of students, including those who are naturally bright as well as those who struggle academically, those who feel secure as

well as those who are less sure of themselves. The second kind, by contrast, assists only a small segment of students—either those who are
already very knowledgeable or those with incredibly tough skins.

Likewise, when you're teaching sports—or when you're advising
somebody else who is—make sure they're set up so that boys at all skill
levels can participate and master the game, so that boys receive plenty of
encouragement, so that winning is not hailed as being everything. Remember that shaming—in word or deed—is never an acceptable coaching technique.

Do all that you can to foster the transformative experience of sports.
This means encouraging boys to be emotive (but cautioning them against
being overly aggressive or hostile toward others); supporting the close,
affectionate relationships they develop with their teammates (but interrupting excessive teasing or taunting); providing as much positive feedback as possible to help boost their feelings of confidence (but not pushing
them to become obsessive about how strong or successful they are as athletes); and modeling a good attitude about losing, one that helps them, in a
positive way, to learn from their weaknesses and failures. All of this can be
achieved whether you do it by getting directly involved or by overseeing
how your son is coached.

*Insist upon multitiered athletic programs that address boys' varying
levels.* Just as most schools assign students to various classes based on
their relative scholastic abilities, athletic programs should ideally be structured so that they embrace all boys at all skill levels. For example, in an
after-school soccer program, some coaches have found it helpful—rather
than just having varsity and junior varsity teams—to set up three, four, or
even five different teams. In some cases these teams are divided by skill
level, and in some cases they are set up so that boys with top athletic skills
are mixed in with boys with less advanced skills. Another approach is to
create an intramural system where teams that are not ready to play against
teams from other schools practice side by side with teams that are ready to
take on such outside competition. Insist that your boy's school implement
programs that are creative in providing such diverse opportunities for boys
at all levels of athletic achievement.

Encourage your boy's school to "guy-ify." Just as during the 1960s
and 1970s schools began to give girls increased opportunities to play
female versions of sports traditionally enjoyed exclusively by boys—such
as baseball, basketball, and hockey—I believe the time has come for

schools to broaden their perspective by "guy-ifying" aspects of sports typically thought of being appropriate only for girls. For example, some school systems have "guy-ified" cheerleading so that boys who are less comfortable on the field—and more comfortable encouraging their teammates from the sidelines—can become cheerleaders without fear of ridicule and without feeling left out of the game.

Encourage coed sports. In a similar vein, coed sports provide an excellent opportunity for many boys. This means not only allowing girls to play on boys' teams or to play sports typically thought of as being "for boys only," but also allowing boys to play on the girls' teams and to play sports typically thought of as being "for girls only." I know some schools, for instance, that now have coed field hockey, lacrosse, basketball, and volleyball. On the whole, coed sports tend to be set up in a way that allows for a greater level of participation (and confidence building) among kids of all different shapes, sizes, and abilities. Coed sports can be wonderfully transformational for boys (and for girls) and should be vigorously encouraged.

Use sports to teach boys to respect their bodies and learn respect for their limits. Finally, as we saw earlier in this chapter, some boys go too far in how they play and train for sports. Some extend themselves physically in excessive ways. Some become too aggressive or reckless in how they play a sport, injuring themselves or others. And some actually harm themselves by developing eating disorders, such as bulimia and anorexia nervosa. Most often, there are always some boys who just seem to overdo it, pushing their bodies beyond their natural limits. While it's wonderful to encourage boys to be devoted to themselves and their teams and to try to reach new levels of athletic performance, it's quite another thing to allow boys to hurt themselves or others. So don't stand on the sidelines. Get involved, encourage your boys in a healthy way, and intervene if things go too far. As one boy, age eleven, recently said following his recovery from a serious track injury: "I've really learned that all you can do is your very best. As our coach always tells us, '*There is no finish line!*' "

The Greeks, who gave us the legacy of the Olympics, believed that all life must be seen in balance, and that even heroes (including sports heroes), must face tragedy and loss, along with the glory of victory. Sports, when genuinely appreciated under the tutelage of a wise mentor coach, can both uplift and humble boys—at once at the top of their game and almost simultaneously confronted with injury, loss, and defeat, turning real boys into strong, healthy, confident men:

And he, who in his youth secures a fine advantage, gathers hope and flies on wings of manly action, disdaining cost. Men's happiness is early ripened fruit that falls to earth from shakings of adversity.

Men are duty bound. What is a man? Man is a shadow's dream. But when divine advantage comes men gain a radiance and a richer life. (Pindar, *Odes*)

The radiance and the shadow's dream—both are parts of boys that sports may help to reveal and draw out. In the hands of the proper coach, sports provide a place where the rougher edges of boys' love may be softened and expressed freely. To keep sports in proper perspective and balance, boys need to cultivate the spirit of play, so easily lost to the cult of victory or competition. Then, and only then, will sports fulfill its true mission, releasing boys from the restrictions of the old Boy Code and offering them genuine opportunities for personal transformation.

PART THREE

WHEN THE BOUGH BREAKS

The toil of growing up;
The ignominy of boyhood; the distress
Of boyhood changing into man;
The unfinished man and his pain.

—WILLIAM BUTLER YEATS
"The Dialogue of Self and Soul"

–12–

HAMLET'S CURSE: DEPRESSION AND SUICIDE IN BOYS

"There's a mold you should fit into if you're a guy. You're supposed to be on the strong aggressive side, have social strength, and strength of will, and strength of body. You can't break like a twig in the wind."—Mark, age fifteen

THE HIDDEN EPIDEMIC OF BOYS' DEPRESSION

Duncan Casner and his mother both appeared surprised when I first said the word "depression." Tall, lean, and athletic-looking, with large brown eyes and stylish-looking wire-rim glasses, Duncan, at age sixteen, probably would not have fit anyone's stereotype of a depressed human being.

"He's getting into all sorts of trouble at school," his mother, Jocelyn, explained before sending Duncan to see me. "He's cutting classes and coming home early. And he tells my husband and me that he's been getting bad headaches. When the school called me to complain and I asked Duncan what was going on, he told me he thought he had a problem with migraines. But when I get home most days, he's always in his room playing around with his computer. His grades are dropping, and I want to see him succeed like his older brother, Graham, who's a freshman at Bates. Duncan's always been such a good kid and we just really can't figure out what's gotten into him."

Duncan and I began to meet shortly after my phone call with his mother, after his family doctor had ruled out any physical basis for his headaches.

"Maybe you could tell me a little bit about the headaches," I asked Duncan during his third visit with me.

"Lots of times at school, by the afternoon, my head hurts. It starts killing me. I can't take it, so I go home, lie down, and just fall asleep. Then I usually surf the Net, or just watch TV."

"It sounds kind of lonely," I suggested.

"Nah—not really. I'm a loner anyway. I don't really like many people. I'm just as happy doing my own thing. I'm sort of the independent type."

And then I seemed to say the magic words. "What was it like when your brother was still around? I understand he's off at college now."

"Who, Graham? Well, Graham used to be, like, one of my best friends. But he's older than me."

"Do you miss him?"

"Not really. I mean, yeah sort of. Maybe at school." Duncan seemed uncertain, deeply confused.

"You mean school's not quite the same without him?"

Duncan began to cry; in fact he cried so heavily his words became almost incoherent. "He used to . . . he used to help me."

"Help you deal with the other kids?" I asked.

"No. Not with the other kids. With the teachers."

"What do you mean?"

"Well, they always give way too much homework than you can get done. And then I start messing things up. I make mistakes in spelling. You see, I'm dyslexic and so I have some problems at school."

"Dyslexic?"

"Yeah."

"So Graham helped you?"

"Every afternoon he'd go over my homework with me and make sure I understood my mistakes. And then in the afternoons we'd hang out together."

"Do your parents know that you're dyslexic?"

"Yeah. But they don't like to talk about it. And they never knew how much Graham helped me."

As our discussions continued, I learned that Duncan had been diagnosed with dyslexia just four years earlier. Since he came from a family with two incredibly driven, highly successful parents and a talented older brother, apparently his disability was discovered rather late and was still hardly discussed. Both of his parents had basically kept his dyslexia a secret from the outside world.

It turned out that in addition to skipping classes and developing bad headaches, Duncan had developed serious problems with sleeping that were making it close to impossible for him to concentrate at school, his energy level had dropped enormously, and teachers reported that he often seemed irritable. Unbeknownst to either him or his parents, Duncan was significantly depressed. Yet because he hadn't come home and opened up to his parents about his difficulties at school, because he had not really told them how much he missed his brother Graham, Duncan simply seemed to them to have developed "problems with his behavior."

"Duncan is just acting out, isn't he?" asked Jocelyn.

"Actually," I answered, "I think he may be somewhat depressed. I'd recommend we continue talking and in addition that we seek consultation with a psychiatrist to see if he might also benefit from a short-term intervention with appropriate antidepressants."

"You've got to be kidding me," his mother replied incredulously, "You're not telling me my Duncan is clinically depressed, are you?"

"Well, yes, I think he may be."

"This isn't a common problem with boys his age, is it?" she then asked.

"It's not as uncommon as you might think," I explained. "In fact, recent research tells us there may be at least as many boys who are depressed as there are girls who are depressed. And that means there may actually be millions of depressed boys out there, many of whom may not look depressed on the outside."

"It sounds like a hidden epidemic," offered Jocelyn.

"I think you may be right," I said.

BIG BOYS DON'T CRY

Of all the cultural prohibitions that limit our boys, I have found that one of the most unrelenting is the taboo against expressing sadness. It's so common as to be a cliché: "Big boys don't cry," boys are told. "Get over it. Snap out of it!" Though every boy naturally feels sad from time to time, boys learn early on not to cry or talk about sadness, and not to turn to others for help. The Boy Code enforces these restrictions.

Our male cultural icons reinforce them too. It's hard to think of Michael Jordan, Muhammed Ali, Tom Cruise, Bruce Willis, Arnold Schwarzenegger, or John Wayne expressing feelings of personal sadness in public. The typical action hero underscores the idea that tough men don't get sad—they just get even. The hero finds his enemies have burned down his home, his car's tires are slashed, and his friend has been slaughtered—does he scream, weep, or collapse? No, he glares off into the distance, and the only sign of emotion is a tightening muscle in his cheek, the growing fury in his stony gaze. Then he bursts into action, leaping into a high-tech vehicle and roaring off to seek revenge.

Because society trains boys to cover their sadness, it becomes very difficult for others to know when a boy is not doing well emotionally. Add to this the fact that we generally do not *expect* boys to be sad or depressed— and the fact that if we do suspect depression in boys, *we often use inappropriate methods of diagnosis originally designed to ascertain depression in adult women*—and it should not be surprising that we frequently have a hard time realizing when our sons are unhappy, and often fail to detect (or to accept) depression when it occurs in young and adolescent boys.

By "depression" I mean the disorders that range from dysthymia (which is something like being in a very bad mood a lot of the time) up to and including what is generally referred to as a major depression or a clinical depression. Another form of depression is what psychologists call bipolar disorder, or manic-depressive illness. Since many of the symptoms in this disorder overlap with the symptoms we discuss in clinical depression, much of our discussion of how to detect and treat depression in boys will also be helpful to anyone trying to detect these and other forms of depression as well.

As reflected in Duncan's story, when parents first learn that their sons are unhappy or clinically depressed, they are often utterly surprised. "We had no idea he felt that way," they say. "He seemed so with it and upbeat." Or: "We knew he seemed grouchy and tired a lot, but we thought it was just a normal teenage thing." A boy can be severely depressed, even suicidal, and his parents may not be able to tell the boy's troubled state.

Learning to uncover whether a boy, especially a young boy, is merely discontented or is actually depressed can be quite difficult. It's hard to discern a boy's feelings of sadness or vulnerability, and the line between short-lived unhappiness and clinical depression is sometimes hard to make out.

Take, for instance, eight-year-old Devon Washington. Large for his age, Devon was sent to see one of my colleagues when one of his teachers discovered that he was hitting his playmates during recess each day. These weren't everyday playful taps but truly forceful injurious punches. The teacher realized there was a problem when another boy came to her and revealed a large black-and-blue mark on his upper arm. The teacher told my colleague, "Devon is not doing well in our school. He doesn't listen in class. He's very aggressive, acts out a lot, and now is punching other kids. We think he may be hyperactive."

The teacher's proposed diagnosis was plausible. Devon was inattentive in class, was not doing well in his schoolwork, and now had begun to direct aggression toward other students. But, it turned out, according to my colleague, that Devon was actually depressed. He did not exhibit any of the classic symptoms we generally associate with depression—for example, he wasn't quiet, melancholic, or withdrawn. He wasn't weepy. He wasn't expressing despair or hopelessness. Instead, Devon was rebellious and full of rage—he resisted doing his schoolwork, acted defiant and distracted, and now was lashing out at others. It was only through the prescription of cognitive behavioral therapy and appropriate antidepressant medications that Devon was able to overcome his illness.

THE MANY FACES OF DEPRESSION

Depression affects boys in a variety of ways. It may make them feel sad, anxious, or numb. The depressed boy may act sullen and withdrawn or, like Devon, may become agitated, overly aggressive, and full of rage. He may misbehave in school or become dependent on drugs or alcohol. Or he may just seem glum.

Depression in boys is a syndrome involving a whole range of behavioral difficulties and symptoms. While just about any adult who's been diagnosed with clinical depression will tell you that the experience is quite different from a "bad mood," it's essential, especially in the case of boys, to see depression as this kind of wide-ranging syndrome with symptoms that fall along a continuum from mild to extreme. I believe that if we dwell merely on the most extreme—and obvious—instances of full-blown, or "clinical," depression, we risk failing to help boys cope with emotional states that, though less intense on the surface, are actually very painful for them, emotional states that without appropriate intervention may very well evolve into a major depression or provoke suicidal feelings. There's also a risk that by ignoring certain related behaviors, most notably irritable conduct and the abuse of substances, we may also fail to recognize the onset of a serious depression.

THE BIOLOGY OF DEPRESSION

We now know that in addition to psychological elements, depression can often be caused by biological factors, most notably by an imbalance in certain neurotransmitters, such as serotonin, that seem to directly affect emotional well-being. Medications that correct these imbalances—so-called SSRIs (selective serotonin reuptake inhibitors) such as Prozac (fluoxetine), Zoloft (sertraline), and Paxil (paroxetine)—have been shown to be helpful to many people, including children, suffering depression. But neurotransmitter levels are also affected by psychological phenomena, such as daily stress, loss of a loved one, or an early trauma, all of which may change the biological and chemical workings of the brain, leaving it vulnerable to depression. Exercise levels can change neurotransmitter levels in a different way, improving your mood and your biology.

We are just beginning to understand the complex interrelationships between the biological and psychological aspects of our emotional systems. As with the heart, some people are born with a genetic predisposition to heart disease; they inherit a weak heart, high blood pressure, or a tendency to atherosclerosis. Such individuals will have to work hard to prevent heart disease. But heart disease doesn't have to come about through genetics. If a previously strong heart receives enough abuse—a poor diet, chronic smoking, or a habitual lack of exercise—it will become vulnerable to a heart attack. Likewise, depression seems to run in some families, but a *vulnerability* to it can be created at any point, through early deprivation, a lack of healthy loving relationships, or repeated blows to one's self-esteem.

While I believe the biological, or "organic," components of clinical depression (and the medical treatments for them) are of paramount importance and need to be carefully studied, my primary focus here is on what other psychologists and I have discovered about *external* psychological factors that can lead boys toward serious sadness or depression—factors such as a boy's family life, how he's treated at school, the quality of his friendships, and what kind of emotional support he gets on a regular basis.

THE COST, AGAIN, OF SOCIETY'S DISCONNECTION

In my view, so many of the symptoms of depression that boys experience are caused by gaps in how we, as a society, address the inner emotional worlds of our boys. As discussed in earlier chapters, boys are often pushed too early to be independent of those people—their parents—who have so far been their main source of comfort and nurturance. I believe that the pain of being separated from and losing these people, in and of itself, is enough to depress just about any boy. While neither the trauma of premature separation nor "abandonment" leads all boys to become depressed, either may create a deep sadness in many boys, making them vulnerable to depression later, either as boys or as men.

Further, I believe that many boys become susceptible to depression because of the emotional scarring they receive through society's shame-based hardening process. No matter how healthy a boy's emotional system was when he started life, it quickly becomes compromised by the hardening he feels is necessary to avoid feelings of shame, and by his denial (because of shame) of vulnerable emotional states such as sadness, disappointment, and despair. Every boy needs to cry sometimes, to seek the comfort of loving arms, to tell someone how much he hurts and to have them respond with empathy. Yet because of the gender straitjacket that inhibits boys from ever completely *experiencing* these feelings (let alone expressing them) and insists that they don't need help, boys actively repress feelings of sadness in an unhealthy way that can lead them to feel lonely and frightened, or push them toward more severe forms of depression.

But the straitjacket also brings about sadness and depression in boys in yet another important way. As we've discussed, our gender-stereotyped myths about boys mislead us to believe that boys do not care much about their relationships with friends and families and that boys are generally tough, "cocky," and independent. Yet we've also learned that, in reality, most boys experience all sorts of insecurities, feel tremendously dependent on their friends and families, and in many areas (for example, at school or when dating) are prone to large fluctuations in self-esteem. Boys yearn for connection—they care a lot about their relationships and about how they are liked by others. But because we are so often confused by the old myths, we may tend not to pay attention to the emotional ups and downs in our sons' friendships and relationships and thus be unaware of the devastating feelings of shame our sons may experience when these friendships or relationships are not going well or have come to an end. Such shame in a boy, if no one detects it and explores it with him, can lead him to feel profoundly sad, afraid, and disconnected from the rest of the world, and even to become clinically depressed.

DEPRESSION OVER RELATIONSHIPS

Yet researchers have perennially doubted the intensity or basic emotional importance of boys' relationships and so have assumed that problems in them would be unlikely to cause boys to become sad or depressed. Thus a study on depression in adolescent boys and girls conducted by Joan Girgus and her colleagues at Princeton University hypothesized that "levels of depression in early adolescent girls are more closely related to their popularity with peers than in early adolescent boys"—an assumption based on "the frequent argument that women are more likely than men to base their self-esteem on their relationships with others and on the approval of others." But the results of the study were not as expected. "Surprisingly, the boys' depression scores were significantly correlated with both popularity and rejection, whereas the girls' depression scores were only significantly correlated with rejection. Thus, girls and boys are apparently equally vulnerable to depression as a function of poor peer relationships."

Another study, by Paul Rohde, John Seeley, and David Mace, in Eugene, Oregon, also found that boys suffer when they don't have healthy relationships. This study focused on the extent to which delinquent adolescents develop ideas about suicide, and it found that boys were more likely to think about suicide if they were suffering stressful life events and if they lacked social supports in situations such as when they were lonely and had few close relatives. The authors concluded that suicidal behavior for boys is closely linked to their social connections.

We now know that the opposite is also true—that strong relationships can *prevent* boys from sliding into depression or engaging in risky, self-destructive behaviors in the first place. The National Longitudinal Study on Adolescent Health, also mentioned in Chapter 7, found that teenagers who felt connected to their families were less likely to experience emotional distress. They were also less likely to engage in violence, attempt suicide, or use harmful substances. The key factors were parents who "shared activities" with teens, who were physically present at key times during the day, and, most important, who expressed warmth, love, and caring. Also, as we learned in our discussion about adolescence, Blake Bowden, at Cincinnati Children's Hospital Medical Center, found that teens who ate dinner with their parents at least five nights a week were significantly better adjusted than classmates who dined alone.

In my opinion, we simply must resist being fooled by a boy's mask. Boys are not Lone Rangers, and at all ages they need to be told that they're good, that they make good friends, that they're needed and loved. And, like all human beings, they particularly need caring support when their relationships are disrupted or come to an untimely end.

CHANGING RATES OF DEPRESSION: IT'S A GUY THING TOO

Perhaps one of the main reasons we often fail to detect (and thus to treat) depression in boys is that depression has been seen as something that girls and women suffer far more often than boys and men do.

The reality, however, does not seem to follow our gender-stereotyped assumptions.

Some 3.5 million children under the age of nineteen are clinically depressed in this country—about 5 percent of children in that age group. According to IMS America, a research company, some 580,000 prescriptions for Prozac, the most popular antidepressant drug, were written for children ages five and older in 1996. In studies conducted in 1990 and 1991, Professor Susan Nolen-Hoeksema and her colleagues at Stanford University found that from ages eight through twelve, *more* boys reported depression than girls, and that these boys' scores for depression were consistently *higher* than those of girls. Interestingly, these Stanford studies reflected that the most important symptoms of depression in prepubescent boys were behavior disturbances (such as being irritable or misbehaving) and anhedonia (a lack of pleasure, especially in relation to friends and friendships). Of course these kinds of symptoms, taken alone, would not generally qualify for a diagnosis of depression. This helps to explain why many boys, especially older boys who may display only these kinds of symptoms, could easily have their depressive states overlooked or misdiagnosed.

In one of the largest studies of depression in children, a survey in 1982 of 2,790 children in rural Pennsylvania, Smucker at Penn State found that there were no differences in the numbers of boys and girls who were depressed, nor in the severity of their depressions—suggesting that girls and boys may be equally susceptible to depression. In another poll of 1,000 teenagers conducted for *Ms.* magazine in 1997, 28 percent of young women aged fifteen to twenty-one stated they feel depressed daily or several times a week, and 20 percent of young men in the same age group reported to the magazine that they feel depressed just as frequently.

These studies on the incidence and severity of depression in boys are staggering. It's quite probable that many of the studies may actually underreport the incidence of depression in boys, especially among older boys, because of boys' reluctance to confess to sadness or vulnerability. Because boys feel pressured to mask their genuine pain, many boys, in the context of psychological studies or surveys, may fail to admit—or even know—that they're experiencing depression.

This has already been shown to be true of men. Angst and Dobler-Mikola in Switzerland found that men and women who are depressed report their problems very differently. *The men tended to minimize their pain.* The researchers started with depressed men and women whose emotional problems had caused them similar levels of impairment at work. One could assume that these men and women were suffering similar levels of emotional pain. Yet the men in this group reported far fewer symptoms of depression than women.

Angst and Dobler-Mikola also found that, over time, men tended to forget how depressed they had been in the past. Men and women who had the same number of symptoms of depression were interviewed one year later. Men recalled many fewer symptoms of depression. Men seem to actively suppress their memories of a vulnerable, sad time.

In a similar way many boys may tend to deny or "forget" their pain when questioned by research scientists. While some studies are designed to evoke more candid responses from boys, many (in fact, probably most) are not. This can lead to research results that, among other things, end up underestimating the actual incidence of depression among boys.

But what's most important, of course, is not to debate which gender is more prone to depression but to understand that all human beings, despite gender, are all too eminently vulnerable to depression and that the only way to help reduce the incidence of depression is first to recognize this, and then to learn how to detect symptoms early on and master what to do when these symptoms begin.

RECOGNIZING SADNESS AND DEPRESSION IN BOYS

Learning how to detect *sadness* in boys is actually a separate process from learning how to recognize an actual *depression*. While there's a lot of overlap, it's important to distinguish the normal strategies a healthy boy uses to cope with feelings of sadness from the symptoms of an actual depression. So much of the difference has to do with the *degree* of a boy's behavior—how much he acts a certain way, how intense his behavior is, and how long the behavior lasts. For instance, a boy who occasionally shuts himself into his room when he's feeling down is probably just momentarily feeling sad. By contrast, the boy who frequently comes home from school, goes into his room, shuts the door, and refuses to talk to anyone is obviously exhibiting behaviors that fall squarely within the continuum of depression. Likewise, a boy who has a bad day and doesn't feel like coming to the dinner table is clearly quite different from one who consistently refuses to eat or dine with his family. Where diagnosing depression in boys becomes more difficult, of course, is when boys' behaviors fall between the temporary "bad mood" and the comportment of somebody who is obviously unwell. Also, as we've seen, adults may not recognize depression in boys when it is expressed as anger or agitation rather than as sadness, hopelessness, withdrawal, and despair.

Sadness but not Depression

Admittedly, recognizing sadness and depression in boys tends to be more difficult than recognizing them in girls. When girls feel sad, they generally rely on a very different coping style than boys. Girls, according to psychologist Susan Nolen-Hoeksema of Stanford University, tend to "ruminate" on their sadness, its symptoms, and its possible causes. Also, research shows that most girls are more likely to cry, admit their feelings of unhappiness, hopelessness, or helplessness, and seek out support from friends and family. In a recent poll, researchers found that when girls feel sad, almost half (45 percent) say they talk to friends. Only 26 percent of the boys polled said they would turn to friends for support.

In contrast, when boys feel sad, they do not tend to dwell, or "ruminate," on their unhappiness. And while certainly some will go directly to friends or family for comfort and support, the majority attempt either to simply "let go" of their painful feelings or instead to take an "action-oriented" strategy to resolve them. Fourteen-year-old Ross told me how he deals with being sad. "About once a week, I get upset about something, but I forget about it pretty soon. I find a friend and go play ball or just hang out. I put it aside and just move on."

Other times, Ross says, he just gets mad. He told me about a time he got in a fight with a friend. "I came home really sad and went up to my room. I just sat on my bed and listened to music. I was sad, then I got mad—really tense and really mad—and then I yelled and punched my pillow a bunch of times. That's how my sadness is, mixed in with a lot of aggression. Being sad is the same as being mad for me."

Ross's response is typical of many boys who cope with mild sadness by distracting themselves. They play ball, hang out with friends, listen to music, or watch TV. When emotions are running so high that simple distraction doesn't work, a boy will tend to withdraw for a while, needing to be alone to ride out the storm and reemerging from his sadness only after the worst of the pain is passed. Many boys in the "Listening to Boys' Voices" study spoke of the need to "let things blow over."

Listen, for instance, to Mark, a bright and energetic fifteen-year-old:

"There's a mold you should fit into if you're a guy. You're supposed to be on the strong, aggressive side, have social strength, and strength of will, and strength of body. You can't break like a twig in the wind."

"So how do you deal with things when you're feeling weak, when things aren't going so great?" I asked.

"When I get angry," Mark answered, "I try to just let it go. I usually try to rationalize it in my head, to explain to myself that I shouldn't be that angry about it. I try to either think about it calmly, or not think about it at all so it won't bother me anymore. When I feel sad, I look for something to throw it into perspective. . . . *It kind of goes away or I concentrate on something else.*"

Because he has internalized the sense that showing too many unresolved feelings can be counterproductive, Mark feels critical of other boys who are unable to keep a lid on their emotions. "Some guys get obsessed with one annoying point in their life, but if they only let go of it, their life would be much better. It wouldn't take them a lot of effort to let go of it. I wish they would just act rationally or calmly, just kind of take it a little quieter and less vocally, like everyone else told them to."

Mark seems to equate expressing his vulnerability with an acute sense of shame, fearing severe penalties for failing to adapt to the mold. "If you don't fit in, then you're a loser, you're worthless, you look stupid, and no one likes you. People tend not to associate with you. They push you off in the corner. After a while, if you respond badly, if you just respond by getting more and more depressed, people don't react well to that." Mark's comments reflect how any gap in a boy's self-confidence—any admission that he's feeling sad or depressed—becomes a cause for others to reject him. And then again if a boy continues to internalize his feelings of sadness and pain and doesn't learn how to suppress them, he may fear they're only going to get worse. Mark explains:

"If you try to shut yourself inside your head and not ever come out, then it's just going to be worse. There's no way to get away from it."

But if some boys like Mark deal with sadness by simply attempting to "let it go," others rely on the "timed-silence syndrome" we discussed earlier. When a boy feels hurt or unhappy, he may prefer to lick his wounds in private, where he will not be shamed by others. He comes up for air—and may seek out help from parents or friends—only after experiencing a period of silence and private grieving. The advantage of this strategy for a boy is that no one ever sees his sadness. He averts shame. The disadvantage, of course, is that unless parents know this syndrome when they see it, they may have a difficult time detecting his sadness.

My sense is that boys who successfully use distracting and withdrawing strategies including "timed silence" still need other people to help them recover from their emotional pain. After withdrawing to let the worst of the storm pass, most boys go out of their way to reconnect with family and friends. When he's ready to reemerge, a boy needs to interact with others: to play a mindless game of ball with friends, to have mom say, "Glad things seem better," to have dad offer a special trip for ice cream, or even to have the same old argument with his sister about the TV schedule. When this happens, a boy knows that life goes on. His shame melts away. The people who care about him are still around and can be counted on.

One ten-year-old boy told us that he could count on his grandfather to help him feel better. After Jim got diagnosed with a serious eye-related disability, he said he was "embarrassed" to have to wear thick prescription glasses and to have to go to special classes with other disabled children. He started getting really sad—coming home and not talking to anyone—and his grandfather noticed. His grandfather didn't ask what the matter was—he just told Jim to get his coat on. They went to the park and started tossing a baseball—a practice that continued every afternoon for a while. "He told me stories about his life, about coming over on a boat and working in a restaurant. He's had a tough life. It made me feel a lot better," says Jim. Jim may not be able to put it into words, but his grandfather's stories probably helped so much because they expressed the clear message: we all have hardships that we have to bear, I too have felt sad and overwhelmed; I found a way of dealing with it and you'll get through it too—we still care about you.

When boys have family and friends who offer this kind of sensitive support, they often can get over even difficult situations. The following steps should help when a boy needs some extra attention:

Create a safe space. Create a safe space in which your boy can express his feelings openly without fear of being shamed or reproached. Usually this means finding a time when there aren't other distractions and explaining to the boy that he can say or express anything, that nobody will judge or punish him for what he shares.

Listen carefully. Listen very carefully to what a boy says. He may not open up immediately, and you might need to just listen patiently until he feels comfortable enough to explain exactly what he's going through. Sometimes the boy may simply not yet be ready to talk. He may still need some private time. If you detect that this is the case, simply allow the boy to take that time and try to be completely available to him (i.e., don't give him half your attention while also doing something else) when he emerges from his silence and seeks your help.

Be especially careful about shaming your son. When it's your turn to talk, it's best if you avoid saying anything that might humiliate or embarrass your son. Just about the most helpful thing you can say is that you understand the way he feels and that you are there to help him through in any way you can. Let him know how much you empathize with what he's experiencing. Although sometimes it may seem easier to tease him a bit, to give advice, or to tell him that "everything will be fine," these types of responses tend to cut off the boy's ability to express his feelings genuinely. Instead, simply tell your boy that "it sounds like things are rough right now"—let him know that you care about the pain he's feeling. In the end, all you need to do is be available, ask thoughtful questions that show that you care, really listen carefully, avoid judgments and lecturing, and express your love and concern genuinely.

WHEN THINGS GET WORSE

When a boy sees no sympathy at hand or if distressing circumstances beyond his control continue, his normal "action-oriented" coping strategies may become overwhelmed. He may no longer be able to forget his sadness by playing a hard game of hoops, punching pillows, or spending an evening alone listening to music. Attempting to repress his unhappiness and his shame over it may instead thrust him toward turbulent self-conflict, painful emotions jumbling his thoughts and churning his stomach. A young boy may become restless and impulsive, unable to focus and unable to behave appropriately. He may turn irritable or hostile, expressing his inner confusion by attempting to hurt others or taking dangerous risks like high-speed driving. He may express the physical aspect of his turmoil by getting sick, having chronic headaches or stomachaches.

Or he may withdraw, becoming more and more sullen and estranged from those who care about him. All of these in moderation are normal coping mechanisms when a boy is in pain. But when boys act this way, it's important to look beneath the surface, ask questions, express concern, and attempt to determine what the boy is experiencing; for when these behaviors become persistent or extreme, the boy may very well be on his way to depression.

Kenny Robinson, aged sixteen, was fortunate enough to have a mother who recognized that his angry and aggressive behavior was a nonverbal cry for help and did what she could to bring him back to health. Kenny started seeing a therapist weekly. In these conversations, Kenny was able to let down his mask of anger and express his underlying sadness about his father's leaving home so abruptly.

"Nothing's the same without my dad around," he said. "Mom never has time anymore either. She's too busy talking on the phone to her lawyer or her sister."

"You feel like you've lost both your mom and your dad," suggested the therapist.

Kenny's eyes filled with tears. "Yeah. I don't know what's going on."

His therapist brought Kenny's mother into several sessions and helped her see how much Kenny needed her at this terrible time. Mrs. Robinson was clearly distraught and anxious about the family crisis, but was also concerned about Kenny.

The therapist suggested they institute "special time," where Mrs. Robinson played whatever game Kenny suggested, as long as it didn't hurt anyone (and with a spending cap if needed). They started with one hour a week of special time. Mrs. Robinson had trouble at first getting the energy to follow Kenny's active play, but she saw how important it was to him.

Within a few weeks, the two developed a special game. Kenny was a detective who searched for missing persons and sent home good men who had been lost. Mrs. Robinson played her part with increasing enthusiasm. She realized Kenny needed to work through his father's leaving in his own way.

She also realized how little she had been telling Kenny about why his father left. Now she made a conscious effort to sit down with him and give him any news she received. They imagined what it would be like to see his father again. She talked to Kenny and helped him sort through the confusing issues. She told him that she knew his father was trying to be a good man, but sometimes people do things that are wrong even when they're trying their best.

Kenny and his mother and the therapist also spent two sessions talking about how Kenny could stop fighting with other kids. He said quietly, "I fight because the other kids say rotten things about my dad." At this point, Mrs. Robinson started crying and reached over to hug Kenny, who also began to cry. Kenny agreed to try to find ways to talk to kids about his dad, instead of hitting them.

Over the months of therapy, Kenny's school problems have abated. The family has many rocky times ahead, but at least now mother and son are going through them together.

Kenny was lucky that his mother dealt with his angry behavior by sending him to therapy instead of sending him to his room. All too often, a boy's action-oriented coping style confuses the most well-meaning parents and teachers. We take the actions at face value and react accordingly. We punish the angry or impulsive child and medicate the overactive one. We push the "malingering" boy to toughen up and get back into the swing of things. And, worst of all, we tend to isolate the withdrawn or angry boy. We see his tough, sullen exterior, and say, "He's a teenager, what do you expect? It's a phase. He's just being a boy." And so we let him drift away.

Some of us may not recognize these signs of sadness in boys, in part because we're eager not to. It's painful to have to admit that someone we love is suffering. It's hard to realize that a boy, whom we prefer to see as tough and strong, can be weighed down by extreme unhappiness. Some parents just accept the outward action behaviors as if they were an inevitable fact of nature, that all young boys act up and that teenagers are rebellious. But behind many of these external displays of boyhood energy and activity are often boys in trouble, boys in pain.

THE DIFFICULTY OF DIAGNOSING DEPRESSION IN BOYS

Diagnosing depression in boys is difficult for several reasons. First, as we've already seen, it's often hard to draw the line between the normal strategies a boy uses to deal with day-to-day hurts and disappointments from the symptoms of actual depression (these symptoms will be described later in this chapter).

Second, depression is hard to diagnose in boys because boys so often mask the very behaviors we traditionally associate with depression—sulking, crying, withdrawing.

The third and, I believe, most important reason recognizing boys' depression is so difficult is that we tend to look for it using benchmarks more appropriate to girls and women. Some of the classic symptoms of depression in women include becoming weepy, openly expressing hopelessness, helplessness, and despair, showing dependence on others or seeking out—and then rejecting—help from others. Yet these symptoms are less common in boys, and in fact many depressed boys may exhibit none of them.

If we are to recognize depression when it strikes boys, I believe we need to understand the unique constellation of symptoms that occur in boyhood depression. When we comprehend the specific ways in which boys show—or mask—their unhappiness and other symptoms of depression, it becomes easier to catch depression in its early phases before it becomes severe and difficult to reverse.

Consider, for example, fifteen-year old Ed, a quiet boy who actively denied that he had any emotional problems or that he was experiencing any emotional pain. When I first met Ed, he sat across a desk from me in a small hospital office, rubbing his head in his hands and saying over and over again. "I don't know how I got here."

"You tried to kill yourself," I replied softly. "You took a lot of pills and booze, then tried to use your father's pistol to finish the job." Luckily, the gun had discharged accidentally, the neighbors had called the police, and here was Ed—alive and showing no scars.

He smiled wanly at me. "It's a mistake, just a big mistake."

But I knew better. In the emergency room, he had upset the doctors by cursing them when he realized he was still alive. This was no mere "attempt" and certainly no "mistake" but a determined end run toward death.

But unlike some of the girls on this locked ward, Ed showed no outer signs that he had narrowly survived a suicide attempt. He had no slashed wrists, no teary, red-rimmed eyes, no sad, needy look about him. Indeed, Ed denied being depressed.

Ed reluctantly answered my questions about his family. He hadn't seen his dad in three years, since dad remarried and had another child. His older brother and sister were "getting by" on their own. His brother was an electrician; his sister, a nurse. He, the baby of the family, was living at home with mother. He was barely passing any of his classes and had been threatened with suspension for truancy.

After we worked together for a while, Ed was able to talk about his anger at his family. Brother Greg was drinking heavily and abusing his wife. Dad, also an alcoholic, was flatly refusing to pay child support and refusing to see Ed and his siblings. "I guess the Grady men don't give a shit about the future," said Ed with his typical half-grin.

"I think a lot of young men aren't sure what their future could be," I offered.

"Yeah. What's there to look forward to? Life sucks and then you die."

As we worked together, it was clear that Ed felt deeply hurt by his father's abandonment. But instead of grieving, Ed learned to put on a false front, to grin and crack jokes. That was easier than pretending he still cared about his father. He had quite a vocabulary around angry words: "Pissed off," "fed up," "Po'd." But he vehemently denied he was depressed. And he vehemently denied he needed help. "All I want is a pack of Winston's and a chance to get out of here. I'll be fine."

Despite his pain, despite his clear suicidal intent, Ed might not have been diagnosed with depression by a mental health worker who was focused too strictly on current methods of diagnosis, which rely heavily on the criteria in the *Diagnostic and Statistical Manual of Mental Disorders,* or the *DSM.* In this reference book for clinicians, we find that diagnosing depression is done according to a checklist: a patient must show a certain minimum number of symptoms. First and foremost, he must be suffering a depressed mood or have lost the ability to take any interest or pleasure in the world. In addition, he must suffer at least *four* other symptoms from a list that includes: weight loss, sleep disturbances, agitation or retardation, fatigue or loss of energy, feelings of worthlessness or guilt, trouble concentrating, trouble making decisions, and thoughts of suicide.

Such criteria are not designed specifically for children and are based on a narrow model of depression, one heavily influenced by the way depressed *women* tend to behave. According to these criteria we would have trouble diagnosing Ed as depressed, yet we know that he was so despairing that he was ready to end his life. It's not that the traditional *DSM* criteria are never helpful in diagnosing depression in boys, for they are. It's just that they're incomplete and do not recognize the broad range of symptoms in boys that we've been discussing.

Nonetheless, most mental health professionals currently use these adult criteria to diagnose depression for children as young as nine years of age. For children younger than nine, especially preschool-age children who are not yet necessarily able to articulate their feelings in a clear way, depression is usually inferred primarily from a sense of the child's outward demeanor (how sad his face looks) or mood—that is, through the child's conduct (especially acting out or problems with disobedience) or through complaints about physical problems (such as headaches or stomachaches). In children of school age up to and including the prepubescent years, features such as mood disturbance, irritable behavior, and more adultlike sadness are also considered. In addition, both preschool and prepubescent children may express feelings of worthlessness, low self-esteem, and a type of apathy or lack of pleasure called anhedonia. Finally, mental health professionals look for certain anxieties, phobias, and even the mention of suicide in children within this age range.

In addition to the fact that this approach uses too narrow a set of symptoms to identify depression in boys, there's another problem. Making a diagnosis based on such criteria often depends on a patient's telling a clinician about his problems and the clinician's understanding and acting upon what the patient reports. Yet we know that boys and men minimize their problems, underreport their symptoms, and forget about troubles as soon as possible. We also know that medical professionals may actually "collude" with men's reluctance to see or discuss their feelings of sadness. In 1991, Potts, Burnam, and Wells, from the Rand Corporation, compared the way doctors diagnosed male patients suffering from depression-like symptoms to how these patients responded to a more objective—and anonymous—questionnaire, something called the Diagnostic Interview Schedule. The surprising result was that about 65 percent of the men diagnosed as healthy by the doctors were actually suffering from depression, according to their answers on the questionnaire. In other words, the physicians failed to catch over three out of five male depressions. Many depressed men don't tell their doctors about their troubles, and many doctors aren't asking the right questions or aren't "hearing" the answers men are giving them. Potts, Burnam, and Wells concluded that physicians are unlikely to press men about symptoms or to inquire in any depth once their male patients assure them that things are fine. Physicians, believing that they are helping men to avoid feelings of shame, go along with the code of silence.

With boys, especially young boys, the dialogue between the child and his parent, physician, or other caregiver, may be even more limited. The boy may not be able to find words to express his feelings or the adult listening to the boy may not be closely enough attuned to the boy's subtle cries for help to realize how much the child is hurting. Given this important communication gap—and, additionally, if the adult is looking for symptoms that are more typical in women such as sudden teary out-breaks—it's little surprise that depression in boys so often goes undetected and thus untreated.

How Do You Tell if a Boy Is Depressed?

What type of criteria should we use to better diagnose boys who are depressed? I would propose creating a new diagnostic tool specifically designed to identify depression in boys. This would recognize that boys (and men) tend to act out depression through myriad behaviors, some of which look the same as those traditionally associated with depression in women *but many of which look different.* Bearing in mind too that every depressed boy is likely to have symptoms that look different from those of the next boy and that these symptoms will also vary depending on the specific age of the boy, I would recommend that we diagnose depression by watching carefully for the following symptoms:

1. **Increased withdrawal from relationships and problems in friendships.** Though a boy may deny that he's doing so, he may tend to spend less time than usual with friends and family. He may become further disconnected from them emotionally, acting more and more like something of a loner. He may stop talking and respond to questions reluctantly. At home he may spend long periods of time in his own room, shrinking from interactions with other family members. At school he may retreat from students and teachers and avoid participating in classroom discussions and activities. He may try to sit in the back of the room, sequester himself during recess or study-breaks, and sit alone during lunch. He may try to avoid going to gym class, skip other courses, or become completely truant. When asked who his friends are, he may report that he has very few or none. He may seem unable to keep a "best" friend. This group of symptoms may appear in boys of all ages.

2. **Depleted or impulsive mood.** The boy may act tired, dispassion-ate, bored, depleted. He may stop showing interest or taking plea-sure in activities he used to seem to enjoy. If normally he is vivacious and talkative, he may become increasingly sluggish, less talkative, and less outgoing. Alternatively, he may act impul-

sively, unpredictably, or irrationally. He may seem more anxious or fearful than usual, perhaps reporting to you that he feels "nervous," "worried," or "tense." It's important for us to distinguish normal mood swings, especially during adolescence, from shifts in a boy's moods that reveal deeper problems. This is a subtle distinction, so I suggest parents err on the side of asking a boy how he's feeling rather than simply dismissing or ignoring his mood changes. Note that depleted mood is a common symptom of depression in boys of all ages; however, the occurrence of impulsive mood increases with age.

3. **Increase in intensity or frequency of angry outbursts.** Even the smallest provocation may lead the boy to become full of rage and to verbally or physically lash out at others. What may at first seem to be a boy's tendency to be "in a bad mood" may escalate into temper tantrums or frequent outbursts of anger or ongoing irritability. It's important to remember that anger or "being mad" is one of the main ways boys indirectly express other feelings like grief, disappointment, and hopelessness. But when a boy becomes persistently angry or "grouchy," he may very well be suffering a depression. Although the nature of a boy's angry outbursts may vary with age, this symptom is significant for boys of all ages.

4. **Denial of pain.** Even when questioned directly about difficult situations—a divorce, a death, an alcoholic parent, academic troubles—the boy may deny he's feeling unhappy. His mantra may be something like "Everything's fine" or "What's the big deal?" or "Nothing's wrong—why are you bugging me?" Behind these hardened responses may be a frightened, hurting boy. It's important to probe behind the mask to help the boy express his authentic feelings. A boy in denial is often a boy in pain. He may also be severely depressed. Because this symptom is closely linked with the mask that emerges over time, it is unlikely to occur in preschool children; but with age, it may arise with increasing frequency.

5. **Increasingly rigid demands for autonomy or acting out.** The boy may say things such as "Leave me alone." He may resist adult authority. Younger boys may resist following rules at home or at school. They may act out in the classroom or at home. Older boys may come home late, take long drives alone, and resist participat-

ing in family events (even locking themselves in their rooms) or following family rules (such as curfew or "lights out"). While sometimes the boy may simply be rebellious or working through the normal process of individuation, he may in reality be isolating himself to cope with depression. Studies have confirmed that many boys who are depressed tend to develop conduct disorders. In 1986, Denise Kandel and Mark Davies, at the Department of Psychiatry at Columbia University Medical School, found that for boys, depressed mood was associated with minor delinquency and school absences. In 1990, Jeff Mitchell and Christopher Varley, at the University of Washington School of Medicine, found that 25 percent of preadolescent boys who were depressed also had a conduct disorder, whereas none of the preadolescent girls did. It's important not to see boys who misbehave as "bad" or "toxic." They may be sensitive, thoughtful boys who are actually depressed.

6. **Concentration, sleep, eating, or weight disorders, or other physical symptoms.** The boy may find it difficult to concentrate on any one task without becoming quickly distracted or uninterested and might actually be diagnosed with attention deficit disorder. He may have trouble falling asleep, wake up abruptly in the middle of the night, or awaken prematurely in the morning. Alternatively, he may find himself tired a good deal of the time and sleeping too much each day. He may also suffer eating or weight disorders such as anorexia, bulimia, or obesity. These disorders do not happen only to girls. Also, he may have frequent headaches and stomachaches or report other persistent physical symptoms. Any of these problems with concentration, sleeping, eating, or maintaining body weight, or other physical symptoms should be discussed thoughtfully with the boy, as they are frequently associated with depression and/or may be connected with other serious medical disorders. In one form or another, these problems suggesting depression may occur in boys of any age.

7. **Inability to cry.** The boy may appear unable to cry. Thus, for instance, if he is physically injured or is obviously in the middle of an emotionally traumatic experience, he may fail to shed a tear, appearing more stoic and hardened than usual. When any boy "shuts down" his emotions in this way, he may be trying to numb out what are actually symptoms of depression. Tragically, research

shows that this symptom can occur in boys as early as elementary school.

8. **Low self-esteem and harsh self-criticism.** The boy may seem very unsure of himself. He may utter self-effacing remarks such as "I'm such a jerk" or "Nobody cares about me" and focus on his failures more than on his successes. He may blame himself for things that clearly are not his fault. When offered compliments, he may deny them and try to persuade others of his weaknesses and shortcomings. Low self-esteem can be both a cause and a result of depression in boys. When you determine that a boy doesn't feel good about himself, not only should you try to encourage and support him but you should also make sure that his low self-confidence isn't linked to a more generalized sadness. Research has shown that this symptom can surface in depressed boys as early as the third grade.

9. **Academic difficulties.** Often closely linked with low self-esteem, the depressed boy may have problems doing well at school. His grades may plummet, and he may get a bad report insofar as his conduct is concerned. These problems may stem not only from his lack of self-confidence but from his tendency to be distracted by his latent sadness. He may simply feel too unhappy to do his school work, much in the way that an adult who is depressed may begin to have problems focusing on work-related obligations. Also, when a boy is depressed, he may experience general difficulties concentrating on any given task, become withdrawn and tired, and thus find it very difficult to apply himself to his class work. This symptom can occur as early as the age when the boy leaves home to begin school.

10. **Overinvolvement with academic work or sports.** The boy may become almost obsessive about his schoolwork or sports activities. He may spend all his free time on homework, studying compulsively, or out on the playing fields, avoiding contact with friends or family. While working hard at school or playing sports are obviously positives, some boys may use such activities to distract themselves from depressive states much in the way that men who are "workaholics" will use career-related work for such distraction. This symptom is more common as boys move toward adolescence.

11. **Increased aggressiveness.** The boy may exude an overabundance of aggressive energy. He may act "wild," become difficult to control, pick fights, or even intentionally injure others. His aggressiveness may actually spiral into sheer violence. Aggressiveness, like anger, is an approach boys take to cover up vulnerable feelings. Again, it's critical that we not rush to the conclusion that an aggressive boy is merely a boy who is "bad" and doesn't know how to behave. His rough behavior—especially if it becomes chronic and extreme—may actually be his way of calling for help. This symptom occurs in boys of all ages.

12. **Increased silliness.** Perhaps to mask his genuine feelings of sadness, the boy may actually act silly or outrageous. He may, even as a very young boy, become the class clown at school or become the family comic at home. As his self-confidence deteriorates, he may also have a tendency to become the brunt of other people's jokes. This is perhaps the most deceptive symptom of depression in boys. Not only does the boy seem to be doing all right, he seems amusing, entertaining, funny. But under the cheerful exterior may reside deep feelings of pain or desperation.

13. **Avoiding the help of others.** The "I can do it myself" syndrome. When offered help on a task or given the chance to get emotional support from others, the boy will insist that he can handle things himself. This is another way in which the boy attempts to remove himself from the mainstream of his family and social circles and isolate himself. While a boy taking initiative should usually be encouraged, if he consistently or inappropriately protests others' offers to help him out, he may be falling into a withdrawn or antisocial behavioral pattern not atypical of depressed boys. As a boy begins to be oppressed by the Boy Code—as early as the elementary school years—he may manifest this symptom of depression.

14. **New or renewed interest in alcohol or drugs.** In older boys there may be a tendency to become more and more involved in alcohol or drug use. A boy who might have enjoyed a beer from time to time may begin spending time with friends who drink until they're drunk. He may smoke marijuana regularly or begin experimenting with more serious drugs. Nearly one million eighth-graders say they have gotten drunk, according to a 1997 survey of 1,115 teens. This survey also found that 56 percent of those between the ages of twelve to seventeen have a friend or class-

mate who has used LSD, cocaine, or heroin, up from 39 percent in 1996. Sadly, many of these self-destructive behaviors are considered "cool" by teenagers and can confer social acceptance on a boy, a valuable benefit for a lonely, disconsolate boy. Such excessive use of drugs and alcohol is a classic sign of depression in boys and men and appears to be occurring in children of younger and younger ages.

15. **Shift in the interest level of sexual encounters.** In older teenagers who are sexually active, there may be either a pronounced increase or decrease in his dating behavior or sexual activity. While obviously a healthy adolescent libido does not generally lead to depression, a boy who exhibits radical changes in his sexual behavior may be engaging in obsessive/compulsive behavior that reflects depression.

16. **Increased risk-taking behavior.** During the teenage years the boy may begin to take inappropriate or unnecessary risks that show poor judgment. Examples include a new and unexplained tendency to engage in unprotected sexual activity, to drive at excessive speeds, or to engage in such sports as extremely risky skiing or bungee jumping that have high morbidity rates.

17. **Discussion of death, dying, or suicide.** Especially during adolescence—but in some cases as early as the elementary school years—boys who are depressed may initiate discussions of or make casual or even joking references to death, dying, or suicide. While a child's curiosity about his own mortality (or that of others) is only natural, it's important to listen closely to any boy who talks about these issues. Especially if he's exhibiting some of the other symptoms of depression, his reference to death, dying, or suicide may actually be an indirect way of letting others know that he's not feeling good about himself, that he may be depressed. It's *always* better to be wary, to question him about such a reference, even if turns out that he was simply curious or trying to be humorous.

While it would be extremely rare for any boy who is depressed to exhibit all of these symptoms, it may also be unlikely that he'd exhibit just one. Typically, several of these symptoms will appear in a boy who is depressed. Yet because depression occurs along a continuum from "mild" to "severe," I think it's important to take immediate steps to help the boy as soon as *any* of the symptoms outlined above are detected. With depression, it's better to be safe than sorry.

ROBERT

At the beginning of third grade, eight-year-old Robert started getting into trouble at school. He picked fights at recess, taunting other kids. In class, he seemed unable to concentrate. Full of restless energy, he couldn't sit still or stay quiet. He began to be known as a troublemaker and his grades started to slip. Prior to this year, Robert had always been an easygoing boy who got good grades.

If we analyze his behavior, we can detect several of the criteria from our diagnostic model: acting out, excessive aggressiveness, problems with concentration, and academic difficulties. Robert, whose father was a prominent banker who had been convicted for fraud, had been traumatized by his father's abrupt departure from home. Now Robert was exhibiting symptoms that, in my opinion, constituted mild to moderate depression.

PHILIP

Fourteen-year-old Philip also showed dramatic behavior changes when he entered high school. He started hanging out with the tough kids and smoking pot. Soon, he was staying up late at night and was unable to get up in the morning. He skipped school often and started failing courses. He and his mother started fighting constantly, and Phillip would often shout at her loudly and inappropriately.

Philip's behaviors also fall directly within our diagnostic model—his use of drugs, problems sleeping, truancy, difficulty at school, excessive anger, resisting authority. Through discussions with Philip, I learned that his parents had recently divorced and that both he and his mother were having a difficult time coping with his father's absence and dealing with life in a new and quite tense mother-son household. I diagnosed Philip as moderately to seriously depressed.

PETER

After Peter's best friend, Brad, died in a car accident, sixteen-year-old Peter suddenly quit the basketball team and shut himself up in his room every afternoon, listening to loud music. He consistently refused to join the family for dinner, just saying sullenly, "I'm not hungry." He started having thoughts of suicide.

Peter, by seeking to isolate himself, refusing to eat, and thinking about suicide, satisfied several of the diagnostic criteria for boyhood depression. In fact, he was in the midst of a major clinical depression.

Often as I consult with schools or talk to parents, I hear of boys like Robert, Philip, and Peter. It's hard to think of depression when you first observe these boys' problem behaviors. But armed with our list of diagnostic criteria, we can become more effective at knowing when the boy is actually depressed. Also, I find that if one has the chance to ask a few questions, it may turn out that the boy has suffered a recent unacknowledged difficulty that may have precipitated his symptoms. For instance, on further investigation it was uncovered that in Robert's case, his father, a prominent banker in town, was indicted and sent to jail for fraud. Philip's marijuana smoking started soon after his parents announced they were getting divorced. Peter lost his best friend in a fatal car accident when Brad and some other boys drove home from a party drunk.

Underneath Robert's restlessness and aggression, Philip's marijuana habit, and Peter's sullen withdrawal are sad, scared, and lonely boys. Though each is at a different stage on the continuum of depression, each has emotional problems severe enough to affect not only his present ability to function but also his future lot in life. These boys have suffered serious life crises, but not insurmountable ones. But what has made these boys unable to cope with their situations, and caused them to sink into depression, is that these boys, like most boys, do not know how to talk about their sadness or openly grieve over their losses and are not receiving the personal or professional help they may need.

STEVE AND MARIJUANA: WHEN PARENTS MISS THEIR CUE

To prevent boys from being trapped in the self-destructive spiral of depression, it's important that parents and other concerned adults intervene early. One family I worked with missed several early chances to reach their son, Steve, and brought him to me when he was sixteen years old because he was by then a chronic marijuana user and in trouble with the local police. At this point, unfortunately, hostility and drug-induced numbness were Steve's habitual ways of coping with the world. "Sure, I smoke pot every day," he told me. "Sometimes once in the afternoon and once at night. What about it?" He also said he smoked two to three packs of cigarettes a week.

I asked him when he started smoking. "I don't know. Maybe three years ago for cigarettes. Two years ago for pot. Whatever."

After months of weekly meetings, he still doesn't see his addictions as a problem. But he has begun speaking more openly—and with less hostility—about why he smokes.

"It doesn't matter what I do," Steve says. "I used to get along with my mom. But I don't anymore. She just complains all the time. All she ever says is 'Comb your hair' and 'Turn down your music' and 'Study more' and 'Clean your room.' The other day, when my report card came, she said I'm 'good for nothing' like my father. I hate her."

"My dad doesn't talk. He says like, one word a year. My sister just talks on the phone all day and all night. I have guys I hang with in school, but I never see them outside of school."

I asked Steve if his father really was good for nothing. "Yeah," he says. "He has this lousy job so we can't buy anything and he just watches TV every night. We'd be better off without him."

Is Steve like his father? "I don't know," he says. "Maybe. But at least I talk once in a while."

Steve is slow to acknowledge the cycle of disappointment and disconnection with his parents that has taken place over the years. But he did tell me about a formative event that happened when he was eleven years old, which clearly made an impression on him and set the stage for his hardened attitude toward his parents.

"The day after school started, my dog got run over. He really was *my* dog, no matter what my sister says. My mom got him for me before she was even born. So anyway, my mother, sister, and I heard a car slam on its brakes and we ran outside. My sister started crying. My mom was talking to the lady in the car who hit Sam. I walked away and nobody even noticed. I went and hid in this old junk car we have in the garage. I kept feeling this lump in my throat, but I didn't want to cry, so I swallowed the lump."

"That night when my father came home from work, my mother told him about Sam. Dad yelled at me, 'I told you not to let him in the front yard!' which wasn't even true. I just walked away. I went to my room and didn't come out until the morning."

I asked if anyone came in to talk to him. "Nope," said Steve. "Nobody cared. They just had dinner without me."

Steve's family wasn't there when he needed them. When he was sad about his dog, so many years ago, he would have been greatly helped by a kind word or a sympathetic hug. Instead, he was yelled at, ignored, and shut out of the family. No one in his family even acknowledged his grief. At that point, Steve's sadness over his loss was compounded by sadness over the lack of caring from his family. In return, Steve began to shut them out and adopt a studiedly nonchalant attitude, a pose he has probably perfected in the five years since his dog died. Maintaining that tough attitude—completely covering up his grief and his longing for an emotional connection to his family—is a difficult act, one made immensely easier by the daily administering of emotion-deadening substances.

But even if we didn't know the exact source of Steve's grief and disappointment, we could more easily determine that he's depressed by using our diagnostic criteria for boys. His persistent denial of pain, his withdrawal from his family, his problems at school, his low self-esteem, and his increased drug use, all signal that Steve may be seriously depressed.

THE LORDS OF DESTRUCTION

Depression in boys can be fatal. In addition to suicide, many of its other symptoms—abuse of drugs or alcohol, increased aggressiveness, conduct disorders—can end up being lethal.

Consider the true story of the so-called Lords of Destruction. In the summer of 1997 nine boys, aged fifteen and sixteen, living in rural upstate New York, got together and started calling themselves the Lords of Destruction. It seemed at first that this was just typical teenage boasting, because these boys were more aimless than dangerous. They were poor students, not very popular with girls, and unsure of their futures. Their backgrounds were similar, but not shocking: a history of learning disabilities and failure at school, combined with parents who didn't care enough or have time enough. The boys became known for skipping school, drinking beer, stealing small items from local merchants, throwing rocks at cars, and just being generally annoying small-town punks. One night the boys drank too much. Four of them got into a car and, driving 100 mph in a 40 mph zone, ended up running the car into a tree. They were killed instantly.

Just a few months later at a drunken sleepover, two other Lords got into a fight. One brandished his grandfather's shotgun, which accidentally went off, killing the other. A seventh boy, depressed over his friends' deaths, was sent to a drug rehabilitation center. An eighth member of the group, after a petty theft, was sent to a juvenile detention facility. In the fall, there were nine boys. By the spring, only one boy was still alive and living at home.

In the words of one of their peers, these boys were just aiming to "live fast and die young."

I wonder what it might have taken to save these boys from dying quite so young. Part of the problem is that we explain away so much in our teenage boys as just the wilder side of "boys will be boys." We respond as though boys were biologically driven by some sort of testosterone-inspired desire to drive too fast, to drink too much, and to play with guns, as though it were normal for boys to be so filled with so much despair that they don't care whether they live or die.

Unfortunately, sometimes we see drugs and alcohol and our minds snap to a moral judgment. We blame our boys for having a weak will, and tell them to "Just say No." We blame the addictive power of substances, the drug lords in Colombia, or the persuasive junkies in the next town. As long as we can find someone else to blame, we don't have to admit that perhaps, just perhaps, our boys are taking drugs because they're suffering intense emotional pain. But in the rush to judgment we can again miss the chance to understand our boys and the compulsions that might drive them to drug use.

These Lords—these ordinary boys—satisfied many of the diagnostic criteria for depression we have proposed be used for boys. They were socially withdrawn, abused drugs, acted aggressively, suffered learning disorders, disrespected authority, performed poorly at school, and obviously had low self-esteem. In my opinion, each of them was significantly depressed.

SUICIDE

Tragically, a disproportionate number of our boys are turning to the most desperate of solutions to depression and emotional pain—suicide. Since the 1950s, suicide rates for young white men have nearly tripled and remain twice as high as the suicide rate for all Americans. For African American young men, the suicide rate has increased a staggering 165 percent over the past twelve years. Suicide is the third leading cause of death among young adults between the ages of fifteen and twenty-four, behind only accidents and homicide. While more girls attempt suicide, four times as many boys than girls actually succeed in killing themselves. We are losing almost five thousand teens every year to their own despair in what has truly become an epidemic.

In the tight-knit community of Evansville, this epidemic of suicides became shockingly real last year. In October 1997, James Scali walked inside his house to find his seventeen-year-old son, Kurt, hanging from his closet railing.

Shocked and horrified, James and his wife were completely unable to answer the question Why? Kurt was a warm, friendly, sandy-haired boy, who was popular with his buddies and with girls. Recently his life had been going well. He had landed a job he wanted. He had a girlfriend he liked.

Some parts of his life were less rosy. His brother had been arrested recently and was being held without bail on a charge of robbing the local grocery store. Kurt had been caught in a minor accident after uncharacteristically driving drunk. Still, it didn't seem to add up to the kind of sadness that drives a boy to suicide. How—his family, friends, and the entire community wondered—could he have done this to himself?

Kurt was part of a string of suicides in Evansville that summer. He was the eighth teenage boy to take his life in the span of only six months, while during the same time another sixty-five or so young men from the neighborhood had attempted suicide and had been treated in local hospitals and clinics.

Some blamed the deaths on the hard times in the neighborhood. Evansville, a clannish, tight-knit community of Italian-American families, had once been a source of pride for them and now had fallen on hard times. What hadn't changed was the community's belief in a code of tough masculine behavior and its pride in the boys who excelled at that code. An uncle of one of the suicide victims described how he had taught his boy to be a real man. He said, "I taught him not to back down. Stick up for yourself. Don't let anyone push you around. If you can't hit them with your hands, pick up something and whack them with that."

Sadly, this boy and the other suicide victims must have faced demons that couldn't be whacked with sticks, demons that they had no tools for combating. Apparently Kurt had told a friend the day before, "I wish life would end." Kurt had tried to communicate his agony, yet sadly it went unheeded.

Part of the problem is that boys don't know how to communicate their despair. Kurt's statement "I wish life would end" the day before his suicide was something that could be passed off as hyperbole, a remark with no more emotional weight than the common expression "Life sucks." Certainly, Steve, before he descended into a life of drugs and school failure, never told anyone he was sad about his dog's death. By adolescence, boys have submerged their feelings so well they are no longer in touch with them and therefore don't know how to ask for help even when they most desperately need it.

BOYS' DEPRESSION—WHAT ARE WE TO DO?

To prevent our boys from drifting away from us, I believe it's important to take proactive steps to help prevent tragedies like those described.

Be alert about your boy's friendships and relationships. Try to know how their relationships are going. Take the lead and try to break through the silence about relationship talk; ask your son whom he spends time with, who his friends are, how he likes his teachers at school, how he's feeling about his siblings, if he feels that everything is going well with *you.* Strong relationships can prevent boys from sliding into despair or risky behaviors in the first place. Boys need to feel connected to significant people who care about them, who make time for them and who listen to them. This is among the best protections we can give our boys.

Be watchful for signs of depression and intervene early. One of the worst kinds of family tragedy occurs when the signs of depression are present but nobody sees them or acts upon them. When you notice your boy exhibiting any of the behaviors associated with depression—or if your boy just seems to be a little bit "down"—don't waste a moment before asking him what's going on with him. Intervene early. If he lets you know he needs some time before talking, give him that time. But keep yourself available for talks and, when he's ready, listen to what he says empathically. Tell him stories about your own experiences feeling sad or disappointed and how you were able to cope with these situations. Let him know that you care, that he's a good person, and that you'll always be there for him.

Don't be afraid to consult with a therapist. If it seems as if your boy's symptoms aren't going away, don't be afraid to consult with a therapist. Many times parents don't feel comfortable approaching a therapist because they're afraid they might be overreacting and fear they'll embarrass their boy by suggesting therapy. If you develop these kinds of reservations, contact the therapist yourself and see whether he or she might meet with you separately first to hear about your boy and his situation. I would strongly recommend that therapy for boys be conducted with someone who not only appreciates children's or adolescents' needs in general, but who also understands boys' needs in particular. A therapist must be sensitive to the shaming culture that boys grow up in and be sure not to further shame the boy. At best, a therapist can provide a boy with a new, safe relationship, in which he can continue to grow and develop.

If a boy's depression is severe, medical intervention may be necessary. When a boy's depression becomes severe, I would certainly suggest consulting with a psychiatrist knowledgeable about intervening with appropriate medications. More and more frequently doctors are prescribing antidepressants to young adults and children when appropriate. Some studies suggest that the newer antidepressants—such as some of the SSRIs (selective serotonin reuptake inhibitors)—may be effective in cases of serious clinical depression. Medications can be a huge benefit to a boy sunk in the depths of clinical depression. But it's important to realize that medicating a boy is rarely enough. Therapy—with the psychiatrist who is also trained in such specialized counseling or with a psychologist or other appropriate mental health clinician with such training—is also needed to ensure that the boy understands the problems that led him to depression and learns how to detect the early signs of these problems if they recur.

Try to address the big picture. It's critical that we try to understand our sons in the larger context of what their lives are like at home, at school, and in society in general. It's so easy to think that a boy who becomes sad or depressed is somehow to blame, that somehow he's not a "real boy" or a "good boy." But in so many cases, the problem goes beyond the boy himself. He may be being bullied. He may be struggling at school. His friendships may not be working out well. Perhaps he's dealing with parents who don't get along or who have their own troubles. Perhaps he's getting teased because, in one way or another, he's not quite following the Boy Code.

To help boys conquer sadness and avoid depression, we must be sure to look at the big picture. It's not enough just to know the boy and his behaviors. We need to find out what his life is really all about. So in addition to asking him about his relationships, try to find out what his days at school are like. Does he enjoy his classes? Are his teachers fair to him? Do the other students treat him well? Has he had any disappointments recently? What does he do after school? Does he feel fulfilled? Is he lonely?

Also, find out whether biological factors might be contributing to a boy's unhappiness or depressive state. Inquire whether there's any family history of depression. Because some studies have shown that a vulnerability to depression may actually be inherited, figuring out whether a pattern of depression exists within a family is a logical step to assessing the possibility of depression in a child. Even if such a pattern does not exist, it's also important to consider that internal biological factors—for instance, an imbalance in certain neurotransmitters in the boy's brain—may be leading to the change in his behavior more than something intrinsic to his personality or to his life experiences. Determining whether such a chemical imbalance may exist obviously requires consultation with a knowledgeable clinician.

In addition to looking at these biological aspects, we need to ask appropriate questions about what the boy's family life is like. Do his parents get along? Are both his parents living with him or are they separated or divorced? Does he have a close relationship with both his mother and father? Do they both treat him well? Is there any possibility of abuse or neglect in the household? Does the boy have siblings? If so, does he get along well with them? Do they treat him with love? Have there been any recent major traumas or losses in the family—a chronic illness, an accident, a divorce, a death? Have any of the boy's siblings or one of his parents recently suffered depression or other psychological disturbances?

By probing behind the mask to learn as much as we can not only about our boy's inner emotional world but also about all aspects of his daily life experiences at school, on the playground and at home, we begin to understand the many factors that may be contributing to his sadness or depression. Since only rarely is a boy's unhappiness or depression caused by something entirely within himself, it's critical that we see the big picture and address all of the conditions, internal and external, that may be bringing him down.

Stay on top of the facts about depression and talk about them openly. Finally, try to keep informed about depression and encourage others who care for your boy—especially teachers and adult youth leaders—to learn more about these issues. If yours is a two-parent family, make sure your spouse participates in the learning process. Once your children are old enough, explain to them that you understand how sad life can sometimes be. As adults it's not unusual to feel as though it's "inappropriate" to talk to children about things that aren't happy. Yet having honest talks about how tough and disappointing things can get is important. So talk about the mask. Talk about gender and the straitjacket. Talk about how society can be unfair to boys. By letting young people know that life isn't always so easy, we set the stage for honesty and open the door for sharing emotions without embarrassment or shame.

Following each of these steps is just the beginning for helping boys overcome pain and ward off depression. Though they may not guarantee that a boy will always be happy, these strategies can surely help him through some of the tough times. And they may make the difference between life and death.

—13—

VIOLENCE:

SLAY OR BE SLAIN

*"You better know how to fight. If you don't,
people will just walk all over you."—Dean, age eleven*

IT BEGINS WITH DISCONNECTION: THE ROOTS OF MALE VIOLENCE

Today, most violence in our society is perpetrated by young males against other young males. Violence is the most visible and disturbing end result of the process that begins when a boy is pushed into the adult world too early and without sufficient love and support. He becomes seriously disconnected, retreats behind the mask, and expresses the only "acceptable" male emotion—anger. When a boy's anger grows too great, it may erupt as violence: violence against himself, violence against others, violence against society. Violence, therefore, is the final link in a chain that begins with disconnection.

Violence is also about shame and honor. For many boys, failing to "know how to fight"—or refusing to fight when challenged to do so—may be considered disgraceful, a sign of dubious masculinity. By learning how to fight and striking out against others who may be younger, weaker, or less skilled at combat, our young aggressor attempts to respect old Boy Code rules that call on him to do everything possible to protect his honor and prevent shame. We've already spoken of a boy's exquisite sensitivity to shame and the toughening up he does to protect himself against it. Violence, of course, is a boy's attempt to go yet one step further—to thwart shame and dishonor by going on the offensive, by hurting another human being.

Ironically, violence in boys also sometimes represents a vain attempt on their part to reconnect with others, to make and keep friends. Whether it's winning a fight and thus impressing one's peers, helping other boys to beat up another kid, or actually joining a gang, violence may give some boys a false impression that they're somehow growing closer to one another, bonding, in effect, through their individual and collective acts of aggression and malevolence. We've spoken of how sports can be transformative—enabling boys in a positive, healthy way to express a wide range of emotions, bond as friends, and boost their feelings of self-esteem. For some boys, violence is an unhealthy and, of course, futile attempt to gain similar social benefits.

A WORLD OF VIOLENCE

Most of us think that violence is about other people's children. We think of violence as a netherworld occupied by street criminals, gang members, serial killers, vicious rapists—the dregs of society, not our children or the children of people we know. But talk with almost anyone and eventually you will uncover some incidence of violence that has touched someone in or close to his or her family. The lawyer uncle who committed suicide. The son at the prestigious university who was mysteriously murdered. The marketing manager who was seriously injured in a late-night car crash. The family friend who was accused of physically abusing his wife. The nine-year-old who was killed in a bicycle accident. The four unsuspecting students and their teacher killed in cold blood during school one Tuesday morning, allegedly at the hands of two young Arkansas boys.

The fact is that we all live in a world of violence, and that our boys are particularly vulnerable to its many manifestations. Only a small percentage of boys perpetrate or participate in the worst sort of violence—violent crime—or are direct victims of it. But every one of them is a witness to extreme violence of one kind or another: in school, on the street, in the news, on television programs, in the movies, at the computer, in books and magazines, and, sadly too often, at home.

Most parents of boys will have to contend with the issue of violence very early in their sons' lives, just as every boy must contend with it himself. The challenge for parents is to understand the difference between action, which boys love, and violence, which most boys don't—and to learn how to help boys keep on this side of the line that separates the two.

When does roughhousing get too rough? When does teasing become bullying? When does boldness cross the line into unnecessary risk-taking?

As parents we want to encourage our boys in their pursuit of action but keep them from becoming part of the national statistics that pertain to violence in our society. We can do so through the potency of connection we've discussed throughout this book—by staying closely involved with our sons, teaching them how to handle the anger that can turn to violent rage, and imparting as much information as we can to help them avoid becoming victims of others' hurtful acts.

A NATIONAL CRISIS

The fact that most violence in our society is done by or to males will come as no surprise to most people. But what's alarming—and less well known—is that the violence that surrounds us in this country increasingly involves *young men and boys.*

For example, consider a seemingly commonplace and nonlethal example. The American Medical Association determined that one in ten boys has been kicked in the groin by the age of sixteen. Twenty-five percent of those kicks result in an injury. We might shrug off this finding, and assume that many of the kicks are unintentional or that they are simply part of normal boyish roughhousing and play. But the AMA also discovered that most boys don't tell their parents about the groin kick or the injury. And, even more significant, about 25 percent of the injured boys exhibited signs of depression within a year after the injury. In other words, these boys did not consider a kick in the groin as just a routine part of boyhood. The event bothered them, they felt shame about the injury. They were disturbed by the violence but felt they couldn't or shouldn't talk about it, so they hid their emotions behind the mask. Neither boy involved in the incident—the kicker or the one kicked—may end up as a spouse-beater or a gun-toting criminal, but both have experienced violence.

Young men and boys also suffer a great deal of violence that falls into the category of risk-taking behavior gone wrong. Michael Kennedy, the sixth child of Robert Kennedy, was killed in late 1997 while playing a game of football on skis. Although he was thirty-nine, hardly a boy, when he slammed into the tree, he was engaging in the kind of violent, "boys-will-be-boys" behavior that our society not only tolerates but has come to respect, encourage, and even revere. Statistics show that Michael Kennedy was not alone—although males account for about 60 percent of all skiers, 85 percent of all skiers killed are men. Although no crime was involved, no weapons, no malice of intent, Michael Kennedy was, in effect, a victim of violence.

And of course one of the most tragic manifestations of male violence is self-mutilation and suicide. As we discussed earlier, in the United States the suicide rate among fifteen- to twenty-four-year-olds tripled between 1950 and 1990, and suicide is now the third leading cause of death within this age group. Among Americans of all ages, the rate of suicide among males is about four times the rate among females.

Indeed our boys and young men are at risk from all kinds of violence—from fighting and accidents, violent crime, murder, and suicide. "The major causes of mortality and morbidity among teenagers have shifted from infectious to behavioral etiologies," writes Dr. C. Wayne Sells, a specialist with the Department of Pediatrics at the University of California. In other words, young people have more to fear from their own behavior than they do from disease. Here are a few statistics:

- 78 percent of all unintentional deaths of youth result from motor vehicle accidents; 75 percent of those are young men.
- About one third of all victims of violent crime are twelve to nineteen years of age.
- Homicides are the second leading cause of death among adolescents, accounting for 22 percent of all deaths among youths fourteen to twenty-five in 1991. Males are more than 400 percent likely to be murdered than are females.
- Between 1979 and 1991, almost 40,000 kids aged fourteen to nineteen died from firearms. The firearms death rate among male teenagers, aged fifteen to nineteen, more than doubled from 1985 to 1994, reaching 49.2 deaths per 100,000—*the highest level ever.*
- As stated above, suicide is the third leading cause of death among people aged fifteen to twenty-four and the rate of suicide within this age group has tripled from 1950 to 1990. Suicide among the very young, from age ten to nineteen, has also increased significantly. The rate of suicide for males of all ages is four times that of the female rate.

These facts demonstrate that young people have become increasingly involved in and vulnerable to violent crime, and that the young people most at risk are boys. Boys begin their involvement with violence very early. In fact, research shows that after the age of two, boys get injured up to four times more often than girls. Parents simply come to expect their boys to use up more Band-Aids and make more trips to the emergency room than their girls.

Yet, curiously, boys themselves take a rather blithe attitude toward injury. A Canadian study shows that boys tend to blame injury on bad luck rather than on any correctable circumstance, such as their own behavior. This tendency of boys to blame injury on external factors is also borne out by an intriguing study recently conducted by the Gillette Company that investigated the shaving habits of male and female adults. When a man cuts or nicks himself shaving, the study found, he generally blames the razor. When a woman draws blood, she tends to blame herself.

But, even if a boy never gets entangled in violent crime directly as a perpetrator or a victim—as he probably won't—he still must find his way to healthy manhood in an environment that is replete with violence.

IT CAN START WITH THE BULLY

For many boys, the earliest and most vivid experience with violence is provided by the school bully. Charlie is a child whose whole first-grade year was made utterly miserable by a bully named Ben. Ben was a thoroughly modern bully. The bullies of the 1990s must operate differently from those of the 1950s. Overt and obvious physical aggression is not tolerated on many American playgrounds today. The child who pushes or slaps or kicks or punches is swiftly dealt with; the child who bites, in this age of AIDS, is considered a dangerous potential health hazard. Today's bullies have developed a subtler set of strategies that include ridicule, shaming, making others feel inadequate.

So, rather than physical violence, Ben used primarily verbal weapons— the insult, the taunt, the jeer—but was skillful enough in wielding them that they caused Charlie great distress, even though he himself was seldom the victim of Ben's aggression. Seeing his classmates abused caused Charlie to develop a chronic stomachache that sometimes kept him out of school or sent him home early. Charlie's mother identified Ben as the principal cause of Charlie's woes and resulting stomachaches, and alerted the classroom teacher. The teacher, however, was in her first year on the job and did not have enough experience to deal effectively with the problem.

As a result, she downplayed Charlie's stomachaches and implied that he just needed to "tough it out."

Charlie and his parents worked on a number of strategies for dealing with the "Ben issue," but the problem remained until summer finally came, and Charlie escaped the bully for the beach. In fact, that was no solution at all—it merely provided a temporary escape. The fact is that the disruptive effect of the chronic bully can be a difficult problem for everyone involved in the situation—students, teachers, and parents, including the parents of the bully himself—but it can be alleviated and even solved, as we'll discuss later in this chapter.

Bullies like Ben can cast a pall over an entire classroom and playground, and bullies remain a fixture on playgrounds throughout the world. In fact, the National Association of School Psychologists estimates that, in the United States, some 160,000 children miss school every day for fear of being bullied. One colleague told of a mother whose child was being tormented by a playground bully, but could get no action from the school authorities. So concerned was she for her child, she began hiding behind a shed on the school grounds, hoping to catch the bully in the commission of one of his crimes.

But what causes a boy to bully or to allow himself to be bullied? Is a bully a "naturally" violent boy—or is he a boy desperate for connection who is only able to express his need through violent action?

Is It Action or Violence?

When thinking about boys and violence, it's essential to make a distinction between violent behavior and action behavior. Although most boys aren't violent, they often love physically vigorous activities, intense games, loud play, rough play. For the most part, however, that inclination to action does not cross over the line into violence. Most roughhousing ends abruptly when one of the participants gets hurt—a bump on the head, a twisted arm, or an elbow in the gut—and so does not escalate into a fistfight. Most teasing and joshing trails off without crossing over into physical violence. Most intense activities, such as sports, conclude with the participants exhausted and the players shaking hands rather than in a melee. In fact, sports, as I've emphasized, generally bring boys closer to one another.

So what makes for the difference between an active boy and a violent one? In my opinion, there are virtually always important psychological factors that come into play. It's rarely just chance that escalates a boy's natural craving for action into an unnatural one for violence. In the case of Ben, Charlie's bully, the boy's parents had recently gone through a difficult divorce. Ben felt disconnected from his parents, the family he had once been part of, his friends, and his community. Ben also suffered from a learning disorder. He felt inadequate and ashamed. And he had just moved to the town and knew few people. He felt alone and powerless and still more disconnected. Because his mother now had to work full-time and his father wasn't around, Ben got little help with these difficult emotions. Left on his own, trying to appear stoic, he channeled all his fears into anger and aimed it at his classmates. Interestingly enough, however, Charlie was, in fact, an unusually empathic child; he liked Ben—when he wasn't in his bully mode—and even accepted invitations to his house to play. Perhaps, in some way, Ben was asking for connection and empathy and recognized Charlie as a boy who might be able to give it to him. As explained above, in some cases boys like Ben perpetrate violence not because they want to injure others, but rather because they believe it will somehow win them friendship and approval from others. And sometimes the person they most especially desire to win over is not a co-aggressor but instead their victim.

Of course, a bully may be more likely to meet with retaliation by his victim than with friendship. Gordon, a seven-year-old African American, was a frequent target of Leonard, the bully of his second-grade class. "Leonard is really mean to everybody," Gordon said. "He pulls girls' hair, he hits boys, and he spits on you. I hate him!"

When their class finished a unit on the history of African Americans, Leonard used what he had learned to add shaming to his bullying. When he encountered Gordon on the playground, he took to calling him "slave." "At first I wanted to punch him," Gordon told me. "But I was afraid I'd get in trouble. I was going to tell on him, but I was scared he would get even worse to me after that."

Gordon did not punch Leonard, nor did he go to his teacher with his problem. Instead, he endured the insults for several days—"like a man"—and then decided to confide in his mother. She listened, with steadily growing fury, and then made her recommendation. "I told Gordon it was OK to slug Leonard," she admits. "There are some things that just aren't acceptable."

So, the next time Leonard called him a slave, Gordon punched him. Both boys were promptly hauled off to the principal's office, where the

principal counseled Gordon that he should "not use fists to solve problems." Leonard's parents were summoned. After a lengthy meeting, both
Gordon and Leonard were sent home for the day.

The next day Leonard the bully had backed off. "He's still mean to me
and everybody," Gordon said, "but he doesn't call me slave anymore." And
Gordon pointed out that he had gotten a half day off from school to boot!

The mother's recommendation worked, but it didn't help to solve the
long-term problem of either the bully or his victim. Plus, Gordon ended up
with a confusing set of mixed messages. On the one hand, the principal
delivered the message that violence is neither acceptable nor the "best"
way to solve problems. On the other hand, Gordon gathered some overwhelming empirical data that, in fact, a solid slug at the right moment can
sometimes provide a short-term solution to the problem.

One thoughtful researcher into men's and women's anger, Jean Baker
Miller, believes that this kind of violent behavior stems from fear. Boys are
"made to fear *not* being aggressive," she writes, "lest they be found wanting, be beaten out by another, or (worst of all) be like a girl. All of these
constitute terrible threats to a core part of what is made to be men's sense
of identity—which has been called masculinity." The phenomenon of
which Miller speaks, in my opinion, affects boys in at least two central
ways. First, it makes the potential instigator of violence more likely to leap
into action. Rather than risk an affront to his honor or a blow to his sense
of "masculine" self-esteem, the boy defends himself by going on the
offensive, by lashing out at others. Second, this same fragility—the trepi-
dation a boy feels about being shamed, about being considered less that a
"man"—may lead the *victim* of other boys' violence to take the beatings in
silence, even to smile and attempt to shrug them off. So if he does not tat-
tle or retaliate (as, for example, Gordon did), he may instead try to bear the
violence quietly, to cover any outward signs that he is the victim, that he is
too scared to take on the bully. As I've learned in my years of counseling
men, many adult males would rather die than be shamed. So I suppose it
should be little surprise that many boys feel similarly.

In my view, today's boy bully is often, but not always, tomorrow's
adult violent offender. Sometimes the high school bully learns to control
his anger along the way to manhood, and former classmates, cautiously
greeting him at their twenty-year reunion, are stunned to find the young
tormentor has turned into a charming and engaging adult. On the other
hand, sometimes the quiet victim, the shy loner, or the troubled bystander
suddenly turns violent in an unexpected eruption of rage, either in later

boyhood or as an adult. This might explain the case of the mild fourteen-year-old Kentucky high school student who, in 1997, killed three fellow students with a rifle, much to the disbelief and incomprehension of his parents, teachers, and classmates. The question on everybody's lips at the time was "Why?" The boy had shown no signs of violent behavior; he was no bully. But, clearly, something caused him to "snap"; such violent acts do not just "happen." I believe that among other things it is *shame* that makes a boy like this snap. When enough shame collects inside of him—when he feels disconnected, unpopular, less than "masculine," maybe even hated—the boy tries to master his feelings and reconnect with others through violence.

The good news is that we now know a great deal about how shame fuels anger, what can trigger it to turn into rage and violence, and how to think about and behave with boys differently, so they can feel better about their genuine selves, turn away from anger, avoid violent behavior, and still retain the qualities and pursue the activities that are more positively "boy"—the vigorous action, the productive intensity, the boldness of individual endeavor, the empathy found in group play and team sports.

WHAT CAN WE DO?

First, we can understand *why* boys may harbor anger and why their inclination for action and rough play may turn that anger into rage or violence. In Chapter 3, I talked about the biology of boys. I argued that many people base their thinking about boys on the myth that "testosterone = aggressiveness = boys," but that nothing in the research, mine included, proves that equation to be true. We now see the old "nature vs. nurture" debate as outdated and simplistic, and have come to understand that the behavior of boys results from a combination of biological and environmental factors. All boys are not biologically destined to be more aggressive than girls. Biology creates *tendencies* for boys and girls to behave differently, but it is not an absolute. In fact, all the behavioral qualities that we traditionally associate with girls—such as empathy, sensitivity, and compassion—are also basic male traits. Research shows that boys begin their lives with a natural sense of empathy, which is antithetical to violence. Boys as young as twenty-one months display a well-developed, natural, "hard-wired" ability to feel empathy, including a wish to help other people who are in pain.

And yet, as we discussed in Chapter 2 on shame and the trauma of separation, by the second grade, boys seem far less attuned to feelings of hurt
and pain in others, and begin to lose their capacity to express their own
emotions and concerns in words. This, of course, is the self-hardening
boys do when they begin to feel society's pressure to avoid feelings and
behaviors that might bring them shame. This is the process that pushes
boys to wear a mask of bravado. And this, in large part, is what makes
them violent.

And so the statistics show that violence is overwhelmingly a male
"thing." Young men are violent with other young men, with young women,
and with themselves. "Most violent behavior is and always has been the
work of men," writes James Gilligan. "It is clear that both cross-culturally
and trans-historically, men have been the more violent sex."

So why do men behave so much more violently than women do, if
there is no male "violence chromosome"? The answer, again, lies in the
themes we have been discussing throughout this book. When boys feel disconnected and afraid of being shamed, when they harden themselves and
then put on the macho mask, the one emotion they feel it's acceptable to
show, and thus the only emotion that they will show, is anger. That anger
can come out as risk-taking behavior or, as I sometimes call it, "death-
oriented bravado." The boy has such a phobia of showing his shame that he
counteracts it or overcompensates for it, by showing its opposite—reck-
lessness and risk-taking and even violence against himself.

That anger can easily turn to violence against others when the right
factors are present or come into play. We had a glimpse of some of these in
the story of Ben, the first-grade bully. There is generally a triggering event
for any violent act—a threat, a betrayal, or an insupportable loss. The man
who loses his job and goes on a shooting spree. The teenager whose girlfriend dumps him for somebody else and beats her up. The second-grader
whose friend excludes him from a party or special event and screams at his
mother. Whether the boy engages in risk-taking behavior or commits violence against others, it is often fueled by a reservoir of anger, fear, and
shame, that has gradually accumulated over the years since the trauma of
separation from his parents.

A group of Danish doctors conducted a study to try to determine a link
between early disconnection from the mother and adult behavior. They
found that "individuals who suffered both birth complications and early
childhood rejection were most likely to become violent offenders in adult-

hood." But if these unlucky guys were "most likely" to become violent offenders, I believe a boy need not suffer birth complications or outright rejection by his mother to feel the *loss* of being prematurely pushed out into the "man's world." As we've seen, the push to disconnect is ubiquitous—it comes not only from parents but from peers, other adults, and from our popular culture in general. From a very early age, the boy is thrust out into the world and placed in what we've seen is a painful, shame-inducing male straitjacket. Throughout boyhood, the strings are pulled tighter and tighter until either the straitjacket snaps or the boy does.

ON THE FRONTIER

One way to think about our boys today is that they exist on a kind of frontier. Writers and historians—and our own intuition and experience—tell us that the frontier, any frontier, is generally a more violent place than civilization, the world of cities and towns and well-established communities. The American West has long been considered the quintessential violent frontier, and the American cowboy the quintessential example of the true man—laconic, tough, self-contained, unemotional, and, above all, action-oriented. Countless legends and songs and books and movies and television programs have helped to create and sustain the image of the lone man surviving on the wild and violent frontier—the Marlboro Man. When I was growing up, in the fifties, the macho hero was generally a cowboy or a ranger or a lawman. John Wayne in *Stagecoach* and *The Searchers*. Gary Cooper in *High Noon*. They didn't say much. They focused on an active mission: to get the bad guys. Women were, for the most part, a distraction—if a necessary, and sometimes pleasant, one. Emotion was expressed haltingly. Vulnerability and weakness could get you killed, and fast. The father (if he hadn't already been shot or eliminated in some other violent way) expected his son to wrangle the horse or wrestle the bully or shoulder the rifle as soon as possible, with no whining and without much instruction.

For boys, these images of the frontier can be immensely powerful, even if they don't think of themselves as particularly violent or imagine themselves as future cowboys. Of course, the West is currently pretty much out of vogue, but the idea of the frontier—and its stereotype of the lone, violent male hero—continues to provide the setting for some of our most popular media. The current favorite frontier is outer space, with aliens now taking the roles of the bad guys.

I believe one of the reasons boys find the frontier so appealing is that they feel they are inhabiting a kind of emotional and physical frontier of their own. They are made to feel isolated from one another. They feel disconnected from their families. They are admired and rewarded for physical strength and emotional courage, while physical weakness and emotional vulnerability are ridiculed. On the frontier, risk-taking behavior is commonplace. It should be no surprise that boys who are forced to live on such a frontier act out the role in real life—by punching, shooting, or taking a risk that leaves them dead.

MALE AND FEMALE STEREOTYPES AT SCHOOL

The traditional stereotypes for boys and girls, men and women, endure in the classroom, as well as in the popular media. "Teachers and parents bemoan the fact that gender dynamics at school are hardly different than they were forty years ago. Forty years? Try forty thousand!" writes Lawrence Cohen in an article called "Hunters and Gatherers in the Classroom." Indeed, for all the progress we have made in changing attitudes and redefining roles for men and women, particularly women, it seems that the most basic of stereotypic behaviors linger on in the classroom. "Boys roughhouse; girls play house," writes Dr. Cohen. He describes asking two six-year-olds, a boy and a girl, "What makes a child popular? The girl said, 'Being nice, having a lot of good ideas, being smart.' The boy said, 'Shooting missiles.' " Boys are admired by their peers for physical prowess— who can run fastest, who can kick the soccer ball farthest, who can ring the bell first at the top of the climbing rope—as well as intellectual vigor and prowess at verbal sparring. Boys also can gain admiration, or at least notoriety, through acts of daring. Who dares cross the street not at the crosswalk? Who dares jump over a ditch? Who dares talk with the strange janitor? Who dares eat a sandwich made of peanut butter, salami, and ketchup? Who dares bring a knife to school, when it's strictly forbidden? Who dares kill a stranger?

Girls, however, tend to gain status through building and maintaining relationships, being nice and sociable, dressing well and looking good, participating in class, speaking articulately, scoring well on tests, reading difficult books, pleasing the teacher. In other words, boys are constantly being rewarded—by their peers, and even by their teachers and parents— for behavior that fits the traditional male stereotype.

The stereotypes apply to insult and ridicule and bullying, as well as to admiration and reward. As soon as a kid steps out from behind the mask, as soon as he defies the old Boy Code, he may encounter trouble. Boys who act "like girls" may be labeled sissies or babies. Boys who "can't fight"—or who won't fight—may be relegated to the bottom of their peers' friendship hierarchy. As eleven-year-old Dean warned me: "You better know how to fight. If you don't, people will just walk all over you." And so boys harden themselves, learn how to fight, and give themselves over to society's stereotyped vision of how they should behave.

And yet, as prevalent as these stereotypes are, there are lots of kids— maybe even the majority—who do not fall prey to them. There are plenty of boys who show empathy with one another, who back away from violence when things get out of hand, who talk with one another about their thoughts and emotions, who accept a wide range of people with a wide range of behavioral, physical, and cultural differences.

How do they become that way? Many of them say, "It's my friends that get me through." As Preston, age thirteen, explained to me when I asked him how he deals with kids who fight and act violently: "It's not so much about fighting. It's about standing up for yourself and for your friends." So just as peers can join together into a violent gang, they can also support one another in resisting society's stereotypes, finding their own path, and avoiding violence. In other words, the prevention for violence can be found in connection—with friends, with family, with parents.

MAKING CONNECTIONS AND PROVIDING MODELS

People who care about others and feel connected to them are rarely the ones who allow their anger to get out of control or commit acts of violence. A boy who is cared about will be more likely to care about others. If he feels connected to his parents and his family, he will feel more connected to other people. If he feels that his parents understand him and empathize with him, he will have the ability to do the same with others.

The difficulty for many parents is that it is not always an easy task to find the best way to express caring for their boy child or to make and keep a connection with him, especially as the child goes through adolescence. Most boys respond to hugs and kisses, but not always in public. Most boys respond to parents when they praise them, but not if the praise seems excessive or unwarranted. Some boys want to be active with their parents—to go swimming or to the supermarket or to the movies—but others need less active contact. Fathers, may do fine "doing things together," but also need to recognize when the boy only requires that the father *be* there, and take full notice of what his son is up to. We've heard a lot about parents who fail to attend the big baseball game or the recital or the school play and how disappointing that can be to the boy. But we've also seen parents who do make it to the big event, and then spend most of their time on the cell phone or reading the newspaper. The point is that boy knows when the parent is truly involved and genuinely cares, and when he or she is merely going through the motions. No parent is perfect and every child's threshold of need is different, but there is a kind of running tally being kept in every boy's head. When the debits outweigh the credits, the boy starts to feel deprived of love, nurturing, and caring. That's when he begins to focus more on his own needs than those of others; that's when he starts to feel anger. That's when all his vulnerable feelings may funnel into rage, and when his rage may bubble over into violence.

So, it's what the parent *does* and how the parent *behaves* that is most important. A parent or teacher may talk about caring and the importance of being empathic until he or she is blue in the face, but if they don't act with empathy themselves, the talk is meaningless. The best way for parents to help their boys express their emotions and avoid anger and rage is also the most difficult: they must provide a model for their children in the way they themselves behave. Parents are good at telling a boy not to shout, not to hit, not to tease or ridicule others. But all those reasonable and time-honored lessons are instantly negated as soon as the father gets angry and kicks a chair himself, or the mother describes a neighbor boy who acts like a baby, or both parents get in an argument that ends with the father slamming out of the house and the mother insulting him as he storms out of the driveway.

Linda found that her ten-year-old son, Jonah, was translating his father's actions into his own violent behavior at school. As early as age three, Jonah had begun behaving aggressively, and she would receive calls from the day-care center complaining that he was biting other kids. "I'd tell him to stop it, and I'd give him time-outs like everyone suggested, but it just kept getting worse."

By the time Jonah reached fourth grade, Linda had grown accustomed to getting the calls. "Jonah gave so-and-so a black eye. Jonah knocked so-and-so's tooth out. I didn't know what to do. I never thought I'd be the mother of a violent kid."

Finally, Linda set up a meeting with Jonah's teachers and the school psychologist. Together, they probed for possible causes for Jonah's behavior. "It was very, very hard to admit," she told me, "but I had to face it. Jonah was just imitating his dad." It seems that Jonah's father, Mike, had worked at an insurance company for almost ten years and had never received a promotion. Often, he would take out his professional frustrations on his family. Jonah took the brunt of his father's anger, in the form of frequent spankings and harsh verbal insults. "Mike always calls Jonah our good-for-nothing kid," Linda admitted. "He's easier on the girls, but with Jonah, he's quick to fly off the handle."

Our boys are watching us, carefully. By the time they're three or four, they have started to notice the disparity between what they are told to do and what you actually do yourself. How many times have you heard a child say, after being told not to raise his voice or call someone an idiot, "But, Daddy does it!"

So, in addition to doing things with your child, what kinds of modeling behavior will help boys understand that males can be empathic and express emotions and still be active "real boys"?

PERSPECTIVE-TAKING

Encourage your boy's innate ability to feel empathy for others. This can be done by a practice called "perspective-taking." It simply means that, in any situation, you help your child to understand the point of view of the other people involved. Why does Ben pick on others? (He's sad because his parents just got divorced. He needs a friend but he doesn't know how to make one.) Why did so-and-so not invite you to the party? (Maybe he was worried you wouldn't come.) Why did the teacher get mad at the kids? (Maybe because his wife is very sick and he's distracted and scared.) Why did your mother snap at you? (Because she's trying to finish a paper for her advanced degree and feels stressed right now.) Taking the perspective of others tends to create empathy. When boys feel empathy for others' worries and concerns, they feel less shame about their own vulnerabilities. Boys can, in fact, learn the value and ways of empathy, if they see it practiced by their parents and those around them.

You can also allow yourself to express emotions other than anger. Research shows that both mothers and fathers are more apt to express anger around boy children than around girls. In addition, boys' more vulnerable emotions are shamed away. As a result, for boys, anger, as we've seen, becomes the final common pathway for an entire range of other suppressed feelings and the most or only acceptable way to express themselves emotionally. But when parents, fathers in particular, admit to feelings of fear, uncertainty, and vulnerability boys feel more able to do so themselves. One father, when he received a rejection notice for a book manuscript, told his son how *sad* he felt as a result. The boy comforted him and said how sorry he was the publisher didn't like the book. It immeasurably heartened the father, who thought of himself as hardened to such professional disappointments. And it helped form a very strong, lasting emotional bond between man and boy.

Don't get me wrong. I do not expect every boy, or every parent, or every household to be anger-free. We've all visited homes where the parents are so intent on removing "negative emotions" from their lives that every interaction becomes sugarcoated and the environment seems as unnatural as a home filled with anger and violence. Anger is part of life and can be a useful and productive emotion—to right a wrong or fix a problem, help a friend, or spur others to action.

As a parent, you can engage in your own acts of empathy and caring, by doing favors for friends and neighbors, taking care of aged parents, getting involved in community affairs, or volunteering for charity work. And you can recognize and reward acts of empathy and caring in others. Boys often show wonderful empathy for a friend when he is hurt or disappointed. Tell him you admire it. When you see or read about similar acts of empathy, point them out to your son. And, as much as possible, you can help to surround your boy with other people—friends, coaches, teachers, and relatives—who can act as additional models of caring and connection.

CREATING VIOLENCE-FREE ZONES

Any parent of boys knows that, no matter how cared for and connected they may feel, they have less predilection for talking openly about their feelings than girls do. In response to a direct question about how things went at school or what a boy thought of a movie or how he feels about a relationship with a friend, the parent may get little more than an "I don't know" or "Fine" or "I don't want to talk about it." Sometimes the parent, like a cross-examiner, feels compelled to press the issue, asking one follow-up question after another until both participants in the lopsided conversation are frustrated or annoyed. Then, at some unexpected moment (often at bedtime, just when the light is supposed to be going out) the answer will come tumbling out. Things are going badly at school. The movie was scary and upsetting. The friend turned out to be less of a friend than the boy had thought.

When it comes to talking about violence, it's very important that a boy have a "violence-free zone," a place where he can remove the mask and speak about fighting and violence without fear of suffering shame, belittlement, or retaliation. The zone may look different for each boy, and the parent needs to discover how to create one that works best for his or her son. But it will likely not be in front of a group of his friends while riding home in the car after a movie. It will likely not be at the family dinner table if older sister and younger brother are listening. It may not be while sitting around the table in the office of the guidance counselor or school principal. It may not be predictable at all. The parent needs to be ready to listen when the boy is ready to talk. If it's five minutes past bedtime, it may be more important to have a conversation than it is for the child to get to sleep on schedule.

Robert talks about how bedtime chats helped his son, Henry, avoid violent behavior. "My son is a 'softy,' " he says, intentionally using a term that we have come to see as derogatory for boys. "And I like it that way."

"Henry has always been a sensitive kid," Robert says. "When an apartment building near here burned down, he put some of the clothes he'd outgrown into a bag and asked us to mail them to the families who lost their things. He's like a little father to our one-year-old, always telling him stories and cuddling with him in the rocking chair. I always wanted my son to grow up knowing that being male doesn't mean not having a heart."

About a year ago, however, Henry started to change. "It was like a hard shell was building up around him. You could still see the Henry we know inside there, but there was a wall there," his mother, Andrea, explains. "It took us a while to get it out of him. It turned out there was this older kid in the neighborhood who went after him all the time. We had no idea. We thought he was having fun with a bunch of kids playing outside in the afternoons, but instead he was the butt of a lot of cruel teasing, and sometimes some physical stuff, pushing and shoving, that kind of thing." The bully was clever enough never to use enough physical force to cause a cut or a noticeable bruise.

"When Henry started to act differently, I got angry at first," Robert recalls. "My first reaction was 'What's wrong with you? Why are you acting so nasty? I want my little boy back!' But getting irritated with him only made him close up more. One time I overheard him calling his little brother a 'stupid crybaby' in a mean voice—which was totally unlike him—and I lost it."

Robert and Andrea talked about the problem, and tried to find books to read that would help them. "Andrea encouraged me to stop blaming Henry," says Robert, "and to assume that something was happening to him to make him act this way, something that was not his fault. She knew the world isn't always kind to gentle boys."

Eventually, the parents developed a new ritual with Henry. "As often as we could, we'd put the one-year-old to sleep first," says Robert. "Then we'd both go into Henry's room to tuck him in. Before lights out, we'd each tell one good thing about our day and one hard thing about our day. I purposely tried to show him even a grown-up man has feelings. I talked about real things that are hard in my life, like dealing with my parents' aging, and trying to figure out why my secretary seems so unhappy with me all the time.

"One night, Henry started talking about this neighborhood kid as his example of a hard thing for the day. Once he felt safe talking about it, it became an open topic. Now we're like a team dealing with it. We try out different options, like playing inside with just the kids he gets along with, or joining the Boy Scouts so he has less time to hang around at home after school, or talking about why this bullying kid might be acting that way."

"It seems like we're getting our 'softy' back," his mother concludes. Meaning, of course, a good kind of soft—not weak, but empathic.

Often, a boy will find a space to safely express his concerns outside the home. These may be of his own making—in a school group, a sports team, a community organization, a neighbor's home. Or they may be within programs organized for the purpose. Voices of Love and Freedom is a program developed by Patrick Walker, a professor of education at the University of Massachusetts, and Robert Selman, a psychologist with appointments at Harvard's Graduate School of Education and Medical School. The intent of the program is to help kids learn how to resolve conflicts without resorting to violence. The program uses storytelling to provoke the participants into discussing the characters and events and making connections to their own lives. The idea is to help kids see actions and situations from the perspectives of the different characters, and to understand that we can all feel vulnerable and threatened, and that we all have a shared humanity. As I said earlier, this kind of perspective-taking makes it more likely that a boy will feel empathy for others' weaknesses and concerns, and less shame about his own. *When a boy feels empathy for another, and diminished personal shame, it is unlikely he can so dehumanize that person as to want to commit violence against him.*

BULLY-PROOFING

Another program, at the Cherry Creek School District in Englewood, Colorado, seeks to help boys deal with violence through what they call "bully-proofing." The kids start by identifying what a bully is and how a bully behaves. Victims and potential victims learn what makes them attractive targets for bullies. Not surprisingly, a key attribute of the victim is a lack of self-esteem—rather than characteristics such as race, size, physical appearance, clothing, or eyeglasses. Students then acquire skills in defusing situations in which bullies approach them. Bullies get a sharp talking-to at their first transgression. If that doesn't work, they face a variety of consequences.

One of the most intriguing aspects of the program is that it finds ways to redirect all that bully energy into positive activities. "School officials heard that a fifth-grader was terrorizing kindergartners and first-graders," said a Cherry Creek school psychologist. "A school counselor took the bully aside and told him that someone was picking on the younger kids and asked the bully for help. In short order, the bully became a guardian." Perhaps he even stumbled upon a future profession—as a professional bodyguard! Teachers and administrators in Cherry Creek say the program has reduced the dominance of bullies, reduced the vulnerability of victims, helped teachers improve their conflict-resolution skills, and made parents feel better about the safety and well-being of their kids.

You'll notice, however, that the school does not claim to have solved the bully problem. In fact, research indicates that most teachers and school administrators do not know what to do about bullies. The problems that make a bully a bully are often well outside the authority or expertise of the school system to solve. Moving a bully from one class to another may not be an effective solution. And there is generally no way to remove a bully from school altogether.

So, what can parents do for children who face a bully at school? First, they can make their child aware that they support him and understand what a difficult problem he is dealing with. They can help him understand the methods of a bully and work with the boy to develop strategies and tactics for counteracting his techniques. Tell him: Never get angry; admit your own imperfections; make a joke of his verbal attacks; and surround yourself with friends. In fact, a child with strong friendships is seldom at risk from bullying behavior.

If the boy cannot solve the problem himself, some parents feel it necessary to intervene themselves. Child-violence experts SuEllen and Paula Fried describe a mother who—after gaining agreement from her son—decided to confront a bully who was beating up her son on the way home from school. One day she approached the bully and informed him—in a calm and level voice—that there are laws against assault and battery, and that if the problem continued, she would have to discuss the matter with his parents, and then the school, and, if necessary, law enforcement officials. The strategy worked and the beatings stopped.

The parent should be sure that the school authorities know there is a bully in their midst. Bullies are skilled at hiding their activities from teachers and playground monitors. Finally—and this is a very delicate task, and one that many parents may not want to undertake—the parent can talk about the problem with the bully's own parents. Like Linda, whose son Jonah was imitating his father's bullying behavior, the parents may not know—or not yet have admitted—that their child is terrorizing kids at school.

VIOLENCE IN THE MEDIA

Most parents I talk with feel daunted in their efforts to keep violence out of their boys' lives by the seemingly inexhaustible amount of violence that pervades the media, over which they have little or no control. Many homes now receive cable television, which offers dozens of channels of programming. You can't channel-surf without stumbling onto a violent news story, a violent movie, a violent made-for-TV drama, a violent cartoon, or a violent sports event. Television advertising, although rarely violent, does its share of reinforcing the traditional stereotypes, particularly of the young, cool male. Risk-taking behavior—sky surfing, bungee-jumping, fast driving—is everywhere in TV commercials. Young men in advertising are often depicted as loners or as members of cool all-male groups; rarely are they seen as sons in happy home settings with caring parents.

Some parents feel a little better when their kids abandon the television to play video or computer games. After all, there are plenty of games that require real skill to play and involve an element of education—building and maintaining cities, word games, and math programs. But so many video and computer games involve little more than shooting an assortment of bad guys with the help of an array of monster weapons and massively armored vehicles and impossibly adroit aircraft. Many of the games celebrate their violence. In *Doom,* for example, the levels of play are designated as:

I'm Too Young to Die! (easiest)

Hey, Not Too Rough

Hurt Me Plenty

Ultra Violence

Nightmare (hardest)

When it comes time to quit the game, the computer sneers at the player, "You know, the next time you come in here I'm gonna toast you!"

An intriguing aspect of the video/computer-game phenomenon, however, is the way boys play the games when together. I have seen groups of boys as young as five and as old as twelve gather around the screen to watch as one player does battle with the alien or monster or Nazi criminal of the day. They don't talk much; they stare at the screen as if entranced, occasionally calling out "Yes!" when the boy player makes a good hit, or moaning when he is blown prematurely to smithereens. The odd contrast is that these boys—while they watch macho-man mayhem unfolding before them—often seem very connected to each other, supportive of the player, and nonjudgmental about his performance. In other words, they are behaving very differently than the big boys portrayed in the game.

If a parent prevails on the boy to turn off the TV, shut down the computer, and read a good book, he may still gravitate toward stories that involve risk-taking, murder, mystery, and violence—from the Hardy Boys to Goosebumps to Jon Krakauer conquering Mount Everest. The question is not whether we live in a society awash with violent images. We do. The question is, what effect does exposure to all that violence have on boys? And, if we think it's harmful, what can we do to manage and mitigate the effect?

Some kids, of course, are more affected than others by what they see on TV, and it may disturb them in clearly defined ways. Eleven-year-old Ray, for example, had had trouble sleeping for about six months. Ray is an expressive boy, and readily shared what precipitated his problem. "My parents don't let me watch much TV, and definitely not any violent TV shows," he said. "One time when they were out, this baby-sitter let us watch whatever we wanted. Me and my brother watched this show where this robber came and tied up the whole family and then killed everybody except the little kid. I started getting these nightmares after that, and then I started not wanting to sleep at all. I keep thinking that a robber might come. I hear all these sounds and I get really scared."

Nothing has helped Ray sleep since then. His grandmother came for an extended visit and shared a room with him for a while, and that provided a temporary respite. But since then his sleeplessness has returned, and his parents are at their wit's end. "We tell him over and over that things like that almost never happen, but he won't believe us," Ray's mother says. "That scene is etched in his mind, and it just won't go away. His pediatrician has recommended we see a psychologist for a few sessions."

There has been a great deal of research into this subject, and many of the findings are inconclusive or contradictory. A National Institute of Mental Health study found that children who see kindness on television tend to imitate it. Just through casual observation, it is obvious that boys, as they play, will assume the roles of characters they see on TV or in the movies. They become James Bond, or the Terminator, or Beavis, or Darth Vader, or Freddie Kruger. They may also use language and threats, often as part of the bullying vocabulary, that come from the violent media.

Eight-year-old Evan, for example, is a third-grader at an urban elementary school. Students there often watch hours of television a day, battle one another in elaborate video games at home or at the local arcade, and sometimes accompany older siblings or their parents to films that require an adult for admittance. I asked him what kids call one another on the playground. "All kinds of things," Evan told me. "I heard a kid calling somebody 'condom' today. That same kid called me 'cocksucker' once. Another kid got real mad yesterday and said he was going to put this kid in cement and drop him in the river." Where did the idea about the cement come from? "Everybody heard on TV about this fourth-grader who got murdered that way," Evan explained.

And there are more chilling examples of violent crimes being committed by young men who, when caught, confessed that they were inspired by a specific television program or movie. The fourteen-year old North Carolina killer of three classmates claimed that he was influenced by *The Basketball Diaries*. In that movie, the star, Leonardo DiCaprio, opens fire on his classmates while in a drug-induced dream. In Kentucky, a group of six young men and women who murdered three people say they admired the action in *Natural Born Killers*. John Hinckley, the man who tried to assassinate President Reagan to prove his love for the actress Jodie Foster, said he was inspired by Martin Scorsese's movie *Taxi Driver.* Even with such examples, it is not possible to make a general, direct link between exposure to media violence and inclination to personal violence. Exposure to media violence sometimes has the effect of satiating a natural appetite for violence. Or witnessing extreme violence may frighten and even sicken or repel a boy, and turn him away from it.

We can, however, draw a few conclusions about the relationship of media violence to real-life violence. Boys who see a great deal of violence in the media tend to become desensitized to it. Violence seems to be a "normal" part of life. This may heighten the possibility that they will tolerate violence on the part of their friends or in themselves. Boys, in fact, may come to think that the world is actually a more violent place than it really is. A steady diet of murders, plane crashes, car wrecks, robberies, shootouts, hostage takings, emergency-room crises, football injuries, and alien abductions can lead a young male mind to imagine that the TV landscape accurately mirrors the real landscape. That may lead a boy, especially an angry boy, to expect violence, prepare for it, and react with violence more quickly than is warranted.

But I do not believe that a boy who feels truly connected and loved and who has safe settings where he can express his emotions will be motivated to violence by exposure to violent acts in the media. He may imitate those acts in play, he may revere his action heroes, he may spend more hours in front of the television than a parent would wish, but it is unlikely he will cross over the line into rage and violence. Even so, parents continue to worry about the negative effects of media violence—desensitization, glorification of hurting others, and the sheer amount of time and energy wasted on watching violence that could be applied to far more positive and productive pursuits.

There are a number of strategies that parents can employ to better deal with this chronic problem of violence in the media, particularly television.

· **Discuss the issue.** Your kids should know *why* you think the viewing of media violence is a problem, and why you don't want them to rack up three hours a day in front of the set, watching "real men" shoot big guns. Just getting angry or just shutting off the television does not help them understand the serious issue involved.

- **Restrict and monitor.** Some parents limit the amount of time their kids can watch television each day or each week. Others limit the types of programs they are allowed to watch, by channel or by rating. At the very least, parents should monitor what the kids are looking at. Know what's on, what it's about, how long the kids have watched.
- **Watch together.** Many parents don't really know the content of the shows and movies their kids like to watch. They've "heard about" that movie or they saw two minutes of one episode of that show. You can't make an informed decision about what you will allow your boys (and girls) to watch if you don't know what it's really about.
- **Talk about what you've seen.** When you watch together, then you can talk together. Review the show together. Ask questions. Was it good? Was it realistic? Why did the characters act as they did? Would you ever act that way? What do you think will be the consequences of the violence we just saw?
- **Make better selections.** When it's mom and dad's turn to pick the television show, video, movie, or book, choose something you think is good and does not glamorize violence. There are movies and books out there that have exciting action that don't promote violent or excessive risk-taking behavior, and that show boys as connected and caring people. *Iron Will* is one of them. *Home Alone 3* is not.

I can hear some parents chuckling or shaking their heads in resignation as they read the above. Some parents have simply thrown up their hands and given up trying to wrestle with the TV dragon. I encourage you to keep thinking about the problem and talking about it with your kids. At the very least, it's important that they know how strongly you feel. The *potency of parental connection* is a vital force in combating the negative images of violence in the media. Its power should not be underestimated.

HARNESSING ANGER AND AGGRESSIVE ENERGY

Another important kind of antiviolence intervention is what I call "harnessing." By teaching boys how to harness their anger and aggressive energy and redirect them into healthy outlets, we can help them to avoid hurting others or themselves. Harnessing, in my opinion, can take at least two important forms. First, boys can be taught to release their anger and pent-up aggression through what's traditionally known as catharsis. This simply involves giving your boy permission—in an appropriate private space—to vent his feelings openly and without inhibition. In your presence you can invite him to shout, scream, cry, or voice whatever he needs to—and as loudly and vigorously as he needs to—so that he can purge himself of the painful feelings that plague him. If noise is a concern, he can use a pillow to muffle the sound. If he feels the need to punch something, he can punch away at a pile of pillows and cushions. What's most important, of course, is that he feel free to "let it all out," to express his angst, anger, and aggression in your warm, loving presence. This kind of closely supervised catharsis is a normal healthy process that can help defuse much of the painful rage that may be inside your son.

Second, I suggest using sports and athletic activities as another venue for the healthy expression of these feelings. As long as *strict limits are set*—and, if necessary, *proper safety equipment is utilized*—the boy can engage in activities such as boxing, wrestling, or just playful roughhousing to release his rage and aggression. I recently observed a game where one boy wore a helmet and safety pads and then mounted a balance beam (with lots of well-cushioned mats below to catch him safely when he fell). Other boys, wearing protective foam-rubber equipment, were permitted to try to bounce up against the boy on the beam, and were even allowed to try to knock him off it. The boys I observed playing this game appeared to love it. Clearly it gave them a chance to let out their aggressive energy and, for some of them, it probably provided a measure of relief from internalized feelings of anger. These kinds of safe, low-risk activities, supervised by an adult, provide healthy channels for such feelings and, in my opinion, can do much to remove the need boys may feel to act out their feelings in less healthy, more violent ways.

ENCOURAGE ACTION, DISCOURAGE VIOLENCE

Boys have fantastic energy and exuberance, a willingness to venture into the unknown, to test their limits, to take action. When these traits are applied to positive endeavors and relationships, the results can be spectacular—boys will build and create wonderful things and manage and sustain long-term friendships and productive collaborations. It is when boys are not allowed to express the full range of their emotions—when they are forced to wear the mask—that's when their energy and need for action may come out as violence. We must let them know that power need not mean power *over* another person; it can mean power *with* other people. To do that, we must begin by acknowledging the pain they have experienced themselves, allowing them to speak their feelings, and ridding them of the seeds of shame that too often grow into the thorns of violence.

_14_

DIVORCE

"Why do my parents hate each other so much?
Is it my fault?"—Vinnie, age eleven

THE THIRD TRAUMA

When Oliver turned seven, his parents began to go through a difficult period. His mother, Anne-Marie, was not happy in her job; his father, Carey, was working long hours to start a small business. They both agreed that Anne-Marie would stick with her job until Carey could get his business off the ground. They were both tired; money was tight and so was time. At first they bickered only now and again, but then their relationship began to disintegrate into a perpetual series of heated arguments. As Carey's business went through problem after problem, his tendency to drink a glass of wine at dinner spiraled into nightly binges that left him drunk, loud, and incoherent.

One morning, Anne-Marie woke up Oliver and explained to her son in a whisper: "Oliver, it's time for you and me to go live in our own apartment."

"But what about Daddy?" Oliver wondered.

"Daddy's staying here. Don't worry—you'll have plenty of chances to visit him. But right now Daddy and Mommy need to live in two separate places. So you're gonna come with me for starts."

"But . . ."

"There'll be no 'buts' about it. Get up and take your bath. And then it'll be time to go on a trip together—to our new apartment," Anne-Marie said, struggling to cover her anger with a cheerful tone.

When the two left the family home that morning, what neither knew was that they would never return again. Anne-Marie and Carey never reconciled. In fact, the daily arguments they had had when they lived together simply continued over the phone.

"I really don't think I can take this much longer," Anne-Marie had said to Carey, talking about her job during one of their early-morning phone calls that always started in whispers but ended in shouting.

"All right," Carey snapped, "then quit! It'd be better than hearing you complain all the time."

"I would if it weren't for Oliver," she replied.

"It's not about him," said Carey.

"Of course it's about him," Anne-Marie snapped back. "If I don't earn any money, how are we going to send him to camp? Who's going to pay for his needs?"

Carey took her comments as a personal affront to his ability to support the family. "I'm doing the best I can!" he barked. "You know what I'm trying to do."

"All you can think of is yourself," she snapped back. "I'm sick of it. I'm sick of everything," she shouted. And, with that, she hung up.

Ann-Marie, who always tried her best to keep the fights to these early-morning phone calls when Oliver was still asleep, turned to discover her son standing at the other side of the kitchen. He obviously had heard the entire encounter, but said nothing. But Anne-Marie, who realized she was late for an appointment already, sidestepped the issue. "Daddy and I were just talking about work," she said. "Let's get you ready to go." Oliver went off to the bus stop without saying a word.

Anne-Marie felt guilty. After several months of couples therapy, she and Carey both realized that their differences were irreconcilable and that divorce was the only viable solution. Yet both of them found it hard to face, and neither one of them could find a way to tell Oliver.

That afternoon, Oliver said nothing to his mother when he got home from school. He dashed up to his room and slammed the door. Before she could follow him, the phone rang. It was the mother of one of Oliver's friends, a boy named Lee. It seemed that, on the bus coming home, Oliver had jumped on Lee, pushed him down, sat on him, and bounced on him, hard. The driver had stopped the bus, and hauled Oliver away from his friend. Fortunately, Lee's mother was as concerned for Oliver, whom she knew well, as she was for her own son, who, after all, had not been hurt.

According to Lee, it was just a bit of roughhousing that got a little out of hand.

At last, Anne-Marie realized that something was seriously bothering her son. She went to Oliver's room to talk about it, but he refused to let her in. Finally, she told him—through the door—that she knew what had happened, that she wasn't mad at him, and just wanted to talk about what was bothering him.

After a moment the door opened and Oliver appeared, his cheeks streaked with tears.

"What is it, Oliver?" she asked tenderly. "What's bothering you?"

"Are you and Dad going to get divorced?" he blurted out, and then burst into sobs and threw his arms around his mother.

Anne-Marie was stunned. Although she had known for weeks that she and Carey would be getting divorced, somehow she had thought she should wait awhile before discussing it with Oliver. But now it was obvious that Oliver was well aware of the seriousness of the situation. She hugged Oliver tightly.

"It's all my fault," Oliver said in a confessional tone.

"Oh, honey," Ann-Marie consoled him, "it is not your fault. That's just not true."

"What you said this morning," Oliver explained, his voice cracking. "You said it was all because of me and you were sick of everything. So now you're sick of me. Are you going to get divorced from me too?"

Now Anne-Marie began to cry with him. "I'm sick of what's happening at work," she said. "I'm sick of not having enough money sometimes. But I could never be sick of you. Never!"

It is a fact of our lives that divorce affects millions of children every day. Even for children whose parents' marriages remain intact, the fear of divorce hangs over them ominously. Almost every little boy knows another little boy who sees his dad only on weekends, or whose mother expects him to do more chores than most other little boys. By the time he is a teenager, it is the rare boy who doesn't have a friend with a stepparent, or whose mother has a live-in boyfriend, or has become a member of a blended family with three new siblings, or whose father has left the family. "It seems like everybody's divorced," nine-year-old Timmy told me.

Divorce has become such a pervasive phenomenon today that, for the millions of boys whose parents do divorce, I believe it amounts to a third trauma of boyhood. All the issues we have discussed in relation to the other two traumas of boyhood come into play during divorce—and, often, more intensely so: the disconnection from parents, the shame, the wearing of the mask to cover painful feelings of loss and loneliness, and the gender straitjacket that restricts boys from expressing these emotions.

The divorce itself is a wrenching disconnection for a boy. He feels disconnected from the family and home that once were that safe space. The majority of boys are in the custody of their mothers, so they may feel especially disconnected from their fathers. A boy may see his dad only on weekends or never see him at all. At the same time, he may feel distanced from his mother, who may herself be so upset and overburdened that she simply has little time or energy left for her son. The boy has, in essence, been pushed away from family and home—just as he may be pushed away during the other two typical disconnections of boyhood.

But with divorce, there is no positive benefit claimed for the disconnection, and there is no sanction or support from society for it. Unlike the pushing away at age six that is supposed to help a boy "cut the apron strings" or the separation at adolescence that is supposed to encourage a boy to become an independent man, any positive result from a disconnection by divorce *for the boy* is much harder to discern. A divorce may bring relative peace to the couple after a particularly strife-torn period of marriage. Or it may bring relative emotional health to one or, sometimes, both of the divorced parents. But society does not tell the boy that divorce is good for him, and rarely does he see it that way.

Fifteen-year-old Dennis explained: "Everyone says to me, like, 'When are your parents coming to pick you up?' or 'Are you going away with your parents this summer?' And I'm like 'No. My parents are divorced. My father doesn't even speak to my mother anymore.' "

Jake, age twelve, told me: "I don't tell anybody about my parents. It's not their business and anyway they won't say anything nice about it."

David, seventeen, emphasized: "As a guy, I'm not about to go around talking about my parents. I mean, the other kids will be, like 'Grow up— get a life. You're not the only one!' "

Even given the prevalence of divorce, the boy still behaves in accordance with the Boy Code. Rather than show his feelings of sadness, vulnerability, helplessness, despair, and loss, he will retreat behind the mask. He may act out, become difficult, fight, talk back to the teacher, argue, hit things and people, but—whatever he does—he knows that he must not show the shame that torments him—the shame that he feels at not measuring up, feeling weak, not being a real man.

And divorce is seldom as simple and "clean" as two adults separating and one of them taking primary custody of the boy. The divorce rearranges all the members of the family, the extended family, and everyone who comes in contact with the family—like pieces on a chessboard. The relationship of mother and son changes, the relationship of father and son changes. The relationship of mother, father, and other caregivers, including teachers, changes. What's more, a whole new set of players may come on the scene, all of whom have differing and bewildering stakes and roles in the matter: counselors and lawyers, baby-sitters or nannies, grandmothers or family friends, boyfriends and girlfriends, new "parents" and siblings in a remarriage. Even the family pet may leave home.

The problem for boys of divorce is that their reactions to it are often misinterpreted and misunderstood. There has been a great deal of discussion in recent years about the relative effects of divorce on boys and girls. Judith Wallerstein, founder of the Center for the Family in Transition, talks about the "sleeper effect" of divorce on girls. During a divorce, girls may seem to be coping successfully, they seem "fine." But, years later—sometimes many years later—the dormant negative feelings will surface and disrupt their lives. Boys, on the other hand, are more likely than girls to act out during the divorce. Their voices, in fact, may become loud and strident. But what we are hearing is not a boy's true inner voice—it is an angry cry, disconnected from the genuine pain he feels within. So while boys and girls tend to behave differently in a divorce situation—boys often make noise, girls tend to suffer in silence—both behaviors are meant to cover the deeper pain they feel within.

"I'm not ever getting married," seventeen-year-old Jason once told me, "it's just gonna be all day long arguing about money, arguing about who said this and who said that, and yelling at the kids. You'll just end up alone, so why even get married in the first place?"

If divorce were a rare phenomenon in our society, perhaps we would not need to pay such close attention to this third childhood trauma. But, according to Lawrence Beymer of Indiana State University, the parents of some three-thousand kids get divorced or separated every day. Half of all Caucasian boys live in a single-parent home (usually headed by the mother); three quarters of all African American boys are in the same situation. Most of these boys are under the age of eighteen. Many studies show that boys of divorced families are more at risk for a range of problems than boys of intact families. Author S. H. Kaye reports that they tend to be more aggressive, are absent from school more often, and score less well in both reading and math. A study by D. M. Fergusson of more than one thousand New Zealand children from birth to age fifteen, showed that the children of divorced families were more likely to become sexually active earlier, more likely to abuse drugs, and were twice as likely to drop out of school altogether.

The good news is that boys *can* cope successfully with divorce, as can girls and parents. The third trauma of boyhood—like the other two—can be ameliorated. The problem comes if a family has been unsuccessful at dealing with either of the other two traumas. If parents expect their boy to "tough it out" when he goes to school or when he reaches puberty, they may well expect him to do the same during divorce. On the other hand, if parents have developed a strong relationship with their boy that provides him with ample opportunities to be himself and express his true emotions, he is more likely to get through a divorce without retreating behind the mask. To do so, however, parents must separate their feelings about each other, and the situation they are in, from their feelings about their son. Although this can be extremely difficult to do, it can and must be done.

LEARNING TO READ THE ACTION "BAROMETER"

The emotions involved in a family on the brink of divorce, during divorce, and after divorce, are extremely complex and constantly changing—sometimes gradually, sometimes violently and suddenly. A boy may respond to these changes through various types of action: sometimes a wild and unexpected spike of activity, such as Oliver's episode on the school bus, sometimes a new and obsessive kind of activity such as constant talking or teasing, and sometimes it may be "anti-activity"—the boy will withdraw into silence and sullenness. A parent must learn to read the boy's action barometer.

The most typical emotions for a boy of divorce include shame, guilt, vulnerability, and anxiety. He may suffer intense feelings of shame, that he is unable to be a man and cope with this difficult storm alone. "I'm always wondering now—if I hadn't been such a baby about everything, maybe my parents would still be together," Raphael, aged sixteen, explained. "My father always yelled at my mother and told her she was too easy on me. He said I was a spoiled brat, that I got everything I wanted. I think he was sick of both of us." Indeed, a boy like Raphael may feel guilt, that somehow he is to blame for the breakup of his parents and the destruction of his family. He often feels vulnerable and powerless—there is nothing he can do to repair his family or to connect with them. He feels fear and anxiety about the future. What will happen to me? Who will look after me? Will I have to move to a new house, a new neighborhood, a new school? Above all, he feels a tremendous sense of disconnection. Not only is the connection to an intact family shattered, he may be unable to connect with his father or mother individually, because they are so distraught themselves. They may be so consumed by their own anger, remorse, worry, and guilt, they may have difficulty focusing on the feelings of their son. All of which causes the boy to disconnect from his own genuine feelings.

J. W. Santrock, who interviewed forty-five fifth-grade boys, argues that divorce is so traumatic and painful, it is actually more difficult for a boy to deal with than a parent's death. A death, even a tragic and unexpected one, is more clear-cut than a divorce. The boy will long for the parent and miss him or her, but the parent is gone; there is no possibility of his or her return. Sons of a divorced couple, by contrast, may harbor hopes that their parents will reunite, and may work very hard—for years, in some cases—to bring about a reconciliation, when none is possible. "I tried everything," Kent, now aged eighteen, remembers, "I tried getting them to come to my tennis matches together; I tried organizing a Christmas party where we could all be a family; once, when I was only eight years old, I ran away from home to go see my dad to beg him to come back to be with us. Nothing worked. It was definitely over. I was pretty much devastated."

Societal attitudes also contribute to the relative negative consequences of divorce. Society shares grief over the death of a parent and may even make an exception to the Boy Code by allowing a boy to cry and express feelings of sadness and loss. For the most part, however, we expect the boy—especially the adolescent boy—to endure a parent's death with stoicism and a stiff upper lip. Think of Prince Harry as he marched behind Lady Diana's hearse, his face calm and emotionless. But what was he thinking and feeling inside?

Society, in my opinion, is far less accepting of divorce—despite its prevalence—and is even less likely to accommodate a boy's feelings about it. The divorced family is often viewed as an unsuccessful one, and seems to pose a threat to intact families, especially those that may be having problems of their own. Other parents aren't sure of what to say to divorcing parents, whom to take sides with, or how to relate to the children involved. Often the result is that neighbors and friends say very little. They don't deliver hot cooked meals, as they might after a death. They don't go out of their way to call on the divorcing family, as they would attend a grieving family. And so a boy may feel yet another disconnection—this time from his community.

For many boys, the only way to handle the seething emotions involved in divorce is to express them through action, as they do in many other contexts, as we have discussed. They will throw and hit and break things. They will get involved in fights at school and in the neighborhood. They will yell and play loudly. They will refuse to go to bed, refuse to go to school, refuse to do whatever a parent asks. They will step on ants, pull branches off trees, skateboard off high jumps, steal things from the local convenience store, set fires, rip their clothes, get lost in the woods, spit on the sidewalk, throw rocks at windows, play game after video game of mayhem and violence, lose their homework, talk back to a teacher, and commit a thousand other acts that look like those of a "bad kid" but are actually the cries of a boy in pain. Or, as I've said, a boy may take the opposite of action. He may withdraw, stop talking, retreat to his room, lie for hours on the couch, shoot a thousand paper wads into his wastebasket, wander around the house, watch excessive amounts of television, put on his headphones and listen to music all day long, stand by the window and stare into space.

These actions—or a boy's failure to act—can indeed be read like a barometer of a boy's feelings. The more extreme his behavior, the greater his pain is likely to be.

SINGLE-PARENT FAMILIES: MOTHERS

The majority of boys of divorce who live in single-parent households live with their mothers, and a vast majority of those are in the sole custody of their mother, with little or no contact with their father. With a lot of hard work and dedication, a mother can successfully raise a boy without a father in the picture, and even mentor a boy who has no significant male figure in this life. But the relationship of mother and son is very different from that of father and son, and it can take time for a mother to understand in what ways it is different and to adjust to them.

When Ron was nine, his mother left his father, after many months of arguing, counseling, reconciliation, and renewed bitterness. Finally, after another argument that covered the same old emotional territory, Ron's father stormed out of the house and his mother reached the end of her tolerance. She packed up Ron and his two sisters, got in the car, and set off for a relative's house many hours away.

Along the way, the family stopped for a meal. Once settled in a booth, Ron's mother went to the ladies' room with his two sisters. He was left to go to the men's room alone. "I had always gone into the bathroom with my father," Ron remembered. "I didn't like going in there alone with all those strange men. What made it worse was I imagined my mother and my sisters in the ladies' room together, commiserating, talking, hugging each other. I don't think my mother really thought about it. She just assumed that I could go in alone. I had never discussed my nervousness about public bathrooms with her because I didn't need to. But my father knew all about how I felt. He told me he'd felt the same way when he was a kid."

"From that moment, I really felt like I was on my own. My mother and my sisters had each other. They could retreat to the ladies' room. But I couldn't. I had no one to cry with, and I didn't think I should cry alone."

It took Ron years—through counseling and as a member of a support group—to break out of his silence and finally talk about the breakup of his family. "Thirty years later, I can cry and seek comfort not only from my wife, but from friends whom I have come to trust. But from the time I was nine years old until just the last few years, I was almost completely cut off from my emotions."

I do not suggest that mothers of divorce intentionally shun or ignore the feelings of their male children. But, just as a father can never have the same deep and instinctual understanding of a daughter's needs as a mother can, even the most caring and intuitive mother will be unable to completely anticipate and understand the idiosyncrasies and concerns of her boy. As Cindy, the divorced mother of two boys, put it to me: "I know I do a pretty good job and that my boys are usually comfortable with how I handle things. But there's a sadness I see in them sometimes, like a longing they have that's not getting satisfied. When I see that look, I know it's about their father. They miss him—his style, his laugh, his way of doing things. I love my boys a lot but I feel like there's just nothing I can do when they're feeling that way. We all just have to live through it together."

The mother-son relationship in mother-only families may be further complicated by the roiling emotions the mother is experiencing, and particularly her attitudes toward the boy's father and men in general. While it is not always the case, the mother may feel strong negative emotions toward the father—disappointment, exasperation, anger, hatred, jealousy, disgust. She may expand these feelings and apply them to men in general for a while or, sometimes, for many years after the divorce. When a boy witnesses such emotions displayed toward the central male figure in his life and toward his gender as a whole, he may be confused about what role models he should follow—whom *should* he act like if all men are bad?

But the greatest danger is that the mother's feelings about the father could spill over onto her attitude toward her son. If she begins to think of her own son as "just like his father," or "acting like all men do," he may come to see himself as toxic. Now he feels that he is not only unable to talk with his only parent, but that his very presence is unwanted by her. He may feel he has nowhere to turn for solace and help. Whom can he tell that his mother thinks he is bad?

Some mothers may have a very different reaction. Rather than seeing their son as toxic, they may expect him to become the "little man of the house." They may seek emotional support, and even physical comforting, from him after the divorce. They may expect the boy to take on tasks and responsibilities of the father, such as looking after younger children in the family and doing chores around the house. Although there is nothing wrong with a boy helping out around the house, this push to become the "little man" can exacerbate the trauma of the divorce. Not only must he adjust to a new life with only one parent, he may also be being asked to become a man too soon.

Boys in such mother-only families can have a very difficult time of it. Stephanie Kasen conducted a study of 648 children, eight years after their parents' divorce. It showed that boys in mother-only households were five times more at risk for major depressive disorders than girls in mother-only families. They were also far more at risk than boys who had a consistent, adult-male relationship with their biological or stepfather or with another male figure, such as a mother's boyfriend, uncle, or a family friend.

But the determining factor of how well a boy in mother-only families survives divorce is not the presence or absence of a father or male figure. If a mother can keep her feelings for her husband from negatively affecting her attitudes toward men in general, and her son in particular, and learn to recognize how boys express emotion—often through action—she can help her son get through the divorce, not without pain, but without *unnecessary* pain.

In fact, there is plenty of evidence that demonstrates that a boy can still achieve adulthood successfully without a father and with no dominant male figure in his life. Single mothers often do a wonderful job of raising their sons without help from a man.

Roberta, for example, married Jeff when both were seniors in a college in Vermont. They had two children within three years, Ryan and Kim. Jeff went on to get an advanced degree at a university in Massachusetts, while Roberta took a part-time job and raised the kids. The family members saw one another mostly on weekends. When Jeff graduated, he took a job near home, and Roberta went back to school and got her teaching certificate. A few years after she graduated, Jeff was offered a lucrative and exciting job in Utah. Roberta did not want to move; he did. After seven years of marriage, they both realized that they had drifted apart and wanted different things from their lives. They separated in a reasonably amicable way. Jeff lived alone in Utah for a year, and visited the family only twice. After another year, Jeff and Roberta decided to divorce. Ryan was seven, Kim was six.

"I realized that I had to shoulder the responsibility for bringing up my kids," Roberta said. "I could either do it with caring and intelligence, or I could do it with remorse and recrimination. When I think about it, there really was no choice. I wanted to do what was best for my kids, and for me. I knew they'd be better off if I was positive about things, and I knew I'd feel better about myself, too. No one wants to live with a complainer."

Roberta got a job that enabled her to be home most of the after-school hours. She refused to demonize Jeff, and although he never visited, she encouraged her children to call him when they wanted to. From time to time she dated, but did not actively seek to replace Jeff with another man. Above all else, she talked with both her children about their lives, and tried to do things with Ryan that he particularly liked. "When we went to our first hockey game together, he taught me the team cheer, and, I tell you, I yelled it as loud as anybody in the arena."

When Ryan turned twelve, Jeff invited him for a visit to Utah. "My first reaction was to say no," Roberta remembers. "I thought Ryan might like it better out there. He might want to stay. He might form some incredible bond with his father and I would lose him. But I knew I had to let him go. So, I told him that I was going to miss him a lot, and that I hoped he had a great time."

"Ryan did have a great time, doing all kinds of things, going to rodeos and horseback riding and whitewater-rafting. But it was like a vacation. He knew it wasn't home. What we have is very strong. And, to give Jeff credit, he didn't make a play for Ryan's affections. They established a relationship, which is good, but he didn't manipulate Ryan or try to turn him against me."

"If I could do it all again, I guess I wouldn't have married so young. I would have had kids later. I would have tried harder to keep the marriage together. But, I can't do it all again. And I have two great kids. That's a lot."

THE DEADPAN DAD

In mother-custody families, the role of the father varies tremendously. Some fathers disappear altogether. Some, like Jeff, are distant and play only a minor role in their sons' lives. We can make some generalizations, however, about the relative status of mother and father. Statistics show that most mothers are worse off financially than they were before the divorce, but that fathers more often suffer depression. This is often because the mother has been the one who creates the social connections in and for the family, she has been the emotional glue, and the father feels separated and lost without the social environment he once knew. This can cause the father to become despondent or depressed, and adversely affect his capacity to be with his son. He may continue to meet his financial obligations (unlike so-called deadbeat dads), but may be unable to meet his emotional obligation—he becomes a "deadpan" dad, as we discussed in Chapter 6. The deadpan dad is a man who is there for his son only through prescribed visits or through his monthly support payment. He is not irresponsible so much as he is confused, depressed, or emotionally "numbed-out" about being separated from his son.

Sometimes, particularly in the cases of well-to-do families, a boy will force a deadpan dad to substitute money when no love is available. Martin, sixteen, had idolized his father, a wealthy executive in a global corporation. But when his parents divorced, the father moved out of the suburban town where they had lived and took a luxurious penthouse apartment in the city. Martin's mother was well provided for, but his father, who was terribly upset by the divorce, soon became deeply involved in a relationship with a much younger woman and often took her with him on his extensive business travels around the world. "I almost never saw my dad," said Martin. "He never sent me any letters. Once in a while I'd get a postcard from London or Beijing or someplace. I remember on one of them my dad's girlfriend had written a little note. 'Hi sweetheart.' I hardly knew her."

Martin's father made up for his absence in his own way. He bought Martin a car, and sent him tickets to rock concerts and basketball games—always the best seats. Every weekend, Martin could be seen whizzing off to some event, an attractive girl at his side. He was, in fact, considered by many of his classmates as the ultimate in cool. He had plenty of money. He had his own car. He could do whatever he wanted.

Gradually, Martin learned to speak the language of money that his deadpan father had taught him. "For my eighteenth birthday, I asked my father if I could have my own credit card, and he gave it to me. The first thing I did was take my girlfriend on a vacation to St. Bart. We stayed in the best suite in the best hotel. We had an incredible time. I didn't tell him about it. But when he got the credit-card statement, he went ballistic. He called me up and screamed at me. I screamed back at him. I told him that he owed me. He owed me big-time for leaving my mother, and putting us all through such incredible shit."

Although many fathers vacate their son's lives, many do not. Sometimes it is the mother who works to keep the connection.

Louise's marriage ended just a few days before her son, Will, was born. Her husband married the woman he was having an affair with and moved halfway across the country. "Raising Will by myself meant I had to find ways to bring men into his life. I knew I could give him a lot, but I knew there were some things only a man could give him," Louise said. She determined that, as he grew up, Will would have a positive relationship with his father. "I was furious at Max for the affair and for leaving me to raise a child on my own, but I never let Will know that. I've encouraged their relationship ever since Will was an infant. I still have to call his father and say, 'You know you haven't called Will in three weeks, do you think maybe you can give your son a call?' For my son's sake, I have basically orchestrated this relationship over the years. So my son has a great relationship with his father, and feels very close to him although it's long-distance."

Louise also arranged for Will to have a Big Brother. "Starting when Will was seven, he had Blair for three years. Blair's a really good guy. That was great." Then Louise built a relationship with a man named Gary and, eventually, he moved in with Louise and Will. "When Gary first moved in, I had to explain to him that as the adult he needed to reach out to the child. The first few weeks were a bit tense, but since then it's worked out. There is no animosity, and now he would rather share things with Gary than with me. You know, get approval from Gary as opposed to approval from me, the mother. And I support that."

Sometimes a relationship with a "substitute" man doesn't take. A mother may try to help her son form a bond with her new boyfriend if the father is not in the picture, and even push a little too hard to make it work. But, if that boyfriend is replaced by another, and then another, naturally the boy will feel even greater disconnection. He has already been "abandoned" once by a male role model. A string of disappointments in male relationships can further damage his already fragile sense of self-esteem.

Some fathers, too, are less willing to stay involved with their son's lives after the mother enters a new relationship. One who fell out of touch with his son after the mother remarried says, "Her new husband is a nice guy. He gets along really well with my son. I don't think he needs me anymore." Even when a son gets into a stable family relationship with his mom and a stepfather he likes, that does not mean he has lost his need for his father. The only message he gets from the noncommunicative dad is "I don't care about you. You're not important."

But not all fathers, of course, become separated from their boys after the divorce. And some actually take sole or primary custody. The number of father-custody families is on the rise, although the percentage is still very small. There is new, and controversial, research that shows that some boys who live with their father may fare better than those who live with their mother. Whether or not this is true, the research underscores for me just how important it is for a father not to fade out of his son's life because he assumes he is not needed or wanted. As fourteen-year-old Tony puts it: "You've only got one mom and you've only got one dad. So I think you really want to have both of them in your life."

A SOCIETY BUILT ON AN OUTDATED STEREOTYPE

Just as society expects boys to behave in certain ways, it expects families to do the same. As prevalent as divorce is, and as politically correct as our schools and community organizations have become in talking about it, society is still structured in favor of two-parent intact families. The boy without a father will find himself at a disadvantage, or at least in an awkward situation, far more often than he would like. The parent-teacher conference will always be with his mother. If he plays a team sport, his coaches will almost always be men—but not his father. At the Cub Scout sleepover, his mother may come along, but she will be in the minority. He may be invited on an outing with several friends, to a ball game or a campout. There may be four sons there, but only three fathers.

Even when teachers, parents, friends, neighbors are exquisitely sensitive to the boy's situation, the fact remains: the boy is without a father—he does not have what the other boys have. And, as much as his pals may complain about curfews or disagreements with their fathers, the boy can see that these are but minor problems in otherwise strong relationships. He does not want to be different, but there is nothing he can do to about it. This, of course, leads the boy to feel shame, which begins the cycle we've seen in so many other difficult situations—he puts on the mask and tries to harden himself against the painful feelings of being part of a different kind of family.

FINDING A SAFE SPACE IN A "BLENDED" FAMILY

The two-parent intact family may be the model that society chooses to idealize, but more and more families do not fit the stereotype. Boys of divorce may find themselves in all manner of blended and reconstructed families that bring with them problems every bit as complicated as dealing with a stressed mother or an absent father. When either parent remarries, the boy may become part of an enlarged family that includes an adult who suddenly assumes the place of the missing parent. The stepparent may also bring along his or her children from a previous marriage. Society has developed a stereotype of the happily chaotic blended family, a Brady bunch in which the stepparents embrace their new foundlings with boundless love and understanding and create a family-like group that is even more fun and interesting and loving than the two-parent family. Of course, it's seldom that easy.

After six years of sole custody of her son and daughter, Barbara London married a man named Arthur; he had never been married and had no experience in parenting. Cameron is ten, Willa is six.

"Cameron has had a hard time adjusting to having a stepfather," Barbara told me. "My daughter has seemed to settle in pretty well, but Arthur and Cameron are still having a hard time."

Cameron was acting out regularly. "There have been calls from the school, and things at home have become crazy. At dinner one night, we had barely started eating when Cameron wanted to leave the table. Arthur told him he was not excused yet. Cameron started talking back to him, shoving his plate around. Arthur got mad at him, which made Cameron even madder himself. Finally, he swore at Arthur and called him a filthy name. Arthur went nuts. He couldn't believe a ten-year-old had called him that. Next thing I knew, Cameron was slamming the door to his room and Arthur was ready to walk out and never return."

Barbara tried to mediate between the two. She tried to explain to Arthur how Cameron must feel, with this stranger suddenly trying to exert authority over him. She also tried to explain to Cameron that Arthur had never had kids and needed practice to learn how to be a stepparent. "Neither one of them had much patience with me," Barbara said.

I asked her if she thought Cameron's behavior was related to his age or his gender. She thought for a while. "I think this is partly because Cameron's a boy. He tends to get angry and act out. Willa gets sad and mopey. When I think about it, I realize she's having a hard time, too, but it's much easier for Arthur and me to cope with a cute, teary-eyed, six-year-old girl than with an angry, shouting ten-year-old boy. Willa tells me about her feelings. She points to the stuffed elephant her dad gave her and says she misses her 'real father.' When I ask Cameron what he's feeling, he says he hates Arthur."

Many stepparents feel as though no matter how hard they try, whatever they do is wrong. If they try to be a pal to their stepchildren, the children reject them. If they try to become a replacement parent, the children resist their attempts to wield authority over them. If they try to ignore the stepchildren, they find it is, of course, impossible.

For many boys, as we've seen, the solution is to toughen themselves up and don the mask. They hide their feelings and act as if everything is OK while they continue to suffer inside. For other boys, the solution is to act out, go wild, get in trouble.

Boys in unhappily blended homes face an additional difficulty. They may no longer think of home as a safe space, in which they can express themselves. When that happens, they may seek to create a safe space outside the home—at a friend's house, a gang hangout, a girlfriend's place, or some school activity. Although he may be lucky enough to make a positive connection in one of these places, it is often at the expense of connection at home.

HOW TO KEEP A BOY OF DIVORCE FROM DONNING THE MASK

No one would argue that divorce in itself is a positive thing, although it may have some positive results. One parent or both may create a better, more satisfying life for themselves outside the marriage. Children may find themselves freed from a depressing home environment or from physical or verbal abuse. But divorce itself and the process of becoming divorced are anything but positive. Divorce puts sons at risk, just as it does daughters. We must learn to recognize the warning signs that a boy is headed for trouble.

No two boys will react the same way to a divorce. One boy may feel intense anger toward one or both parents, another may not. One boy may become extremely depressed, even suicidal, during a divorce, another may not. Many boys will act out their emotions and become disruptive and wild. Other boys may fall silent. It's important not to make any assumptions about the boy's emotions. The only solution is to carefully observe your son's behavior, and to find ways to discuss the divorce and his emotions with him. To misinterpret your son can be as damaging for your relationship as not to hear him at all.

There are many behaviors, of course, that clearly indicate that a boy is having trouble with his feelings. He may have psychosomatic symptoms, become "hypermature," or do poorly at school. He may have trouble making or keeping friends. He may fight or disrupt class or engage in aggressive dialogues with a teacher. As disturbing as these behaviors are for a parent, they also offer the opportunity to begin talking. If a boy refuses to go to school, for example, that may be a time when you can start a discussion of what's really bothering him. Is it the spelling test, as he says, or is it that he misses his father?

REALIZE THAT NOTHING STAYS THE SAME

Stephen's father and mother divorced when he was eleven, and his mother returned to work full-time. She was so stressed with work, financial worries, and the emotional turmoil of the divorce, that Stephen decided he had to help out. He tried to assume a stoic presence, and did his best to take over the running of the household. He helped with cooking, cleaning, and caring for his six-year-old brother. He even screened his mother's telephone calls, hoping to protect her when the credit card company called about late payments. By the time Stephen reached sixteen, his mother had worked through her financial problems, was more comfortable at work, and was much more stable emotionally. After five years of allowing Stephen to play the role of the father, she unwittingly expected Stephen to return to his old role as the little boy in the house.

One Friday evening, Stephen decided to go out and asked his mother if he could borrow the car. "Not until you clean up your room," she said.

Stephen snapped. "I've been cleaning my own room for five years, and the kitchen, too. I didn't need you to tell me to take care of my brother and mow the lawn and buy the groceries, and I don't need you to tell me to clean up my room now. You can't suddenly decide to be my mother." He took the car keys and dashed out of the house.

His mother cried when she thought about the truth of Stephen's statement: she had placed a great demand on him during the divorce. Now she wanted things to return to "normal," but it was too late. The point is that a parent can *never* stop looking at and listening to the boy of divorce. His emotions at the moment of divorce will be different from those six months after the divorce. And, like Stephen, they are likely to continue to change—sometimes quite unexpectedly—for years thereafter.

MAKE SAFE SPACES AND SPECIAL TIMES

We have talked about the need to create safe spaces for boys, where they feel unpressured, free of the gender straitjacket, and able to talk. For boys of divorce, it may be useful to formalize those safe spaces by creating regular times at which a parent will always be available and during which the child can expect complete attention.

After Philip's parents got divorced, his father, Jack, was soon involved with a new woman. On weekdays Philip lived with his mother, Ariana. On weekends Philip stayed with his father and his new girlfriend, Joyce, and Joyce's five-year-old daughter, Charlotte.

"On school days, I missed my dad. I love my mom and everything, but she doesn't like to do things with me that he likes, like play Nintendo or help me practice my batting and stuff. Then on weekends, I missed my mom. Dad wanted to be with Joyce and would tell me to go outside and play. Plus Charlotte was always hanging around, bugging me."

Philip had suffered from mild asthma for many years. After a few months of the visits to his father's new home, the asthma got worse. He began wheezing two or three times a week, badly enough that he found himself in the nurse's office at school.

"At first I thought Philip's asthma had taken a terrible turn for the worse," Ariana remembers. "I would be called out of an important meeting at work and rush to his school. When I got there, he would look suspiciously healthy. I understood that the nurse wanted to take every precaution and keep me informed, but I suspected something was going on besides an asthma attack."

Ariana looked for help from a parents' support group that she was attending, and the group leader suggested a technique called "special time." As we've discussed elsewhere in this book, special time is when a parent follows the child's lead to do whatever he or she wants for a specified period, as long as the activity does not harm anyone—and with a spending cap if necessary. Ariana and Philip began doing special time for an hour twice a week.

"At first Philip wanted to drag me outside to play baseball or watch him ride his bike, things I wasn't always in the mood to do after a long day at work," Ariana told me. "But I did it, because I had to prove that I really was willing to play on his terms."

Within a few weeks, Philip invented a new activity for special time— a game in which he pretended to have an asthma attack. "I was supposed to pick him up, carry him to the hospital, and then play the concerned doctor with magic medicine."

Gradually, Ariana came to understand what Philip was trying to accomplish with the game—and with his asthma episodes at school: he wanted to be reassured that Ariana would always be there to help him when he needed it. "Pretty soon, I started embellishing my performance. I acted terrified that he was so sick. I would tell him how much I loved him. I promised that I would always be there whenever he needed me. I even pretended I had a beeper so he could always get in touch with me, even when he was at his father's for the weekend."

Philip responded so positively to the pretend beeper, Ariana decided to get a real one. The special time, and the asthma game, worked. Philip's visits to the school nurse became more infrequent and, then, at last, ended. "I don't wheeze anymore," Philip says. "I feel a lot better now." I asked him why he thought his asthma had improved. "I guess I just didn't feel good when my dad started living with Joyce," he said.

Philip and Ariana have continued to do special time at least once a week. "He's moved on to other activities," Ariana reports with a smile. "Like making me risk my neck going Rollerblading with him."

During these special times, the subject of discussion is not always divorce, nor even Philip's feelings. Sometimes mother and son just spend time together, doing "whatever." It isn't necessary to push the boy into conversation, or to "make him" talk—any mother of a boy knows that too many direct and probing questions are the shortest route to turning a boy off. But the special place assures the boy that *when he wants to talk* he will have a willing ear. Often, that's as important to a boy as actually saying anything at all.

REASSURE, BUT DON'T DISSEMBLE

When a boy starts to talk about his feelings about divorce, all sorts of statements, perceptions, ideas, and concerns may come tumbling out, some of which may strike you as misguided or just plain wrong. It will not help to "correct" his ideas or in any way judge his feelings with comments such as "How could you feel that way?" Or "That's crazy!" Or "You're wrong to feel that way."

The important thing is to reassure your son that you are there for him and that you love him. At the same time, it won't help to make things sound better than they are. If you know that the other parent is moving away or getting remarried, don't hide the fact. If your son wants an expensive new sound system but it's not in the budget, don't say, "We'll see," or "That's not important." Tell him when it might be possible to buy the system. Or suggest other ways he might get one—by working for it or buying a used one. Your boy needs to rebuild his trust in you, and the best way to help him do that is to be open, honest, and straight with him.

At the same time, try to avoid unburdening all of your stress on him. Sharing your concerns and worries will encourage him to do the same, but revealing that you're feeling out of control may cause him to keep his worries to himself in the future. You want to be honest with him, yes, but you don't want to force him into the role as your counselor or therapist. It's an inappropriate role for him to play and is likely to make him feel awkward; it may inhibit him from expressing his own thoughts and healing his own hurts, as well.

THE BENEFITS OF CONSISTENT CO-PARENTING

Relations between ex-spouses may be full of anger, blame, and sadness, but much research shows that boys fare better when both parents remain involved in his life. Joint-custody children tend to fare better both economically and emotionally than single-custody kids, unless the relationship between mother and father is so acrimonious it provides more grief than support.

It is important for a boy to feel that his parents don't hate each other and that he need not choose sides—mom or dad. So even if you would rather have nothing to do with your ex-spouse, ideally you will overcome your own reservations and help your son maintain a relationship with him or her. It will help your boy to be more honest about his feelings about the divorce if he feels he has both parents to support his feelings, and that they are not trying to make him see the other parent as the villain.

With all the changes that boys face after divorce—seeing one parent less or not at all, perhaps moving to a new home, facing judgment as a kid from a "broken home"—it is important to try to provide consistent parenting. If your son splits his time between two homes, try to make joint parenting decisions on discipline strategies and rules. Don't accept negative behavior because of the divorce. If he is suddenly acting out, try to get him to understand *why* he is doing it, and help him see which behaviors are inappropriate. When he's handling the situation well, tell him. Let him know that you know how tough things are for him, and that you respect how he's dealing with his concerns.

Sometimes responsibilities around the house will change after a divorce, especially when a mother returns to work full-time or parents begin to develop active social lives. Helping around the house with younger children or with cleaning and maintenance can make a boy feel that he is contributing to the family and assisting in making a positive transition after the divorce. Asking your son's advice on where he would like to move, or what the visitation schedule he thinks would work best, enables him to feel less powerless in spite of so many changes. But, when doing so, be careful of forcing him into the role as the "little man of the house." Don't ask him to advise you on adult decisions that he isn't mature enough to understand, such as your career, or give him too much responsibility, like staying home with younger children every night. Let him make decisions he can make; you make those that require an adult's judgment.

PEERS CAN SUPPORT AS WELL AS PRESSURE

Studies show that boys from families of divorce spend more time with peers than boys from intact homes. This can be a positive or a negative factor in a boy's ability to deal with divorce, depending on who the peers are, how they view divorce, and what they do together. If a boy gets involved with other kids who genuinely like him, are willing to listen to him, and who don't judge him, his group can provide much of the connection and love that he has lost at home. The same need for peer connection and acceptance can also lead a boy to join with groups of kids who have similar feelings of anger, and research shows that—in extreme cases—it may even lure him into gangs and cults.

The responsibility of the parent is to be especially vigilant in knowing who the boy's friends are, what they do together, where they do it, and to set limits on where they can go and how long they can be away from home. When the parent watches a boy closely and is positively involved in his life, the boy is less likely to skip school, become involved in gangs or criminal activities, become sexually active too early, or abuse drugs or alcohol.

Families in transitions such as divorce are generally more at risk for "parenting problems," such as inability to manage children's negative behavior. However, a study of families at risk for these parenting problems shows that parents who are significantly more involved in their sons' activities and who offer more supervision than they did before the divorce were more successful in positively influencing their son's behavior.

TEACHERS AND BOYS OF DIVORCE

School is often the arena where boys act out their emotions about divorce, and, often, teachers are the ones who take the brunt of it. I believe that teachers can do a great deal to help a boy through these difficult times. Some thoughts:

- Teachers should be aware of changes in children of divorce, in behavior, attitude, and performance, but not *expect* that a child will exhibit certain problems.
- Teachers should be sensitive to school situations that may affect the child (such as Mother's Day art projects, or family discussions) and avoid comments that will make the child feel stigmatized or ashamed.
- Outbursts shouldn't be taken personally by teachers, as boys often react at school outside the real problem at hand.
- Teachers and parents should work together to understand how the divorce may be affecting the boy's academic behavior and social situations.

- Teachers may need to support the child more than usual, and should express a sincere interest in his well-being, whenever possible and appropriate.
- Teachers should be aware of custodial arrangements and the role of the noncustodial parent.
- Teachers should understand that there may be a lowering in the standard of living for homes without a father, which may affect a child's ability to participate in class activities such as special field trips or to get private tutoring if necessary.

AN EXTRA NOTE FOR TEACHERS: THE BOY'S BEHAVIOR AS BELLWETHER

Teachers should be especially alert to changes in a boy's social behavior or academic performance even when the family is intact and no divorce is contemplated. If a boy misbehaves, fails, or rebels in some uncharacteristic way, the cause could possibly be a problem at home. The boy's difficulty at school may, in fact, be a precursor to more serious troubles at home, such as divorce. In this way, a boy's behavior may serve as a kind of bellwether for the behavior of the family as a whole.

SURVIVING DIVORCE: A PRIMER FOR BOYS

There is a beautiful Jewish folktale which suggests that all human beings are originally conceived with both a male and a female side that are split apart at birth as we are sent down from heaven to earth. During our youth we search for our soul mate. Then, at the time we are ready to be married, God gathers together the original kindred souls, helps them to fall in love, and rejoins them in marriage for life. It is a beautiful story, but so painfully different from the marital realities—and casualties—of today's complex world.

For us and our children, divorce is an everyday fact of life. Living with divorce, as I have shown, poses a unique set of painful problems, often forcing boys into yet another premature and painful separation—a third trauma. Already forced to leave the holding nest of maternal love at a very young age, and pushed over time to hide his continuing need for succor behind apathy and stoicism, a boy finds himself in a particularly fragile state if his family—his one remaining emotional anchor—is then torn asunder by parental separation. And if at that moment he is an adolescent also dealing with the second pull to be separate—a time when he probably needs adult supervision and guidance the most—his parents' divorce can cause lasting confusion about who he is, who he can trust, and who will provide him with a relationship, and a love, that will last.

The voices we have heard of boys and teens caught in the web of divorce—and the staggering statistics reported on the dramatic impact a divorce can have on a boy's self-esteem, temperament, and academic performance—testify to the potential of trauma in this all too common occurrence. And yet we must be careful not to fall prey either to moralistic blame or to callous shaming. Although some couples may enter into both marriage and divorce too lightly, many have tried their best to make a go of the marriage. Many discover, despite the most intense and genuine efforts to keep the marriage going, that they'll truly thrive best on their own.

And while the trauma of divorce is especially bound to hit a boy hard—because it's unexpected, because it's painful, and because the old Boy Code continues to deprive him of the emotional support he needs to deal with it—I believe that all need not be seen from the vantage point of total pessimism. Boys can and do survive divorce. Indeed, to the astonishment of psychologists, some boys eventually end up doing quite well— much better than we would ever have imagined. It is of vital importance to know what makes for these differences.

First, as we have seen, parents must be on the lookout for boys' sadness and distress, which often lies hidden behind the mask, constricted by the gender straitjacket. We must all be wary of the boy who tells his struggling mom and tearful dad, "Don't worry, I'm fine." Recognize that nothing is more likely to be further from the truth.

Try, within bounds, to tolerate and harness his rage, remembering that anger is often a boy's first and most familiar way to express feeling. Show that you accept his need to withdraw and be silent by neither withdrawing in return nor pushing the process too quickly, but by "hanging in there" with patience and love.

Second, assure your son, that although things cannot remain the same, the divorce is between (and for) the parents—it is not meant to be another separation where he is concerned. Except under the most extreme circumstances (such as where one parent is abusive or mentally ill), strive to keep the parental turmoil away from the boy and out of the ongoing co-parenting arrangement.

Third, don't be afraid to lean on other adult loved ones for help. Interdependence is a normal part of our human condition. When you form new friendships and relationships with other adults, you're giving your boy this essential message. In other words, not only are you giving yourself new companionship and support, but you're opening your boy to the reality that the same is possible for him.

Fourth, stress to your son that it's OK to be afraid—that mom may worry about bringing up a son without a dad, and that dad too may worry about how sad and lonely he may become if the ties to his son are weakened or cut off. Be honest and keep these discussions out in the open—within reasonable limits and in a way that is appropriate to your son's age—so that your son gets the message that his pain is normal, that you don't expect or want him to bury his emotions or become disconnected from you, that he, after all, is not alone.

As counterintuitive—or overly optimistic—as this may seem, it's important to attempt to teach connection throughout the divorce process, an enduring connection between a boy and his parents that no legal marital realignment will ever destroy. In your own darkest moments of confusion and despair, do your best not to fall prey to guilt and shame. Your boy is yearning for your love and affirmation. And seeing him through this complex life change with a minimum of pain is also an antidote to the feelings of loss and helplessness that *you* may feel.

Focus on a future in which you can create a safe space for your boy to express all his pent-up emotions—positive and negative—and follow your heart's desires to remain connected to him throughout this process. In the end, no matter what the outcome of the divorce, through the power of ongoing emotional parental commitment, you and your son can share a lifetime of healthy connection and the possibility for individual and mutual renewal.

PART FOUR

STAYING CONNECTED: REAL BOYS/ REAL MEN

My boy, as gently on my breast,
From infant sport, thou sink'st to rest;
And on my hand I feel thee put,
In playful dreams, thy little foot,
The thrilling touch sets every string
Of my full heart to quivering;
For, ah! I think, what chart can show
The ways through which this foot
    may go?

Its print will be, in childhood's hours,
Traced in the garden, round the
    flowers;
But youth will bid it leap the rills,
Bathe in the dew on distant hills,
Roam o'er the vales, and venture out
When riper years would pause and
    doubt,
Nor brave the pass, nor try the brink
Where youth's unguarded foot may
    sink.

But what, when manhood tints thy
    cheek,
Will be the ways this foot will seek?
Is it to lightly pace the deck,
Helpless, to slip from off the wreck?
Or wander o'er a foreign shore,
Returning to thy home no more,
Until the bosom now thy pillow,
Is low and cold beneath the willow?

Or, is it for the battle-plain,
Beside the slayer and the slain?
Will there its final step be taken?
There, sleep thine eye no more to
    waken?
Is it to glory or to shame—
To sully, or to gild thy name?
Is it to happiness or wo
This little foot is made to go?

But wheresoe'er its lines may fall,
Whether in cottage or in hall;
O, may it ever shun the ground
Where'er his foot was never found,
Who, on his path of life, hath shed
A living light, that all may tread
Upon his earthly steps; and none
E'er dash the foot against a stone!

Yet, if thy way is marked by fate,
As, guilty, dark and desolate;
If thou must float, by vice and crime,
A wreck, upon the stream of time!
Oh! rather than behold that day,
I'd know this foot, in lightsome play,
Would bound, with guiltless, infant
    glee,
Upon the sod that sheltered me!

—H. F. GOULD
    "The Little Foot"

Epilogue:
The "Real Boy" Code—Revising
the Boy Code and Staying
Connected

For me, one of the most heartwarming experiences in listening closely to boys is hearing one of them share a thought or tell a story that reflects his resistance to the Boy Code—an unconscious and almost imperceptible rebellion against the gender straitjacketing that most of our sons experience every day. Often arising from what seems to be his gut sense that "I've just got to do what's right" or "I'm just going to have to be myself," these touching moments seem to surface when the boy—despite society's rigid gender-based expectations and his own years of stoic suppression of real emotion—finally connects with a new voice within.

When a boy utters these words to assert himself, when he takes on the old Boy Code, he is engaging in an act of heroism, a first attempt to dismantle our society's double standards and toxic views about the male gender. He may be blazing the path for a far more expansive, far less oppressive set of guidelines and expectations—a New Boy Code that respects what today's boys and men are really about—one that will be based upon honesty rather than fear, communication rather than repression, connection rather than disconnection.

My recent conversation with Chris revealed one such boy, one such hero.

Towering over me at nearly six feet, Chris Jackson, with his shock of red hair and intense greenish-brown eyes, seemed unusually self-confident for his seventeen years. Though at first he seemed somewhat shy and reserved, as he began speaking to me I was impressed by his candor and guileless manner. Chris, I had been told, was a top athlete at his school, an able pupil, and one of his school's most respected student leaders. Our conversation covered a range of issues, but Chris seemed most interested in talking about his friends and about the ups and downs of his relationships with them.

"I've got a good group of friends," he boasted with a proud smile. "I've never had any major problems with them."

"No conflicts whatsoever?" I asked.

"Well," he confessed, "now that you mention it, there was that whole scene with Dan that started out as just a hassle but really upset me."

Chris explained to me that Dan Norton had been his friend since kindergarten, that they had lived in the same working-class suburb of Chicago for as long as he could remember. The two had been T-ball team-mates and soccer team cocaptains, and now they were varsity co-captains of the high school football team. "We were pretty close for a long time," Chris volunteered, "We went through a lot together. Dan's parents got divorced, and my mother had breast cancer recently, although she's doing fine now."

"It sounds like a pretty important friendship," I offered.

"Well, we used to spend a lot of our free time together," Chris continued, "and, yes, we were good friends, actually very close friends,"

Chris seemed relaxed when talking about his feelings and comfortable about sharing with me how much he had cared for Dan. But apparently things had recently changed between the two childhood buddies.

"I guess I should say that we *were* good friends. I used to really like the guy until he started to have this one big problem that just completely annoyed me."

"And what was that?" I asked Chris.

"Well," he answered, "Dan would always be late and keep me waiting, like when we were supposed to meet up in the morning to take the bus to school. It took me a while to say anything to him—you know, I sort of needed time to sort things out in my own mind."

"So, did you confront him?" I asked.

"Yep. And when I did, he was really mean, really negative in response. He said some awful things like 'Who do you think *you* are?' and that kind of thing. I didn't want to react right then, so I walked away and tried to think about it—to let it blow over."

But Chris found that the more he puzzled about this incident the more upset he became. "Somehow I couldn't let go of it in my head, and then it dawned on me why. It wasn't just the stuff he was doing to me. You see, he was also starting to pull pranks and hassle the younger kids at our school. Like, ever since he made varsity, he'd rank on the freshmen, hide stuff from their lockers—and sometimes he'd just rough them up. He didn't do anything real bad, but I could see he was, like, terrorizing these younger kids."

"So what did you do about it?"

"That's when I told him he was becoming a jerk, that he was going too far. These kids didn't deserve to be ranked on or beat up. You know, I asked how he would feel if one of the seniors started giving *him* a hard time."

"And how did Dan respond to that?"

"Well, he was like: 'C'mon, Chris. What's gotten into you? Have you become a little wimp or something? Don't you remember what those seniors used to do to us when we came up from junior high? It's just part of being a guy.' " Chris, in fact, did remember all the hazing, even some of the roughhousing that—though never physically harmful—always left him with a deep sense of shame. He even remembered one kid who teased him when his mother had to go through a mastectomy.

"It sounds like going to your high school can be pretty rough," I suggested.

"Yeah. Back then, my older brother, who was a junior at the time, was like, 'Chris, just act tough and ignore them, and they'll lay off you.' "

"Did his advice work well for you?"

"Well, yes and no. I mean, yes, it kept the other guys from hassling me. But, you know, it's stupid to have to act tough all the time. You get all wound up inside, like maybe you're going to have a heart attack or something. You feel awful about yourself, like you're just a big dopey loser. And now that I'm on the other side and I see what these little kids have to go through, I don't really think it's worth it. So, when I see Dan roughing up the little guys, I'm like, 'No way.' I told Dan, 'Why don't you just cut the shit—all it does is screw kids up, like it did us. It's just not right.' "

"So what did Dan say to that?" I asked.

"Well, Dan and I were still friendly for a while, even though the way he treated the other kids—almost like a bully—bothered me a lot. But then Allison moved to town."

"Allison?"

"Yeah. She was this really neat girl, kind of funky, artistic, and real smart. You know in English class, when the teacher would ask all those tough questions, she always had the right answer. I liked her right away."

"She was a friend of yours?"

"Well, she wasn't like a girlfriend or anything. I mean she was just a friend, more like a sister. We started to spend some time together. Unfortunately this wasn't the cool thing to do."

"Why not?"

"First of all, she was new, and kids weren't sure they liked her. But she was 'different'—her clothes, the music she listened to, and that stutter she had. You see, when Allie was a little girl, she was real shy and would stutter when she talked in front of the class. She told me that she used to be like, 'That, that, that's right.' Her parents got her help for this, speech therapy I think it was, and it mostly went away. But even these days, if she gets real nervous, sometimes it comes back. And when we started at high school with the older kids and everything—she had some bad days, with a lot of stuttering."

"So Dan wasn't too supportive of Allison?" I asked.

"For some reason," Chris explained, "He seemed to really hate her, and I knew he ranked on her behind her back. But then one day in math when she was trying to answer a question the stutter came out and it was real hard for her to stop. 'The ger . . . the ger . . .' Finally the teacher realized it and just tried to change the subject. But from the back of the class I could hear this big old horse laugh. I knew that laugh. It was Dan's. I wanted to do something right then and there, but I knew Allie wanted to fight her own battles and so I respected that—I kept quiet. I didn't want to make her feel even worse than she probably already did."

"Good for you," I offered.

"But after class," Chris continued, "it got worse. After the teacher had left, Dan and a couple of other guys surrounded Allie and were saying: 'GERR . . . GERR . . . what's the matter Allie, cat got your tongue?' "

"Was everyone involved in the teasing?"

"Some of the other kids were giggling, but most just seemed pretty angry and so they took off. Funny thing, all the girls and other guys mostly left and it was only Dan and a couple of other boys who hung around and teased her. Allie started to defend herself, but the stutter wouldn't stop. She started crying and ran from the room, with Dan laughing the whole time. It was pretty awful."

"What did you do about it?"

"I just couldn't stand it anymore. I walked right up to Dan and said. 'Dan, cut this crap out! I've told you before to stop the bullying. Can't you see you're hurting Allie?' "

"How did Dan respond to that?"

"He stepped real close to me—you know, his face right into mine—and said real loudly, 'What you going to do about it, you wuss?' It was a direct challenge. He was shouting at me. I knew he was looking for a fight. I don't really know what I would have done, and maybe never will. Because just when he was trying to pick a stupid fight with me, these other kids came up to us and were like, 'What the hell?' A bunch of guys from the football team were there and they were just shouting: 'Hey, back the hell off, Dan.' My friend Kevin was shouting: 'Chill out, Dan' and pulled him away. Then Greg said something like 'Hey, Chris is right—why are you bullying her? She's a nice kid, so lay off.' And then, four of the guys went up to Dan and said, 'You lay off Chris and you leave Allie alone. And if you lay a hand on either of them, we know just where to find you.' "

"How did you feel about that?" I asked Chris.

"I was really happy that they sided with me. Me and Allie were sort of the underdogs—and the other guys were taking our side. Like maybe my older brother would have told me to just stick with Dan and act cool and tough. But here were four of the other guys from our team defending me and Allie, sticking up for her rights. And my parents told me I handled it well too."

"So, how did it turn out?"

"Well, Dan never bothered Allie again and I think he got a little less rough with the other kids too. I'd known him for a long time, though. So, after a while, I tried to talk to him, to explain my feelings, and he just went, 'Well, Chris, I guess we're in different worlds now.' You know I felt bad for a couple of days but then I kept thinking—OK, why did I finally stand up to the guy? And the thought that kept coming to mind was: *It just isn't right—somebody's got to try to change these things.*"

"What things do you mean exactly?"

"Like that guys have to act mean and rank on other people. Or that kids like Allie who have problems get teased. It just seems like a big waste. I think everybody's human so everyone should be treated the same. This year when I was going for class president, my campaign message was 'At Hickman High, there's a place for everyone.' I thought some people might think I was a nerd or whatever, but I decided that I just don't mind anymore. It's a good thing, because now I'm class president and Dan seems to be coming around too. I think I know why he felt pressured to act like such a jerk, and so maybe now we can just let the past be the past and someday even be friends again."

As this story reflects, it's quite possible for a boy today to break out of the gender straitjacket, buck the old Boy Code, and still win the approval and love of family, friends, and society at large. Despite the pressure on him to behave otherwise, Chris stood up for himself and for his friend Allie and triumphed in the end. Unbeknownst to Chris, he was acting like something of a pioneer, rebelling against our old rules about masculinity, and thus breaking new ground for boys and for men.

About forty years ago, society began the process of discarding its old rules about girls and women that tied them down to traditional feminine and maternal obligations, required them to forfeit higher education (and then depend financially on men), and barred them from participating in the many professions, activities, and pursuits once thought to be either "un-ladylike" or "for men only." While we've hardly finished the process, we've come a long way in opening a broad range of opportunities to girls and women and in helping them feel comfortable sounding their true voices and being their true selves without fear of being seen as anything less than a hundred percent "feminine." We've come a long way in liberating girls and women from the gender straitjacket that for years they've been forced to wear.

Boys like Chris show us that society seems to be ready to begin an equivalent process of liberation for boys and men. We are starting to revise the old Boy Code that for ages has cut our boys and men in two, calling upon them to suppress their loving, sensitive, emotionally expressive sides, and then bemoaning the lack of these qualities in them as adults, especially in their relationships with women.

Boys like Chris are beginning to question the double standard of masculinity that has pushed boys and men to feel they must choose between being the kind of tough, competitive, unfeeling, uncommunicative man traditionally celebrated as "masculine" and being the kind of open, expressive, egalitarian man now heralded as ideal by much of contemporary society.

Boys like Chris show us that, yes, boys can have some or all of these qualities without having to choose between them arbitrarily, that there is a way for boys to be at once tough and gentle, vulnerable and courageous, dependent and independent. Like Chris, they can handle some tough situations on their own, but decide to lean on their peers without being shamed.

Like him, they can play a rugged sport like football and yet steer clear of unnecessary physical fighting. Perhaps at last we're beginning to cherish all the emotions and qualities that boys naturally have inside themselves. Love, fear, empathy, guilt, anger, sadness, bravado, loyalty, courage—all of these are normal, healthy parts of the real boy.

It seems we're getting ready for a second gender revolution. The boys we've met in this book all seem to be telling us, some directly and some more subtly, "I want out of the old Boy Code," "I'm sick of hiding important parts of who I really am," and "I want to be able to be myself."

Today it would be virtually unheard of to require a girl to stick to old rules about being a "good little girl," refrain from showing qualities historically celebrated as "masculine," such as assertiveness or independence, or restrict herself to expressing only half of the person she genuinely is. I believe that boys like Chris are finally catching on that, in a very similar way, it's simply no longer acceptable for boys to have to follow the old Boy Code rules, stuff away feelings and behaviors once labeled "feminine," and suppress half of themselves to avoid being shamed.

I hear boys telling us "Enough already" and "Let's move on." Boys seem eager to unite their private and public selves, to feel proud of who they really are, to be freed of the shackles of shame that have held them back for centuries.

Chris teaches us that boys do care; they do love; they do nourish; they can be tough; they do flex their muscles; and, they greatly value their friendships. Boys like Chris are helping us to codify a new set of rules for boys and men, a code for the Real Boy. Here at last will be a set of rules, much like those we've been striving to enforce for girls and women, that say "Every door is open to you," "There's not just one right way of doing things," and "You are good just the way you are."

I believe the time has come for us to allow boys to craft this new, far more flexible code of manhood. As we've seen, boys are not biologically wired to act in just one "boylike" way; they are not mean-spirited, violent, or "toxic"; there is not one single way of acting or being that is more "masculine" than the next; boys are simply not the stoic, self-confident loners of procrustean myths.

As tough, cool, independent as they may sometimes seem, boys yearn desperately for friendships and relationships. Despite the bragging and bravado, boys like Chris, just like most girls and women, may feel devastated when these friendships or relationships suffer or fail. They too can become sad, frightened, and lonely, suffer low-self-esteem, and tumble toward serious depression.

And as we've seen, boys may actually become traumatized if emotionally they're pushed away from their closest loved ones before they're truly ready. In spite of all of society's messages to the contrary, parents cannot love their boys too much or somehow spoil them with too much caring or affection. In fact, boys with parents who remain emotionally connected to them do better in school, are more healthy psychologically, and, when they become adults, achieve greater success in their careers and relationships.

Unless they are conditioned not to be, boys are eminently loving and caring human beings. Like Chris, today's real boy sincerely wants to help others. He's sensitive to what other people feel and he does not want to hurt them. He takes action not only because he knows that it's right or just, but because he feels genuine empathy. But as we've seen, if this empathy is to stay alive, a boy must feel that others will reciprocate. If we withhold our love and affection, our boy feels ashamed and then hardens himself. If we don't stay active in his emotional life and listen to his feelings well, he comes to believe that his emotions are not welcomed. In sum, if we don't give him our empathy, he won't give empathy to us.

Real boys need people to be with who allow them to show *all* of their emotions, including their most intense feelings of sadness, disappointment, and fear. Real boys need to hear that these feelings are normal, good, and "masculine." They need to know that there really isn't any feeling, activity, or behavior that is forbidden to them as boys (other than those that could end up seriously hurting them or somebody else). They need to be taught connection rather than disconnection. They need to treated with the same kind of caring and affection we hope they'll be able to express when they become men in the next century. They need to be convinced, above all, that both their strengths and their vulnerabilities are good, that all sides of them will be celebrated, that we'll love them through and through for being just the boys they really are.

SOURCES

Much of the material found in each chapter comes from the "Listening to Boys' Voices" study and other related research by the author. Other sources for each chapter are listed below.

INTRODUCTION

Betcher, R. W., and Pollack, W. S. (1993). *In a Time of Fallen Heroes: The Re-Creation of Masculinity.* New York: Atheneum.

Brown, L. M., and Gilligan, C. (1992). *Meeting at the Crossroads: Women's Psychology and Girls' Development.* New York: Ballantine Books.

Gilligan, C. (1982). *In a Different Voice.* Cambridge: Harvard University Press.

Jordan, J. (ed.) (1997). *Women's Growth in Diversity.* New York: Guilford Press.

Jordan, J. V., Kaplan, A. G., Baker Miller, J., Stiver, I. P., and Surrey, J. L. (1991). *Women's Growth in Connection.* New York: Guilford Press.

Pipher, M. (1994). *Reviving Ophelia.* New York: Grosset/Putnam.

Pollack, W. S. (1996). "Becoming Whole and Good: A New Psychology of Men." International Coalition/Boys' Schools Symposium, June.

———— (1996). "Boys' Voices: Can We Listen, Can We Respond? Toward an Empathic Empirical Agenda." International Coalition/Boys' Schools Symposium, June.

PART ONE. REAL BOYS

CHAPTER 1

Brody, L. R. (1993). "On Understanding Gender Differences in the Expression of Emotion." In S. Ablon, D. Brown, J. Mack, and E. Khantazian (eds.), *Human Feelings: Explorations in Affect Development and Meaning* (pp. 87–121). Hillsdale, N.J.: Analytic Press.

———— (1996). "Gender, Emotional Expression and the Family." In R. Kavanaugh, B. Zimmerberg-Glick, and S. Fein (eds.), *Emotion: Interdisciplinary Perspectives.* Hillsdale, N.J.: Lawrence Erlbaum.

————, and Hall, J. (1993). "Gender and Emotion." In M. Lewis and J. M. Haviland (eds.), *Handbook of Emotions.* New York: Guilford Press.

Brown, L. M., and Gilligan, C. (1992). *Meeting at the Crossroads: Women's Psychology and Girls' Development.* New York: Ballantine Books.

Bushweller, K. (1994). Turning Our Backs on Boys. *The American School Board Journal, 181,* 20–25.

Gilligan, C. (1982). *In a Different Voice.* Cambridge: Harvard University Press.

Jordan, J. V., Kaplan, A. G., Baker Miller, J., Stiver, I. P., and Surrey, J. L. (1991). *Women's Growth in Connection.* New York: Guilford Press.

Miller, J. B. (1976). *Toward a New Psychology of Women.* Boston: Beacon Press.

———, and Stiver, I. P. (1997). *The Healing Connection.* Boston: Beacon Press.

Pipher, M. (1994). *Reviving Ophelia.* New York: Grosset/Putnam.

Pollack, W. S. (1982). " 'I'ness and 'We'ness: Parallel Lines of Development." (Ph.D. dissertation, Boston University). University Microfilms International, 82-13517.

——— (1992). "Boys Will Be Boys: Developmental Traumas of Masculinity—Psychoanalytic Perspectives." Paper presented as part of a symposium "Toward a New Psychology of Men" at the Centennial Meeting of the American Psychological Association, Washington.

——— (1995). "No Man Is an Island: Toward a New Psychoanalytic Psychology of Men." In R. Levant, and W. S. Pollack (eds.), *A New Psychology of Men* (pp. 33–67). New York: Basic Books.

——— (1995). "Becoming Whole and Good: A New Psychology of Men." International Coalition/Boys' Schools Symposium, June.

——— (1996). "Boys' Voices: Can We Listen, Can We Respond? Toward an Empathic Empirical Agenda." International Coalition/Boys' Schools Symposium, June.

Ravitch, D. (1994). "Blackboard Bungle." *Men's Health,* October, 110.

Rotundo, E. A. (1993). *American Manhood: Transformations in Masculinity from the Revolution to the Modern Era.* New York: Basic Books.

CHAPTER 2

Barkley, R. A. (1995). *Taking Charge of ADHD.* New York: Guilford Press.

Brody, L. R. (1993). "On Understanding Gender Differences in the Expression of Emotion." In S. Ablon, D. Brown, J. Mack, and E. Khantazian (eds.), *Human Feelings: Explorations in Affect Development and Meaning* (pp. 87–121). Hillsdale, N.J.: Analytic Press.

——— (1996). "Gender, Emotional Expression and the Family." In R. Kavanaugh, B. Zimmerberg-Glick, and S. Fein (eds.), *Emotion: Interdisciplinary Perspectives.* Hillsdale, N.J.: Lawrence Erlbaum.

———, and Hall, J. (1993). "Gender and Emotion." In M. Lewis and J. M. Haviland (eds.), *Handbook of Emotions.* New York: Guilford Press.

Chodorow, N. (1978). *The Reproduction of Mothering.* Berkeley: University of California Press.

——— (1989). *Feminism and Psychoanalytic Theory.* New Haven: Yale University Press.

David, D., and Brannon, R. (eds.) (1976). *The Forty-nine Percent Majority: The Male Sex Role.* Reading, Mass.: Addison-Wesley.

Fivush, R. (1989). "Exploring Sex Differences in the Emotional Content of Mother-Child Conversations about the Past." *Sex Roles, 20,* 675–91.

Greif, E., Alvarez, M., and Ulman, K. (1981, April). "Recognizing Emotions in Other People: Sex Differences in Socialization." Paper presented at the biennial meeting of the Society for Research in Child Development, Boston.

Jordan, J. (1984). *Empathy and Self-Boundaries* (Stone Center Working Paper Series, Work in Progress No. 16). Wellesley, Mass.: Wellesley College, Stone Center.

———— (1989). *Relational Development: Therapeutic Implications of Empathy and Shame.* (Stone Center Working Paper Series, Work in Progress No. 39). Wellesley, Mass.: Wellesley College, Stone Center.

Koch, J. (1997). "The Interview: Sam Gash." *Boston Sunday Globe Magazine,* August 24, 16.

Krugman, S. (1991). "Male Vulnerability and the Transformation of Shame." In W. S. Pollack, chair, "On Men: Redefining Roles." The Cambridge Series, The Cambridge Hospital, Harvard Medical School, Cambridge.

Malatesta, C. Z., and Haviland, J. M. (1982). "Learning Display Rules: The Socialization of Emotion Expression in Infancy." *Child Development, 53,* 991–1003.

————, Culver, C., Tesman, J., et al. (1989). *The Development of Emotion Expression During the First Two Years of Life.* Monographs of the Society for Research in Child Development, *50*(1–2, Serial No. 219).

Morrison, A. (1989). *Shame: The Underside of Narcissism.* Hillsdale, N.J.: Analytic Press.

Osherson, S., and Krugman, S. (1990). "Men, Shame and Psychotherapy." *Psychotherapy, 27,* 327–39.

Pollack, W. S. (1995). "No Man Is an Island: Toward a New Psychoanalytic Psychology of Men." In R. Levant, and W. S. Pollack (eds.), *A New Psychology of Men,* (pp. 33–67). New York: Basic Books.

———— (1995). "Deconstructing Dis-identification: Rethinking Psychoanalytic Concepts of Male Development." *Psychoanalysis and Psychotherapy, 12(1),* 30–45.

USA Today Poll. (1997). "Children's time spent with family." *USA Today.*

CHAPTER 3

Blum, D. (1996). Boys May Be More Emotionally Fragile. *Sacramento Bee,* June 10.

———— (1997). *Sex on the Brain.* New York: Viking.

Fausto-Sterling, A. (1992). *Myths of Gender.* New York: Basic Books.

Halpern, D. F. (1997). Sex Differences in Intelligence: Implications for Education. *American Psychologist, 52(10),* 1091–1102.

Kimura, D. (1992). Sex Differences in the Brain. *Scientific American,* September, 119–25.

Pleck, J. (1981). *The Myth of Masculinity.* Cambridge, Mass.: MIT Press.

Pollack, W. S. (1995). "Reframing Masculinity: Men, Empathy, and Empathy for Men." Paper presented at the Cambridge Symposium, Cambridge, Mass. Winter.

——— (1995). "Men's Erotic Desires: Love, Lust, Trauma, Sex, Biology, and Psychoanalysis." Paper presented at the 103rd annual convention of the American Psychological Association, New York, August.

CHAPTER 4

Gilligan, C. (1982). *In a Different Voice.* Cambridge: Harvard University Press.

Jacklin, C. N. (1989). Female and Male: Issues of Gender. *American Psychologist, 44,* 127–33.

Maccoby, E. (1990). Gender and Relationships: A Developmental Account. *American Psychologist, 45,* 513–20.

———, and Jacklin, G. N. (1974). *The Psychology of Sex Differences.* Stanford: Stanford University Press.

———, and Jacklin, G. N. (1980). Sex Differences in Aggression: A Rejoinder and Reprise. *Child Development, 51,* 964–80.

Pollack, W. S. (1996). "Becoming Whole and Good: A New Psychology of Men." International Coalition/Boys' Schools Symposium, June.

——— (1996). "Boys' Voices: Can We Listen, Can We Respond? Toward an Empathic Empirical Agenda." International Coalition/Boys' Schools Symposium, June.

PART TWO. CONNECTING TO BOYS

CHAPTER 5

Barnett, R. C., and Marshall, N. (1991). "Physical Symptoms and the Interplay of Work and Family Roles." *Health Psychology, 10,* 94–101.

———, Marshall, N. L., and Pleck, J. H. (1992). "Men's Multiple Roles and Their Relationship to Men's Psychological Distress." *Journal of Marriage and the Family, 54,* 358–67.

———, and Rivers, C. (1996). *She Works, He Works.* New York: HarperCollins.

Betcher, R. W., and Pollack, W. S. (1993). *In a Time of Fallen Heroes: The Re-Creation of Masculinity.* New York: Atheneum.

Grossman, F., and Pollack, W. (1984). "Good Enough Fathering." Paper presented at the annual meeting of the National Council on Family Relations, San Francisco, October.

———, Pollack, W. S., Golding, E. R., and Fedele, N. M. (1987). "Autonomy and Affiliation in the Transition to Parenthood." *Family Relations, 36,* 263–69.

Herzog, J. (1982). "On Father Hunger: The Father's Role in the Modulation of Aggressive Drive and Fantasy." In S. Cath, A. Gurwitt, and J. Ross (eds.), *Father and Child* (pp. 163–74). Boston: Little, Brown.

Jordan, J. V., Kaplan, A. G., Baker Miller, J., Stiver, I. P., and Surrey, J. L. (1991). *Women's Growth in Connection.* New York: Guilford Press.

Miller, J. B., and Stiver, I. P. (1997). *The Healing Connection.* Boston: Beacon Press.

Pollack, W. S. (1995). Deconstructing Dis-identification: Rethinking Psychoana-lytic Concepts of Male Development. *Psychoanalysis and Psychotherapy, 12(1)*, 30–45.

————, and Jordan, J. V. (1997). "Breaking 'The Rules' for Men and Women: Generating Genuine Empathy." Paper presented at the Symposium: "Break-ing 'The Rules'—New Models of Male-Female Relationships" at the 105th annual convention of the American Psychological Association, Chicago.

Weingarten, K. (1994). *The Mother's Voice: Strengthening Intimacy in Families.* New York: Harcourt and Brace.

CHAPTER 6

Adler, J. (1996). "Building a Better Dad." *Newsweek,* June 17, 58–64.

Barnett, R. C., and Marshall, N. (1991). "Physical Symptoms and the Interplay of Work and Family Roles." *Health Psychology, 10,* 94–101.

————, Marshall, N. L., and Pleck, J. H. (1992). "Men's Multiple Roles and Their Relationship to Men's Psychological Distress." *Journal of Marriage and the Family, 54,* 358–67.

————, and Rivers, C. (1996). *She Works, He Works.* New York: Harper-Collins.

Bernadett-Shapiro, S., Ehrensaft, D., and Shapiro, J. L. (1996). "Father Participa-tion in Childcare and the Development of Empathy in Sons: An Empirical Study." *Family Therapy, 23(2),* 77–93.

Betcher, R. W., and Pollack, W. S. (1993). *In a Time of Fallen Heroes: The Re-Creation of Masculinity.* New York: Atheneum.

Blankenhorn, D. (1995). *Fatherless America.* New York: Basic Books.

Brody, L. R. (1996). "Gender, Emotional Expression and the Family." In R. Kavanaugh, B. Zimmerberg-Glick, and S. Fein (eds.), *Emotion: Interdisci-plinary Perspectives.* Hillsdale, N.J.: Lawrence Erlbaum.

Buck, R. (1977). "Non-verbal Communication of Affect in Pre-school Children: Relationships with Personality and Skin Conductance." *Journal of Personal-ity and Social Psychology, 35,* 225–36.

Cath, S., Gurwitt, A., and Ross, J. (eds) (1982). *Father and Child.* Boston: Little, Brown.

D'Angelo, L. L., Weinberger, D. A., and Feldman, S. S. (1995). "Like Father, Like Son? Predicting Male-Adolescents' Adjustment from Parents' Distress and Self-restraint." *Developmental Psychology, 31(6),* 883–96.

DeLuccie, M. F. (1995). "Mothers as Gatekeepers: A Model of Maternal Mediators of Father Involvement." *Journal of Genetic Psychology, 156(1),* 115–31.

Dorsey, S. A. (1995). "Father Figures." *Boston Globe.* June 19, 21.

Elias, M. (1996). Teens Do Better When Dads Are More Involved. *USA Today,* August 22, D1.

Fox, E. (ed.) (1993). *The Five Books of Moses.* New York: Schocken Books.

Grossman, F., and Pollack, W. (1984, October). *Good Enough Fathering.* Paper presented at the annual meeting of the National Council on Family Relations, San Francisco.

———, and Golding, E. (1988). "Fathers and Children: Predicting the Quality and Quantity of Fathering." *Developmental Psychology, 24,* 82–91.

———, and Fedele, N. M. (1987). "Autonomy and Affiliation in the Transition to Parenthood." *Family Relations, 36,* 263–69.

Herzog, J. (1982). "On Father Hunger: The Father's Role in the Modulation of Aggressive Drive and Fantasy." In S. Cath, A. Gurwitt, and J. Ross (eds.), *Father and Child* (pp. 163–74). Boston: Little, Brown.

Homer (1963). *The Odyssey.* Trans. by Robert Fitzgerald. New York: Anchor.

Jain, A., Belsky, J., and Crnic, K. (1996). "Beyond Fathering Behaviors: Types of Dads." *Journal of Family Psychology, 10(4),* 431–42.

Lamb, M. (1975). "Fathers: Forgotten Contributors to Child Development." *Human Development, 18,* 245–66.

——— (1977). "The Development of Parental Preferences in the First Two Years of Life." *Sex Roles, 3,* 475–97.

——— (1981). *The Role of the Father in Child Development.* New York: Wiley.

———, and Oppenheim, D. (1989). Fatherhood and Father-Child Relationships. In S. Cath, A. Gurwitt, and L. Gunsberg (eds.), *Fathers and Their Families* (pp. 11–16). Hillsdale, N.J.: Analytic Press.

Levant, R. F. (1992). "Toward the Reconstruction of Masculinity." *Journal of Family Psychology, 5,* 379–402.

McGaw, J. (1997). "Doing It Their Way." *The Boston Parents' Paper,* June, 28–31.

Negri, G. (1995). "When Dad's in the Lunch Bunch." *Boston Globe,* March 31, 33.

Osherson, S. (1986). *Finding Our Fathers: The Unfinished Business of Manhood.* New York: Free Press.

Pollack, W. S. (1991). "Managers as Fathers." *The Levison Letter.*

——— (1995). "A Delicate Balance: Fatherhood and Psychological Transformation—A Psychoanalytic Perspective. In J. L. Shapiro, M. J. Diamond, and M. Greenberg (eds.), *Becoming a Father: Social, Emotional and Clinical Perspectives.* New York: Springer.

———, and Grossman, F. K. (1985). "Parent-Child Interaction." In L. L'Labate (ed.), *The Handbook of Family Psychology and Therapy* (pp. 586–622). Homewood, Ill.: Dorsey.

Pruett, K. D. (1987). *The Nurturing Father.* New York: Warner Books.

——— (1989). "The Nurturing Male: A Longitudinal Study of Primary Nurturing Fathers." In S. H. Cath, A. Gurwitt, and L. Gunsberg (eds.), *Fathers and Their Families* (pp. 389–405). Hillsdale, N.J.: Analytic Press.

Roberts, P., and Mosley, B. (1996). "Fathers' Time." *Psychology Today,* May/June, 48–55.

Segell, M. (1995). "The Pater Principle." *Esquire,* March, 121–27.

Shapiro, J. L., Diamond, M. J., and Greenberg, M. (eds.) (1995). *Becoming a Father: Social, Emotional, and Clinical Perspectives.* New York: Springer.

Shellenbarger, S. (1996). Work and Family: High-powered Fathers Savor Their Decisions to Scale Back Careers. *The Wall Street Journal,* June 12.

Snarey, J. (1993). *How Fathers Care for the Next Generation: A Four-decade Study.* Cambridge: Harvard University Press.

CHAPTER 7

Coopersmith, S. (1981). *Self-Esteem Inventories (School Form).* Palo Alto, Calif.: Consulting Psychologist Press.

DeAngelis, T. (1996). "Young Girls Engage in Some Sexually Inappropriate Behavior as Often as Boys." *APA Monitor,* October. American Psychological Association.

Elias, M. (1997). "Family Dinners Nourish Ties with Teen-agers." *The Wall Street Journal,* August 15.

Erikson, E. (1959). "Identity and the Life Cycle." *Psychological Issues, 1.* New York: International Universities Press.

——— (1963). *Childhood and Society.* New York: W.W. Norton.

Feldman, S. S., and Wentzel, K. R. (1995). "Relations of Marital Satisfaction to Peer Outcomes in Adolescent Boys: A Longitudinal Study." *Journal of Early Adolescence, 15*(2), 220–37.

Gant, L. M., et al. (1994). "Increasing Responsible Sexual Behavior among High-risk African-American Adolescent Males: Results of a Brief, Intensive Intervention." *Journal of Multicultural Social Work, 3*(3), 49–58.

Guttmacher Institute. (1994). *Sex and American Teenagers.* Alan Guttmacher Institute: New York.

——— (1996). *Readings on Men.* New York: Alan Guttmacher Institute.

——— (1997). *Facts in Brief: Teen Sex and Pregnancy.* New York: Alan Guttmacher Institute.

Hales, D. (1996). "How Teenagers See Things." *Parade Magazine,* August 18.

Jordan, J. (1987). "Clarity in Connection: Empathic Knowing, Desire and Sexuality." (Stone Center Working Paper Series, Work in Progress No. 29). Wellesley, Mass.: Wellesley College, Stone Center.

King, L. A., and King, D. W. (1993). *Sex-Role Egalitarianism Scale (SRES).* Port Huron, Mich.: Sigma Assessment Systems.

Kutner, L. (1993). "Heroes Offer Ways to Explore Feelings and Situations." *The New York Times,* December 23.

Lewin, T. (1997). "Teen-agers Alter Sexual Practices, Thinking Risks Will Be Avoided." *The New York Times,* April 5.

Madaras, L., and Madaras, A. (1995). *My Body, My Self for Boys.* New York: Newmarket Press.

Manning, A. (1997). "Teens Starting Substance Abuse at Younger Ages." *USA Today,* August 14, 8D.

Murray, B. (1996). "Debates Over Sex Education May Put Teen Health at Risk." *APA Monitor, November.* American Psychological Association.

Nottelmann, E. D. (1987). "Competence and Self-Esteem during Transition from Childhood to Adolescence." *Developmental Psychology, 23*(3), 441–50.

Pleck, J. H., Sonenstein, F. L., and Ku, L. C. (1993). "Masculinity Ideology: Its Impact on Adolescent Males' Heterosexual Relationships." *Journal of Social Issues, 49(3),* 11–29.

———— (1994). "Social-Psychological Influences on Condom Use." (Center for Research on Women Working Papers Series, Work in Progress No. 273). Wellesley, Mass.: Wellesley College.

Pollak, S., and Gilligan, C. (1982). "Images of Violence in Thematic Apperception Test Stories." *Journal of Personality and Social Psychology, 42(1),* 159–67.

Resnick, M. D., Bearman, P. S., Blum, R. W., et al. (1997). "Protecting Adolescents from Harm: Findings from the National Longitudinal Study on Adolescent Health," *Journal of the American Medical Association, 278(10),* 823–32.

Shapiro, L. (1997). "The Myth of Quality Time." *Newsweek,* May 12, pp. 62–69.

Steinhauer, J. (1995). "At a Clinic, Young Men Talk of Sex." *The New York Times,* September 6.

CHAPTER 8

Bednall, J. (1996). *Bi-linguality of Gender in Single Sex Schools for Boys.* Huntington Valley, Ohio: University School Press.

Gilligan, C. (1982). *In a Different Voice.* Cambridge: Harvard University Press.

Jones, D. C., and Costin, S. E. (1995). "Friendship's Quality During Preadolescence and Adolescence: The Contributions of Relationships Orientations, Instrumentality, and Expressivity." *Merrill-Palmer Quarterly, 41(4),* 517–535.

Levant, R. F. (1992). "Toward the Reconstruction of Masculinity." *Journal of Family Psychology, 5,* 379–402.

Lever, J. H. (1976). "Sex Differences in the Games Children Play." *Social Work, 23,* 78–87.

Maccoby, E. (1990). "Gender and Relationships: A Developmental Account." *American Psychologist, 45,* 513–20.

————, and Jacklin, G. N. (1974). *The Psychology of Sex Differences.* Stanford: Stanford University Press.

———— (1980). "Sex Differences in Aggression: A Rejoinder and Reprise." *Child Development, 51,* 964–80.

McIntosh, H. (1996). "Research on Teen-age Friendships Dispels Old Myths." *APA Monitor,* June. American Psychological Association. Washington, D.C.

———— (1996). "Adolescent Friends Not Always a Bad Influence." *APA Monitor,* June. American Psychological Association. Washington, D.C.

Pollack, W. S. (1995). "No Man Is an Island: Toward a New Psychoanalytic Psychology of Men." In R. Levant and W. S. Pollack (eds.), *A New Psychology of Men,* (pp. 33–67). New York: Basic Books.

————, and Jordan, J. V. (1997). "Breaking 'The Rules' for Men and Women: Generating Genuine Empathy." Paper presented at the Symposium "Breaking 'The Rules'—New Models of Male-Female Relationships" at the 105th Annual Convention of the American Psychological Association, Chicago, Ill.

Swain, S. (1989). "Covert Intimacy: Closeness in Men's Friendships." In B. J. Risman and P. Schwartz (eds.), *Gender in Intimate Relationships: A Microstructural Approach* (pp. 70–93). Belmont, Calif.: Wadsworth Publishing.

Tannen, D. (1990). *You Just Don't Understand.* New York: William Morrow.

Thorne, A., and Michaelieu, Q. (1996). "Situating Adolescent Gender and Self-esteem." *Child Development, 67,* 1374–90.

Zachary, G. P. (1997). "Male Order: Boys Used to Be Boys, But Do Some Now See Boyhood as a Malady?" *The Wall Street Journal,* May 2, A1.

CHAPTER 9

American Psychiatric Association (1994). *The Diagnostic and Statistical Manual IV.* Washington, D.C.: American Psychiatric Association.

Center for Disease Control and Prevention (1997). *Statistics on AIDS.* Washington, D.C.: U.S. Department of Health and Human Services.

The Committee on Adolescence (1993). "Homosexuality and Adolescence." *Pediatrics, 92(4),* 631–34.

Friedman, C., and Downey, J. (1993). "Psychoanalysis, Psychobiology, and Homosexuality." *Journal of American Psychoanalytic Association, 41(4),* 1159–98.

———, and Downey, J. (1994). "Homosexuality." *The New England Journal of Medicine, 331(14),* 923–30.

Gray, S. (1997). "Not Content with the Closet." *Boston Globe,* August 23, B1.

Isay, R. A. (1989). *Being Homosexual: Gay Men and Their Development.* New York: Farrar, Straus & Giroux.

Kallman, F. J. (1953). *Heredity in Health and Mental Disorder: Principles of Psychiatric Genetics in the Light of Comparative Twin Studies.* New York: Norton.

Schwartzberg, S., and Rosenberg, L. G. (in press). "Treating Gay and Bisexual Men." In W. S. Pollack and R. L. Levant (eds.), *New Psychotherapy for Men.* New York: Wiley.

Slater, B. R. (1988). "Essential Issues in Working with Lesbian and Gay Male Youths." *Professional Psychology: Research and Practice, 19(2),* 226–35.

CHAPTER 10

Bednall, J. (1996). *Bi-linguality of Gender in Single Sex Schools for Boys.* Huntington Valley, Oh.: University School Press.

Bushweller, K. (1994). "Turning Our Backs on Boys." *The American School Board Journal, 181,* 20–25.

Cohen, L. (1997). "Hunters and Gatherers in the Classroom." *Independent School Magazine, Fall, 57(1),* 28–36. National Association of Independent Schools.

Crossen, C. (1997). "Mind Field." *The Wall Street Journal,* June 5.

deGroot, G. (1994). "Do Single-Sex Classes Foster Better Learning? *American Psychological Association Monitor, July,* 60–61.

ERIC/AE Digest Series EDO-TM-96-01 (1996). Multiple Intelligences: Gardner's Theory.

Finger, J. P. K. (1995). "A Study of Professed and Inferred Self-Concept-as-Learner of African-American and Caucasian Middle Grade Students." The University of North Carolina at Greensboro. Unpublished dissertation.

Halpern, D. F. (1997). "Sex Differences in Intelligence: Implications for Education." *American Psychologist, 52(10),* 1091–1102.

Harper, K. L., Purkey, W. W. (1993). "Research in Middle Level Education." *National Middle School Association, 17(1),* 79–89.

Hawley, R. A. (1991). "About Boys' Schools: A Progressive Case for an Ancient Form." *Teachers College Record, 92(3),* 433–44.

———— (1998). Personal communication. University School, Chargrin Falls, Oh.

Hedges, L. V. and Nowell, A. (1995). "Sex Differences in Mental Test Scores, Variability, and Numbers of High-Scoring Individuals." *Science, 269,* 41–45.

Hulse, D. J. (1997). *Brad and Cory: A Study of Middle School Boys.* Huntington Valley, Ohio: University School Press.

Jordan, E. (1995, March). "Fighting Boys and Fantasy Play: The Construction of Masculinity in the Early Years of School." *Gender and Education, 7(1),* 69–86.

Melvoin, R. I. (1998). *Beyond Politics: Boys, Biology, Values and Character.* Huntington Valley, Oh.: University School Press.

"Men: Tomorrow's Second Sex." *Economist,* September 28, 1996, pp. 23–26.

Pollack, W. S. (1995). "Becoming Whole and Good: A New Psychology of Men." International Coalition/Boys' Schools Symposium, June.

———— (1996). "Boys' Voices: Can We Listen, Can We Respond? Toward an Empathic Empirical Agenda." International Coalition/Boys' Schools Symposium, June.

Pottorff, D. D., Phelps-Zientarski, D., and Skovera, M. E. (1996). "Gender Perceptions of Elementary and Middle School Students about Literacy at School and Home." *Journal of Research and Development in Education, 29(4),* 203–11.

Ravitch, D. (1994). "The War on Boys." *Men's Health,* October, 110.

Riley, R. W. (1994). Notes of Secretary Richard W. Riley during release of the 1992 National Assessment of Educational Progress Trend Report, August 17.

———— (1997). Testimony of Secretary Richard W. Riley before the Senate Labor, Health and Human Services and Education Subcommittee of the Senate Appropriations Committee, September 4.

Zachary, G. P. (1997). "Male Order: Boys Used to Be Boys, But Do Some Now See Boyhood as a Malady?" *The Wall Street Journal,* May 2, A1.

CHAPTER 11

Betcher, R. W., and Pollack, W. S. (1993), *In a Time of Fallen Heroes: The Re-Creation of Masculinity.* New York: Atheneum.

Carlat, D. J., Camargo, C. A., and Herzog, D. B. (1997). "Eating Disorders in Males: A Report on 135 Patients." *American Journal of Psychiatry, 154(8)*, 1127–32.

Giamatti, A. B. (1989). *Take Time for Paradise.* New York: Summit.

Harris, M. (1956). *Bang the Drum Slowly.* Lincoln: University of Nebraska Press.

Isenberg, P. (1980). "An Essay." *Harvard Magazine,* November–December, 6–10.

Miedzian, M. (1991). *Boys Will Be Boys: Breaking the Link between Masculinity and Violence.* New York: Anchor Books.

Pindar (1974). *Pindar's Odes.* Trans. by Arthur Swanson. New York: Bobbs-Merrill.

Pollack, W. S. (1996). *Boys at Play: Sports and Transformation.* Hunting Valley, Ohio: University School Press.

Winnicott, D. W. (1974). *The Maturational Process and the Facilitating Environment.* New York: International Universities Press.

PART THREE. WHEN THE BOUGH BREAKS

CHAPTER 12

American Psychiatric Association (1994). *The Diagnostic and Statistical Manual IV.* Washington, D.C.: American Psychiatric Association.

Angst, J., and Dobler-Mikola, A. (1984). "Do the Diagnostic Criteria Determine the Sex Ratio in Depression?" *Journal of Affective Disorders, 7,* 189–98.

Brooks-Gunn, J., and Petersen, A. C. (1991). "Studying the Emergence of Depression and Depressive Symptoms During Adolescence." *Journal of Youth and Adolescence, 20(2),* 115–19.

Centers for Disease Control. (1985). *Suicide Surveillance, 1970–1980.* Washington, D.C.: U.S. Department of Health and Human Services.

——— (1995). *Suicide in the United States, 1980–1992.* Washington, D.C.: U.S. Department of Health and Human Services.

——— (1997). *Suicide Death and Rates per Hundred Thousand, United States, 1989–1995.* Washington, D.C.: U.S. Department of Health and Human Services.

Compas, B. E., and Hammen, C. L. (1994). "Child and Adolescent Depression: Covariation and Comorbidity in Development." In R. J. Haggerty, L. R. Sherrod, N. Garmezy, and M. Rutter (eds.), *Stress, Risk and Resilience in Children and Adolescents,* (pp. 225–67). New York: Cambridge University Press.

Girgus, J., Nolen-Hocksema, S., and Seligman, M. E. (1989). "Why Do Sex Differences in Depression Emerge During Adolescence?" Paper presented at the annual meeting of the American Psychological Association, New Orleans, August.

Gross, J. (1997). "Among Nine Friends, Too Many Funerals and Too Many Scars." *The New York Times,* July 31, B1.

Hochman, G. (1995). "Is Your Child Moody or Depressed?" *Child Magazine,* February, 58–61.

Kandel, D. B., and Davies, N. (1986). "Adult Sequelae of Adolescent Depressive Symptoms." *Archives of General Psychiatry, 43*(*3*), 255–62.

Mannuzza, S., Klein, R., Bessler, A., Malloy, P., and Hynes, N. (1997). "Educational and Occupational Outcome of Hyperactive Boys Grown-Up." *Journal of the American Academy of Child and Adolescent Psychiatry, 36*(*9*), 1222–27.

Marttunen, M. J., Henriksson, M. M., Aro, H. M., Heikkinene, M. E., et al. (1995). "Suicide among Female Adolescents: Characteristics and Comparison with Males in the Age Group 13 to 22 Years." *Journal of the American Academy of Child and Adolescent Psychiatry, 34*(*10*), 1297–1307.

McIntosh, J. L. (1996). "Suicide Rate Data 1994." *Fact Sheet: American Association of Suicidology,* Washington, D.C.

Mitchell, J., and Farley, C. (1990). "Isolation and Restraint in Juvenile Correctional Facilities." *Journal of the American Academy of Child and Adolescent Psychiatry, 29*(*2*), 251–55.

National Center for Health Statistics (1996). *Report of Mortality Statistics.*

Nolen-Hocksema, S. (1990). *Sex Differences in Depression.* Stanford: Stanford University Press.

——— (1995). "Gender Differences in Coping with Depression Across the Lifespan." *Depression, 3,* 81–90.

———, and Girgus, J. S. (1994). "The Emergence of Gender Differences in Depression During Adolescence." *Psychological Bulletin, 115*(*3*), 424–43.

———, Girgus, J. S., and Seligman, M. E. P. (1991). "Sex Differences in Depression and Explanatory Style in Children." *Journal of Youth and Adolescence, 20*(*2*), 233–45.

——— Girgus, J. S., and Seligman, M. E. P. (1992). "Predictors and Consequences of Childhood Depressive Symptoms: A Five-Year Longitudinal Study." *Journal of Abnormal Psychology, 101*(*3*), 405–22.

Peterson, K. S. (1996). "Teens Unlikely to Talk about Depression." *USA Today,* August 7.

Pollack, W. S. (in press). "Mourning: Melancholia and Masculinity: Recognizing and Treating Depression in Men." In W. S. Pollack and R. L. Levant (eds.), *New Psychotherapy for Men.* New York: Wiley.

Potts, M. K., Burnam, M. A., and Wells, K. B. (1991). "Gender Differences in Depression Detection: A Comparison of Clinician Diagnosis and Standardized Assessment." *Psychological Assessment: A Journal of Consulting and Clinical Psychology, 3*(*4*), 609–15.

Public Health Service. (1956). "Death Rates by Age, Race and Sex, United States, 1900–1953: Suicide." *Vital Statistics Special Reports, 43*(*30*).

Resnick, M. D., Bearman, P. S., Blum, R. W., et al. (1997). "Protecting Adolescents from Harm: Findings from the National Longitudinal Study on Adolescent Health," *Journal of the American Medical Association, 278*(*10*), 823–32.

Rohde, P., Seeley, J. R., and Mace, D. E. (1997). "Correlates of Suicide Behavior in a Juvenile Detention Population." *Suicide and Life-Threatening Behavior, 27*(*2*), 164–75.

Smucker, M. (1982). "The Children's Depression Inventory: Norms and Psycho-metric Analysis." Unpublished Ph.D. dissertation, Pennsylvania State University, University Park.

Tanouye, E. (1997). "Antidepressant Makers Study Kids' Market." *The Wall Street Journal,* April 4, B1.

CHAPTER 13

American Psychological Association. (1997). "What Makes Kids Care? Teaching Gentleness in a Violent World." Fact sheet.

Bower, B. (1997). "Navy Recruits Report Abusive Legacy." *Science News, 152,* 116.

Boyd, M. (1997). "Study Offers Insights into Why Boys Have More Injuries than Girls." University of Guelph, Canada. Fact sheet.

Canada, G. (1995). *Fist Stick Knife Gun: A Personal History of Violence in America.* Boston: Beacon Press.

Crick, N. R., and Casas, J. F. (1997). "Relational and Overt Aggression in Preschool." *Developmental Psychology, 33(4),* 579–88.

DeAngelis, T. (1996). "New Interventions Address Teen-age Behavior Problems." *American Psychological Association Monitor,* October.

Fishman, S. (1997). "Teenage Boys Teach in Parenting Program." *Boston Sunday Globe,* March 23, E16.

Friend, T. (1996). "Kick in Pants Exposes Boys to Groin Pains." *USA Today,* August 7.

Gewertz, K. (1996). "Voices Against Violence." *Harvard University Gazette,* May 2.

Gilligan, J. (1996). *Violence: Our Deadly Epidemic and Its Causes.* New York: Putnam.

Herbert, W., and Daniel, M. (1996). "The Moral Child." *U.S. News & World Report,* June 3, 52–59.

Koch, J. (1997). "The Interview: Sam Gash." *The Boston Sunday Globe Magazine,* August 24, p. 16.

McIntosh, J. L. (1996). *Suicide in the U.S.A.* American Association of Suicidality, Washington, D.C.

Miedzian, M. (1991). *Boys Will Be Boys: Breaking the Link between Masculinity and Violence.* New York: Anchor Books.

Miller, J. B. (1983). "The Construction of Anger in Women and Men" (Stone Center Working Paper Series, Work in Progress No. 4). Wellesley, Mass.: Wellesley College, Stone Center.

Murray, B. (1995). "Kids Learn Keys to Healthy Relationships." *American Psychological Association Monitor,* September.

Pollack, W. S. (1995). "Reframing Masculinity: Men, Empathy and Empathy for Men." Paper presented at the Cambridge Symposium, Cambridge, Mass., Winter.

Raine, A., Brennan, P., and Mednick, S. A. (1997). "Interaction between Birth Complications and Early Maternal Rejection in Predisposing Individuals to

Adult Violence: Specificity to Serious, Early-Onset Violence." *American Journal of Psychiatry,* 154, 1265–71.

Resnick, M. D., Bearman, P. S., Blum, R. W., et al. (1997). "Protecting Adolescents from Harm: Findings from the National Longitudinal Study on Adolescent Health." *Journal of the American Medical Association, 278(10),* 823–32.

Sells, C. W., and Blum, R. W. (1996). "Morbidity and Mortality among U.S. Adolescents: An Overview of Data and Trends." *American Journal of Public Health, 86(4),* 513–19.

Seppa, N. (1996). "Keeping Schoolyards Safe from Bullies." *American Psychological Association Monitor.*

Sleek, S. (1995). "APA Is Raising Money for Violence-Prevention Effort." *American Psychological Association Monitor,* October.

Thomas, P. (1997). "U.S. Crime Rate Falls Again in 1996." *Boston Globe.* June 2.

U.S. Department of Justice. (1994). *Violent Crime: National Crime Victimization Survey* (NCJ-147486).

——— (1997). *Males and Firearms Violence.*

——— (1997). *Victim Characteristics.*

CHAPTER 14

Allison, P. D., and Furstenberg, F. F. (1989, July). "How Marital Dissolution Affects Children: Variations by Age and Sex." *Developmental Psychology, 25(4),* 540–49.

Beaty, L. A. (1995). "Effects of Parental Absence on Male Adolescents' Peer Relations and Self-Image." *Adolescence, 30(120),* 873–80.

Beymer, L. (1995). *Meeting the Guidance and Counseling Needs of Boys.* Alexandria, Va.: American Counseling Association.

Bonkowski, S. E., Boomhower, S. J., and Bequette, S. Q. (1985). "What You Don't Know Can Hurt You: Unexpressed Fears and Feelings of Children from Divorcing Families." *Journal of Divorce, 9(1),* 33–45.

Burns, C. (1985). *Stepmotherhood.* New York: Times Books.

Fergusson, D. M., Horwood, L. J., and Lynskey, M. T. (1994, October). "Parental Separation, Adolescent Psychopathology, and Problem Behaviors." *Journal of the American Academy of Child and Adolescent Psychiatry, 33(8),* 1122–31.

Forehand, R., Neighbors, B., and Wierson, M. (1991). "The Transition of Adolescence: The Role of Gender and Stress in Problem Behavior and Competence." *Journal of Child Psychology and Psychiatry and Allied Disciplines, 32(6),* 929–37.

Guidubaldi, J., Cleminshaw, H. K., Perry, J. D., and McLoughlin, C. S. (1983). "The Impact of Parental Divorce on Children: Report of the Nationwide NASP Study." *School Psychology Review, 12(3),* 300–23. Kent State University.

Guidubaldi, J., and Perry, J. D. (1985, September). "Divorce and Mental Health Sequelae for Children: A Two-Year Follow-up of a Nationwide Sample." *Journal of the American Academy of Child Psychiatry, 24(5)*, 531–37.

Hetherington, E., Cox, M., and Cox, R. (1986). "Long-Term Effects of Divorce and Remarriage on the Adjustment of Children." *Annual Progress in Child Psychiatry and Child Development*, 407–29.

Hodges, W. F., and Bloom, B. L. (1984). "Parents' Report of Children's Adjustment to Marital Separation: A Longitudinal Study." *Journal of Divorce, 8(1)*, 33–50.

Kasen, S., Cohen, P., Brook, J. S., and Hartmark, C. (1996). "A Multiple-Risk Interaction Model: Effects of Temperament and Divorce on Psychiatric Disorders in Children." *Journal of Abnormal Child Psychology, 24(2)*, 121–50.

Kaye, S. H. (1988–89). "The Impact of Divorce on Children's Academic Performance." Special issue: Children of Divorce: Developmental and Clinical Issues. *Journal of Divorce, 12(2–3)*, 283–98.

Parke, R. D. (1981). *Father.* Cambridge: Harvard University Press.

Peretti, P. O., and di-Vitorrio, A. (1993). "Effect of Loss of Father through Divorce on Personality of the Preschool Child." *Social Behavior and Personality, 21(1)*, 33–38.

Reinhard, D. W. (1977). "The Reaction of Adolescent Boys and Girls to the Divorce of Their Parents." *Journal of Clinical Child Psychology, 6(2)*, 21–23.

Wallertsein, J. S., and Blakeslee, S. (1989). *Second Chances.* New York: Ticknor and Fields.

———, and Kelly, J. B. (1980). *Surviving the Break-up: How Children and Parents Cope with Divorce.* New York: Basic Books.

Whitehead, B. D. (1993, April). "Dan Quayle Was Right." *Atlantic Monthly, 271,* 47–84.

Zaslow, M. J. (1988, July). "Sex Differences in Children's Response to Parental Divorce: I. Research Methodology and Postdivorce Family Forms." *American Journal of Orthopsychiatry, 58(3)*, 355–78.

BIBLIOGRAPHY

Adler, J. (1996). "Building a Better Dad." *Newsweek,* June 17, 58–64.

Allison, P. D., and Furstenberg, F. F. (1989, July). "How Marital Dissolution Affects Children: Variations by Age and Sex." *Developmental Psychology, 25(4),* 540–49.

American Psychiatric Association. (1994). *The Diagnostic and Statistical Manual IV.* Washington, D.C.: American Psychiatric Association.

———— (1997). "What Makes Kids Care? Teaching Gentleness in a Violent World." Fact sheet.

Angst, J., and Dobler-Mikola, A. (1984). "Do the Diagnostic Criteria Determine the Sex Ratio in Depression?" *Journal of Affective Disorders, 7,* 189–98.

Barkley, R. A. (1995). *Taking Charge of ADHD.* New York: Guilford Press.

Barnett, R. C., and Marshall, N. (1991). "Physical Symptoms and the Interplay of Work and Family Roles." *Health Psychology, 10,* 94–101.

————, Marshall, N. L., and Pleck, J. H. (1992). "Men's Multiple Roles and Their Relationship to Men's Psychological Distress." *Journal of Marriage and the Family, 54,* 358–67.

————, and Rivers, C. (1996). *She Works, He Works.* New York: HarperCollins.

Beaty, L. A. (1995). Effects of Parental Absence on Male Adolescents' Peer Relations and Self-Image. *Adolescence, 30(120),* 873–80.

Bednall, J. (1996). *Bi-linguality of Gender in Single Sex Schools for Boys.* Huntington Valley, Oh.: University School Press.

Bergman, S. J., and Surrey, J. (1992). "The Woman-Man Relationship: Impasses and Possibilities." (Stone Center Working Paper Series, Work in Progress No. 55). Wellesley, MA: Wellesley College, Stone Center.

Bernadett-Shapiro, S., Ehrensaft, D., and Shapiro, J. L. (1996). "Father Participation in Childcare and the Development of Empathy in Sons: An Empirical Study." *Family Therapy,* 23(2), 77–93.

Betcher, R. W., and Pollack, W. S. (1993), *In a Time of Fallen Heroes: The Re-Creation of Masculinity.* New York: Atheneum.

Beymer, L. (1995). *Meeting the Guidance and Counseling Needs of Boys.* Alexandria, Va.: American Counseling Association.

Blankenhorn, D. (1995). *Fatherless America.* New York: Basic Books.

Blum, D. (1996). "Boys May Be More Emotionally Fragile." *Sacramento Bee,* June 10.

———— (1997). *Sex on the Brain.* New York: Viking.

Bly, R. (1986). *Selected Poems.* New York: Harper & Row.

———— (1990). *Iron John: A Book about Men.* Reading, Mass.: Addison-Wesley.

Bonkowski, S. E., Boomhower, S. J., and Bequette, S. Q. (1985). "What You Don't Know Can Hurt You: Unexpressed Fears and Feelings of Children from Divorcing Families." *Journal of Divorce, 9(1)*, 33–45.

Boszormenyi-Nagy, I., and Ulrich, D. N. (1981). "Contextual Family Therapy." In A. S. Gurman and D. P. Kniskern (eds.), *Handbook of Family Therapy*. New York: Brunner/Mazel.

Bower, B. (1997). "Navy Recruits Report Abusive Legacy." *Science News,* 152, 116.

Boyd, M. (1997). "Study Offers Insights into Why Boys Have More Injuries than Girls." University of Guelph Fact Sheet, Canada.

Brody, L. R. (1985). "Gender Differences in Emotional Development: A Review of Theories and Research." *Journal of Personality, 53,* 14–59.

——— (1996). "Gender, Emotional Expression and the Family." In R. Kavanaugh, B. Zimmerberg-Glick, and S. Fein (eds.), *Emotion: Interdisciplinary Perspectives*. Hillsdale, N.J.: Lawrence Erlbaum.

——— (1993). "On Understanding Gender Differences in the Expression of Emotion." In S. Ablon, D. Brown, J. Mack, and E. Khantazian (eds.), *Human Feelings: Explorations in Affect Development and Meaning* (pp. 87–121). Hillsdale, N.J.: Analytic Press.

———, and Hall, J. (1993). "Gender and Emotion." In M. Lewis and J. M. Haviland (eds.), *Handbook of Emotions*. New York: Guilford Press.

Brooks-Gunn, J., Petersen, A. C. (1991). Studying the Emergence of Depression and Depressive Symptoms during Adolescence. *Journal of Youth and Adolescence, 20(2),* 115–19.

Brown, L. M., and Gilligan, C. (1992). *Meeting at the Crossroads: Women's Psychology and Girls' Development*. New York: Ballantine Books.

Buck, R. (1977). "Non-verbal Communication of Affect in Pre-school Children: Relationships with Personality and Skin Conductance." *Journal of Personality and Social Psychology, 35,* 225–36.

———, Miller, R. E., and Caul, W. F. (1974). "Sex, Personality, and Physiological Variables in the Communication of Affect via Facial Expression." *Journal of Personality and Social Psychology, 30,* 587–96.

Burns, C. (1985). *Stepmotherhood*. New York: Times Books.

Bushweller, K. (1994). "Turning Our Backs on Boys." *The American School Board Journal,* 181, 20–25.

Canada, G. (1995). *Fist Stick Knife Gun: A Personal History of Violence in America*. Boston: Beacon Press.

Carlat, D. J., Camargo, C. A., and Herzog, D. B. (1997, August). "Eating Disorders in Males: A Report on 135 Patients." *American Journal of Psychiatry, 154(8),* 1127–32.

Cath, S., Gurwitt, A., and Ross, J. (eds.) (1982). *Father and Child*. Boston: Little, Brown.

Centers for Disease Control. (1985). *Suicide Surveillance, 1970–1980*. U.S. Department of Health and Human Services, Washington, D.C.

———— (1995). *Suicide in the United States, 1980–1992.* U.S. Department of Health and Human Services, Washington, D.C.

———— (1997). *Suicide Death and Rates per Hundred Thousand, United States, 1989–1995.* U.S. Department of Health and Human Services, Washington, D.C.

———— (1997). *Statistics on AIDS.* U.S. Department of Health and Human Services, Washington, D.C.

Chodorow, N. (1978). *The Reproduction of Mothering.* Berkeley: University of California Press.

———— (1989). *Feminism and Psychoanalytic Theory.* New Haven: Yale University Press.

Cohen, L. (1997). "Hunters and Gatherers in the Classroom." *Independent School Magazine, Fall, 57(1),* 28–36.

Coles, R. (1986). *The Moral Life of Children.* New York: Atlantic Monthly Press.

The Committee on Adolescence. (1993). "Homosexuality and Adolescence." *Pediatrics, 92(4),* 631–34.

Compas, B. E., and Hammen, C. L. (1994). "Child and Adolescent Depression: Covariation and Comorbidity in Development." In R. J. Haggerty, L. R. Sherrod, N. Garmezy, and M. Rutter (eds.), *Stress, Risk and Resilience in Children and Adolescents* (pp. 225–67). New York: Cambridge University Press.

Coopersmith, S. (1981). *Self-Esteem Inventories (School Form).* Palo Alto, Calif.: Consulting Psychologist Press.

Crossen, C. (1997). "Mind Field." *The Wall Street Journal,* June 5.

Cunningham, J., and Shapiro, L. (1984). "Infant Affective Expression as a Function of Infant and Adult Gender." Unpublished manuscript, Brandeis University, Waltham, Mass.

David, D., and Brannon, R. (eds.) (1976). *The Forty-nine Percent Majority: The Male Sex Role.* Reading, Mass.: Addison-Wesley.

D'Angelo, L. L., Weinberger, D. A., and Feldman, S. S. (1995). "Like Father, Like Son? Predicting Male-Adolescents' Adjustment from Parents' Distress and Self-Restraint." *Developmental Psychology, 31(6),* 883–96.

DeAngelis, T. (1996). "New Interventions Address Teen-age Behavior Problems." *American Psychological Association Monitor,* October.

———— (1996). "Young Girls Engage in Some Sexually Inappropriate Behavior as Often as Boys." *American Psychological Association Monitor,* October.

deGroot, G. (1994). "Do Single-Sex Classes Foster Better Learning?" *American Psychological Association Monitor,* July, 60–61.

DeLuccie, M. F. (1995). "Mothers as Gatekeepers: A Model of Maternal Mediators of Father Involvement." *Journal of Genetic Psychology, 156* (1), 115–31.

Diamond, M. J. (1986). "Becoming a Father: A Psychoanalytic Perspective on the Forgotten Parent," *Psychoanalytic Review, 73,* 445–60.

Dorsey, S. A. (1995). "Father Figures." *Boston Globe.* June 19, p. 21.

Dunn, J., Bretherton, I., and Munn, P. (1987). "Conversations about Feeling States between Mothers and Their children." *Developmental Psychology, 23,* 132–39.

Eagly, A. H., and Steffen, V. J. (1986). "Gender and Aggressive Behavior: A Meta-Analytic Review of the Social Psychological Literature." *Psychological Bulletin, 100,* 309–30.

Elias, M. (1996). "Teens Do Better When Dads Are More Involved." *USA Today,* August 22, D1.

——— (1997). "Family Dinners Nourish Ties with Teen-agers." *The Wall Street Journal,* August 15, D 4.

Eisenberg, N., and Lennon, R. (1983). "Sex Differences in Empathy and Related Capacities." *Psychological Bulletin, 94,* 100–131.

ERIC/AE Digest Series EDO-TM-96-01. (1996). Multiple intelligences: Gardner's Theory.

Erikson, E. (1959). "Identity and the Life Cycle." *Psychological Issues, 1.* New York: International Universities Press.

——— (1963). *Childhood and Society.* New York: W.W. Norton.

Faludi, S. (1991). *Backlash: The Undeclared War against American Women.* New York: Crown.

Fausto-Sterling, A. (1992). *Myths of Gender.* New York: Basic Books.

Fedele, N. M., Golding, E. R., Grossman, F. K., and Pollack, W. S. (1988). "Psychological Issues in Adjustment to First Parenthood." In G. Y. Michaels and W. A. Goldberg (eds.), *The Transition to Parenthood* (pp. 85–113). New York: Cambridge University Press.

Feldman, S. S., and Wentzel, K. R. (1995). "Relations of Marital Satisfaction to Peer Outcomes in Adolescent Boys: A Longitudinal Study." *Journal of Early Adolescence,* 15(2), 220–37.

Fergusson, D. M., Horwood, L. J., and Lynskey, M. T. (1994). "Parental Separation, Adolescent Psychopathology, and Problem Behaviors." *Journal of the American Academy of Child and Adolescent Psychiatry,* 33(8), 1122–31.

Finger, J. P. K. (1995). "A Study of Professed and Inferred Self-Concept-as-Learner of African-American and Caucasian Middle Grade Students." The University of North Carolina at Greensboro. Unpublished dissertation.

Fishman, S. (1997). "Teenage Boys Teach in Parenting Program." *Boston Sunday Globe,* March 23, E16.

Fivush, R. (1989). "Exploring Sex Differences in the Emotional Content of Mother-Child Conversations about the Past." *Sex Roles, 20,* 675–91.

Forehand, R., Neighbors, B., and Wierson, M. (1991). "The Transition of Adolescence: The Role of Gender and Stress in Problem Behavior and Competence." *Journal of Child Psychology and Psychiatry and Allied Disciplines,* 32(6), 929–37.

Fox, E. (ed.) (1993). *The Five Books of Moses.* New York: Schocken Books.

Friedman, C., and Downey, J. (1993). "Psychoanalysis, Psychobiology, and Homosexuality." *Journal of American Psychoanalytic Association, 41(4),* 1159–98.

Friedman, C., and Downey, J. (1994). "Homosexuality." *The New England Journal of Medicine, 331(14),* 923–30.

Friend, T. (1996). "Kick in Pants Exposes Boys to Groin Pains." *USA Today*, August 7.

Frodi, A., Macaulay, J., and Thorne, P. R. (1977). "Are Women Always Less Aggressive than Men?: A Review of the Experimental Literature." *Psychological Bulletin, 84*, 634–60.

Fuchs, D., and Thelen, M. (1988). "Children's Expected Interpersonal Consequences of Communicating Their Affective State and Reported Likelihood of Expression." *Child Development, 59*, 1314–22.

Gant, L. M., et al. (1994). "Increasing Responsible Sexual Behavior among High-Risk African-American Adolescent Males: Results of a Brief, Intensive Intervention." *Journal of Multicultural Social Work, 3(3)*, 49–58.

Gewertz, K. (1996). Voices against Violence. *Harvard University Gazette*, May 2.

Giamatti, A. B. (1989). *Take Time for Paradise*. New York: Summit.

Gilligan, C. (1982). *In a Different Voice*. Cambridge: Harvard University Press.

Gilligan, J. (1996). *Violence: Our Deadly Epidemic and Its Causes*. New York: Putnam.

Gilmore, D. D. (1990). *Manhood in the Making*. New Haven: Yale University Press.

Girgus, J., Nolen-Hocksema, S., and Seligman, M. E. (1989). "Why Do Sex Differences in Depression Emerge during Adolescence?" Paper presented at the annual meeting of the American Psychological Association. New Orleans, August.

Gleason, J. B., and Greif, E. G. (1983). "Men's Speech to Young Children." In B. Thorne, C. Kramarae, and N. Henley (eds.), *Language, Gender and Society* (pp. 140–50). London: Newbury House.

Googins, B. (1991). *Work-family Stress—Private Lives, Public Responses*. Westport, Conn.: Greenwood Press.

Gray, S. (1997). "Not Content with the Closet." *Boston Globe*, August 23, B1.

Greenson, R. (1968). "Dis-identifying from Mother: Its Special Importance for the Boy." *International Journal of Psychoanalysis, 49*, 370–74.

Greif, E., Alvarez, M., and Ulman, K. (1981). "Recognizing Emotions in Other People: Sex Differences in Socialization." Paper presented at the biennial meeting of the Society for Research in Child Development, Boston, April.

Gross, J. (1997). "Among Nine Friends, Too Many Funerals and Too Many Scars." *The New York Times*, July 31, B1.

Grossman, F., and Pollack, W. (1984). "Good Enough Fathering." Paper presented at the annual meeting of the National Council on Family Relations, San Francisco, October.

———, Pollack, W. S., and Golding, E. (1988). "Fathers and Children: Predicting the Quality and Quantity of Fathering." *Developmental Psychology, 24*, 82–91.

———, Pollack, W. S., Golding, E. R., and Fedele, N. M. (1987). "Autonomy and Affiliation in the Transition to Parenthood." *Family Relations, 36*, 263–69.

Guidubaldi, J., Cleminshaw, H. K., Perry, J. D., and McLoughlin, C. S. (1983). "The Impact of Parental Divorce on Children: Report of the Nationwide NASP Study." *School Psychology Review, 12(3)*, 300–323.

———, and Perry, J. D. (1985). "Divorce and Mental Health Sequelae for Children: A Two-Year Follow-up of a Nationwide Sample." *Journal of the American Academy of Child Psychiatry, 24(5)*, 531–37.

Guttmacher Institute. (1994). *Sex and American Teenagers.* New York: Alan Guttmacher Institute.

——— (1996). *Readings on Men.* New York: Alan Guttmacher Institute.

——— (1997). *Facts in Brief: Teen Sex and Pregnancy.* New York: Alan Guttmacher Institute.

Hales, D. (1996). "How Teenagers See Things." *Parade Magazine,* August 18, 4–5.

Hall, J. A. (1978). "Gender Effects in Decoding Nonverbal Cues." *Psychological Bulletin, 85,* 845–57.

Halpern, D. F. (1997). "Sex Differences in Intelligence: Implications for Education." *American Psychologist, 52(10),* 1091–1102.

Harper, K. L., and Purkey, W. W. (1993). "Research in Middle-level Education." *National Middle School Association, 17(1),* 79–89.

Harris, M. (1956). *Bang the Drum Slowly.* Lincoln: University of Nebraska Press.

Harrison, J. (1978). "Warning: The Male Role May Be Dangerous to Your Health." *The Journal of Social Issues, 34,* 65–86.

Haviland, J. J., and Malatesta, C. Z. (1981). The Development of Sex Differences in Nonverbal Signals: Fallacies, Facts, and Fantasies. In C. Mayo and N. M. Henly (eds.), *Gender and Non-verbal Behavior.* New York: Springer-Verlag.

Hawley, R. A. (1991). "About Boys' Schools: A Progressive Case for an Ancient Form." *Teachers College Record, 92(3),* 433–44.

——— (1998). Personal communication, University School, Chargrin Falls, Ohio.

Hedges, L. V., and Nowell, A. (1995). "Sex Differences in Mental Test Scores, Variability, and Numbers of High-Scoring Individuals." *Science, 269,* 41–45.

Herbert, W., and Daniel, M. (1996). "The Moral Child." *U.S. News & World Report,* June 3, 52–59.

Herzog, J. (1982). "On Father Hunger: The Father's Role in the Modulation of Aggressive Drive and Fantasy." In S. Cath, A. Gurwitt, and J. Ross (eds.), *Father and Child* (pp. 163–74). Boston: Little, Brown.

Hetherington, E., Cox, M., and Cox, R. (1986). "Long-Term Effects of Divorce and Remarriage on the Adjustment of Children." *Annual Progress in Child Psychiatry and Child Development,* 407–29.

Hite, S. (1981). *The Hite Report on Male Sexuality.* New York: Ballantine Books.

Hochman, G. (1995). "Is Your Child Moody or Depressed?" *Child Magazine,* February, 58–61.

Hodges, W. F., and Bloom, B. L. (1984). "Parents' Report of Children's Adjustment to Marital Separation: A Longitudinal Study. *Journal of Divorce, 8 (1),* 33–50.

Hoffman, M. I., and Levine, I. F. (1976). "Early Sex Differences in Empathy." *Developmental Psychology, 12,* 557–58.

Homer (1975). *The Iliad.* Trans. by Robert Fitzgerald. New York: Anchor Books.

Homer (1963). *The Odyssey.* Trans. by Robert Fitzgerald. New York: Anchor Books.

Hulse, D. J. (1997). *Brad and Cory: A Study of Middle School Boys.* Huntington Valley, Oh.: University School Press.

Isay, R. A. (1989). *Being Homosexual: Gay Men and Their Development.* New York: Farrar, Straus & Giroux.

Isenberg, P. (1980). "An Essay." *Harvard Magazine,* November–December, 6–10.

Jacklin, C. N. (1989). "Female and Male: Issues of Gender." *American Psychologist, 44,* 127–33.

Jain, A., Belsky, J., and Crnic, K. (1996). "Beyond Fathering Behaviors: Types of Dads." *Journal of Family Psychology, 10(4),* 431–42.

Jones, D. C., and Costin, S. E. (1995, October). "Friendship's Quality during Preadolescence and Adolescence: The Contributions of Relationships Orientations, Instrumentality, and Expressivity." *Merrill-Palmer Quarterly, 41(4),* 517–35.

Jordan, E. (1995). "Fighting Boys and Fantasy Play: The Construction of Masculinity in the Early Years of School." *Gender and Education, 7(1),* 69–86.

Jordan, J. (1984). "Empathy and Self-Boundaries" (Stone Center Working Paper Series, Work in Progress No. 16). Wellesley, Mass.: Wellesley College, Stone Center.

———— (1987). "Clarity in Connection: Empathic Knowing, Desire and Sexuality" (Stone Center Working Paper Series, Work in Progress No. 29). Wellesley, Mass.: Wellesley College, Stone Center.

———— (1989). "Relational Development: Therapeutic Implications of Empathy and Shame." (Stone Center Working Paper Series, Work in Progress No. 39). Wellesley, Mass.: Wellesley College, Stone Center.

———— (ed.) (1997). *Women's Growth in Diversity.* New York: Guilford Press.

Jordan, J. V., Kaplan, A. G., Baker Miller, J., Stiver, I. P., and Surrey, J. L. (1991). *Women's Growth in Connection.* New York: Guilford Press.

Juster, F. T., and Stafford, F. P. (1985). *Times, Goods, and Well-Being.* Ann Arbor, Mich.: Institute for Social Research.

Kallman, F. J. (1953). *Heredity in Health and Mental Disorder: Principles of Psychiatric Genetics in the Light of Comparative Twin Studies.* New York: W. W. Norton.

Kandel, D. B., and Davies, N. (1986). "Adult Sequelae of Adolescent Depressive Symptoms." *Archives of General Psychiatry, 43(3),* 255–62.

Kaschak, E. (1992). *Engendered Lives: A New Psychology of Women's Experience.* New York: Basic Books.

Kasen, S., Cohen, P., Brook, J. S., and Hartmark, C. (1996). "A Multiple-Risk Interaction Model: Effects of Temperament and Divorce on Psychiatric Disorders in Children." *Journal of Abnormal Child Psychology, 24(2),* 121–50.

Kaye, S. H. (1988–89). "The Impact of Divorce on Children's Academic Performance." Special issue: Children of Divorce: Developmental and Clinical Issues. *Journal of Divorce, 12 (2-3)* 283–98.

Kessler, R., and McRae, J. (1981). "Trends in the Relationship between Sex and Psychological Distress: 1957–1976." *American Sociological Review, 46,* 443–52.

———, and McRae, J. (1983). "Trends in the Relationship between Sex and Attempted Suicide." *Journal of Health and Social Behavior, 24,* 98–110.

Kimmel, M. S. (1987). *Changing Men: New Directions in Research on Man and Masculinity.* Newbury Park, Calif.: Sage Publications.

Kimura, D. (1992). "Sex Differences in the Brain." *Scientific American,* September, 119–25.

King, L. A., and King, D. W. (1993). *Sex-Role Egalitarianism Scale (SRES).* Port Huron, Mich.: Sigma Assessment Systems.

Koch, J. (1997). "The Interview: Sam Gash." *Boston Sunday Globe Magazine,* August 24, 16.

Krugman, S. (1991). "Male Vulnerability and the Transformation of Shame." In W. S. Pollack, chair., "On Men: Redefining Roles." The Cambridge Series, Cambridge Hospital, Harvard Medical School.

Krystal, H. (1979). "Alexithymia and Psychotherapy." *American Journal of Psychotherapy, 33,* 17–30.

Kutner, L. (1993). "Heroes Offer Ways to Explore Feelings and Situations." *The New York Times,* December 23.

Lamb, M. (1975). "Fathers: Forgotten Contributors to Child Development." *Human Development, 18,* 245–66.

——— (1977). "The Development of Parental Preferences in the First Two Years of Life." *Sex Roles, 3,* 475–97.

——— (1981). *The Role of the Father in Child Development.* New York: Wiley.

———, and Oppenheim, D. (1989). "Fatherhood and Father-Child Relationships." In S. Cath, A. Gurwitt, and L. Gunsberg (eds.), *Fathers and Their Families* (pp. 11–16). Hillsdale, N.J.: Analytic Press.

Lennon, R., and Eisenberg, N. (1987). "Gender and Age Differences in Empathy and Sympathy." In N. Eisenberg and J. Strayer (eds.), *Empathy and Its Development* (pp. 195–217). New York: Cambridge University Press.

Levant, R. F. (1992). "Toward the Reconstruction of Masculinity." *Journal of Family Psychology, 5,* 379–402.

———, and Pollack, W. S. (1995). *A New Psychology of Men.* New York: Basic Books.

Lever, J. H. (1976). "Sex Differences in the Games Children Play." *Social Work, 23,* 78–87.

Lewin, T. (1997). "Teen-agers Alter Sexual Practices, Thinking Risks Will Be Avoided." *The New York Times,* April 5.

Maccoby, E. (1990). "Gender and Relationships: a Developmental Account." *American Psychologist, 45,* 513–20.

————, and Jacklin, G. N. (1974). *The Psychology of Sex Differences.* Stanford, Calif.: Stanford University Press.

————, and Jacklin, G. N. (1980). "Sex Differences in Aggression: A Rejoinder and Reprise." *Child Development, 51,* 964–80.

Madaras, L., and Madaras, A. (1995). My Body, My Self for Boys. New York: Newmarket Press.

Majors, R. G., and Billson, J. N. (1992). *Cool Pose: The Dilemmas of Black Manhood in America.* New York: Lexington Books.

Malatesta, C. Z., and Haviland, J. M. (1982). "Learning Display Rules: The Socialization of Emotion Expression during the First Two Years of Life." *Monographs of the Society for Research in Child Development, 50* (1-2, Serial No. 219).

Manning, A. (1997). "Teens Starting Substance Abuse at Younger Ages." *USA Today,* August 14, 8D.

Mannuzza, S., Klein, R., Bessler, A., Malloy, P., and Hynes, N. (1997). "Educational and Occupational Outcome of Hyperactive Boys Grown-up." *Journal of the American Academy of Child and Adolescent Psychiatry, 36*(9), 1222–27.

Marttunen, M. J., Henriksson, M. M., Aro, H. M., Keikkinene, M. E, et al. (1995). "Suicide among Female Adolescents: Characteristics and Comparison with Males in the Age Group 13 to 22 Years." *Journal of the American Academy of Child & Adolescent Psychiatry, 34*(*10*), 1297–1307.

Melvoin, R. I. (1998). *Beyond Politics: Boys, Biology, Values and Character.* Huntington Valley, Oh.: University School Press.

McGaw, J. (1997). "Doing It Their Way." *The Boston Parents' Paper,* June, 28–31.

McHale, S., and Crouter, A. (1992). "You Can't Always Get What You Want: Incongruence between Sex-Role Attitudes and Family Work Roles and Its Implications for Marriage." *Journal of Marriage and the Family, 54,* 537–47.

McIntosh, H. (1996). "Research on Teen-age Friendships Dispels Old Myths." *American Psychological Association Monitor,* June. Washington, D.C.

———— (1996). "Adolescent Friends not Always a Bad Influence." *American Psychological Association Monitor,* June. Washington, D.C.

McIntosh, J. L. (1996). "Suicide Rate Data 1994." American Association of Suicidology, Washington, D.C. Fact sheet.

"Men: Tomorrow's Second Sex." (1996). *Economist,* September 28, 23–26.

Miedzian, M. (1991). *Boys Will Be Boys: Breaking the Link between Masculinity and Violence.* New York: Anchor Books.

Miller, J. B. (1976). *Toward a New Psychology of Women.* Boston: Beacon Press.

———— (1983). "The Construction of Anger in Women and Men" (Stone Center Working Paper Series, Work in Progress No. 4). Wellesley, Mass.: Wellesley College, Stone Center.

————, and Stiver, I. P. (1997). *The Healing Connection.* Boston: Beacon Press.

Mitchell, J., and Farley, C. (1990). "Isolation and Restraint in Juvenille Correctional Facilities." *Journal of the American Academy of Child and Adolescent Psychiatry, 29*(2), 251–55.

Mitscherlich, A. (1963). *Society Without the Father.* New York: Harcourt, Brace, and World.

Morrison, A. (1989). *Shame: The Underside of Narcissism.* Hillsdale, N.J.: Analytic Press.

Murray, B. (1995). "Kids Learn Keys to Healthy Relationships." *American Psychological Association Monitor,* September.

———— (1996). "Debates over Sex Education May Put Teen Health at Risk." *American Psychological Association Monitor,* November.

The National Center for Health Statistics (1996). *Report of Mortality Statistics.*

Negri, G. (1995). "When Dad's in the Lunch Bunch." *Boston Globe,* March 31, p. 33.

Nolen-Hocksema, S. (1990). *Sex Differences in Depression.* Stanford: Stanford University Press.

———— (1995). "Gender Differences in Coping with Depression across the Lifespan." *Depression, 3,* 81–90.

————, and Girgus, J. S. (1994). "The Emergence of Gender Differences in Depression during Adolescence." *Psychological Bulletin, 115(3),* 424–43.

————, Girgus, J. S., and Seligman, M. E. P. (1991). "Sex Differences in Depression and Explanatory Style in Children." *Journal of Youth and Adolescence, 20(2),* 233–45.

————, Girgus, J. S., and Seligman, M. E. P. (1992). "Predictors and Consequences of Childhood Depressive Symptoms: A Five-Year Longitudinal Study." *Journal of Abnormal Psychology, 101(3),* 405–22.

Nottelmann, E. D. (1987). "Competence and Self-Esteem during Transition from Childhood to Adolescence." *Developmental Psychology, 23(3),* 441–50.

Osherson, S. (1986). *Finding Our Fathers: The Unfinished Business of Manhood.* New York: Free Press.

Osherson, S., and Krugman, S. (1990). "Men, Shame and Psychotherapy." *Psychotherapy, 27,* 327–39.

Parke, R. D. (1981). *Father.* Cambridge: Harvard University Press.

Peretti, P. O., and di-Vitorrio, A. (1993). "Effect of Loss of Father through Divorce on the Personality of the Preschool Child." *Social Behavior and Personality, 21(1),* 33–38.

Peterson, K. S. (1996). "Teens Unlikely to Talk about Depression." *USA Today,* August 7.

Pindar (1974). *Pindar's Odes.* Trans. by Arthur Swanson. New York: Bobbs-Merrill.

Pipher, M. (1994). *Reviving Ophelia.* New York: Grosset/Putnam.

Pleck, J. (1981). *The Myth of Masculinity.* Cambridge: MIT Press.

———— (1994). "Social-Psychological Influences on Condom Use." (Center for Research on Women Working Papers Series, Work in Progress No. 273). Wellesley, Mass.: Wellesley College.

————, Sonenstein, F. L., and Ku, L. C. (1993). "Masculinity Ideology: Its Impact on Adolescent Males' Heterosexual Relationships." *Journal of Social Issues, 49(3),* 11–29.

Pollack, W. S. (1982). " 'I'ness and 'We'ness: Parallel Lines of Development." Ph.D. dissertation, Boston University. *University Microfilms International, 82-13517.*

—— (1983). "Object-Relations and Self Psychology: Researching Children and Their Family Systems." *The Psychologist-Psychoanalyst, 4,* 14.

—— (1989). "Boys and Men: Developmental Ramifications of Autonomy and Affiliation." Paper presented at the midwinter meetings of the Division of Psychotherapy, American Psychological Association, Orlando, Fl.

—— (1990). "Men's Development and Psychotherapy: A Psychoanalytic Perspective." *Psychotherapy, 27,* 316–21.

—— (1991). "Can Men Love? Psychoanalytic and Developmental Perspectives on Men and Intimacy." Paper presented at the Symposium on Men and Intimacy at the 99th Annual Meeting of the American Psychological Association, San Francisco.

—— (1991). "Managers as Fathers." *Levinson Letter.*

—— (1992). "Boys Will Be Boys: Developmental Traumas of Masculinity—Psychoanalytic Perspectives." Paper presented as part of a symposium "Toward a New Psychology of Men" at the centennial meeting of the American Psychological Association, Washington.

—— (1992). "Should Men Treat Women? Dilemmas for the Male Psychotherapist: Psychoanalytic and Developmental Perspectives." *Ethics and Behavior, 2,* 39–49.

—— (1994). "Engendered Psychotherapy: Listening to the Male and Female Voice." *Voices, 30(3),* 43–47.

—— (1995). "No Man Is an Island: Toward a New Psychoanalytic Psychology of men." In R. Levant and W. S. Pollack (eds.), *A New Psychology of Men* (pp. 33–67). New York: Basic Books.

—— (1995). "A Delicate Balance: Fatherhood and Psychological Transformation—A Psychoanalytic Perspective." In J. L. Shapiro, M. J. Diamond, and M. Greenberg (eds.), *Becoming a Father: Social, Emotional and Clinical Perspectives.* New York: Springer.

—— (1995). "Reframing Masculinity: Men, Empathy and Empathy for Men." Paper presented at the Cambridge Symposium, Cambridge, Mass. Winter.

—— (1995). "Deconstructing Dis-identification: Rethinking Psychoanalytic Concepts of Male Development." *Psychoanalysis and Psychotherapy, 12(1),* 30–45.

—— (1995). "Men's Erotic Desires: Love, Lust, Trauma, Sex, Biology, and Psychoanalysis." Paper presented at the 103rd annual convention of the American Psychological Association, New York. August.

—— (1995). "Becoming Whole and Good: A New Psychology of Men." International Coalition/Boys' Schools Symposium, June.

—— (1996). "Boys' Voices: Can We Listen, Can We Respond? Toward an Empathic Empirical Agenda. International Coalition/Boys' Schools Symposium, June.

———— (1996). "Living on the Fault Line of Gender—Finding Common Ground: Searching for Our Soulmates." Paper presented at the 104th annual convention of the American Psychological Association, Toronto, Canada. August.

———— (1996). *Boys at Play: Sports and Transformation.* Hunting Valley, Oh.: University School Press.

———— (1998). "The Trauma of Oedipus: Toward a New Psychoanalytic Psychotherapy for Men." In W. S. Pollack and R. L. Levant (eds.), *New Psychotherapy for Men.* New York: Wiley.

———— (1998). "Mourning: Melancholia and Masculinity: Recognizing and Treating Depression in Men." In W. S. Pollack and R. L. Levant (eds.), *New Psychotherapy for Men.* New York: Wiley.

————, and Grossman, F. K. (1985). "Parent-Child Interaction." In L. L'Abate (ed.), *The Handbook of Family Psychology and Therapy* (pp. 586–622). Homewood, Ill.: Dorsey.

————, and Jordan, J. V. (1997). "Breaking 'The Rules' for Men and Women: Generating Genuine Empathy." Paper presented at the Symposium "Breaking 'The Rules'—New Models of Male-Female Relationships" at the 105th Annual Convention of the American Psychological Association, Chicago.

Pollack, W. S., and Levant, B. F. (1998). *New Psychotherapy for Men.* New York: Wiley.

Pollak, S., and Gilligan, C. (1982). "Images of Violence in Thematic Apperception Test Stories." *Journal of Personality and Social Psychology, 42(1),* 159–67.

Pottorff, D. D., Phelps-Zientarski, D., and Skovera, M. E. (1996). "Gender Perceptions of Elementary and Middle School Students about Literacy at School and Home." *Journal of Research and Development in Education, 29(4),* 203–11.

Potts, M. K., Burnam, M. A., and Wells, K. B. (1991). "Gender Differences in Depression Detection: A Comparison of Clinician Diagnosis and Standardized Assessment." *Psychological Assessment: A Journal of Consulting and Clinical Psychology, 3(4),* 609–15.

Pruett, K. D. (1987). *The Nurturing Father.* New York: Warner Books.

———— (1989). "The Nurturing Male: A Longitudinal Study of Primary Nurturing Fathers." In S. H. Cath, A. Gurwitt, and L. Gunsberg (eds.), *Fathers and Their Families* (pp. 389–405). Hillsdale, N.J.: Analytic Press.

Public Health Service. (1956). "Death Rates by Age, Race and Sex, United States, 1900–1953: Suicide." *Vital Statistics Special Reports, 43(30).*

Raine, A., Brennan, P., and Mednick, S. A. (1997). "Interaction between Birth Complications and Early Maternal Rejection in Predisposing Individuals to Adult Violence: Specificity to Serious, Early-Onset Violence." *American Journal of Psychiatry, 154,* 1265–71.

Ravitch, D. (1994). "The War on Boys." *Men's Health,* October, 110.

Reinhard, D. W. (1977). "The Reaction of Adolescent Boys and Girls to the Divorce of Their Parents." *Journal of Clinical Child Psychology, 6*(2), 21–23.

Resnick, M. D., Bearman, P. S., Blum, R. W., et al. (1997). "Protecting Adolescents from Harm: Findings from the National Longitudinal Study on Adolescent Health," *Journal of the American Medical Association, 278*(10), 823–32.

Riley, R. W. (1994). Notes of Secretary Richard W. Riley during release of the 1992 National Assessment of Educational Progress Trend Report, August 17.

——— (1997). Testimony of Secretary Richard W. Riley before the Senate Labor, Health and Human Services and Education Subcommittee of the Senate Appropriations Committee, September 4.

Roberts, P., and Mosley, B. (1996). "Fathers' Time." *Psychology Today,* May/June, 48–55.

Rohde, P., Seeley, J. R., and Mace, D. E. (1997). "Correlates of Suicide Behavior in a Juvenille Detention Population." *Suicide and Life-Threatening Behavior, 27*(2), 164–75.

Rotundo, E. A. (1993). *American Manhood: Transformations in Masculinity from the Revolution to the Modern Era.* New York: Basic Books.

Sadker, M., and Sadker, D. (1994). *Failing at Fairness.* New York: Scribners.

Schwartzberg, S., and Rosenberg, L. G. (in press). "Treating Gay and Bisexual Men." In W. S. Pollack and R. L. Levant (eds.), *New Psychotherapy for Men.* New York: Wiley.

Segell, M. (1995). "The Pater Principle." *Esquire,* March, 121–27.

Sells, C. W., and Blum, R. W. (1996). "Morbidity and Mortality among U.S. Adolescents: An Overview of Data and Trends. *American Journal of Public Health, 86*(4), 513–519.

Seppa, N. (1996). "Keeping Schoolyards Safe from Bullies." *American Psychological Association Monitor.*

Shapiro, J. L. (1993). *The Measure of a Man: Becoming the Father You Wish Your Father Had Been.* New York: Delacorte.

———, Diamond, M. J., and Greenberg, M. (eds.) (1995). *Becoming a Father: Social, Emotional, and Clinical Perspectives.* New York: Springer.

Shapiro, L. (1997). "The Myth of Quality Time." *Newsweek,* May 12, 62–69.

Shellenbarger, S. (1996). "Work and Family: High-Powered Fathers Savor Their Decisions to Scale Back Careers." *The Wall Street Journal,* June 12.

Sherrod, D. (1987). "The Bonds of Men: Problems and Possibilities in Close Male Relationships." In H. Brody (ed.), *The Making of Masculinities: The New Men's Studies.* Cambridge, Mass.: Unwin Hyman, Ltd.

Siegal, M. (1987). "Are Sons and Daughters Treated More Differently by Fathers than by Mothers?" *Developmental Review, 7,* 183–209.

Silverman, D. K. (1987). "What Are Little Girls Made of?" *Psychoanalytic Psychology, 4,* 315–34.

Silverstein, O., and Rashbaum, B. (1994). *The Courage to Raise Good Men.* New York: Viking.

Slater, B. R. (1988). "Essential Issues in Working with Lesbian and Gay Male Youths." *Professional Psychology: Research and Practice, 19(2),* 226–35.

Sleek, S. (1995). "APA Is Raising Money for Violence-Prevention Effort." *American Psychological Association Monitor,* October.

Smucker, M. (1982). "The Children's Depression Inventory: Norms and Psychometric Analysis." Unpublished Ph.D. dissertation, Pennsylvania State University, University Park.

Snarey, J. (1993). *How Fathers Care for the Next Generation: A Four-decade Study.* Cambridge: Harvard University Press.

Steinhauer, J. (1995). "At a Clinic, Young Men Talk of Sex." *The New York Times,* September 6.

Stern, D. N. (1985). *The Interpersonal World of the Infant.* New York: Basic Books.

Stiver, I. (1984). "The Meanings of 'Dependency' in Female-Male Relationships" (Stone Center Working Papers Series, Work in Progress). Wellesley, Mass.: Wellesley College, Stone Center.

Stiver, I. (1986). "Beyond the Oedipus Complex: Mothers and Daughters" (Stone Center Working Paper Series, Work in Progress No. 26). Wellesley, Mass.: Wellesley College, Stone Center.

Strickland, B. (1988). "Sex-Related Differences in Health and Illness." *Psychology of Women Quarterly, 12,* 381–99.

Sullivan, H. S. (1953). *Conceptions of Modern Psychiatry.* New York: W.W. Norton.

——— (1953). *The Interpersonal Theory of Psychiatry.* New York: W.W. Norton.

Surrey, J. (1984). "The 'Self-in-Relation': A Theory of Women's Development" (Stone Center Working Paper Series, Work in Progress No. 13). Wellesley, Mass.: Wellesley College, Stone Center.

Swain, S. (1989). "Covert Intimacy: Closeness in Men's Friendships." In B. J. Risman and P. Schwartz (eds.), *Gender in Intimate Relationships: A Microstructural Approach* (pp. 70–93). Belmont, Calif.: Wadsworth Publishing.

Tannen, D. (1990). *You Just Don't Understand.* New York: William Morrow.

Tanouye, E. (1997). Antidepressant Makers Study Kids' Market. *The Wall Street Journal,* April 4, B1.

Thomas, P. (1997). "U.S. Crime Rate Falls Again in 1996." *Boston Globe.* June 2.

Thorne, A., and Michaelieu, Q. (1996). "Situating Adolescent Gender and Self-Esteem." *Child Development, 67,* 1374–90.

Tronick, E. (1989). "Emotions and Emotional Communication in Infants." *American Psychologist, 44,* 112–19.

———, and Cohn, J. (1989). "Infant-Mother Face-to-Face Interaction: Age and Gender Differences in Coordination and the Occurrence of Miscoordination." *Child Development, 60,* 85–92.

Tyson, P. (1982). "A Developmental Line of Gender Identity, Gender Role, and Choice of Love Object." *Journal of American Psychoanalytic Association, 30,* 61–86.

USA Today Poll. (1997). "Children's Time Spent with Family." *USA Today.*

U.S. Department of Justice. (1994). *Violent Crime: National Crime Victimization Survey* (NCJ-147486).

——— (1997). *Males and Firearms Violence.*

——— (1997). *Victim Characteristics.*

Vaillant, G. E. (1977). *Adaptation to Life.* Boston: Little, Brown.

Wallerstein, J., and Blakeslee, S. (1989). *Second Chances.* New York: Ticknor and Fields.

———, and Kelly, J. B. (1980). *Surviving the Break-up: How Children and Parents Cope with Divorce.* New York: Basic Books.

Weinberg, M. K. (1992). "Sex Differences in 6-Month-Old Infants' Affect and Behavior: Impact on Maternal Caregiving." Ph.D. dissertation, University of Massachusetts.

——— (1992). "Boys and Girls: Sex Differences in Emotional Expressivity and Self-Regulation during Early Infancy." In L. J. Bridges (chair), "Early Emotional Self-Regulation: New Approaches to Understanding Developmental Change and Individual Differences." Symposium conducted at the International Conference on Infant studies, Miami, Fl.

Weingarten, K. (1994). *The Mother's Voice: Strengthening Intimacy in Families.* New York: Harcourt, Brace.

Weiss, R. S. (1990). *Staying the Course: The Emotional and Social Lives of Men Who Do Well at Work.* New York: Fawcett Columbine.

Whitehead, B. D. (1993, April). "Dan Quayle Was Right." *Atlantic Monthly, 271,* 47–84.

Winnicott, D. W. (1974). *The Maturational Process and the Facilitating Environment.* New York: International Universities Press.

Zachary, G. P. (1997). "Male Order: Boys Used to Be Boys, but Do Some Now See Boyhood as a Malady?" *The Wall Street Journal,* May 2, A1.

Zaslow, M. J. (1988, July). "Sex Differences in Children's Response to Parental Divorce: I. Research Methodology and Postdivorce Family Forms." *American Journal of Orthopsychiatry, 58(3),* 355–78.

INDEX

ABOUT THE AUTHOR

WILLIAM S. POLLACK, Ph.D., a clinical psychologist, is the codirector of the Center for Men at McLean Hospital/Harvard Medical School, an assistant clinical professor of psychiatry at the Harvard Medical School, and a founding member and Fellow of the Society for the Psychological Study of Men and Masculinity of the American Psychological Association. He is coauthor of *In a Time of Fallen Heroes: The Re-Creation of Masculinity* and coeditor of *A New Psychology for Men*. He and his family live in Massachusetts.

ABOUT THE TYPE

This book was set in Times Roman, designed by Stanley Morison specifically for *The Times* of London. The typeface was introduced in the newspaper in 1932. Times Roman had its greatest success in the United States as a book and commercial typeface, rather than one used in newspapers.